The Shaping of ‘Abbāsid Rule

PRINCETON STUDIES ON THE NEAR EAST

The Shaping of ʿAbbāsid Rule

By Jacob Lassner

PRINCETON UNIVERSITY PRESS, PRINCETON, NEW JERSEY

Published by Princeton University Press, Princeton, New Jersey
In the United Kingdom: Princeton University Press, Guildford, Surrey

Library of Congress Cataloging in Publication Data will be
found on the last printed page of this book

Publication of the book has been aided by a grant from The
Andrew W. Mellon Foundation

This book has been composed in Linotype Granjon

Clothbound editions of Princeton University Press books
are printed on acid-free paper, and binding materials are
chosen for strength and durability.

Printed in the United States of America by Princeton
University Press, Princeton, New Jersey

To
Phyllis, Elizabeth, and Jason

Contents

List of Illustrations

List of Maps

Acknowledgments

This is a book that has developed over a rather long period of time. Certain notions concerning political symbolism and urban planning were, in fact, derived from an earlier investigation of medieval Baghdad, and the contents of various chapters were originally presented over several years in a series of papers before different learned societies. During these years, I have benefited from numerous discussions with many colleagues. Any attempt to express my appreciation to all of them would require a statement of interminable length; I would like, therefore, to single out a few individuals whose encouragement and cooperation have been truly invaluable. Moshe Sharon, of the Hebrew University, is one with whom I have shared long and animated conversations about the 'Abbāsids for over a decade. My colleague Leonard Tennenhouse read the entire manuscript with a discerning eye and offered stylistic suggestions that were indispensable to the final version of the text. I am particularly grateful to Susan Garr and Lia Wiss, who had to struggle with all the strange names and symbols in preparing the manuscript. Above all, there is my wife, Phyllis, who has been a constant source of encouragement and good counsel.

The material dealing with the 'Abbāsid military organization was researched with the help of a J. S. Guggenheim fellowship, and an A.C.L.S.-S.S.R.C. grant made it possible to complete those sections concerned with 'Abbāsid clientage.

Preface

The present work on the formation of the 'Abbāsid government is largely based on a series of smaller studies originally intended for separate publication. These were, in turn, the outgrowth of an earlier unpublished effort: the explication of a short, but unique, historical tradition that preserves an alleged conversation between two 'Abbāsid notables, the Caliph al-Mahdī and his great uncle 'Abd al-Ṣamad b. 'Alī. It may seem incongruous that so ambitious a final project has originated with a single text of fifteen lines. The account is, however, of considerable significance, for, in a few unsolicited words of advice, the outspoken uncle suggests an important triangular relationship between the 'Abbāsid ruling family and its instruments of rule: the civilian bureaucracy and the imperial army.

Although the complex relationship between the various segments of the ruling institution will be seen as crucial to an understanding of early 'Abbāsid government, it cannot be said that the broader issues raised by these relatively obscure passages have been given full recognition. Indeed, given the dearth of serious research on the polity of the new dynasty, it is not surprising that this text and others like it have gone largely unnoticed. What is more revealing is that no substantive effort has yet been undertaken to study the foundations of 'Abbāsid power, that is to say, those elements that shaped the political attitudes and institutions of the emerging regime. The need to address this subject is compelling, not only on its own merits, but also because the period and events under review were generally important to the formation of medieval Islamic society.

Perhaps it is understandable that scholars have tended to shy away from studying the emergence of an 'Abbāsid polity. In the absence of archival materials and similar documentation, it has been necessary to rely on the medieval chronicles and belles lettres as primary sources. The Arabic historiography dealing with the critical events is, however, highly tendentious, and many of the traditions show evidence of considerable shaping under the aegis of an official patronage. As yet, no one has devised a way to isolate and catalogue the major literary conventions that are woven into the medieval texts—the codes, so to speak, by which the embellishment can be unraveled in order to reveal the residual historicity of the documents. Although even a casual reading of the chapters that follow will reveal a sensitivity to, if not overwhelming concern with, precisely these sorts of textual problems, the reader will note that a systematic methodological statement has not been included. Nonetheless, traces of such a statement and the method it implies are to be found throughout the explication of the sources. In fact, a second series of studies dealing specifically with 'Abbāsid historiography is in preparation and, when finished, should represent a companion volume to the present study.

With the materials currently available, it would have been premature to attempt an all-encompassing history of the emergent 'Abbāsid regime. It may very well be that scholars will never possess the documentation necessary to write a descriptive account even limited to its political institutions. A different format, tailored to the realities of current research, was therefore required. It was decided to base the present book on a series of independent studies that had been structured earlier. Although each chapter focuses in detail on a specific salient problem, there is a thematic unity throughout, so that, when viewed as a whole, the book suggests a broad reading of early 'Abbāsid history.

Taking into account the serious gaps in information, a measure of caution has been necessary, so that the language of analysis has often been chosen with an eye to circumspection. The best of intentions could not, however, prevent the encroachment of some impressionistic readings, particularly when one has had to deal with unique traditions of a highly suggestive nature. One can perhaps answer that, in the end, Islamic history remains a discipline that is susceptible to impressionistic analysis, and that *mea culpas,* if required, might best be reserved for those who would pretend otherwise.

A popular Hebrew ballad of the past states: *ha-shīr lō tam hū raq mathīl* "the song [of labor] is not ended, it has only begun." This book does not represent a definitive statement on the formation of 'Abbāsid government—quite the contrary. The publication of new manuscript materials that are at present inaccessible, together with a systematic review of all the literary texts in current circulation, will, no doubt, add considerably to our understanding of the central issues and events of the second century A.H. That which the reader will encounter in the pages to follow should, therefore, be regarded as a preliminary statement, one that will serve, one hopes, as a modest point of departure for future studies shedding light on the institutions of medieval Islamic society.

The Shaping of ‘Abbāsid Rule

Introduction

Until quite recently, investigators concerned with the formation of 'Abbāsid political institutions tended to rely on a conventional wisdom that was derived from European scholarship of the nineteenth century. Many orientalists of that age tailored their data to fit a conceptual framework strongly influenced by the growth of nationalism and current theories of race and society. They therefore depicted the emergence of the 'Abbāsid dynasty as the culmination of a long struggle between the "Arab Kingdom" of the Umayyads and the conquered population of a shattered Iranian Empire. Or, put somewhat differently, the conflict they perceived was between a ruling institution predicated on the special privilege of a relatively small Arab aristocracy and a more broadly defined coalition of revolutionary forces whose ethnic origins were largely rooted in the former Sassanian provinces to the east.

An exaggerated emphasis was thus given to the role played by the indigenous population of Khurāsān during the years of clandestine operations and, especially, during the open revolt which followed. Moreover, concurrent with this enlarged role for the native Khurāsānīs, there developed the rather seductive notion that Islamic government became increasingly Iranized under the aegis of 'Abbāsid rule. Seen in this light, the revolutionary triumph signified more than a military victory; it heralded the creation of a new order, in which the narrowly defined political structures of Arab society were replaced by a polity of universal outlook and composition. Although no formal consensus emerged among modern scholars as to whether these supposed developments suited their own notions of progress, those sympathies that could be detected seemed to echo a bias of the medieval sources in favoring the new regime.

At the extreme, such views led to the picture of an 'Abbāsid state that was essentially a new Iranian empire, albeit one dressed in the formal attire of a Persianized Islam. A more cautious formulation described the Arab contribution to the ideological and military struggle against the Umayyads and recognized that the 'Abbāsids, whose cause was embraced by the native populace, were themselves blood relatives of the Prophet, the most distinguished Arab of all. Nevertheless, even such a meticulous and sensitive scholar as J. Wellhausen could not resist concluding that "under the guise of International Islam, Iranianism triumphed over the Arabs." Although the author's following remarks imply that he had no clear idea what this statement meant in substantive terms, the apparent sentiments embodied in this observation and others like it took on a formulaic significance, and the alleged Iranization of 'Abbāsid rule was generally regarded as orthodox doctrine by subsequent generations of scholars.[1]

This traditional view has slowly given way to a new consensus. Revisionist historians, returning to the original sources, have attacked the idea of a native uprising against the Umayyads in Khurāsān, with all that this implies for the concept of an Iranian style of government in Islam. Present conceptualizations dramatize instead the critical role of eastern-based Arab tribal armies in the ultimate victory and, at the same time, emphasize the intricate development of 'Abbāsid political ideology within the context of early Shī'ism, a movement deeply rooted in the Arab past. It is recognized that the Iranized Arab settlers in the villages of Khurāsān played a role disproportionate to their numbers in directing the military and administrative affairs of the emergent regime, but these partially assimilated elements of local society are viewed as retaining their Arab identity. Moreover, the settlers' conception of the struggle between the new order to come and the entrenched Umayyad state was firmly based on the events of an earlier Islamic history. The 'Abbāsid mandate, as they understood it, was to restore a pristine Islam that had existed in the time of the Prophet, and not to reverberate to the echoes of a dim foreign past. Although this does not preclude a later susceptibility to lingering Persian influences, any assertion of a transplanted Iranian style of rule for the nascent 'Abbāsid state is highly problematic. Some cultural borrowing was no doubt inevitable, but, despite marriages to women drawn from the native population and an acquired facility with the Persian language, it is not clear that any prominent cultural and political legacy was inherited from the Iranian past by these old Arab settlers. Residual mythologies die slowly, however, and the effects of conventional scholarly wisdom are all too often experienced even after new research has displaced earlier insights from current view.

It may at least be said on Wellhausen's behalf that his general remarks on the changed style of government in Islam are casually presented in a few pages at the conclusion of his ground-breaking work *Das Arabische Reich und sein Sturz*.[2] As the title indicates, his primary concern was not the formation of an 'Abbāsid government, but the history of the regime that preceded it. The detailed historical narrative essentially ends with the accession of the first 'Abbāsid Caliph, Abū al-'Abbās al-Saffāḥ. The brief remarks concerning the vast changes brought about by the 'Abbāsid triumph are therefore merely an appendage that conveniently marks the end of an historic era, as well as a laborious scholarly effort. One has the impression that the author did not fully digest the later course of 'Abbāsid history, and that, in telescoping what he perceived as developments of the future, he relied simply on the traditional outlook of his age rather than on any systematic investigation of his own.

If this is indeed true, it is surely regrettable that he did not turn his considerable talents to a study of the new regime. Despite the imposing contribution of the 'Abbāsids to the development of Islamic government, no synthesis of the period comparable to Wellhausen's work on the Umayyads has yet been attempted. There have been individual studies of varying length and merit on particular events and institutions, but none that suggests an overall pattern of growth for the emerging 'Abbāsid state or even identifies the salient problems of 'Abbāsid rule. Given the nature of the available literary sources, it would be too ambitious, perhaps, to expect a definitive work, but a preliminary statement on the formation of the 'Abbāsid ruling institution is well within reach and long overdue. Had Wellhausen attempted it, it would unquestionably have served as a point of departure for future researchers in early 'Abbāsid history.

A formidable exponent of higher biblical criticism, Wellhausen combined great learning with an acute sense of literary analysis. Although his synthesis of Umayyad times, and, in particular, his treatment of the 'Abbāsid revolution, has undergone revision largely due to the accessibility of new sources, it still remains a model of historical investigation based on a judicious handling of medieval texts. One may add here parenthetically that this model has not always been emulated by the most recent and severe of his critics.[3] The best revisionist studies are indeed outstanding contributions to Islamic historiography, but they remain as yet unpublished and are, in essence, limited to the events surrounding the revolutionary struggle. The most reliable of the works in print is more broadly conceived than these and certainly does not lack detail, but it is at best conventional in its reading of an 'Abbāsid historiography that is both complex and elusive.[4] Even a casual reading of the Arabic sources indicates that the task of reconstructing the earliest decades of 'Abbāsid rule will be extremely difficult, and that, despite recent efforts, it has barely begun.

The present study is restricted to outlining the central problems of 'Abbāsid government during the formative years of the regime. One might begin with an attempt to define what is meant by formative years, for the periodization of 'Abbāsid history continues to be a vexing problem. The lines that separate one historic moment from another are thinly drawn, if not indistinguishable, and the causal effect of events is difficult to ascertain even under the best of circumstances. Nevertheless, the elusive search for coherent blocks of time remains important to the understanding of any given age.

Within the context of the present work, the formative period of the dynasty refers to the time between the years of clandestine revolutionary effort and the creation of the viable political infrastructure that gave formal shape to the emergent 'Abbāsid regime. To all intents and purposes, the process of forming the early institutions of 'Abbāsid rule was completed during the reign of Hārūn al-Rashīd, though it was his grandfather al-Manṣūr who had the most dramatic impact on their development. It will come as no surprise, therefore, that Abū Ja'far 'Abdallāh al-Manṣūr plays the central role in the historical narrative that follows, and that the events of his reign outweigh all others in establishing the incipient pattern of 'Abbāsid government. Yet, since the publication of T. Noeldeke's slim essay of the last century,[5] no individual study of the Caliph has been attempted, nor has any general work successfully integrated al-Manṣūr's remarkable career within the complex history of the period. The general tendency has been to pursue older issues instead of conceptually breaking new ground.[6]

There is no doubt that the more responsible of recent historians have performed a great service in correcting the misconceptions of the past; however, by focusing on the problem of Arab versus Persian influence in the 'Abbāsid rise to power, they may be suggesting to many a reader that the alleged Iranization of government remains an important issue, indeed one that is critical in explaining the foundations of 'Abbāsid rule. It rather appears that the search for the Iranian or Arab origins of various institutions is very much beside the point, for the key to the development of 'Abbāsid rule lies less in cultural borrowings than in the internal dynamics of the 'Abbāsid experience. Among existing scholars, only M. Sharon has shown sufficient sensitivity to this extremely important point. His excellent dissertation, however, is essentially confined to the events of the clandestine revolution and the open revolt that followed.

In a sense, the 'Abbāsid triumph is a most appropriate example of the method by which a loosely controlled revolutionary apparatus is transformed into an established government of imperial capabilities. The specific details of the transformation may often be lacking, but the salient forces that gave rise to an enduring 'Abbāsid state are broadly known, and others can be deduced through persistent detective work, despite the difficulties of weighing the literary evidence. The events pertaining to the revolution have now undergone systematic review, and with the appearance of M. Sharon's detailed thesis, a distinct picture of this exceedingly complex period has emerged. Building on this foundation, the next obvious step will be to investigate the early years of the regime, when the ruling segment of the 'Abbāsid family withstood both internal and external challenges to its legitimacy and, after a rather tumultuous beginning, established the foundations of lasting political power.

Students of comparative history will not find it strange that a turbulent period of transition should have existed between a successful revolution and the establishment of a legitimate and ordered political entity. Some may, however, sense that, by any realistic appraisal, the conditions that prevailed at the conclusion of the 'Abbāsid triumph should have been conducive instead to an era of relative stability, for the ruthless fashion in which the new dynasty obliterated the survivors of the previous ruling house—indeed uprooted every trace of its authority—left the nascent regime without rational fear of a counterrevolution. Moreover, the 'Abbāsids emerged from their long and trying struggle against the Umayyads with virtually their entire military and political apparatus intact. This was the direct result of a prudent policy that consciously avoided alliances with the 'Alid Shī'ites, those kinsmen whose revolutionary efforts invariably turned out to be premature adventures ending in disaster. They chose instead to accept the dictates of historical reality and consolidated their complicated political relationships in Khurāsān before risking an open rebellion from which there was no return.

By opting to delay public exposure, the ʿAbbāsids decisively strengthened their long-range interests. The rather long period of gestation imposed upon their effort not only insured their final success, it also provided the incipient regime with a large number of veteran activists with which to build the administration of a cohesive and enduring society. Aside from the untimely and somewhat mysterious battlefield loss of Qaḥṭabah b. Shabīb, the most able of their commanders, the ʿAbbāsids emerged from the revolution unscathed. Abū al-ʿAbbās, the first of the new Caliphs, could seemingly call upon a loyal core of supporters that included the sons of Qaḥṭabah, capable military men in their own right; Abū Muslim, the creator of the revolutionary army; Abū Salamah, the director of clandestine activities in al-Kūfah; the paternal uncles (*ʿumūmah*) of the Caliph, Ṣāliḥ, Ismāʿīl, Dāwūd, Sulaymān, ʿĪsā, ʿAbdallāh, and ʿAbd al-Ṣamad b. ʿAlī; the Caliph's nephew ʿĪsā b. Mūsā; the future heir apparent, Abū Jaʿfar al-Manṣūr; and various relatives, agents, and operatives of lesser rank.

This impression, though essentially correct, is nevertheless misleading, for the veteran revolutionaries were entirely dependent on the larger constituencies that brought the ʿAbbāsid house to power. The situation caused one politically astute contemporary to observe that the ʿAbbāsid Caliph al-Manṣūr could be compared to the rider of a lion who brings terror to those who see him, but is himself the most terrified of all. In effect, the ʿAbbāsids were prisoners of the revolutionary tradition in which they were spawned. The clandestine nature of the movement's operations, which were critical to its success, called for a revolutionary network of limited size so as to project the lowest possible profile. The linkages between the various cells in the larger apparatus were discreetly arranged to prevent penetration from outside sources. Even at the higher levels, there was no visually identifiable leadership and, more startling yet, no clearly proclaimed ideology. When the broad coalition of forces directed by ʿAbbāsid agents undertook to dislodge the Umayyads by force of arms, it knew neither the inner leadership nor the exact basis of their claims to rule. The name of the "chosen one from the house of the Prophet," whose cause convulsed the Islamic world in civil war, remained a closely guarded secret along with the identity of his family. This condition prevailed until the very moment when the oath of allegiance signifying the election of a new Caliph was publicly taken on behalf of Abū al-'Abbās al-Saffāḥ.

There was, however, an implicit danger in the anonymity that served 'Abbāsid interests so well. By keeping their distance, the family leadership was forced to delegate inordinate power to others within the revolutionary apparatus. In addition, there remained the large Shī'ite constituency that traditionally supported the claims of the 'Alid family. They had suffered through many heartbreaking struggles in the effort to overthrow the Umayyads and counted among their fallen champions a number of distinguished martyrs. In short, they had borne the brunt of opposing the usurpative regime in power, only to be denied the ultimate reward at what should have been their greatest triumph. Despite the long awaited fall of the Umayyad state and the return of authority to the Prophet's family, the denial of the 'Alids gave rise to bitter resentments. The decisive 'Abbāsid victory, which came on the heels of a crushing Shī'ite defeat a few years earlier, may have left the 'Alid pretenders and their hard-core supporters in a state of political disarray. There was no guarantee, however, that the more militant 'Alid leadership would not attempt to topple the new regime at some propitious moment in the future.

The 'Alid relationship with the 'Abbāsid house was extremely complex, for, although the two branches of the Hāshimite clan shared broad political objectives and common support during the Umayyad interregnum, they now emerged as potential rivals for supreme leadership. As a rule, their political instincts failed them, but the 'Alids still merited serious consideration. After all, they too were blood relatives of the Prophet, and, unlike the new rulers, their credentials as martyrs in the cause against the Umayyads were impeccable. This tragic service on behalf of the Faithful carried a powerful emotional appeal and became a recurrent theme of Shī'ite apologists in subsequent generations. There was already sufficient uncertainty surrounding the ideological position of the new ruling family: by what rights did the 'Abbāsids, and Abū al-'Abbās in particular, obtain leadership in the community of Islam? The more cynical observer might have argued that the 'Abbāsids seemingly began as a family in search of a revolution or, at least, in need of an existing revolutionary apparatus. Providentially, they obtained both at the same time. When on his death bed, Abū Hāshim, an heirless grandson of 'Alī b. Abī Ṭālib, secretly transferred his authority, as well as his cadres, to a close friend and kinsman, Muḥammad b. 'Alī al-'Abbāsī. He, in turn, bequeathed his credentials and supporters to his son Ibrāhīm (al-Imām). Following the latter's death, a second son, Abū al-'Abbās, was designated successor under circumstances shrouded with mystery. Even if one were to believe this alleged sequence of events in all its details, there would still be those who denied the original claims of Abū Hāshim; for, who was this descendant of 'Alī by way of a Ḥānafite concubine in comparison with the 'Alids born to Fāṭimah, the daughter of the Prophet himself?

The elements of potential disaster were all there: an 'Alid candidate perhaps capable of subverting the former revolutionary apparatus that now controlled the nascent 'Abbāsid government and, worse yet, a possible disaffection in the ranks of the Khurāsānī military, whose ideological commitment, such as it was, was originally tied to an unknown leader. Is it any wonder that the early 'Abbāsids hounded their potential rivals among the 'Alids, forced the more militant of them into hiding, and crushed them when they emerged on the field of battle?

No less dramatic, however, were the internal problems of the new regime. With the formal declaration of Abū al-'Abbās's Caliphate, the entire family was exposed to public view. The path was thereby cleared for openly mobilizing the numerous relatives who had grown to maturity in anticipation of this moment. After an initial assessment of the situation, the Caliph moved firmly. He dispatched his kin to take direct control of the functioning government bureaucracy. Still more important, he directed the *'umūmah* and 'Īsā b. Mūsā to assume positions of command within the various Khurāsānī regiments that had entered Iraq. In time, the major revolutionary agents, whose extended influence was a source of grave concern, were eliminated by a series of devious strategems culminating in murder. The loyalty of the army, which was the foundation of 'Abbāsid rule, was obtained in turn through a variety of pragmatic measures, not the least of which was the regular distribution of service pay; but the 'Abbāsid house was still not in order.

With the death of Abū al-'Abbās, it became clear that the ruling family itself was torn by dissension. Unfulfilled ambitions eroded the tight discipline that had previously marked the inner coterie. It is sometimes evident that those who achieve power as a result of seditious activities will see sedition about them everywhere, even when it is more apparent than real. The incipient regime was not, however, without problems of a substantive nature. The death of the first Caliph was followed by an internecine struggle for power between his elder brother Abū Ja'far al-Manṣūr and his ubiquitous uncle 'Abdallāh b. 'Alī. In this case, the leading role played by the *'umūmah* and 'Īsā b. Mūsā during the final military campaigns bore seeds that would ripen into bitter conflict. By administering the coup de grace to the previous regime, the Caliph's paternal uncle emerged as the most prominent member of the ruling family and a likely candidate to succeed his nephew. Abū al-'Abbās's eleventh-hour decision to choose his nondescript brother instead set into motion a series of dramatic events that was to have enormous repercussions beyond the field of battle. The military struggle that ended in victory for al-Manṣūr was followed by significant changes in the composition of the 'Abbāsid government, particularly as it affected the Caliph's position with regard to other elements of the ruling house.

Although no comprehensive analysis of the intricate political relationships within the 'Abbāsid family has yet been published, the basic features apparently indicate a confrontation between al-Manṣūr and his paternal uncles, particularly Ismā'īl, 'Abdallāh, 'Abd al-Ṣamad, and Sulaymān b. 'Alī. There were, in addition, eventual difficulties with his nephew 'Īsā b. Mūsā, though the latter, who had become heir apparent, correctly supported al-Manṣūr during the initial challenge to his authority. The critical problem that remained, following 'Abdallāh's defeat, was that of institutionalizing this newly acquired power to withstand the external and internal challenges of the future. This was no simple matter. On the record alone, al-Manṣūr's credentials to rule were decidedly less impressive than those of his nephew and his more illustrious uncles. The Caliph was, however, a remarkably resourceful man. Having successfully fought his way to supreme rule, al-Manṣūr initiated an extremely complex strategy by which he sought to bring about substantive changes in the political alignments of the 'Abbāsid house. Through such measures, he hoped to isolate his relatives from those centers of power that might ultimately give them the necessary leverage to undermine his position. One ramification of this development was an attempt on the part of Abū Ja'far to form a new line of succession based exclusively on his own progeny. A second was the effort to manipulate control of the bureaucracy and the provincial governorships so that key posts did not fall to potential rivals but remained instead in the hands of loyal agents of lesser credentials.

It thus happened that the turmoil within the ʿAbbāsid house was also given geographical expression: in the newly established capitals at al-Hāshimīyah and, later, Baghdad vis-à-vis Syria and the old garrison towns of al-Baṣrah and al-Kūfah. ʿAbdallāh b. ʿAlī had been governor of Syria, as well as a leading commander of the revolutionary armies. As such he inherited the vestigial Umayyad military apparatus of the region and therefore enjoyed the support of the local Arab tribesmen. By using Abū Muslim and the Khurāsānīs against an army consisting largely of these tribal contingents, al-Manṣūr not only turned back the political challenge of his uncle, but he put an end as well to any lingering regional or even dynastic ambitions that there may have been in Syria. At the same time, the Caliph took a major step in reducing the regime's military dependence on Arab tribal organization, thereby paving the way for the formation of more reliable army units based on geographical affiliation.

In related actions, Sulaymān b. ʿAlī, the governor of al-Baṣrah, was eventually forced from the fulcrum of his political strength, and, later, ʿĪsā b. Mūsā was dismissed from the post that he had held at al-Kūfah for no less than thirteen years—this so he could be brought under increasing pressure to give up his place in the line of succession in favor of the Caliph's son, Muḥammad al-Mahdī. Other figures similarly disappear from the active political arena at judicious moments brought about by the ravages of time or a fortuitous, premature demise. It was only some time after al-Manṣūr's death that the noble ʿAbbāsids from the other branches of the family were returned to prominence in the administration of government; but, even then, they did not exercise the dominant authority they had known in the past.

Regardless of the Caliph's attitude toward the *ʿumūmah*, significant changes within the ruling institution were inevitable. The old revolutionary apparatus including the ʿAbbāsid family may have been equal to the task of seeing the fledgling regime through an armed struggle and the period immediately following, but it lacked the capacity to singly administer a state of imperial designs. Under any circumstances the transition between the destruction of one ruling order and its replacement with another is very complicated. The methods that best serve the successful revolutionary are not necessarily conducive to the establishment of a functioning government. Those accustomed to secretive dealings in circumscribed groups may find the delegation of broad authority to outsiders difficult and even unpalatable. Even if the 'Abbāsid family and its cadres emerging from the years of revolutionary activity had the capacity to make this transition successfully, they still lacked the manpower necessary to staff the ever growing government bureaucracy in both the capital and the provinces. Al-Manṣūr, who had been remarkably inconspicuous in earlier times, seemingly compensated for his lack of proper credentials by creating governmental structures of incredible complexity and breadth. Although the Caliph's personal life was characterized by legendary tales of parsimony and an austere behavior of almost comic nature, he encased himself within walls of monumental architecture and surrounded himself with a highly centralized bureaucracy of staggering dimensions. His actions were neither paradoxical nor idiosyncratic; they stemmed from a keen awareness of the desirability of integrating image with function in conducting the affairs of imperial government.

Some prefer to regard this as a residual influence of Iranian origins, though such an attribution is, at best, vague and, at worst, irrelevant. With or without a Sassanian model, the 'Abbāsid ruling institution had to be significantly enlarged. In order to fill the requisite appointments, the Caliph invariably turned to his clients (*mawālī*). To be sure, the institution of clientage had deep historic roots, but no Islamic ruler before al-Manṣūr manipulated those dependent on him with such virtuosity. The Caliph, and his offspring who followed, increasingly preferred to negotiate the business of government through agents tied exclusively to themselves. As a result, they managed to circumvent persons with direct ties to tribal associations or to other powerful interest groups. Although this policy was not specifically designed to disenfranchise the *'umūmah*, it proved very useful in containing their broad influence.

The actual workings of 'Abbāsid clientage are at best elusive, for the historiography of the era does not attempt to define or conceptualize societal institutions. Nor, for that matter, do the extant texts focus in detail on the illustrative careers of individual clients. Nevertheless, the broad outlines of the system can be fairly well understood. Above all, the client was in a dependent status, and, because of this, he had no recognizable constituency of his own. Whatever powers that accrued to him were not derived from and were not transferable to his social class as a whole; they rested solely with his patron, the Caliph. The latter could thus treat the vulnerable *mawlā* as an isolated individual and punish or reward him as he saw fit. The intelligent client was quick to perceive the realities of the situation, and he adjusted his expectations accordingly. This was a far cry from the complex political relationships that enmeshed al-Manṣūr and his relatives within the ruling circle. Despite the engaging accounts of the chroniclers, even ʿAbdallāh b. ʿAlī's challenge to the Caliph's authority did not produce dramatic retribution. For confronting the Caliph in open rebellion, the paternal uncle suffered no more than premature retirement and house arrest.

On the whole, the pool of talent available to the Caliph must have been considerable. To begin with, he had access to those trusted clients already in the employ of the regime, including individuals whose service extended back to the days of clandestine activities and the open revolt that followed. These veterans of the ʿAbbāsid past were entrusted with the most sensitive of posts, such as the distribution of military pay and the commands of various elite security forces. Certain positions were even passed on as family sinecures, thereby extending and strengthening the already existing ties between patron and client. The old political apparatus was deliberately kept flexible and small in keeping with the requirements of the revolutionary effort; with the formal declaration of the ʿAbbāsid regime, however, growth was inevitable, if not desirable. The Caliph would therefore have felt the need to add new clients to his personal service and to that of his government. Existing conditions certainly favored such a policy, for the emergence of an ʿAbbāsid polity on the heels of a crushing Umayyad defeat established the basis for increased social mobility among the enterprising and the talented. Manumitted slaves and freeborn clients alike saw their ties to former patrons severed by the change of dynasty. Having served the Umayyads and others in earlier times, they could now embrace the Caliph's cause and hence obtain entry into the new ruling society, with all that this meant for their personal advancement and that of their relations.

Those *mawālī* at court and within the imperial bureaucracy certainly wielded considerable influence, but it should be pointed out that the substantive power of the regime continued to reside in its military forces. Because the loyalty of the army was, in effect, the only guarantee of the dynasty's continued existence, it was only a question of time before the Caliphs also applied the principles of clientage to that most central of institutions. It was still too early to manipulate the army as an entity, but it was possible to establish powerful personal ties with important elements of the military establishment. This was accomplished in the traditional fashion, by dispensing patronage in a manner beneficial to both subject and sovereign.

Within two decades, a loose coalition of tribal forces, beset by the debilitating effects of narrow group consciousness, was transformed into a well-disciplined professional army. By transplanting a Khurāsānī force to Iraq, the 'Abbāsids were able to instill an esprit de corps in military contingents previously wracked by tribal dissensions. The 'Abbāsid army found a new cohesiveness in unfamiliar surroundings by stressing the common geographical affiliations of the past. In turn, their descendants, a generation removed from the native habitat of Khurāsān, established an identity of their own, based, in part, on the more recent area of geographical settlement provided for them by al-Manṣūr.

The continuous loyalty of the military was not, however, a foregone conclusion. Unlike the isolated client in government service, the professional army was able to effect significant action. Above all, it had a vested interest in the affairs of the 'Abbāsid state and was thus particularly sensitive to stresses of an economic and political nature. Concurrent with a growing instability that eventually led to the erosion of Caliphal authority, the military emerged as an increasingly important, if not decisive, factor in internal government affairs. Difficulties that could not be resolved in localized court intrigues often required the direct intervention of the army, thereby adding a new and volatile dimension to the existing structure of 'Abbāsid society.

The highly personalized system of transforming power within the ruling family—an outgrowth perhaps of the revolutionary experience—served only to exacerbate existing tensions. To be sure, al-Manṣūr, with his rare political cunning and resolve, was able to guarantee, at least initially, a smooth transition of rule. Having overcome the *'umūmah* and his 'Alid kinsmen, he established a precedent for succession based on his immediate family line. However, with the death of his son and heir, al-Mahdī, the internal cohesion of the Manṣūrid household began to crack, and fissures emerged within the innermost circle of the ruling family. Attached as they were to a particular prince of the Manṣūrid line, many leading clients acted as provocateurs in an effort to enhance the positions of their patrons and thereby their own fortunes. Shadow governments were thus created to serve young 'Abbāsid princes who were considered for rule, and the once reliable army of al-Manṣūr's creation became a vested interest group available to the highest bidder with the prerequisite credentials to rule.

The apparent dangers of an independent fighting force were fully comprehended in a subsequent era. In the following century, the Caliph's great grandson al-Mu'taṣim brought the system of clientage to its logical conclusion. He introduced a slave army for the first time in the history of the regime and then attempted to isolate it from the freeborn regiments and society at large. The inheritor of al-Manṣūr's legacy thus established an institution that was to have a most profound effect on the future course of Islamic history. It is well to remember, however, that the seeds of even this development were planted at an earlier time, when the enterprising great grandfather designed the foundations of 'Abbāsid power on a highly complex model of political patronage.

Abū Ja'far al-Manṣūr was the real architect of early 'Abbāsid government, and he drew his plans with much skill and inventiveness. Upon his death he bequeathed to al-Mahdī a viable state that appeared to rest on firm political foundations and a sound fiscal policy. Nevertheless, in the end, his successors were entrapped by a congenital weakness of the imperial polity. Contemporary Islamic society was based less on formal institutional structures than on networks of interpersonal relations, and, when there are a multiplicity of patrons in conflict, clientage can be more of a curse than a blessing. This was particularly true when the progeny of the Manṣūrid house was divided against itself, for clients acting in their own best interests tended to stimulate rather than reduce tensions in an effort to promote the claims of their respective patrons. The process inevitably resulted in a debilitating civil war and set into motion a sequence of events from which the 'Abbāsid Caliphate never fully recovered, though it did manage to survive in a weakened state for another four centuries. The decline of the Caliphate belongs, however, to another era and another book.

PART ONE

The Political Setting

I

THE FIRST INTERNAL CRISIS: THE SUCCESSION TO ABŪ AL-'ABBĀS

Salāmah, the Berber slavegirl:
When pregnant with al-Manṣūr I had a vision. It was as though a lion emerged from my foreparts. He turned his head upward and roared while thrashing about with his tail. The lions then came from all directions, each one prostrating himself before him.

Mas'ūdī, *Murūj* (Beirut), 3: 282

A. The Succession

In A.H. 136, Abū al-'Abbās, the first sovereign of the 'Abbāsid realm, died after a reign of four years. Whatever his accomplishments, one cannot count among them preparations for an orderly succession. Immediately following his death, a convulsive struggle broke out within the ruling family between his distinguished paternal uncle, 'Abdallāh b. 'Alī, and his elder brother, Abū Ja'far al-Manṣūr. The issue between them was ultimately resolved by force of arms, with al-Manṣūr emerging as victor. In part, these circumstances resulted from the reluctance of the 'Abbāsid house to establish a line of succession following the investiture of its first Caliph. If anything, the 'Abbāsids came to power with an abundance of qualified leaders among the blood relatives, a fact that may explain why the Caliph, with so many able and experienced men about, originally chose none to succeed him. The desire to preserve family unity at all costs did not, however, dampen lingering ambitions and aspirations.

Among the prospective candidates, the most compelling presence within the family was, without doubt, Abū al-'Abbās's paternal uncle 'Abdallāh b. 'Alī. He was the commander of the Syrian army, the conqueror of the province, and the extirpator of the Umayyad line. Significantly, 'Abdallāh b. 'Alī was also from a productive branch of the family that provided him with no fewer than six surviving brothers, all provincial governors and distinguished figures in their own right.[1] Despite such impressive credentials (or perhaps because of them), Abū al-ʿAbbās was not moved to declare in his uncle's favor during the formative years of the regime. Moreover, when the decision was finally taken to establish a list of succession shortly before the Caliph's death, ʿAbdallāh b. ʿAlī's name was conspicuous by its absence.

A second choice might have been the Caliph's nephew ʿĪsā b. Mūsā, a distinguished veteran of the political and military campaigns against the Umayyads. Although only a nephew, there was no question of his maturity; he was actually a year older than Abū al-ʿAbbās. ʿĪsā, however, suffered from having been born to an elderly father in a minor and unproductive household. Not only was he a contemporary of his uncles (who presumably stood before him), but the women of his father's house left him with precious few natural allies to support an active bid. In any event, ʿĪsā b. Mūsā was not a man beset by great ambitions or possessed of great talent for political infighting. When Abū Muslim was reportedly prepared to declare Khurāsān in his favor immediately after the death of Abū al-ʿAbbās, he emphatically declined. Instead he chose to follow the dictates of the lamented Caliph's last-minute will by recognizing his uncle, Abū Jaʿfar al-Manṣūr.[2]

At best, the successor to Abū al-ʿAbbās was a person of rather limited distinction. Although his uncles and nephew ʿĪsā b. Mūsā played a predominant part in bringing the ʿAbbāsids to power,[3] al-Manṣūr took no active role either during the formative period of the ʿAbbāsid revolution, or, more significantly, after the secretive stages of the revolution gave way to open insurrection against the Umayyad regime. It may have been wise to remain inconspicuous in the earliest stages of the ʿAbbāsid propaganda; al-Manṣūr's failure to impress, however, was hardly intentional, and, for so ambitious a public figure, it could not remain a policy for long. Once in power, the Caliph was compelled to rehabilitate his image.

The later descriptions of al-Manṣūr's early career therefore took on embellishments that are clearly associated with a historiography assembled under official patronage. He was, for example, reported to have been in control of military operations against Wāsiṭ, the last stronghold of the Umayyads; and tradition has it that his worthy adversary Yazīd b. Hubayrah attributed to al-Manṣūr great talent as a military strategist and tactician. A closer examination, however, reveals that his function was largely political. It was essentially to facilitate the surrender and later, against the terms of the capitulation, the execution of Ibn Hubayrah, the last Umayyad governor of Iraq.[4]

When al-Manṣūr was sent to Wāsiṭ, the city had been under siege for almost a year. Al-Manṣūr was only his brother's agent, as is explicitly stated in a letter forwarded by the Caliph to al-Ḥasan b. Qaḥṭabah, his general in the field: "Indeed the army is yours (*al-'askar 'askaruka*) and the army commanders are yours (*wa al-quwwād quwwāduka*). However, I wish my brother [al-Manṣūr] to be present; so listen to him." The text goes on to indicate that it was al-Ḥasan who was the officer in command, subject to the authority of the Caliph by way of his brother, al-Manṣūr.[5] The only other indication that al-Manṣūr participated in military action in this campaign is a report that, while at Wāsiṭ, he was dispatched by Abū al-'Abbās at the head of a force to relieve pressures in al-Jazīrah. However, even here it appears that his primary function was to arrange a peace with the enemy, and that his future adversary 'Abdallāh b. 'Alī was actually in charge of military affairs. Additional evidence of al-Manṣūr's limited role is found in another version of these events, wherein it is related that 'Abdallāh b. 'Alī, and not his nephew, arranged for the end of the hostilities. Indeed, it was only after this episode, when the region had been pacified, that the future Caliph took over the governorship of the province, his first significant administrative responsibility.[6]

Another tradition that merits consideration is the curious account of Ibn Qutaybah, which attributes to al-Manṣūr nothing less than the conquest of Syria, the execution of Marwān II, and the elimination of vestiges of the Umayyad royal family.[7] The murder of the Umayyads will be treated in detail later in this narrative; it is sufficient to point out here that among the many accounts that depict the end of the Umayyad house, Ibn Qutaybah is unique in describing Abū Ja'far al-Manṣūr as an agent of execution. More significantly, his alleged conquest of Syria is mentioned here only in passing, whereas this difficult campaign is treated in considerable detail by the chroniclers. Ṭabarī, in particular, makes it clear that the principal architect of the 'Abbāsid victory was not al-Manṣūr, but his uncle 'Abdallāh b. 'Alī.

It should be remembered that al-Manṣūr was not at this time an inexperienced youth, but a mature man, as were all the leading revolutionary figures from among the ruling family and its agents. In fact, Abū Ja'far, his younger uncles, and his nephew 'Īsā b. Mūsā were more or less contemporaries. It therefore cannot be said that his inconspicuous performance during the years in question was attributable to a desire on the part of the 'Abbāsid notables to gently ease a youthful future Caliph into the position for which they considered him destined.

Abū al-'Abbās's particular preference for his half brother, therefore, is not so easily explained. If any principle at all was invoked in drawing up the list of successors, it may have been the desire to perpetuate the line of their father, Muḥammad b. 'Alī. One could casually dismiss this as a traditional function of internal family politics, but the issue is somewhat more complex. It was through Muḥammad b. 'Alī that the 'Abbāsids pressed their claims of legitimacy, for it was to him that the revered Abū Hāshim b. Muḥammad b. al-Ḥanafīyah passed on the sacred right to rule (*imāmah*).[8] Through this act, the 'Abbāsids not only inherited the revolutionary apparatus that labored on Abū Hāshim's behalf, they also established their claims to leadership within the community of believers.

Upon the death of Muḥammad b. 'Alī, the *imāmah* was assumed by his son Ibrāhīm (al-Imām), who, in turn, allegedly bequeathed it to his brother Abū al-'Abbās. In all likelihood, the last transfer was hastily and secretly arranged by a group limited to the innermost coterie of the family at the time of Ibrāhīm's sudden and mysterious demise in Ḥarrān. It was greeted with considerable skepticism, if not opposition, by broad segments of the public whose ties to the revolution were exclusively linked to the deceased *imām*.[9] One may therefore assume that within 'Abbāsid family circles, it was Abū al-'Abbās, who was most likely to perceive the critical importance of stressing the ties between the existing regime and Abū Hāshim's legacy to Muḥammad b. 'Alī. The choice of a third son to succeed the father thereby takes on a compelling logic of its own. By every other standard, Abū Ja'far would seem to have fallen short of his nephew 'Īsā b. Mūsā, let alone his paternal uncle 'Abdallāh b. 'Alī.

An additional and rather speculative observation is perhaps in order. If blood descent was a significant factor, the heir presumptive could theoretically have been Abū al-'Abbās's only son, Muḥammad. He was a nondescript youth who himself died heirless in A.H. 150, after what can be most charitably described as an almost invisible career.

His high birth, together with the existence of a literary tradition denigrating him, may perhaps be taken as indication that Muḥammad, bearing his grandfather's name, was actually a potential candidate for rule (why denigrate a noncandidate).[10] However, given his delicate age and the unsettled condition of the nascent regime, it is extremely doubtful that such an option was weighed seriously, if at all. Even in optimal circumstances, Muḥammad's candidacy would have required skillful navigating through rather turbulent political waters, and because his youth had prevented him from participating during the period of revolutionary activity, he did not have the advantage of relationships formed in those years. One can, of course, always speculate that the Caliph might have harbored some vague hopes of passing the *imāmah* on to his progeny. If this was true, the decision to delay drawing up a line of succession might have been an effort not only to preserve family unity, but also to protect Abū al-'Abbās's seed from external pressures until such time as a legitimate case could be made for Muḥammad's candidacy. In any event, if such a strategy was ever conceived, the Caliph's premature death did not allow for sufficient time to bring it to fruition. In the end, Abū al-'Abbās's choice fell upon his elder brother.

Whatever the Caliph's motive, it was only shortly before his death in A.H. 136 that Abū al-'Abbās reportedly nominated his brother Abū Ja'far al-Manṣūr as heir apparent. He, in turn, was to be followed by their nephew 'Īsā b. Mūsā. Abū al-'Abbās then drew up the terms of succession in an appropriate document, which was sealed with the Caliphal signet as well as the seals of the ruling house (*ahl al-bayt*). There is no indication that the contents of the protocol were made generally known before the Caliph died, but it is tempting to regard the document as the last will and testament of Abū al-'Abbās, presumably meant to be released upon his death by 'Īsā b. Mūsā, to whom it was given for safekeeping.[11]

One can readily understand why this arrangement was satisfactory to 'Īsā b. Mūsā, for he could not have foreseen that al-Manṣūr would eventually remove him from the line of succession in favor of his own offspring. On the other hand, 'Abdallāh b. 'Alī was outraged, in view of the disparity between his own accomplishments and those of his less distinguished nephew. That the paternal uncles might have viewed this document with some disappointment, indeed dismay, goes without saying. The *'umūmah* could not have failed to recognize that, given the underlying assumptions of his action, Abū al-'Abbās not only explicitly denied the Caliphate to their branch of the family for at least a generation, but left serious doubts that they would ever come to rule. Moreover, seeds of discontent had been planted, even before Abū al-'Abbās's decision in his brother's favor.

It was during al-Manṣūr's brief tenure as governor of al-Jazīrah that the first inkling of future difficulties with the paternal uncles could be discerned. Ismā'īl b. 'Alī had been given control of al-Mawṣil, an unruly city that was sacked amid great devastation by the Caliph's brother Yaḥyā in A.H. 133. In the events that followed, Ismā'īl executed a local dignitary and was given permission to expropriate his estates, causing the family of the deceased to protest to al-Manṣūr, who, as ruler of al-Jazīrah, presumably had final jurisdiction in the matter. He, in turn, is alleged to have sent his son Muḥammad al-Mahdī to return the properties to the original owners. The *'umūmah* were then obliged to exercise their all-too-ample political muscle when the relatives of Ismā'īl had this decision nullified through the intervention of still another paternal uncle, 'Abd al-Ṣamad b. 'Alī. The estates then remained in the possession of Ismā'īl's heirs until the reign of Hārūn al-Rashīd, when some undisclosed change of status appears to have taken place.[12] This particular incident may have ended to the satisfaction of the *'umūmah*, but it was a harbinger of more troubled times to come. Several years after taking office, al-Manṣūr forcibly removed Ismā'īl b. 'Alī from his post as governor of al-Mawṣil, one of several concurrent moves designed to curtail the power of his paternal uncles.[13]

B. The Claims of al-Manṣūr

The nature of the last-minute arrangement that brought al-Manṣūr to power served only to underscore the weakness of his claim. Seen in this light, he was not the recipient of public acclamation following a long period of recognition as heir apparent. He was, rather, imposed upon the community of believers in hastily orchestrated circumstances. It comes as no surprise, therefore, that the Manṣūrid propagandists created an official hagiology for Abū Ja'far's claims by rooting them in a much earlier perid of history amid familiar apocalyptic settings. Contrasted with the view of a last-minute arrangement, there is, then, a series of traditions that indicate that the succession of al-Manṣūr had been established even prior to the uprising against the Umayyads.

The Persian translator and editor of Ṭabarī (the account is not found in the original Arabic text) relates that Muḥammad b. ʿAlī, before his death in A.H. 125, had already formulated a line of succession through his sons Ibrāhīm (al-Imām), ʿAbdallāh (Abū al-ʿAbbās), and ʿAbdallāh (Abū Jaʿfar). If, indeed, such a convenient plan was ever formulated, it is exceedingly doubtful that it was given public expression. In any event, there is no corroborating textual evidence that this plan existed. It is true that the *Fragmenta Historicorum Arabicorum*, a source that ordinarily merits close reading, preserves a report indicating that, in the year A.H. 132, Abū al-ʿAbbās sent his brother Abū Jaʿfar to Khurāsān where he was to receive the oath of allegiance (*bayʿah*) on behalf of the Caliph and on behalf of himself as successor (*liAbī al-ʿAbbās wa liAbī Jaʿfar baʿdahu*). However, none of the other sources reporting this mission bear witness to such an act. When the *bayʿah* is mentioned, it is reserved for the Caliph alone. Moreover, Abū Jaʿfar was treated in a discourteous, if not humiliating, manner for someone so highly placed in the ruling house.[14] Had, in fact, al-Manṣūr's legitimacy been firmly established at this early date, it is not likely that the revolt of ʿAbdallāh b. ʿAlī would have gathered the momentum it did following the death of Abū al-ʿAbbās, or that ʿAbdallāh's own claims to rule would have been couched in such expressions of outrage.

These reservations notwithstanding, there remain for consideration still other accounts that proclaim the early legitimacy of al-Manṣūr's Caliphate. As if anticipating Muḥammad b. ʿAlī's alleged succession through his sons, there is the tradition of Yaʿqūbī regarding Abū Hāshim b. Muḥammad b. al-Ḥanafīyah, whose transfer of the right to rule to Muḥammad b. ʿAlī, planted the initial seeds of the ʿAbbāsid revolution. It was, indeed, the episode of this last will and testament that defined the earliest ideological claims of the ʿAbbāsids. It is thus noteworthy that, in the account of Yaʿqūbī, the dying Abū Hāshim took time from a didactic lecture on how to overthrow the Umayyads to prophesy the future Caliphate of Abū al-ʿAbbās and his brother Abū Jaʿfar al-Manṣūr after him (*wa iʿlam anna ṣāḥib hādhā al-amr min wuldika ʿAbdallāh b. al-Ḥārithīyah* [that is, Abū al-ʿAbbās] *thumma ʿAbdallāh* [al-Manṣūr] *akhūhu alladhī huwa akbaru minhu*).[15]

These accounts are designed to indicate that a determination had been made long before the revolution was declared and that role in the 'Abbāsid house was to be vested with the offspring of Muḥammad b. 'Alī and not with his brothers, the *'umūmah*. That the paternal uncles were likely to contest this succession was already evident to the family patriarch 'Alī b. 'Abdallāh, who is reported to have foreseen the course of events in a dream.[16] The setting is that of a house filled with vipers. A black snake, emerging from under the mother of 'Abdallāh b. 'Alī, consumes her. A flame emitted from under the mother of Abū Ja'far in turn consumes the black snake. Upon awakening, 'Alī b. 'Abdallāh offered an interpretation of his vision. In effect, his wife, the mother of 'Abdallāh b. 'Alī, will give birth to the son who is destined to liquidate the Umayyads; but his daughter-in-law, the mother of Abū Ja'far, will give birth to the son who will rule the emerging empire. For, in the course of events, the liquidator of the Umayyads will contest his nephew's right to rule and will himself be killed.

The political inferences to be drawn from 'Alī b. 'Abdallāh's analysis are evident even to the uninitiated in dream interpretation. The black snake emerging from his consort is his son 'Abdallāh, whose unsuccessful challenge to rule will mark an end to the pretensions of his branch of the ruling house. Through his failure, 'Abdallāh b. 'Alī will not only deny his progeny a path to the Caliphate, but will also in effect destroy his mother by terminating the political ambitions of her offspring. 'Alī b. 'Abdallāh thus prophesied what later came to pass. His son 'Abdallāh led the army, bearing the revolutionary black standards, and he, more than anyone, was credited with eliminating the last vestiges of the Umayyad house. Alas, having paved the way for an 'Abbāsid dynasty, the black snake fell short of the ultimate prize —the Caliphate itself. For, just as it was predicted in the dream, 'Abdallāh b. 'Alī was consumed by the flame of his nephew Abū Ja'far al-Manṣūr. The impression is given that the unfortunate patriarch offered these views more in regret than in anger, for what is destined by cosmic forces cannot be countermanded or otherwise affected by human intervention; 'Abdallāh b. 'Alī and Abū Ja'far al-Manṣūr were simply actors playing out their roles in the divine scheme.

One should be aware that dreams are not the exclusive domain of those blessed with as noble a genealogy as 'Alī b. 'Abdallāh. Salāmah, the Berber slavegirl who gave birth to Abū Ja'far, also had a vision of the future.[17] It is true her inclination was to lions and not snakes, but the point of the tradition is, nonetheless, clear. When pregnant with al-Manṣūr, she imagined that a lion cub emerged from her foreparts. He turned his head upward and roared while thrashing about. Soon the other lions came from all directions, each one prostrating itself before him. Being a Berber slave, Salāmah may have been reluctant to offer an interpretation of her dream, but for those familiar with the story of Yūsuf, the implied message was abundantly clear. Whereas Yūsuf had to establish primacy over his brothers, al-Manṣūr was called upon to establish himself vis-à-vis his paternal uncles and his nephew 'Īsā b. Mūsā. In both accounts, the interfamily struggle is resolved in favor of the lone individual against the collective group, and in both accounts, there is a suggested rivalry among the mothers. Salāmah's dream, unlike the patriarch's nightmare, was rather pleasant—and why not? The emergence of her son, the victorious lion, over his cousin and his paternal uncles placed the Berber slavegirl on an equal footing with —indeed made her superior to—the other ladies who gave birth to Abū Ja'far's rivals.

The conflict between al-Manṣūr and his close relatives within the 'Abbāsid house is a theme of many variations. Complementing the aforementioned traditions is an anecdote that dates from the reign of al-Manṣūr.[18] The scene, however, is chronologically rooted in the late Umayyad period shortly after Abū al-'Abbās inherited the leadership of the house from his brother Ibrāhīm al-Imām. En route to al-Kūfah (where Abū al-'Abbās was to receive his formal investiture), the two brothers and their uncle 'Abdallāh b. 'Alī were approached by a bedouin girl at a waterhole where they had stopped. "By God," she exclaimed, "I have never seen faces such as these," and then went on to indicate that there were two Caliphs and a rebel present. "This man shall rule," she exclaimed, pointing to Abū al-'Abbās al-Saffāḥ, "and verily, you [al-Manṣūr], shall succeed him." Continuing, she pointed to 'Abdallāh b. 'Alī and said, "and this one will rebel against you."

As if the testimony of a mere bedouin girl were not enough, several years later, when Abū Ja'far reached al-Kūfah to receive the *bay'ah* from members of the ruling family, thereby validating his own succession, he related a similar apocalyptic vision that had previously come to him.[19] Although devoid of snakes and lions, the Caliph's recollection is of particular interest, because, in one well-conceived dream, he was able to express his claims against the 'Alids, against his uncle

'Abdallāh b. 'Alī, and against his nephew 'Īsā b. Mūsā, the original heir apparent, who had been removed in favor of al-Manṣūr's son Muḥammad al-Mahdī.

The time of the dream is fixed before the revolution, when the 'Abbāsids still resided in their ancestral estate at al-Ḥumaymah. The tradition plays on the fact that Abū al-'Abbās, his brother Abū Ja'far, and their uncle 'Abdallāh b. 'Alī share the same personal name. The three of them were in the company of certain notables assembled in Mecca. The Prophet himself was in the Ka'bah, and the door was open but no one came forward. A herald (*munādī*) called out—"Where is 'Abdallāh?"—as if to indicate that the Prophet was granting an audience. Abū al-'Abbās went to the first step and was led by the hand, to return shortly thereafter with a black standard four cubits in length. The meaning of this acquisition is only too clear. The gift of the black flag symbolized that Abū al-'Abbās was destined to lead the family four years subsequent to the overthrow of the Umayyad regime, one year for each cubit in the standard. Although the historical background is unclear, it appears that the black standard had also acquired messianic attributions.[20] The unfurling of such flags later in Khurāsān signified not only an open declaration against the regime in power, but the anticipated coming of a new era as well. With the revolution successfully concluded, Abū al-'Abbās, the first 'Abbāsid Caliph, forsook Umayyad white and officially adopted black as the color of the new dynasty.

Having thus been entrusted with the paraphernalia requisite for the coming messianic age, Abū al-'Abbās was in effect ordained to bring about the collapse of the current Caliphate and to legitimize thereby 'Abbāsid claims to rule. That the Prophet himself gave Abū al-'Abbās the black flags for safekeeping signifies the symbolic transfer of authority directly through God's appointed messenger to a chosen successor, thus bridging the hiatus between "primitive Islam" and contemporary times. This last notion is entirely consistent with 'Abbāsid propaganda, which stressed a return to the ethos of an earlier age when moral authority was vested in the true believers, whose interests were now quite properly represented by the 'Abbāsid family.

The primary function of this tradition, however, is to reinforce the claims, not of Abū al-'Abbās, but, rather, those of his brother and successor, Abū Ja'far al-Manṣūr. Its didactic message is directed not only toward residual supporters of 'Alid causes, but also toward elements that may have questioned the validity of Abū Ja'far's credentials in relation to those of his rivals within the ruling family: his distinguished uncle 'Abdallāh b. 'Alī and his nephew 'Īsā b. Mūsā. In the next sequence of events, the herald again called out, "Where is 'Abdallāh?" By now, the two remaining 'Abdallāhs realized what was to be gained from an audience with the Prophet, so Abū Ja'far and 'Abdallāh b. 'Alī both raced forward. The story indicates that it was al-Manṣūr, and not his uncle, who was led into the Ka'bah where Muḥammad was found sitting. The future Caliph, in all modesty, confessed that the Prophet tied a standard (for him), willed him (*awṣā*) his community (*ummah*), and placed a turban with twenty-three folds on his head saying, "Take it for yourself, Father of Caliphs, until the day of Resurrection." This last reference to resurrection signifies the onset of the end of days when the messianic age is to be ushered in. Just as his brother received the symbolic tools required to overthrow the Umayyads in anticipation of a new era, Abū Ja'far was now granted the symbols of his Caliphate to do the same. To be sure, there could be no better choice than Muḥammad himself to establish al-Manṣūr's claim over that of his uncle. With credentials of this sort, what doubts could there be of the future Caliph's legitimacy?

There are, however, still more subtle nuances to be recognized in this multilayered tradition. Al-Manṣūr did not consider 'Abdallāh b. 'Alī the only threat to himself and the political hopes that he held for his offspring. There remained his nephew, the heir apparent 'Īsā b. Mūsā, who stood directly before the Caliph's son Muḥammad al-Mahdī. A conspiratorial figure by nature, al-Manṣūr could not be sure that, once in power, 'Īsā b. Mūsā would honor his commitment to respect the rights of the Caliph's eldest son. He therefore forced 'Īsā b. Mūsā to relinquish his position, thus guaranteeing the continuous rule of the Caliph's own progeny. These events are also clearly reflected in the tradition. For, in one well-chosen vision, the Caliph not only turned aside the claims of 'Abdallāh b. 'Alī, but, with the gift of the turban, the appellation "Father of Caliphs," and the reference to the Day of Resurrection, he also undercut the legitimate aspirations of his nephew, the heir apparent.

The reference to "Father of Caliphs" clearly indicates that the Prophet revealed, even before the revolution had been formally declared, that the future line of succession would eventually be through

Abū Ja'far's son Muḥammad, thereby eliminating the *'umūmah* and the descendants of 'Īsā b. Mūsā. This is, in itself, not unusual, for Muḥammad followed the designated heir apparent in the line of succession. However, the reference to the turban, which was to be held by the Caliph until the Day of Resurrection, provides an additional meaning. It not only refers to the eternal existence of al-Manṣūr's line (that is, the turban will be held until the end of days), but also represents, in this case, a double entendre, for it also identifies his successor. The rather subtle reference here is not to 'Īsā b. Mūsā, the designated heir apparent, but to the man who was to displace him from the line of succession.

It is no coincidence that the elaborate headdress that was to be held by al-Manṣūr contained twenty-three folds. Although the text offers no explanation for this curious fact, it would have been abundantly clear to all capable of simple arithmetic that the folds specifically represented the twenty-three years of al-Manṣūr's Caliphate. It is therefore implied that the Prophet gave this turban to al-Manṣūr for safekeeping until the latter's death, just as earlier he had presented Abū al-'Abbās with a standard signifying the length of his tenure. The Caliph's passing was, then, to be followed by the Day of Resurrection, an event that clearly denotes the beginning of the messianic age; however, in this context, the allusions to death, resurrection, and the advent of messianic time are intended to be symbolic. The messianic era about to come is but a thinly disguised reference to the reign of the Caliph's son Muḥammad, whose acquired regnal title, al-Mahdī, translated as "Messiah." Therefore, according to this vision, al-Manṣūr was destined to pass the Caliphate directly on to his son, and not to the original heir apparent, 'Īsā b. Mūsā.[21]

The secondary meaning is all too clear. The Prophet legitimized not only al-Manṣūr, but also his sons and grandsons after him. Once acquired, the Caliphate would be held in perpetuity for the Manṣūrid branch of the ruling family. In a fitting touch of irony, Salāmah al-Barbarīyah was thus fated to become the mother of a dynastic order, while the other 'Abbāsid ladies were destined to be consumed by the political failures of their deserving offspring.

No cosmetic touches can hide the fact that all these traditions are, at best, charming fabrications. Upon closer examination, it is clear that they are later inventions representative of a Manṣūrid hagiology that is both prominent and well-defined as a theme in early 'Abbāsid historiography. Its function was to draw attention from the Caliph's humble birth and rather limited career prior to his investiture by promoting a sense of legitimacy derived from invented ideological claims rooted in earlier times, often by way of a prophetic pronouncement or action. Although traditions of this sort may not be factual in detail, according to the critical standards of western scholarship, neither can they be considered outright falsehood. The application of conventional western concepts such as "fabrication" and "invention" to medieval Arabic historiography can be misleading. The legendary history of al-Manṣūr was neither true nor false, but was, in a sense, a meta-truth that transcended the bare particulars of an actual situation by proclaiming what was more real than reality itself.

C. The Claims of 'Abdallāh b. 'Alī

The existence of a Manṣūrid historiography is only a part of the puzzle, for there are echoes also of an historical tradition proclaiming a line of succession through 'Abdallāh b. 'Alī. The rationale for such an arrangement is suggested by M. Sharon in a brilliant analysis of the events surrounding Ibrāhīm al-Imām's sojourn in Syria shortly before his death.[22] The sudden request by the authorities that the hidden leader of the 'Abbāsid revolutionary movement be confined to the capital of the Umayyads is regarded as an act that must have generated considerable anxiety. This would have been true even if one were to accept Sharon's very plausible analysis that the imām was not under arrest, as is often assumed, but that his visit was of a delicate political nature. The possibility that death could overtake Ibrāhīm in hostile surroundings on the eve of the great 'Abbāsid triumph must have weighed heavily on the inner circle of the family, particularly because the revolutionary apparatus may have been exclusively tied to him. Sharon therefore suggests the creation of an initial list of successors chosen from among the members of the 'Abbāsid family who accompanied the imām to Damascus, with the event taking place there in Ibrāhīm's presence. The order is conjectured as first, Abū al-'Abbās, Ibrāhīm's brother, second, his paternal uncle 'Abdallāh b. 'Alī, and third, his nephew 'Īsā b. Mūsā. It may be noted that Abū Ja'far al-Manṣūr was not in their company, and was therefore not among the would-be successors.

Following the mysterious death of Ibrāhīm al-Imām, the inner circle of the family was confronted with a crisis of serious dimensions, that of publicly establishing the legitimacy of Abū al-ʿAbbās, for no public document of Ibrāhīm's last will and testament existed. An initial act was to preserve family unity, and Sharon suggests that the unwritten agreement mentioned above was formally ratified among a somewhat wider body, although not in writing, for full public disclosure would have been still premature. He further conjectures, without explanation, that Abū Jaʿfar's name may have been inserted for that of ʿĪsā b. Mūsā. For Sharon, this proposed list explains the subsequent problem of succession following the death of Abū al-ʿAbbās. Cheated of the right that was clearly his, ʿAbdallāh b. ʿAlī chose to challenge the claims of his nephew. Similarly, Abū Jaʿfar al-Manṣūr's later difficulties with ʿĪsā b. Mūsā may stem directly from the same set of circumstances.

Several questions may be raised with regard to this sequence of events. If this line of succession was, in fact, agreed upon, but, for reasons of security, lacked binding written documents, what was to prevent Abū al-ʿAbbās from drawing up a full bill of particulars, once the ʿAbbāsids were firmly established in power? It surely would have been in the interests of ʿAbdallāh b. ʿAlī to put pressure on the Caliph for an open disclosure, thereby creating an orderly succession. Moreover, why did neither ʿAbdallāh nor ʿĪsā b. Mūsā themselves press any claims on the basis of such a proposed list? The Caliph's uncle did apparently present a case of his own, but it was rooted in events of public distinction and not in silent intrigue. Moreover, it can be demonstrated that the historicity of even these alleged claims is highly questionable.

Interestingly enough, an account is found that resembles the politicized history of al-Manṣūr, but sets forth the credentials of his rival ʿAbdallāh b. ʿAlī. The particular tradition that is of interest plays on the frequency with which the letter *ʿayn* appears in the full name of ʿAbdallāh b. ʿAlī in relation to the *mīm* in that of Marwān b. Muḥammad, the last Umayyad Caliph. The point of the story is to demonstrate that ʿAbdallāh b. ʿAlī had been ordained by fate and the letter structure of his name to eliminate Marwān, thus putting an end to the Umayyad dynasty and heralding a new age. The defeat of the Umayyad armies by ʿAbdallāh in the terminal stages of the revolution and his systematic discovery and destruction of the last vestiges of the Umayyad house were, then, not only the fulfillment of this very prophecy, but, as can be shown, an indication of his right to rule. For, embedded in this apocalyptic tradition is the echo of an historical truth, namely, that ʿAbdallāh b. ʿAlī based his claims to the Caliphate on an alleged statement of Abū al-ʿAbbās, that whoever did combat with Marwān would be chosen as the Caliph's successor.[23]

It is highly unlikely that the Caliph actually made a public declaration of this sort. It is equally unlikely that the promise was the result of a private understanding. The texts describing Abū al-ʿAbbās's pledge seem to indicate that it was made in the presence of a small group of notables, and that the succession was available to anyone in the Caliph's immediate family who would volunteer to engage Marwān in battle. When ʿAbdallāh b. ʿAlī openly courted support for his own Caliphate, he recollected, quite conveniently, that only he had stepped forward to accept this challenge. From a literary point of view, this is even more effective than being chosen by Abū al-ʿAbbās, for it not only reflects the courage of ʿAbdallāh, but also implies the cowardice of the others, particularly of al-Manṣūr, whose lack of military experience was very much a sore point. That this event actually took place in the presence of Abū al-ʿAbbās was affirmed in testimony by various Khurāsānī army officers (*ahl Khurāsān*), including, it is reported, the redoubtable Ḥumayd b. Qaḥṭabah. It led eventually to ʿAbdallāh being recognized by military contingents from Khurāsān, Syria, and al-Jazīrah. The *bayʿah* having been taken to him publicly, ʿAbdallāh now moved to secure Iraq, the central province of the empire and the seat of its administration.

One may be inclined to express some doubt about this tradition, for, if ʿAbdallāh b. ʿAlī was given such assurances, why did the Caliph never give formal expression to his initial sentiments, and why, with the end near, did he have a change of heart in favor of his older brother? Be that as it may, it is clear that, based on a record of service in military and political affairs, ʿAbdallāh b. ʿAlī was the most logical choice as a successor to Abū al-ʿAbbās from the inner circle of the ruling family. Because Abū Jaʿfar al-Manṣūr was, on the same basis, among the least likely, it is not surprising that the claims of the uncle should be wedded to past performance.

This may indeed help to explain the aforementioned tradition of Ibn Qutaybah, which ascribes to al-Manṣūr the conquest of Syria, the death of Marwān II, and the elimination of certain vestiges of the

Umayyad house.[24] Although there are many variant reports concerning the massacre of the Umayyad family, the account of Ibn Qutaybah is unique in describing Abū Ja'far as an agent of execution.[25] Furthermore, the structure of the account and its presentation of detail bear a similarity to a tradition in which 'Abdallāh b. 'Alī took vengeance against the Umayyad family at Nahr Abī Fuṭrus.[26] In both accounts, eighty Umayyad princes were invited to a reception at which they were to receive gifts of honor. In both accounts, the poet al-'Abdī recites the appropriate *qaṣīdah* to commemorate the occasion. In both accounts, the indiscretions of the Umayyad house with respect to the 'Alid line are recalled, and in both accounts, after the brutal series of murders that followed, the principal actor is pictured as casually dining over the bodies, which lay beneath a covering before him. The attribution of all of these details to both 'Abdallāh b. 'Alī and Abū Ja'far al-Manṣūr suggests caution and elicits some comments of a general nature.

It is true that certain of these elements are common to other massacre accounts involving other actors, in particular to those accounts involving Abū al-'Abbās.[27] The difficulties posed by the numerous conflicting traditions have long been recognized, and the suggestion that the extirpation of the Umayyad House was carried out at different historic moments by a number of notables, and over a wide geographic area, seems quite plausible.[28] In this case, Abū Ja'far could well have played a role, along with his uncles 'Abdallāh b. 'Alī, Dāwūd b. 'Alī, and Sulaymān b. 'Alī, as well as his brother the Caliph, Abū al-'Abbās. One may even suggest the proper historic moment. The most likely time for this to have taken place was subsequent to Abū Ja'far's appointment as governor of al-Jazīrah, when he would have been responsible for the Umayyad princes of the region under his jurisdiction just as the others would have had similar responsibilities in their own regions.

The multitude of events, therefore, may explain part of the confusion, and where poetic traditions are similarly garbled as to author and verse, it does not necessarily imply anything more extraordinary than the usual literary embellishment. Nevertheless, the great obfuscation of detail, particularly with regard to the accounts of 'Abdallāh b. 'Alī and his nephews, leads to more speculative thoughts. The conquest of Syria, the execution of Marwān II, and the obliteration of the last vestiges of the house of Umayyah are interrelated events inextricably linked to the career of 'Abdallāh b. 'Alī. Qaḥṭabah b. Shabīb and his Khurāsānīs may have begun the process of destroying the regime in power by military means, but it was 'Abdallāh b. Alī and the *'umūmah* who applied the coup de grace. The massacre of the Caliph's relatives and the exhumation of the graves of his predecessors in Damascus were, as extensions of the military victory over the last Umayyad Caliph, the crowning acts that gave vivid expression to the emergence of a new political order. These established facts notwithstanding, Ibn Qutaybah preserves a tradition that attributes to al-Manṣūr not only the liquidation of various Umayyad notables, something that is well within the realm of possibility, but the conquest of Syria and the elimination of Marwān II as well. The view of this event obtained from Ibn Qutaybah may strain credulity, but it has an inner logic of its own. It is as though the accounts were created to mirror the exploits of Abū Ja'far's distinguished uncle, and as if the last testament of Abū al-'Abbās, which allegedly established Abū Ja'far's claims to the Caliphate, were not really sufficient to displace the great reputation of 'Abdallāh b. 'Alī, forged as it was on the anvil of an authentic history.

Even if the claims of legitimacy on behalf of 'Abdallāh b. 'Alī were rooted in accounts of dubious historicity, his expectations to rule could still be derived from his outstanding public record. One may even suggest that the maneuvers of 'Abdallāh b. 'Alī against his nephew cannot be characterized as a rebellion in the usual sense, for the latter's authority had hardly been established at the outbreak of the conflict. Moreover, despite the final preference of Abū al-'Abbās for his brother, the Caliph's uncle had every reason to believe that his own claims, based on past service, outweighed those of his nephew. Thus, 'Abdallāh b. 'Alī did not see his opposition to al-Manṣūr as a revolt against an entrenched regime, but as the assertion of his own claim to rule in a critical moment when the 'Abbāsid state temporarily lacked established authority.

D. The Revolt of 'Abdallāh b. 'Alī

What mattered in the final analysis, however, was, not the ideological basis of these claims, but the concentration of visible political power, which, translated into realistic terms, meant the army. Any objective assessment on the eve of the conflict between the newly appointed Caliph and his uncle would have invariably led to the conclusion that the scales were heavily weighed in favor of ʿAbdallāh b. ʿAlī. He could be expected to request the support of his distinguished brothers, who, together represented a formidable concentration of political power. Even more significant, he had, at that critical moment, a fully equipped army of both Khurāsānī and Syrian elements ready to depart on a campaign against the Byzantines. In addition, he had secured the oath of allegiance from the officer corps, which included no less important a warrior than Ḥumayd b. Qaḥṭabah, and he had the monetary resources to command their continued support, for he sat on the former treasuries of the Umayyad house.[29] His reputation in the army was equalled only by that of Abū Muslim, a man whose support might have ensured him the Caliphate. Although Abū Muslim followed the dictates of his master Abū al-ʿAbbās in recognizing Abū Jaʿfar as Caliph, there had been considerable enmity between the governor of Khurāsān and the man whose cause he now championed, and there were apparently still some misgivings. ʿAbdallāh b. ʿAlī squandered this clear advantage by brutally eliminating the Khurāsānī constituencies in his force, but that is quite another matter.[30] Abū al-ʿAbbās could not have foreseen that his uncle would attempt to expand what was to be essentially a struggle for succession into a contest for power among regional and ethnic groups. It was to bring about his downfall, for all objective criteria until then indicated a decided advantage for ʿAbdallāh b. ʿAlī.

Seen in this light, Abū al-ʿAbbās's decision to send the document of succession to ʿĪsā b. Mūsā takes on a specific meaning, for the Caliph's nephew was a key element in balancing the forces against ʿAbdallāh b. ʿAlī. Not only had he a military career in his own right, but he commanded as well considerable support from his position as governor of al-Kūfah.[31] Because Abū Jaʿfar was performing the rites of pilgrimage at this time, ʿĪsā was also the only leading ʿAbbāsid not connected with the *ʿumūmah* who was within manageable distance of the state treasuries situated in the administrative capital at al-Anbār. In addition, his own political career was now tied, as a result of these circumstances, to that of his uncle, Abū Jaʿfar. The shape of the emerging political struggle may also serve partly to explain Abū al-ʿAbbās's continued refusal to do away with his trusted agent Abū Muslim despite dire warning from al-Manṣūr. Indeed, Abū Muslim's contacts with the Khurāsānī army made it the critical counterweight to the Syrian contingents commanded by 'Abdallāh b. 'Alī; it was only after his uncle's defeat that al-Manṣūr felt free to move against his client, the governor of Khurāsān.

The defeat of the potent Syrian forces required a major military effort, whose success at the outset of the battle could not be guaranteed despite the boasts attributed to Abū Muslim.[32] In the final analysis, the battle was won not only by the skill of the Khurāsānīs, but also, as previously mentioned, because of internal problems within the Syrian camp. This was brought about by the mixed force that was imposed upon 'Abdallāh b. 'Alī when he left on the summer campaign (*ṣā'ifah*) shortly before the Caliph's death. Fleeing the scene of battle, 'Abdallāh b. 'Alī sought refuge with his brother Sulaymān, the governor of al-Baṣrah, who, as far as can be determined, had remained essentially neutral in the conflict.

The role of the *'umūmah* remains an important part of this puzzle. Ya'qūbī mentions that, following his public acclamation, 'Abdallāh b. 'Alī wrote to 'Īsā b. 'Alī and others (including presumably his remaining brothers), informing them of his investiture based on the alleged promise of Abū al-'Abbās. The letters were no doubt intended to serve as an invitation for open support; however, judging by the accounts of the conflict, only 'Abd al-Ṣamad, 'Abdallāh's heir apparent took an active part in the campaign.[33] This hesitation on the part of the *'umūmah* is perhaps the strongest indication that no line of succession involving 'Abdallāh b. 'Alī had ever been publicly established. Had there been such an arrangement, they would most likely have hastened to his support, especially because all the signs indicated that he was the likely victor in this struggle.

E. The Aftermath

One senses almost that the ferocity of events following the death of Abū al-'Abbās caught all the 'Abbāsids unprepared, and that, even after the conclusion of the unfortunate civil strife, no clear idea emerged of how to handle bruised relations within the ruling house. It appears that the initial inclination was to reduce tensions by conciliatory acts, and that such gestures might have been conditioned in part by al-Manṣūr's continued need for support within circles loyal to the paternal uncles. Furthermore, the essential neutrality of the *'umūmah* is likely to have had an ameliorative effect on the future of the real rebels and so explains the rather lenient punishment meted out to them.

It is reported that, with the battle over in favor of the Khurāsānīs, 'Abd al-Ṣamad was captured at Ruṣāfat al-Shām and delivered to al-Manṣūr, who, in turn, handed him over to 'Īsā b. Mūsā. The Caliph's nephew not only pardoned 'Abd al-Ṣamad, but also bestowed upon him various gifts and raiment. Another account seems to indicate that 'Abd al-Ṣamad went initially to 'Īsā b. Mūsā and was then granted a pardon from the Caliph as well during a period of general amnesty.[34] This course of action was no doubt based on political realities as well as on the residual effects of strong family ties. If, in fact, the remainder of the *'umūmah* was not actively involved in the conflict, the partial function of this general amnesty was to help solidify support within the ruling family behind the new Caliph. The *'umūmah* still retained considerable influence, and there were as well the 'Alid pretenders and Abū Muslim, an ally for the moment, but, in the eyes of al-Manṣūr, a potentially dangerous enemy. Shortly thereafter, both the defeated uncle and his brother-protector took the pledge of allegiance to al-Manṣūr.[35]

However, these acts of apparent reconciliation could not long forestall still other turbulent political confrontations that were destined to rock the house of al-'Abbās and cause a fundamental realignment of political power. The influence of the *'umūmah* was curtailed by isolating them from various provincial assignments. 'Īsā b. Mūsā was at first displaced, and then removed altogether, from the line of succession, and 'Abdallāh b. 'Alī was incarcerated at al-Ḥīrah, where he was to die under extremely mysterious circumstances some years later.

II

FRATRICIDE AND FAMILY POLITICS: DID THE CALIPH MURDER ʿABDALLĀH B. ʿALĪ?

A man said to al-Manṣūr: Revenge is justice, but letting an offense go without punishment is grace. We invoke the protection of God upon the Commander of the Faithful lest he be content with the lesser and not the more dignified of the two.

Ibn Qutaybah, *K. ʿuyūn al-akhbār* (Cairo), 1:98

It is reported that, in the year A.H. 147, the Caliph Abū Jaʿfar al-Manṣūr had his paternal uncle ʿAbdallāh b. ʿAlī put to death by placing him in a house built on a foundation of salt, which then gave way or was caused to collapse about him. This rather bizarre turn marked the finale to an intricate series of events that had begun a decade earlier when ʿAbdallāh b. ʿAlī had contested, by force of arms, his nephew's right to succeed Abū al-ʿAbbās. The broad outlines of this complex and extended episode appear clear, and the principal actors are easily identified; however, the fine detail of the plot remains elusive both at its point of origin and in the concluding act.[1]

Although a military revolt of this importance would ordinarily have called for severe reprisals, in this case it led only to protective custody followed by extended house arrest. Moreover, allowing even for the Caliph's capricious nature, which is well-attested to in a variety of accounts and under different circumstances, no satisfactory answer has yet been advanced as to why the declared rebel against the state should have been spared for so long a period of time and then summarily executed so elegantly at a point in his life when political career and influence were long behind him. At first glance, this may appear to be a rather piquant observation, more interesting for reasons of curiosity than substance, for it is unlikely that any convincing explanation of these events will emerge from a review of ʿAbbāsid historiography. Nevertheless, some tentative remarks are very much in order, particularly because the affair of ʿAbdallāh b. ʿAlī touches directly on the wider subject of relations between the Caliph and various elements of the royal family, one of the more critical if little discussed issues of state and society under the early regime.

A. The Alleged Murder

As a result of the general amnesty that followed the debilitating civil dispute, ʿAbdallāh b. ʿAlī remained in al-Baṣrah with a large retinue. Although an outright rebel against the regime, he could not be disposed of for several years, assuming that this was the Caliph's intention. Not only was he under the protective custody of his brother Sulaymān, the governor of al-Baṣrah, but al-Manṣūr was forced to give legal expression to that arrangement in a document carefully formulated to allow no room for devious exegesis. Although the elegant fashion in which ʿAbdallāh reportedly died may have been worth waiting for, it seems the initial steps leading to his demise could only have been arranged together with a basic realignment of political power within the ruling family.

A significant step in this development was the termination of Sulaymān's tenure as regional governor. Needless to say, prudence dictated that precautions also be taken locally to contain any residual sentiments on behalf of the *ʿumūmah*. In addition to replacing his uncle with a new official, the Caliph prudently built up a force of 12,000 men whom he stationed in the city.[2] Even then, only the agreed upon guarantee of safety for ʿAbdallāh could likely have led his brothers Sulaymān and ʿĪsā b. ʿAlī to deliver him to the Caliph. Once having effected this transfer, al-Manṣūr imprisoned or murdered ʿAbdallāh's following and then incarcerated him at a more secure location in al-Ḥīrah, against the very terms of the agreement.[3] Despite his unilateral abrogation of the "guarantee" (*āmān*), which paved the way for ʿAbdallāh's final imprisonment and death, al-Manṣūr was unwilling or unable to put an end to his uncle for another seven years.[4] These actions may underscore the Caliph's lack of integrity, but they also indicate that, in spite of it, his freedom of movement within ruling circles was somewhat constrained. Although prominent figures serving the ʿAbbāsid house, such as Abū Salamah and Abū Muslim, could be brutally eliminated through a variety of devious stratagems, the Caliph's response to the challenge from within the ruling family was decidedly more subdued and cautious, if not hesitant. Because the issues in the case of ʿAbdallāh involved nothing less than the question of succession itself, the restraint shown by al-Manṣūr regarding his kinsmen is all the more remarkable.

The method of execution reportedly chosen for ʿAbdallāh b. ʿAlī is, in itself, revealing. Even at first glance, one would hardly be disposed to believe the reports of several sources that al-Manṣūr went to the effort of building a structure on foundations of salt that would collapse about his uncle thereby causing his death.[5] A different version of the same story, a unique tradition preserved by Masʿūdī, retains the intent to homicide, although it injects a note of realism into this mysterious scenario. According to Masʿūdī, the Caliph gave orders that the former rebel be strangled along with a concubine by al-Manṣūr's retainer al-Muhallab b. Abī ʿĪsā. The two bodies were then placed in a position of loving embrace, and only at that point was the house demolished about them. After Ibn ʿUlāthah, the chief judicial officer of the city, and other observers were brought to witness the interlocked corpses amid the ruins, the Caliph commanded that the body be removed for burial near the Damascus Gate, an act that earned for the deceased the rather dubious but not insignificant distinction of being the first charter member of the Abū Suwayd Cemetery.[6]

Although the intricacies of Masʿūdī's account contain an undeniable charm, there will no doubt be those who remain skeptical. For them, a more plausible explanation might be that the structural members of ʿAbdallāh's final place of incarceration gave way under more prosaic circumstances; indeed, one notes that a late source, the Khaṭīb al-Baghdādī (5th century A.H.) preserves a tradition wherein it is simply stated that the house collapsed about him on a rainy night.[7] There is no talk of murder, of carefully placed bodies, and, above all, no mention of a foundation of salt. Moreover, the extent of damage that could be sustained to a building in Baghdad because of Mother Nature's tempestuous disposition is ironically best illustrated by the collapse of the domed audience hall that surmounted the very palace of al-Manṣūr (Qaṣr al-Dhahab), an event that is described as having taken place on a night of torrential rain, awesome thunder, and terrible lightning.[8] In light of this, one could very well conclude that the death of ʿAbdallāh b. ʿAlī, though perhaps not regretted, could have been accidental and then subsequently embellished in keeping with his importance and controversiality.

Seen in this context, the alleged testimony of al-Manṣūr himself is of particular interest. Shortly after the death of ʻAbdallāh b. ʻAlī, it is reported that the Caliph went riding with his servant and put the following question before him, "Do you know three Caliphs whose names begin with the letter *ʻayn* who killed three rebels whose names begin with *ʻayn*?" It may be recalled that al-Manṣūr's proper name, like that of his uncle, was ʻAbdallāh. The Caliph's riding companion, whose name quite remarkably also began with an *ʻayn*, then replied, "I only know what is spoken of by the populace (*al-ʻāmmah*). They say, ʻAlī killed ʻUthmān, but in this they lie, that ʻAbd al-Malik b. Marwān killed ʻAbd al-Raḥmān b. Muḥammad b. al-Ashʻath, ʻAbdallāh b. al-Zubayr, and ʻAmr b. Saʻīd. As for ʻAbdallāh b. ʻAlī, the building fell upon him." The Caliph then searchingly asked, "Am I to blame if the building fell upon him?" whereupon his servant responded prudently, "Who said you are to blame?"[9]

This text is, to be sure, a literary invention, but it contains nuances of a real and vexing situation; for, given the conspiratorial climate of the times, it is not difficult to suppose that the general populace spoke of assassination where less sensational circumstances were, in fact, the case. It is therefore necessary for this tradition to emphasize that the *ʻāmmah* are at times misinformed, as in the case of ʻAlī and ʻUthmān. It is, moreover, no accident that ʻAlī's involvement in ʻUthmān's assassination is specifically mentioned here. The purpose of this insertion is to quiet the tongues of the ʻAlid slanderers—in effect saying to them that people who live in glass houses should be forewarned. Furthermore, although the question of al-Manṣūr's involvement in the death of ʻAbdallāh b. ʻAlī is raised, he is not directly accused. On the contrary, the event is described as happening without an agent; it is simply pointed out that the building fell upon ʻAbdallāh. The reader is thereby left with the impression that there may be loose talk among the misinformed, but that there is no hard evidence to incriminate the Caliph of the Islamic realm. Although this is perhaps the most plausible statement, under the circumstances, that could be made to absolve al-Manṣūr, another variant of this tradition cannot resist an even stronger reply to his query. When the Caliph asks, "Am

I to blame?" the answer is not, "Who says you are to blame," but, more affirmatively, "You are not to blame."[10]

B. Historic and Pseudohistoric Precedents

If there is any historicity in the traditions engendered by 'Abdallāh b. 'Alī's death, it is the excruciating difficulty that confronted the Caliph when dealing with an important member of the 'Abbāsid house who was openly disloyal to him. In addition to 'Abdallāh b. 'Alī, one recalls two other paternal uncles who militarily challenged the authority of al-Manṣūr: Ismā'īl b. 'Alī not only went unpunished, he was later awarded the governorships of Fārs and Wāsiṭ; and 'Abd al-Ṣamad b. 'Alī, who was heir apparent to 'Abdallāh during his revolt, was pardoned and served in the administration of three subsequent Caliphs.[11] In contrast, the literature dealing with contemporary justice is replete with numerous accounts of public and private executions down to the goriest details of drawing and quartering (actually halving), to say nothing of other embellishments to the human body. As if this were not enough, there was also the practice of displaying elements of the mutilated torso on public monuments for the edification of the loyal subjects. The purpose of these actions was twofold. On the one hand, the mutilation of the human body degraded the enemy so as to render him harmless even in death, for no miraculous influence from beyond could be conceived of on behalf of someone so grotesquely disfigured. On the other hand, the butcher shop display on public monuments gracing the major arteries of traffic in the capital city addressed itself to the real nature of justice, not the proof of guilt or innocence, but the public demonstration of the authority of the state. Compared with this sort of staged presentation, the elimination of 'Abdallāh b. 'Alī and his discreet burial in a virgin place outside the Damascus Gate, even if true to the last detail, have an almost antiseptic quality about them.

The choice of a collapsed building as the vehicle for an execution is truly an artistic conception. It eliminates the need for the direct hand of an assassin, thereby creating a distance between the act of weakening the foundations and the actual demise of the victim; only the building could be held directly responsible for the death of 'Abdallāh b. 'Alī.

The more complicated staging of Mas'ūdī's account is not, however, without an elegant quality of its own. To be sure, an assassin is required, but the choice of strangulation is clearly intended to leave no telltale marks, and the decision to include a properly posed female companion in death is intended to lead the witnesses who examined the bodies still further away from the conclusion of murder. The function of the legal authorities in the account was, therefore, probably not simply to identify the person of 'Abdallāh b. 'Alī, as has been conjectured, nor to prepare the body for the ritual of burial, as might be suggested; rather, it was to certify, upon examination of the remains, that the body had not been penetrated or mutilated in any way by the ordinary tools of homicide.

The distinction may, at first glance, seem academic (it surely must have appeared so to 'Abdallāh b. 'Alī), but, as illustrated by an important moment in the life of the Prophet at Mecca, it is consistent with a traditional outlook.[12] The particular episode is fixed shortly before Muḥammad's personal hijrah to al-Madīnah, the critical event, as viewed by the traditionists, in the history of the early Islamic "community." The scene is in the Dār al-Nadwah, where the notables of Quraysh have gathered to consider various stratagems for disposing of Muḥammad. Three suggestions are put before the assembly. One is exile. It is rejected at the prodding of the devil, Iblīs, who has fortuitously appeared in order to help the Quraysh solve this rather ticklish problem. It is true that by exiling Muḥammad the Quraysh will be rid of him, but there is the fear that the exiled Muḥammad, a skillful orator, will attract a following beyond Mecca and then return to haunt them. Another suggestion, also rejected, is to chain Muḥammad in irons and leave him unattended in a locked place of confinement until death overtakes him. Although it is also rejected, this second proposal is not without merit. It takes time to consummate, but it does have an air of finality. Moreover, like the suggestion of exile, it does not require the shedding of Muḥammad's blood, thereby avoiding serious retribution by his kinsmen. Unfortunately, this scheme allows sufficient time for others to arrange his escape, and it is therefore also put aside at the recommendation of Iblīs.

Finally, a stratagem is set forth that can win the endorsement of the devil. At the suggestion of Muḥammad's greatest enemy, Abū Jahl, a young lad from each of the clans of Quraysh is recruited and given a sharp dagger with instructions for all to strike the Prophet as if with one blow. This last stipulation is of critical importance, because only in this fashion will his blood be distributed evenly among all the clans, thereby preventing Muḥammad's kinsmen from exacting blood revenge. Unable to overcome the rest of the tribe collectively arrayed against them, the Prophet's relations will be forced to settle for blood money. That Muḥammad was able to foil this attempted assassination with the assistance of Gabriel and God does not necessarily imply that the scheme was not strategically sound, only that it lacked proper tactical support. To be sure, the appearance of Iblīs may leave some doubt as to the historicity of this event. What is interesting, however, is that the thought of spilling the Prophet's blood with a proper instrument for homicide was unthinkable except in those circumstances in which blame could not be directly affixed. Whether legendary or not, the account clearly suggests that murder among kinsmen was a difficult matter, even in the imagination of later literateurs somewhat removed from the tribal life of the Arabian Peninsula.

A brief summary of the legal views touching upon the death of ʿAbdallāh b. ʿAlī and the attempted assassination of Muḥammad is perhaps in order. The relevant opinion is that of the Ḥanafite scholars who were predominant at Baghdad.[13] The proposal that Muḥammad be allowed to languish unattended and the death of ʿAbdallāh b. ʿAlī through the vehicle of a collapsed house both belong to the category called "indirect killing" (*qatl bisabab*), in which someone brings about the death of another without directly killing him; for example, a man digs a well into which someone falls and dies. The legal consequences are the same regardless of whether the death was entirely accidental, or whether the intention was murder from the outset. The punishment, in this case, is a light payment of blood money. This is distinct from "willful murder" (*ʿamd*). The action in willful murder is always premeditated and, significantly, it must be carried out, according to Abū Ḥanīfah, with an instrument that can be used as a weapon to *cut off limbs*—for example, a dagger of the type given to Muḥammad's would-be assassins. For such a murder, the punishment is execution or the payment of substantial blood money. Moreover, the assailant loses any claim of inheritance from the deceased. There is also a third category. Should a person willfully murder another with a weapon that *cannot cut off limbs*, that is, an unsharpened stone or a big stick, the murder is categorized as "similar to *'amd*" (*shabah* or *shibh 'amd*). The punishment under these circumstances is essentially the same as that for *'amd*, but, most important, the assailant cannot be killed in retribution. In light of these considerations, it is not surprising that, when mentioned, fratricide is generally described as a rather complicated matter demanding a delicate method of execution, such as poison, strangulation, or, in the case of 'Abdallāh b. 'Alī, nothing less than a collapsed building.

C. Subsequent Acts of Fratricide

One is inclined to think that the open shedding of blood within the ruling family was considered a reprehensible act that could set undesirable precedents, just as the killing of 'Uthmān allegedly opened the door for the murder of future Caliphs by weakening the moral authority of the Caliphate. To what extent this was due to residual feelings concerning bloodfeuds among kinsmen in earlier times, and to what extent it reflected political considerations within the ruling house cannot be determined with certainty. In any event, among the other 'Abbāsid notables of the eighth century, only the Caliph al-Hādī, and 'Abbāsah, the ill-fated sister of Hārūn al-Rashīd, are said to have met death through violent means. In these cases, however, the facts are so suspect or the extenuating circumstances so extraordinary, that the general thesis suggested here, namely, that fratricide and, beyond that, the actual shedding of blood were unacceptable solutions to political problems within the ruling family, is not seriously, if at all, compromised.

There is first, Mūsā al-Hādī, a Caliph distinguished by a reign that was shorter than his obituary. The mysterious death of Mūsā al-Hādī in his palace at 'Īsābādh has been attributed, in the early medieval tradition, to strangulation (actually smothering with a pillow) and, in some later sources, to poisoning. The choice of these subtle, indeed, undetectable methods of assassination bears out the original contention, that spilling royal blood was to be shunned. However, because the tradition is, in fact, derived from only a single, concise account, one may express reservations about the historicity of al-Hādī's murder. To be sure, there were many individuals within the government who stood to gain by the Caliph's death. These included the brother and heir apparent, Hārūn al-Rashīd (who was about to be deposed), the Queen mother, Khayzurān (a strong-willed presence, whose status was nevertheless falling), the influential politician-client Yaḥyā b. Khālid al-Barmakī (who had been recently imprisoned and was in fear for his life), and numerous retainers whose future depended entirely on the political status of their patrons.[14] Nevertheless, the evidence for regicide is entirely circumstantial. Indeed, one could forcefully argue that it was the political tension within the ruling house with regard to the deposition of the heir apparent that actually gave rise to the dramatic literary invention of al-Hādī's violent death. In less trying times, 'Abbāsid historians might well have been satisfied with a demise occasioned by natural causes.

There is, in fact, every reason to believe that the Caliph died of nothing more dramatic than an ulcerated stomach, although that could hardly have been a source of consolation to him. While this is specified in only a single, terse statement, the various accounts of his lingering illness are filled with significant and interlocking details.[15] The Caliph is reported to have become ill in al-Mawṣil, where he had gone to solicit the support of various military men on the matter of the disputed succession. The illness even then was considered sufficiently alarming as to dissuade the army commanders from making a firm commitment in an uncertain political climate. Because the Caliph's death would have relieved them of the need to choose between factions, they preferred, under the circumstances, to keep their distance and their heads and see if nature would run its course. If the Caliph were to die, they could turn to al-Rashīd. If he were to live, they could always make their peace with him later. It was only when his mission was aborted that the Caliph returned to 'Īsābādh, after a journey that unquestionably took considerable time and effort for the distance of the route along the Tigris was well over one hundred kilometers. It comes as no surprise, then, that, when al-Hādī reached his palace in the suburbs of Baghdad, he was in great discomfort; and, although one may of course conjecture that he was killed on his deathbed, it is highly unlikely. There is, in short, no compelling reason to assume that al-Hādī was murdered unless, of course, one is inclined by tradition to the conspiratorial view of history.

In the early dynasty, only 'Abbāsah, the sister of Hārūn al-Rashīd, is reported to have been given a criminal's execution. But the circumstances were quite unusual. The Caliph was anxious to enjoy the company of his sister as well as that of his client Ja'far the Barmakid under maximum conditions of discretion. To that end, a marriage was required, but good taste demanded that Ja'far and 'Abbāsah never cohabit. 'Abbāsah was, after all, a princess of the ruling house, and Ja'far was only a client of his sovereign. Where embers are kindled there is bound to be fire, and 'Abbāsah not only succumbed to the pangs of her heart, but she managed also to bear children, living testimony of her indiscretion. When the Caliph learned this from one of her servants, he not only had the Barmakid killed, he murdered 'Abbāsah and the children as well.

'Abbāsah's punishment was, however, still confined to a given branch of her family. Who is to say what good brother in similar circumstances would not murder his sister to save his reputation. Nevertheless, even under these most extenuating circumstances, there are serious doubts about the historicity of 'Abbāsah's murder, for only the very late sources deal with the final act to this tragic episode, and not all of them accept it as fact. The earlier accounts say nothing of her death, but relate only those events leading to the discovery of the unwanted offspring. It is not difficult to perceive, however, how the literary imagination of the late medieval authors required the redemption of al-Rashīd's honor and that of his family through the death not only of his presumptuous client, but of his beloved sister and her children as well. Were her indiscretion not sufficient cause, the secret pregnancies and the deceits required to conceal them would have been more than enough to aggravate the Caliph's sense of grievance, thereby explaining the fury of his rage against her, against Ja'far, and against the entire Barmakid family. The Caliph's swift action against the family of the Barmakids, for whatever additional reasons, was, however, quite another matter. They were, after all, his clients and not his blood relatives, and although clientage in a sense made them adoptive members of the 'Abbāsid house, the considerations that entered into dealing with them were altogether different from those due his kinsmen.[16]

The civil war following the death of al-Rashīd may be considered the watershed of 'Abbāsid rule, for it hastened many changes in the fabric of Islamic society. One of the most salient features to emerge in consequence of the prolonged and bitter struggle was the erosion of the veneer of civility that had characterized relations within the ruling family. This was caused not so much by any profound change within the 'Abbāsid house, as by the emergence of the army as a highly independent factor in the politics of the regime. So that even the ill-fated Muḥammad al-Amīn, who was beheaded in the final stages of the siege of Baghdad, can be seen as a victim of this new circumstance rather than of a prearranged plot against his life.

The version generally accepted by the medieval sources is that al-Amīn, faced with impending disaster in the last stages of the siege at Baghdad, decided against breaking out of the city and re-forming his shattered armies for a new campaign. Rather, according to a prearranged plan, he boarded a boat along the Tigris in order to surrender to Harthamah b. A'yan and thus throw himself upon the mercy of his brother, the future Caliph, al-Ma'mūn.[17] In view of all that had happened before, even when serious conflicts had developed within the ruling family, he had every reason to expect that his plea would be recognized. However, when the Caliph reached Harthamah's boat, it was attacked by the vessels of Ṭāhir b. al-Ḥusayn, a fellow general in the army of al-Ma'mūn. The boat was overturned, and, in the skirmish, he swam to safety but was subsequently captured, briefly interned, and murdered by Persian troops. His head was severed and sent to Ṭāhir; his body was left behind and removed the following day. In due time, the head of the deposed Caliph was presented on a platter to his brother in Marw.[18]

The response of al-Ma'mūn and his most trusted political confidant, the wazīr al-Faḍl b. Sahl, would seem to give credence to the view that judges them innocent of the brutal act. Although the new Caliph was overcome by emotion, his chief of state was quick to perceive the political ramifications of this break with precedent. "What has Ṭāhir done to us. He has unsheathed the swords and tongues of the people against us. We commanded that he [al-Amīn] be brought prisoner, instead he is brought mutilated."[19] It is tempting to regard this as crocodile tears, but the underlying sentiment is perfectly consistent with previously observed patterns. Even though his military retainers, and not the future Caliph, had committed the atrocity, it would be many years before al-Ma'mūn dared return to Baghdad; and although the reasons for his absence are admittedly more complex than the mutilation of al-Amīn, the tragic and degrading execution of the Caliph seems nevertheless to have exerted an emotional force. It is not likely that al-Ma'mūn would have willingly brought this situation upon himself. In fact, it was not until A.H. 209 that al-Ma'mūn killed and crucified Ibn 'Ā'ishah, the great grandson of Ibrāhīm al-Imām, in whose name the 'Abbāsid revolution was first begun. This relatively inconspicuous event is explicitly recorded as marking the first time a member of the ruling family was given to execution and public display by executive command.[20]

D. *'Abdallāh b. 'Alī and 'Īsā b. Mūsā*

Although the evidence presented may support the conclusion that 'Abdallāh b. 'Alī's dramatic death was a literary invention, there remains another problem. Why did 'Abbāsid historiography consider it necessary that al-Manṣūr murder his uncle seven years after he had removed him from public life by incarcerating him at al-Ḥīrah? The issue is complex but there is a plausible explanation. Al-Manṣūr's extended difficulties in the affair of 'Abdallāh b. 'Alī came to involve still another potential rival for power, the Caliph's nephew 'Īsā b. Mūsā, who, in accordance with the original scheme of succession, was heir apparent to the throne. In addition to his public service as governor of al-Kūfah, he had had, unlike his uncle, a rather distinguished military career during the revolution, particularly against the 'Alid rebels in A.H. 145.[21] However, there is no indication that 'Īsā was a man of great ambition. There is even the tradition that he was offered the Caliphate when 'Abdallāh b. 'Alī rebelled against al-Manṣūr but rejected it emphatically, preferring to remain loyal to the Caliph and wait for his proper turn.[22] On the evidence available, the potential rivalry between them was always more apparent than real. Nevertheless, this did not save 'Īsā from a series of humiliating experiences that were initiated at the behest of the Caliph and that culminated in 'Īsā being forced to relinquish his position in the line of succession to the Caliph's son al-Mahdī.

One also recalls that 'Īsā had already been seriously compromised by al-Manṣūr in the events leading to the assassination of 'Īsā's friend Abū Muslim at al-Madā'in.[23] The latter had been very reluctant to leave his Khurāsānī army to accompany the Caliph during the *ḥajj* of A.H. 137, for he felt that al-Manṣūr's animosity was potentially hazardous. Nevertheless, after taking precautionary measures, Abū Muslim consented to join the royal party in Iraq, where he enjoyed the hospitality and, indeed, the protection of ʿĪsā b. Mūsā. Upon learning that his guest was summoned by al-Manṣūr for an audience, the Caliph's nephew is reported to have tried to dissuade Abū Muslim from appearing alone. Rather, he suggested that they go together, the clear presumption being that, if al-Manṣūr intended foul play, the presence of the heir apparent would prevent it. However, when ʿĪsā tarried in order to make himself presentable, Abū Muslim foolishly proceeded by himself and became victim to the harsh fate that awaited him.

A second account of this event credits ʿĪsā b. Mūsā with a decidedly less cautious attitude but crystallizes even more clearly the extent to which he was compromised by the Caliph.[24] Abū Muslim, upon learning that he was to appear before the al-Manṣūr, requested that ʿĪsā b. Mūsā accompany him. The latter instructed Abū Muslim to proceed (alone) with a verbal commitment of his protection (*taqaddam wa anta fī dhimmatī*), a promise that ʿĪsā b. Mūsā had every reason to expect would be honored because Abū Muslim was his personal guest. Nevertheless, the governor of Khurāsān was verbally abused and brutally murdered in the presence of the Caliph. Still another tradition[25] relates that ʿĪsā b. Mūsā ultimately made his way to the Caliph's tent, whereupon he first inquired as to the whereabouts of Abū Muslim and then spoke on his behalf. Al-Manṣūr responded by publicly upbraiding the heir apparent (*yā anwaḵu*). He pointed out that Abū Muslim was indeed his greatest enemy as well (*ma aʿlamu fī al-arḍ ʿaduwwan a ʿadā laḵa minhu*) and then called attention to the corpse that lay rolled in the carpet before them. Although these actions wisely brought no act of defiance on the part of the Caliph's nephew, the lesson in character was presumably not lost on him.

In some respects, this event may be regarded as preparation for the murder of ʿAbdallāh b. ʿAlī ten years later; once again, ʿĪsā b. Mūsā was reportedly involved as an unwilling agent in a plan to eliminate an important person who was allegedly his enemy within the regime.[26] Simply put, the following chain of circumstances was set in motion by al-Manṣūr: ʿAbdallāh b. ʿAlī, who had been languishing in prison at al-Ḥīrah, was surreptitiously brought to Baghdad unbeknown to ʿĪsā b. Mūsā, who was himself summoned to the capital from al-Kūfah. Custody of the former rebel was entrusted to ʿĪsā by al-Manṣūr. After secretly delivering his uncle in the middle of the night, the Caliph pointed out 'Abdallāh's past indiscretions against the present line of succession, which coincidentally included 'Īsā b. Mūsā, who was then still heir apparent. Having emphasized this, he further suggested that it was in 'Īsā's interest to protect his position as future Caliph by executing 'Abdallāh, and, significantly, he specified the method of execution as decapitation. Moreover, it was made known, and in no uncertain terms, that any display of weakness on the part of 'Īsā b. Mūsā would undermine the authority of the Caliph himself. As if to reinforce this sentiment, the righteous Caliph sent him a series of letters, while en route as a pilgrim to Mecca, impatiently enquiring if the matter had been brought to a conclusion. 'Īsā did nothing but answered affirmatively lest he arouse the Caliph's anger.

The reconstruction of these events is nevertheless troublesome. Allowing even for the conspiratorial nature that pervaded al-Manṣūr's outlook, no reasonable, let alone logical, explanation can be found to justify a course of action based on a presumed danger from his uncle. What manner of threat was 'Abdallāh b. 'Alī, now seven years incarcerated, to cause any apprehension on the part of al-Manṣūr or his would-be successors. It may, of course, be that the Caliph acted from considerations that were not entirely rational, but this time one suspects the existence of an inner logic to the unfolding scene. If the tradition describing subsequent developments bears any resemblance to historical fact, it becomes evident that 'Abdallāh b. 'Alī was to be the incidental casualty in a much more pervasive and sophisticated plot. The real victim was to be, not the Caliph's uncle, but, rather, 'Īsā b. Mūsā himself.

One recalls that Abū al-'Abbās is reported to have named 'Īsā b. Mūsā second in line to the Caliphate behind Abū Ja'far al-Manṣūr, according to a protocol that was duly affixed in writing. It is not surprising, therefore, that, when 'Abdallāh b. 'Alī set forth his claims to rule following the death of Abū al-'Abbās, 'Īsā b. Mūsā supported al-Manṣūr. By doing so he not only remained faithful to the dying Caliph's will, but he also insured his own right to succeed—or so he thought. Upon assuming the role of Caliph, al-Manṣūr recognized the position of his nephew and placed his own son, Muḥammad al-Mahdī, behind him in the line of succession. However, fearful that 'Īsā might eventually favor his own progeny and thus deprive al-Mahdī of his rightful place, al-Manṣūr became determined to remove him from his position as immediate successor. Such a policy could have been consummated in one of three circumstances. One was premature death by natural causes, the others, assassination or abdication. Taking a realistic assessment and leaving to Allāh that which is His alone, only the last two options were available to the Caliph. In view of al-Manṣūr's inability to do away with 'Abdallāh b. 'Alī, a declared rebel against the regime, it is hardly likely that the loyal governor of al-Kūfah, bearing a legitimate claim duly recognized by the Caliph himself, was in any overt danger. Nor is it more plausible that the dramatic death threat reportedly levied against his son Mūsā would have influenced the heir apparent to give up his obdurate stand against any change involving his status. It is possible that al-Manṣūr was willing to go that far on behalf of his own progeny, but, if that were indeed the case, it would have marked the first time in the history of the realm that so drastic a policy was envisioned where the ruling family was concerned.[27]

One cannot help but assume that the realities of the situation must be weighed somewhat differently. There is nothing in 'Īsā b. Mūsā's career that would suggest great strength of purpose. On the contrary, he gives the impression of a cautious man, able to sustain various slights, and not given to dramatic behavior. Although quite humiliating, the turn of events that inevitably forced him from his position can hardly be said to have brought on a state of deprivation. In the end, he simply exchanged places with al-Mahdī, an exchange for which he received, in a publicly ackowledged agreement, some eleven million dirhams to be distributed to him and his family. But this was still not enough for al-Manṣūr. Although removed from his position as governor of al-Kūfah, 'Īsā remained a formidable figure within the 'Abbāsid hierarchy; and, although by temperament he was not one to initiate action, his continued presence in any line of succession was no doubt regarded with suspicion by a Caliph whose fear of conspiracy was perhaps the most overt flaw of his character.[28]

E. The Plot Analyzed

Viewed in light of these developments, the alleged plot to behead 'Abdallāh b. 'Alī takes on a coloring of its own. Why, indeed, was it necessary to carry on the contacts in secret, and why, in particular, did al-Manṣūr dictate this brutal (or for that matter any) method of assassination as distinct from such delicate means as poison, strangulation or the even more subtle method that was reportedly used somewhat later? Such clandestine maneuvers were clearly not intended to shield ʿĪsā b. Mūsā, but rather the Caliph. It is no small wonder then that al-Manṣūr absented himself from Baghdad during the period in which the crime was to be committed, preferring to keep informed only by way of private messages. Moreover, a murder by the method suggested could not be glossed over as death by natural causes or as some curious accident; nor was there any intention to do so. The reconstruction of these events would seem to indicate that al-Manṣūr was carefully spinning a web of intrigue to entrap ʿĪsā b. Mūsā. ʿAbdallāh b. ʿAlī was to be the instrument by which the Caliph would eliminate both of them with one stroke, for once ʿĪsā b. Mūsā had brutally murdered his great uncle, the first ʿAbbāsid to shed family blood would be given over to the *ʿumūmah* to suffer revenge.

The dangers implicit in al-Manṣūr's intrigue were reportedly not lost on ʿĪsā's scribe, Yūnus b. Farwah, who, with the political cunning of his profession, pieced out the drama that was about to take place. Al-Manṣūr indeed wished to eliminate both notables. To that end, he would have ʿĪsā behead ʿAbdallāh b. ʿAlī in secret and then demand his uncle's presence publicly. When unable to produce him, ʿĪsā would be made a victim of the vengeful relatives, while al-Manṣūr stood in the wings with clean hands. To frustrate the inevitable, ʿĪsā b. Mūsā was advised to hide ʿAbdallāh b. ʿAlī in his residence and deliver him to the Caliph only in public. With al-Manṣūr under the impression that the act had been finalized, the relatives of ʿAbdallāh b. ʿAlī were invited to carry the play through to its conclusion. Needless to say, al-Manṣūr was foiled, as his nephew not only produced ʿAbdallāh b. ʿAlī, but also trapped the Caliph into publicly declaring that which he could hardly refute under the circumstances, namely, that he, al-Manṣūr, had not ordered his uncle put to death. Thus it was not only impossible to accuse ʿĪsā b. Mūsā of murdering his relative, but impossible as well to accuse him of disobeying any Caliphal command. It was only then that al-Manṣūr had ʿAbdallāh b. ʿAlī placed in his prison with foundations of salt.

This last tradition, as it appears here, is unquestionably embellished to heighten the dramatic effect. ʿĪsā b. Mūsā is seen taken to the great central court of the Round City for public execution at the hands of his great uncles, and it is only at the last moment, as his would-be executioner stands before him with sword unfurled, that he reveals his defense. He then confronts the Caliph with his perfidy. "You wished by his death to kill me. This uncle of yours is alive and in one piece. If you command me to deliver him, I shall do so . . . You schemed against me but I was suspicious and it was as I suspected. . . ."[29] One can hardly suppose that these words were uttered publicly before the Caliph, or that ʿĪsā b. Mūsā would have been so casual in the drama that was unfolding about him, waiting until the last moment, with an executioner at his side. Nevertheless, one is inclined to believe that there is an element of truth to this account, and that the snare prepared for ʿĪsā b. Mūsā was not entirely an invention, even if the full details are not altogether clear.

A variant of this account, preserved by Masʿūdī, would seem to indicate a more probable sequence of events.[30] ʿĪsā b. Mūsā, having been approached by the Caliph to kill ʿAbdallāh b. ʿAlī, secretly consulted with Ibn Abī Laylā and Ibn Shubrumah. Ibn Abī Laylā advised following the Caliph's command, but Ibn Shubrumah counseled otherwise. ʿĪsā did not kill ʿAbdallāh b. ʿAlī, but indicated that he had. When the *ʿumūmah* inquired of al-Manṣūr about the condition of their brother, the Caliph responded that he was with ʿĪsā b. Mūsā. They, in turn, asked ʿĪsā about him, and the Caliph's nephew answered that he had had him put to death. The *ʿumūmah* then went to the Caliph with the story that ʿĪsā claimed to have killed ʿAbdallāh b. ʿAlī, and al-Manṣūr registered righteous indignation, "He killed my paternal uncle. By God I will indeed kill him." Since it was clear, according to the report of Masʿūdī, that the Caliph wanted ʿĪsā b. Mūsā to kill ʿAbdallāh b. ʿAlī so he could get rid of them both, ʿĪsā was now called in to explain his action. He pointed out he was only complying with the Caliph's wishes and produced a letter from him to prove it, despite al-Manṣūr's denial. However, when he saw that al-Manṣūr was becoming short-tempered, he became worried and confessed to not having killed ʿAbdallāh b. ʿAlī. ʿĪsā b. Mūsā was then asked to turn his prisoner over to al-Muhallab b. Abī ʿĪsā, who made plans for ʿAbdallāh's ultimate death in the ill-fated house that was collapsed about him. There is no indication here of tantalizing the public executioner or taunting the Caliph with words.

This second tradition pictures ʿĪsā b. Mūsā without bravado and on the horns of a real dilemma: whether to kill his great uncle in a fashion that could well lead the *ʿumūmah* directly to his door, or to spare him and face the wrath of the Caliph. His decision was likely to have been based on the following assumption. If al-Manṣūr did, in fact, wish to have ʿAbdallāh b. ʿAlī killed and meant no harm to him, then the Caliph would intercede to shield his nephew from ʿAbdallāh's vengeful relatives. If, on the other hand, ʿĪsā b. Mūsā was to become the victim of a pervasive plot, the living ʿAbdallāh b. ʿAlī would satisfy the *ʿumūmah* and might even cause them to restrain the Caliph, who could hardly raise suspicions that he was in any way involved in an attempt on his uncle's life. If correctly reported, the presumptive signs, in particular the prescribed method of execution by decapitation, would strongly indicate a pervasive plot. That ʿĪsā b. Mūsā chose to respond positively to the Caliph, though he would not carry out his wishes, is an indication of the dread that al-Manṣūr inspired in him. Be that as it may, the most significant feature to be extrapolated from the entire affair is, once again, the narrow area in which the Caliph could initiate decisive action against elements of the ruling house. When all was said and done, the literateurs who gave final shape to these accounts could not conceive of al-Manṣūr openly killing ʿĪsā b. Mūsā, any more than they could envision ʿAbdallāh b. ʿAlī as the victim of a simple assassination.

To what extent this episode can be related to al-Manṣūr's subsequent desire to remove ʿĪsā b. Mūsā from the line of succession in favor of his own progeny is an open question. In any event, the only realistic course of action open to the Caliph was, not to murder his potential rivals within the ruling house, but to isolate them from their traditional sources of strength, the provincial governorships. Moreover, it was necessary to drive a wedge between them and their would-be constituencies by staged acts of public demonstration that gave expression to the Caliph's authority and to their subordinate status. These measures were no less artistically conceived than the serpentine plans of fratricide so elegantly embroidered into the fabric of ʿAbbāsid historiography. Thus, although ʿĪsā b. Mūsā continued to enjoy the status guaranteed him by high birth and a compliant nature, he was subjected to additional humiliations. Not content with his nephew's earlier abdication in favor of al-Mahdī, al-Manṣūr sought to stage an elaborate series of events to emphasize his point.

Construction of a major palace complex on the east bank of the Tigris was begun in A.H. 151 in order to provide for the future Caliph a residence that could rival the magnificent Round City of al-Manṣūr on the opposite shore.[31] Al-Mahdī was brought home from Khurāsān that very year amid a tumultuous welcome. Delegations from Syria, al-Baṣrah, al-Kūfah, and other districts met him along the way. Some among these visitors were designated by the Caliph to be his son's companions, and they were all clothed in robes of honor and given gifts by al-Mahdī and by the Caliph as well, who presented each man with a sum of 500 dirhams.[32] At the conclusion of these elaborate preparations, al-Manṣūr convened the 'Abbāsid dignitaries in his audience hall and had them renew the pledge of allegiance (*bay'ah*) to himself, to his son and heir apparent, al-Mahdī, and to his nephew, 'Īsā b. Mūsā, who now stood second in line for the Caliphate. Each dignitary taking the pledge was reported to have kissed the hand of al-Manṣūr and that of al-Mahdī; but they only touched the hand of 'Īsā b. Mūsā, as if to indicate, by deliberate breach of protocol, the nature of the political alignment against the Caliph's nephew.[33] The triumphal nature of al-Mahdī's return, the renewal of the pledge, and the obvious snub of 'Īsā b. Mūsā, as well as the construction of the great palace complex at al-Ruṣāfah, were, therefore, all concurrent and apparently related events. They illustrate not only the Caliph's wish to insure the succession of his son, but, equally, his intense desire to give that wish public expression. Not long after the death of al-Manṣūr, 'Īsā b. Mūsā was removed altogether from the line of succession, having been forced into a second public renunciation of high office, this time bought for ten million dirhams guaranteed from the tax revenues of the Zāb estates. Twice rejected, he retired from the active political arena to live out his life in relative seclusion.[34]

III

THE PROVINCIAL ADMINISTRATION: OLD REVOLUTIONARIES AND FAMILY POLITICS

A Christian doctor:

We find it written in one of our books that a man called Miqlāṣ will build a city called al-Zawrā', between the Tigris and the Ṣarāt Canal. When he has laid the foundation and constructed part of the wall, it will be breached from the Ḥijāz thereby interrupting the building of the city. He will undertake to repair this breach, and when it is at the point of being repaired, the wall will be breached again from al-Baṣrah to a greater degree of damage than before. But it will not be long before the two breaches are repaired and he turns to building the city; then he will complete it. He will be granted long life, and his progeny will enjoy life after him.

Al-Manṣūr:

I "by God" am the one. I was called Miqlāṣ when a youth, but then the name passed from me.

Ṭabarī 3/1: 272-3

From the outset of the Abbāsid regime, the crux of the Caliph's dilemma was the possibility of a challenge to the central authorities from an important regional sinecure. This was, in fact, an ever present threat to the Caliphate, for a permanent Islamic presence was established in the wealthy and politically important territories beyond the confines of the Arabian Peninsula. The quintessential problem was how to insure strong local rule while safeguarding the interests of the central regime, at first in al-Madīnah, under the Umayyads in Damascus, and later in the 'Abbāsid capitals of Iraq. Various stratagems included the frequent rotation of governors to prevent the accumulation of power by individuals and the choice of local rulers from among close kinsmen whose loyalty was assured.[1]

A. The Old Revolutionaries and the New Order

It is, in this respect, noteworthy that, following the revolution, the leading members of the 'Abbāsid family were all given provincial governorships by Abū al-'Abbās. Particular branches of the 'Abbāsid house thus came to control various positions of rule, at times replacing the political operatives who had originally secured and run the revolutionary stations. One may see this development as a natural consequence of the relationship between the 'Abbāsid family and the revolutionary apparatus.

During the long period of clandestine activity, caution dictated that the substantive work be carried out by trusted agents rather than by members of the family. As a result, two particularly significant figures emerged: Abū Muslim in Khurāsān and Abū Salamah al-Khallāl in al-Kūfah. Because the majority of the revolutionary constituency established its ties to the cause through these two figures or their representatives, rather than directly through the hidden 'Abbāsid imām, the real power vested in the *wazīr*, or *amīr āl-Muḥammad*, Abū Salamah, and the *amīn āl-Muḥammad*, Abū Muslim, was enough to cause concern within family circles about a potential challenge to their primacy.[2] Although perhaps not given explicit expression, the need for the 'Abbāsids to assert themselves in positions of authority, once it was safe to do so, would therefore seem to have been self-evident.

Abū Salamah was only a client of the 'Abbāsid house, but he had accumulated tremendous power by the time of Abū al-'Abbās's investiture. As soon as the Khurāsānī armies entered Iraq, they technically passed from Abū Muslim's jurisdiction into his.[3] Abū Salamah not only assumed control of military operations in the region, but, of equal importance, he established the administration of the newly conquered areas, appointing governors of his own choosing.[4] The pattern for these developments had been set down previously by Ibrāhīm al-Imām, who, in sending Abū Salamah to al-Kūfah, entrusted him with responsibility for territories in Iraq, Al-Jazīrah, and al-Shām.[5] As the clandestine phase of the revolution came to an end, the revolutionary infrastructure served as the building blocks with which to construct the emerging 'Abbāsid government. The powers that accrued to Abū Salamah before the ruling family emerged in public were therefore considerable, and the geographic scope of his authority included all the major districts between Egypt and present-day Iran.

Moreover, Abū Salamah, through his own actions, provided the 'Abbāsids with additional cause for concern. The untimely death of Ibrāhīm al-Imām, on whose behalf the oath of allegiance had been taken, left a serious problem as to the legitimacy of his successor, Abū al-'Abbās. Without a clearly defined claim to the imāmate, the entire future of the 'Abbāsid cause was left in doubt on the eve of their great victory. The particulars of this last episode have been skillfully pieced together by M. Sharon.[6] Although much of his analysis is admittedly derived from a series of conjectures and is therefore subject to question, his basic thesis is forcefully argued. The full details of the plot are left to Sharon's readers. What is of relevance here is his conclusion that Abū Salamah was genuinely perplexed by Ibrāhīm al-Imām's sudden and mysterious death in Ḥarrān. With no clear directive from the late imām how to proceed, Abū Salamah vacillated in his support for Abū al-'Abbās, the successor secretly chosen by the inner circle of the 'Abbāsid family.

There can be no doubt that Abū Salamah's lack of enthusiasm, together with the growing power at his disposal, represented a potential threat to the emerging regime. Sharon is inclined to view the situation in still more dramatic terms by accepting the basic thrust of those traditions that maintain that the director of the Kūfan station did, in fact, act against 'Abbāsid interests. Whether this took the form of an aborted alliance with 'Alid Shī'ites (which seems improbable) or the call for an electoral college (*shūrā*) to establish a Caliph other than Abū al-'Abbās (which seems highly problematic) is not certain. What is clear is that, when Abū Salamah's ardor for the 'Abbāsid line cooled, the ruling family quite understandably chose to remove him and to seize direct control of the intricate apparatus that he had erected through provincial governorships and military commands.[7] The revolution having been secured, the veteran revolutionary was no longer essential to the broader interests of the dynasty. Although his execution probably resulted from a direct provocation, the mere possession of such power as he had might have insured Abū Salamah's demise.

The problem of Abū Muslim's relationship to the 'Abbāsid house is a more complicated matter. The complexity of the problem stems, in part, from the contradictory traditions that exist concerning his geographic origins, ethnic background, social status, and early associations with Ibrāhīm al-Imām.[8] He is depicted, among other things, as a descendant of Iranian nobility, a freeborn Arab, a manumitted slave, a client of the 'Abbāsid house, and the self-proclaimed grandson of 'Abdallāh b. 'Abbās by way of his illegitimate son Salīṭ. Given the clandestine nature of 'Abbāsid revolutionary activity, there is the suspicion that much of this obfuscation is intentional and based on traditions that appear as early as the revolution itself.[9] Abū Muslim was, in short, intended to serve 'Abbāsid interests as a man for all seasons and for all peoples in Khurāsān.

The trust placed in him by Ibrāhīm al-Imām was borne out by subsequent events. With consummate political skill, Abū Muslim rallied Khurāsān behind the 'Abbāsid cause following the open declaration of rebellion. After the new regime was established, he continued to play a prominent role in service to the 'Abbāsid Caliphs Abū al-'Abbās and Abū Ja'far al-Manṣūr. Despite these substantive contributions to the formation of the 'Abbāsid state, Abū Muslim was brutally murdered by al-Manṣūr in the year A.H. 137. It appears that the circumstances that led to Abū Muslim's death are no less complex than those related to his early career. The traditions dealing with this matter express two central themes: that he combined excessive haughtiness with great power, and that his relations with Abū Ja'far were badly strained because of an accumulation of incidents that began in the reign of Abū al-'Abbās. There is, however, no significant evidence of treason against the state, even in the bill of particulars reportedly levied against Abū Muslim by the Caliph at the moment of his execution.[10] Nonetheless, even if one were to assume that Abū Muslim was entirely trustworthy, he would have to be viewed as a potentially greater threat than Abū Salamah.

Abū Muslim not only had extraordinary power at his disposal, he was, at the same time, decidedly less vulnerable than his counterpart in Iraq. The Kūfan apparatus, though well established, lacked a military experience of its own. It relied primarily on Khurāsānī contingents that entered the region with the geographical advance of the revolution. On the other hand, Abū Muslim was, in effect, the creator of the Khurāsānī army, and, of even greater significance, he had been its central paymaster.[11] Like Abū Salamah, he was entrusted by Ibrāhīm al-Imām with wide ranging administrative powers including jurisdiction over the territories of Khurāsān, Sijistān, Kirmān, Jurjān, Qumis, al-Rayy, Iṣfāhān, and Hamadhān.[12] As supreme governor of the eastern provinces, he traveled with so extremely large a military retinue as to inadvertently cause considerable embarrassment, if not apprehension, to the Caliph.[13] So extensive was his influence that even after the 'Abbāsid family came to power, he is reported to have appointed a district governor without first consulting Abū al-'Abbās.[14]

Relations with the provincial administration in Khurāsān were soon tested. A crisis developed when Muḥammad b. al-Ash'ath, who served as Abū Muslim's governor of Fārs, defied the central authorities.[15] The Caliph had decided to replace the incumbent with his paternal uncle Ismā'il b. 'Alī, but Abū Muslim's appointee was adamant in his refusal to relinquish control, insisting that it was the governor of Khurāsān who had jurisdiction in the issue. When it was pointed out that Abū Muslim was only the servant of the imām, Ibn al-Ash'ath still balked and referred the matter to his patron. Abū Muslim's intervention on behalf of the Caliph's uncle ended the dispute, and Ismā'il b. 'Alī had his province. The real fault may have been that of Ibn al-Ash'ath and was probably based on a misunderstanding. Nevertheless, the Caliph was angered. The affair could only have served to underscore the concern of those who felt that too much power was concentrated in the governor of Khurāsān. Abū Ja'far, in particular, warned his brother, "You are not secure in the Caliphate as long as Abū Muslim lives. . . . It is as though there is none above him or like him."[16]

Still, the impression is created that the governor of Khurāsān was loyal to Abū al-'Abbās, and, despite some misgivings by the Caliph, he was regarded as a valuable political asset. When the decision was taken to liquidate Abū Salamah, the act was carried out by an agent of Abū Muslim, thus shielding the family from any hint of direct involvement.[17] Although Abū Muslim remained in the province where he served as governor, he was informed of all developments at court through his "eyes" and confidant Abū al-Jahm. Through this established liaison, the governor of Khurāsān enjoyed privileged information concerning the affairs of the 'Abbāsid state, and his advice was solicited in critical matters. His long service in Khurāsān made him particularly useful, and during the extended campaign of the Khurāsānīs against Ibn Hubayrah in Iraq, the Caliph made no decision without first consulting his "Trotsky."[18]

Abū Muslim's previous associations with the Khurāsānī commanders then in Iraq, as well as with those under his jurisdiction in the east, were, however, two-edged. As long as he retained the means to meet the payroll of his army, he was no doubt the most powerful figure in 'Abbāsid government outside the ruling family. Within the house, the only reputations to match his were those of the Caliph, by virtue of his position, and 'Abdallāh b. 'Alī, by virtue of his successful military campaigns in Syria and al-Jazīrah.[19] The concentration of such great power, even in the hands of a totally committed ally, would no doubt have given rise to ambivalent feelings. It seems, therefore, that careful thought was given to disposing of the governor of the eastern provinces just as earlier Abū Salamah had been discreetly eliminated.

Such a proposition was reportedly placed before the Caliph by his brother Abū Ja'far, who, despite initial misgivings on the part of Abū al-'Abbās, was left to work out a solution of his own choosing.[20] The Caliph, however, had second thoughts and the matter was then dropped. A somewhat more dramatic version of these events has Abū Ja'far ready to strike while Abū Muslim was visiting at court, with the assassination being prevented only through the last-minute intercession of the Caliph.[21] If Abū al-'Abbās is pictured as reluctant to proceed with the scheme, it was not because of moral or ethical qualms on his part, but because of his recognition of Abū Muslim's hold on a significant following. Despite the assurances of his brother that any opposition would dissipate once the fact of Abū Muslim's death was known, the Caliph ultimately decided against the murder.

The details of these accounts in their present form suggest some shaping. The purpose of the texts is to justify the murder of Abū Muslim in the reign of al-Manṣūr. Although shorn of the usual apocalyptic trappings, there is a sense of déja vu in this tradition that is common to other literary inventions of the Manṣūrid propagandists. As constituted at present, the text may therefore reflect the embellishment of a subsequent period in order to establish that Abū al-'Abbās had also recognized, though somewhat reluctantly, the need to do away with his powerful client. The Caliph's hesitation to involve the ruling house in so drastic a policy is then pictured as caused by practical rather than ethical considerations. Given his brother's lack of decision, it was necessary for al-Manṣūr to act resolutely and put an end to Abū Muslim. In any event, the second of the great revolutionaries who labored on behalf of the 'Abbāsid house was as dispensable as Abū Salamah before him; both were victims of the dynasty's newly defined concerns.

The issue of Abū Muslim's relations with the ruling family is further complicated by the long-standing personal enmity between him and al-Manṣūr. The evidence for their strained relationship is found in a number of traditions. As each account is unadorned by the recognizable techniques of literary embellishment, there is no compelling reason to deny the historicity and importance of the events described. It was Abū Muslim who treated Abū Ja'far in a cavalier fashion when he was sent to do his brother's bidding in Khurāsān,[22] and it was once again Abū Muslim who undermined his position during the delicate negotiations with Ibn Hubayrah at Wāsiṭ.[23] According to one tradition, following the death of Abū al-'Abbās, Abū Muslim quite correctly sent his condolences to the lamented Caliph's brother, but withheld taking the oath of allegiance until a day and a half later.[24] Still other accounts have it that Abū Muslim favored the succession of his friend 'Īsā b. Mūsā, and indeed made overtures to the Caliph's nephew, but 'Īsā refused and respected the terms of the succession.[25] It is true that, when the revolt of 'Abdallāh b. 'Alī broke out immediately thereafter, Abū Muslim reluctantly supported al-Manṣūr.[26] However, it is no small wonder that, once the paternal uncle had been disposed of, the new Caliph turned his attention to an old adversary.

Regardless of the enmity that existed between them, Abū Muslim's murder can be regarded as more than a personal vendetta. The power possessed by the governor of Khurāsān was readily apparent. In the aforementioned tradition, Abū al-'Abbās is pictured as reluctant to do away with his client because he feared the repercussions (and perhaps the failure) of such an act. Although the final form of the tradition may be the product of skillful editing, how and when to deal with Abū Muslim must have been a subject of serious discussion within the councils of the 'Abbāsid family on any number of occasions. The first serious crisis facing the regime was the defection of Abū Salamah. The chronicler preserves a report that the initial response of the 'Abbāsids was to fear possible collusion between the former agents of the two major revolutionary stations.[27] Abū al-'Abbās is pictured as being thoroughly alarmed and, well aware of what this could mean, he ordered a discreet investigation of Abū Muslim's possible involvement. Had Abū Salamah and Abū Muslim opted for concerted action against the

'Abbāsids, the ruling family would have been left with only their dubious claims to legitimacy, for the real instruments of power were in the hands of those agents, who had promoted the revolution on their behalf. Fortunately, not only was Abū Muslim's fidelity verified, but the Caliph made use of his loyalty by turning him against Abū Salamah, while the 'Abbāsids judiciously stood aside in the wings.[28]

The account has an appearance of authenticity. What emerges from a reading of the narrative is a sense of the 'Abbāsid need of Abū Muslim, as well as the fear generated by the power that made him so useful to them. One has the decided feeling that Abū al-'Abbās was well aware that sooner or later Abū Muslim might have to be taken into custody or, beyond that, done away with altogether. To be sure, one can only speculate as to how and when the Caliph thought of dealing with him and what role, if any, he perceived for Abū Ja'far in this matter. If Abū al-'Abbās had any strong feelings in favor of a possible succession by his brother, he may have felt that Abū Muslim had still one more important role to play. Abū Ja'far would need the Khurāsānīs to promote his as yet undeclared claims to rule vis-à-vis the paternal uncles. It would therefore be more advantageous if Abū Muslim were dealt with after his succession.

Ironically, the elimination of 'Abdallāh b. 'Alī as a contender for the Caliphate served only to weaken al-Manṣūr with regard to his client. At the conclusion of the conflict, the major elements of the military apparatus were once again united in Abū Muslim's hands along with the vast treasuries that had been held by 'Abdallāh b. 'Alī.[29] These soon became a source of contention. For Abū Muslim, the grievance was based on the Caliph's lack of confidence in him. "I am trusted with [spilling] blood but not [handling] money." The Caliph, however, was being cautious, for he was no doubt well aware that such huge sums could easily be diverted to undermine the fragile government that emerged in the wake of the civil conflict.[30] There is, to be sure, no indication that Abū Muslim intended to subvert al-Manṣūr's newly established rule at this time. However, given the assent of still another willing candidate from the ruling house, there remained the possibility that he could topple the existing regime at some future moment. A less reticent 'Īsā b. Mūsā comes immediately to mind; he was not only a close friend of Abū Muslim, but stood first in the line of succession as well.

According to an isolated tradition, a proposal to murder al-Manṣūr was actually put before the governor of Khurāsān by his trusted advisor Nayzak.[31] Relations between Caliph and client were then extremely tense, and delicate negotiations were underway to arrange a meeting. Abū Muslim is described as being faced with a difficult decision. He had been ordered by al-Manṣūr to delay his return to Khurāsān. Instead, he was to appear for an audience at the Caliph's camp in al-Madā'in in order to settle the differences between them. As reported in a wide variety of sources, the root of the conflict was the Caliph's demand that Abū Muslim relinquish his hold over Khurāsān (and hence the regional army) in return for a somewhat less sensitive post. Despite the apparent danger and some initial uncertainty, Abū Muslim is seen as determined to meet with the Caliph.[32] One is given the impression that Nayzak is more than anxious about the prospect of this confrontation. Nevertheless, he does see it as presenting a real opportunity for his patron. "If you enter into al-Manṣūr's presence, kill him! Then take the oath of allegiance to whomever you wish. Indeed, the people will not oppose you." If words such as these were ever spoken, there is no indication that Abū Muslim gave thought to the sentiments, let alone the policy they contained. On the other hand, it is clear that al-Manṣūr was not unaware of possible intrigues, and strict precautions were taken to limit the number of individuals in Abū Muslim's entourage, which ordinarily included a large military retinue.

Could the new Caliph have been satisfied with neutralizing Abū Muslim by simply removing him from his position in Khurāsān, thus depriving him of direct contact with major elements of the imperial army? It was, no doubt, the loyalty of the Khurāsānī troops that al-Manṣūr sought, even more than the death of their governor, but it may be argued with some conviction that he could not be sure of one without the other.[33] At best, the offer of a new post may therefore be seen as a subterfuge to isolate the client of the 'Abbāsid house and make him vulnerable to future intrigues. The simplicity of the plot was not lost on Abū Muslim, and he refused to accept a lesser position. If the Caliph ever doubted that execution was a proper course of action, with Abū Muslim's refusal, al-Manṣūr's decision to eliminate him became a forgone conclusion. The final act was carried out in the Caliph's quarters.

The meeting at al-Madā'in was never intended to bring about a reconciliation between the two, but was a carefully laid snare to rid the Caliph of his greatest political burden. A man like Abū Muslim was not to be dealt with by half-hearted or conciliatory measures. There were no restraints of blood ties, only calculated risks. The political wisdom underlying the events of this last episode was appropriately expressed by the Caliph's confidant, Ja'far b. Hanẓalah, "If you take one hair from his [Abū Muslim's] head, kill then kill and kill again." Having seen his advice carried out, he congratulated the much relieved Caliph, "From this day on count the days of your Caliphate."[34]

The defeat of 'Abdallāh b. 'Alī and the murder of Abū Muslim enabled al-Manṣūr to seize firm control of the army and the other levers of power within 'Abbāsid government. Despite some initial discontent, the military commanders remained loyal, having been bought with the distribution of bonuses. The later revolts that were apparently invoked in Abū Muslim's name, were relatively minor affairs.[35] Control of the government was, on the other hand, a rather complex undertaking that required a redistribution of political power, as well as the retention of family loyalty. This was a delicate matter, which no doubt gave rise to somewhat ambivalent feelings. The residual effects of blood ties and the need for active support were balanced against the potential threat that could be mounted against the Caliph from within close family circles. The revolt of his uncle 'Abdallāh b. 'Alī, then governor of Syria, graphically illustrated the danger that existed when influential positions remained in the hands of the most prestigious members of the 'Abbāsid family. It is true, however, that with the exception of 'Abd al-Ṣamad b. 'Alī, the *'umūmah* remained more or less neutral in this struggle, and 'Īsā b. Mūsā's interests were initially linked to those of his uncle, the Caliph.[36]

Although the actual danger from his kinsmen may have been more apparent than real following 'Abdallāh's unsuccessful revolt, the question of their influence continued to weigh heavily on al-Manṣūr. The issue centered on not only the Caliph's position, but also his desire to secure a proper place for his progeny in the line of succession at the expense of the heir apparent 'Īsā b. Mūsā. Because the elimination of the *'umūmah* and 'Īsā b. Mūsā was impossible under any circumstances (it is doubtful that this was ever the Caliph's intention, let alone his expectation), al-Manṣūr instead attempted to curtail their political influence by creating a counterbalance to them from circles outside the ruling family, particularly from elements more easily subjected to tight control.

The Umayyads, in vaguely comparable circumstances, had at times sought out persons who, though of proven ability, nevertheless lacked adequate genealogical credentials for either personally contesting the legitimacy of the regime or for winning the full backing of the local tribal configurations based on the legitimate claims of a third party. In effect, all claims to rule required not only a de facto association with Quraysh, the tribe of the Prophet, but, beyond that, a direct link to the most prestigious elements within it. Given such conditions, the Umayyad appointees could entertain no pretentions of their own, nor would their tribal background allow them to successfully carry any lasting influence with their subjects on behalf of another.

Although not linked as dramatically to tribal considerations, the early 'Abbāsid policy reflected previous patterns in so far as governors were chosen initially from among close kinsmen and were shifted about. Despite established family ties, the provincial appointees later found their positions in political affairs encroached upon by others bearing lesser credentials. Although the precise circumstances governing the rotation of local rulers is frequently missing from the historical accounts, it is clear that the earliest years of the provincial administration were studded with royal names that soon fell by the wayside. Beginning with the reign of al-Manṣūr, a casual perusal of the lists of governors given at the conclusion of the year's events in the annalistic histories indicates a pronounced shift away from elements of the 'Abbāsid house toward others. These include those who can be identified with certainty as *mawālī*, but, in any case, as non-family, thus implying a dependent relationship between governor and Caliph.

There were, nevertheless, several general exceptions to this rule. In the Ḥijāz, in Egypt, and, later, in al-Baṣrah and al-Kūfah, the royal prerogatives were more faithfully respected. However, when all is taken into consideration, Egypt was a territorial enclave. Conditions in the former garrison towns had stabilized, particularly after the founding of a new capital at Baghdad, and it can be forcefully demonstrated that the holy places, despite their religious significance and position in history, were far removed from the center of political power.

B. The Ruling Family and the Ḥaramayn

The decline of Mecca and al-Madīnah as viable foci of political influence is most appropriately illustrated by the abortive revolt of the ʿAlid pretender Muḥammad b. ʿAbdallāh in the year A.H. 145. Although dramatically and somewhat mysteriously described in an interesting, apocalyptic tradition as no less than a "breach (*fatq*) from the Ḥijāz," the rebellion of the ʿAlid fugitive in al-Madīnah was, in reality, a quixotic affair.[37] It was sanctified by numerous religious scholars and was supported by the "cream" of Quraysh and the Anṣār; but this is significant only in so far as it reflects how little the Ḥijazī aristocrats had learned since the time of the Islamic conquest about where the real power of the realm was centered.

A particularly cogent example of the confusion inherent in the thinking of the local Ḥijāzīs is found in an account preserved by Ṭabarī.[38] The setting is that of an approaching royalist army under the command of ʿĪsā b. Mūsā with Muḥammad b. ʿAbdallāh in a quandary over whether to leave al-Madīnah or stay and make his stand there. He therefore solicited the opinions of his various confidants but found their advice contradictory. Among those who participated in these deliberations, a man named ʿAbd al-Ḥamīd b. Jaʿfar is reported to have asked penetrating, and even provocative, questions. He inquired, in effect, if the ʿAlid pretender was cognizant of the limited resources at his disposal and cited the lack of food, horses, weapons, and manpower in the Ḥijāz. When Muḥammad replied affirmatively, ʿAbd al-Ḥamīd pursued this line further and asked if the ʿAlid was not also aware of the relative strength of the enemy, coming as he did from a region abundantly blessed with wealth, weapons, and human resources. Once again Muḥammad b. ʿAbdallāh replied affirmatively. ʿAbd al-Ḥamīd then proposed that Muḥammad set off for Egypt with his immediate following in order to consolidate his position, for not only would he be accepted there, but he would then be able to match the quantitative advantage of his adversary item for item.[39]

No matter how intelligently reasoned and convincingly stated, ʿAbd al-Ḥamīd's tactically modest suggestion served only to bring cries of anguish from another party to the discussion. Neglecting the conventional secular wisdom inherent in Voltaire's aphorism that God is on the side of the big battalions, a second advisor, Ḥunayn b. 'Abdallāh, turned to a more traditional precedent by which to guide his distinguished leader.[40] "God forbid that you should leave al-Madīnah —indeed Muḥammad [the Prophet] had said: 'I see myself in impenetrable armor.'" Although this last phrase is interpreted as meaning the city itself (*faawwaltuhā al-Madīnah*),[41] the metaphor is perhaps more appropriate to the defensive trench that spared the city during the siege of the grand alliance. The Muslims were then able to withstand a large invading army by digging a trench around al-Madīnah. This hitherto unheard of tactic denied the opposing cavalry an open field of charge and forced them to break off the attack, thereby passing the initiative on to the righteous. This reading, that trench equals armor, is reflected in the sequential arrangement of the chronicler and probably suggests his understanding of the passage. For, in the account that immediately follows, Ṭabarī has Muḥammad b. 'Abdallāh reject the Banū Sulaym's advice to fight a campaign based on tactical mobility, in favor of a static defense of the holy city.[42] Encouraged by the example of the Prophet and anxious, no doubt, to be identified with him, the rebel reestablished the trench surrounding al-Madīnah, as if the older stratagem were applicable to his current situation and the magic worked by Salmān al-Fārisī against the Meccan cavalry would repel the army of the 'Abbāsid house. Within a short time, the defensive perimeter was breached and Muḥammad b. 'Abdallāh was seized and executed.

Because the story of 'Abd al-Ḥamīd's advice to Muḥammad b. 'Abdallāh is almost the mirror image of similar traditions concerning Abū Ja'far al-Manṣūr and his confidants, we may doubt the accuracy of various details, if not the historicity of the event itself. A less skeptical inquiry might be satisfied that the text as presently constituted has been subjected to literary shaping but neverheless, contains also elements of an historical truth, specifically that the Ḥijāz declined as a center of political influence due to strategic considerations. This decline is significant for understanding 'Abbāsid policy concerning the choice of governors in that region. For once it can be convincingly demonstrated that al-Manṣūr was no less aware of these strategic factors than was 'Abd al-Ḥamīd, a plausible picture can be worked out to explain the retention of local governors from among the inner circle of the ruling house. The abortive revolt of Muḥammad

b. 'Abdallāh is as good an illustration as any that, regardless of personal credentials, no ruler situated at Mecca or al-Madīnah could be regarded as a serious threat to the regime, because no significant challenge could be launched from so politically emasculated a province.

Tradition has it that al-Manṣūr was indeed an astute student of geopolitics. This is a theme of many variations, as illustrated by still another text of Ṭabarī, which is almost the mirror image of the one previously cited. Instead of the rebel and 'Abd al-Ḥamid, the Caliph and his advisor are the principal actors.[43] After receiving word of the revolt, al-Manṣūr is said to have sent for Ja'far b. Ḥanẓalah al-Bahrānī, whose expertise apparently extended beyond intrigue to military affairs (*a'lam al-nās bi-l-ḥarb*). Upon being asked where the revolt had broken out, the Caliph indicated al-Madīnah, and al-Bahrānī declared, "Then praise God for he [Muḥammad] has made his appearance in such [a place] where there are no financial or human resources, no weapons and no horses." The suggestion was then put forth that the Caliph dispatch a trustworthy client to encamp along the Wādī al-Qurā, cutting off foodstuffs from Syria, and thereby starving the rebels into submission.[44]

The same al-Bahrānī is the principal player in another tradition.[45] Although the format is somewhat altered, the intention is once again to demonstrate that the Ḥijāz alone could not sustain an army large enough to challenge 'Abbāsid rule. When consulted by the Caliph concerning Muḥammad's rebellion in al-Madīnah, al-Bahrānī, without apparent reason, suggested sending an army to al-Baṣrah. He was dismissed until further notice but was recalled when Muḥammad's brother, Ibrāhīm b. 'Abdallāh, fortuitously revolted in Iraq, specifically, in al-Baṣrah. When asked why he came to fear al-Baṣrah would be the source of trouble, al-Bahrānī had a ready explanation. Muḥammad rebelled in the Ḥījāz, which could not sustain an army. Al-Kūfah was firmly under al-Manṣūr's control (the heir apparent, 'Īsā b. Mūsā, was governor, and the Caliph ordinarily stationed contingents of the imperial army in al-Hāshimīyah, the adjoining capital). The Syrians were the enemies of the house of 'Alī b. Abī Ṭālib (the implication is that they could never join forces with one of his descendants), and that left only al-Baṣrah as a source of concern. The Caliph then sent the sons of 'Aqīl, two commanders of Khurāsānī origin, to the governor of that city.

Although this particular account and its several variants are most assuredly highly stylized clichés, there is reason to believe that any evaluation of the 'Alid uprising in the presence of the Caliph would be likely to draw attention to the political impotence of the *ḥaramayn*. There are in some of these traditions, however, subtle nuances that suggest more than this casual observation. They call attention to still another important factor—the relationship of the 'Abbāsid house to the aristocracy of the Ḥijāz. The complex family structures that linked the 'Abbāsids to their kinsmen in the *ḥaramayn* also determined, in no uncertain ways the selection of the local governors for that region.

This is perhaps best illustrated through the detailed exegesis of a particularly intriguing text preserved by Mas'ūdī. The basic theme remains all too familiar; however, in the extensive version of Mas'ūdī, the ubiquitous "military expert" is replaced by a confidant of "practical vision."[46] Al-Manṣūr is reported to have sought the advice of Isḥāq b. Muslim al-'Uqaylī, who, it is said, possessed both ideas and experience (*dhū ra'y wa tajribah*). Asked by al-'Uqaylī for a description of the rebel, al-Manṣūr enumerated his credentials as a distinguished scion of the 'Alid line. Asked about his following, the Caliph listed the aristocratic families from whom Muḥammad b. 'Abdallāh drew his support.[47] Asked for a description of the region in which the revolt had taken place, al-Manṣūr answered, "a place in which there is no agriculture, no stock farming, and no widespread commerce (*balad laysa bihi zar' wa lā ḍar' wa lā tijārah wāsi'ah*)."

Much to al-Manṣūr's surprise, al-'Uqaylī's response, after some thought, was to suggest strengthening the garrison at al-Baṣrah. Because the revolt was then localized in the Ḥijāz and not in Iraq, this seemingly incongruous piece of advice earned for al-'Uqaylī temporary dismissal. Nevertheless, a man who is known for *ra'y* and *tajribah* is never to be taken lightly. As fate would have it, his reputation was soon vindicated when word arrived shortly thereafter of a second revolt, that of Muḥammad b. 'Abdallāh's brother Ibrāhīm in al-Baṣrah.

Having now returned to al-Manṣūr's good graces, al-'Uqaylī explained that his original remarks were based, not on any foreknowledge of events about to take place in Iraq, but, rather, on an assessment of conditions in the Ḥijāz: A rebel that no one (of political influence) would follow, and a region that could not support an army. He therefore assumed that the real danger was elsewhere. Egypt was secure, as were Syria and al-Kūfah, but al-Baṣrah was another matter.[48] Despite the substitution of one advisor for another, the variants of Ṭabarī and Mas'ūdī are essentially the same until this point in the narration. However, the account of Mas'ūdī continues. Now faced with a second revolt, the Caliph asked what was to be done with Muḥammad b. 'Abdallāh in the Ḥijāz, as if no step had been taken until then. Although al-'Uqaylī's suggestion was limited to a program of political propaganda, al-Manṣūr sent the heir apparent, 'Īsā b. Mūsā, to al-Madīnah with a force of 6,000 men and augmented these troops with a large army under the command of Muḥammad b. Qaḥṭabah.[49]

There are several points to this last tradition that merit further explication. Despite the rather compelling charm of the account, the sequence of events described by Mas'ūdī is puzzling. It is not clear why so imposing a force was necessary at al-Madīnah when a much more evident threat existed in Iraq, a province badly depleted of its strategic reserve.[50] Since a reported 70,000 troops of the imperial army were then off on campaigns in Khurāsān and in the Maghrib, there is little if any likelihood that, had Ibrāhīm b. 'Abdallāh already revolted in al-Baṣrah, the Caliph would have sent his nephew with sizeable contingents to the Ḥijāz, and away from al-Kūfah, a city of residual Shī'ite sympathies. Such a move could only have resulted in still further denuding a weakened Iraq of government forces, and in the very areas that required maximum security.

The critical need of the army sent to Khurāsān is suggested in yet another variant of this tradition.[51] As if two consultants giving the same advice under similar circumstances were not sufficient, al-Manṣūr was referred by his military commanders to still a third. This time it was Budayl b. Yaḥyā, a man of ideas (*dhū ra'y*) who had served the Caliph's brother Abū al-'Abbās before him. When he arrived, Budayl was informed that Muḥammad b. 'Abdallāh had revolted in al-Madīnah. Curiously enough, his immediate response was to suggest strengthening the garrison at al-Ahwāz. When the Caliph pointed out that the insurrection was confined to the Ḥijāz, Budayl indicated that he understood, "but al-Ahwāz is the gate through which the rebels will come." Somewhat later, when Ibrāhīm b. 'Abdallāh reached al-Baṣrah, Budayl b. Yaḥyā was again brought in for consultation. His advice was to quickly bring the army into action (from Khurāsān) and to employ al-Ahwāz against the second rebel.

There is, to be sure, no direct reference to the strategic shortcomings of al-Madīnah in this version. It is nevertheless apparent that the Caliph's confidant regarded the real threat to the regime as being elsewhere. The major concern was not Muḥammad b. 'Abdallāh, but the protection of al-Ahwāz, "the gateway" to the central provinces of the empire. When, in fact, al-Ahwāz declared for the 'Alids, the closest available support was the imperial army commanded by al-Mahdī. It was then stationed in al-Rayy, the capital of Khurāsān. Although the Caliph's son immediately dispatched Khāzim b. Khuzaymah with a force of 4,000 men to attack al-Ahwāz, this army still had to march 700 miles along the main roads or 350 miles overland to reach the field of battle.[52]

It was the failure to sustain a strategic reserve at the capital (al-Hāshimīyah)[53] that forced the Caliph to attach the gravest importance to the events unfolding in Iraq and the neighboring provinces. Although, in the end, the 'Abbāsid's victory over Ibrāhīm was decisive, their success was initially uncertain, or, in the language of the aforementioned apocalyptic tradition, a second breach occurred "causing a degree of damage greater than before." What could have compelled the Caliph to commit large forces to a relatively trivial military enterprise in the Ḥijāz at the very time Ibrāhīm was assembling an army in al-Baṣrah and had declarations of support from al-Kūfah, Fārs, Wāsiṭ, and al-Ahwāz? The only plausible explanation is that 'Īsā b. Mūsā was dispatched to al-Madīnah immediately following the uprising of Muḥammad b. 'Abdallāh, and not subsequent to the second revolt. If this is true, the perspicacity attributed to al-'Uqaylī and others in recognizing the inherent danger in Iraq was hardly extraordinary. Not only were the main contingents of the imperial army occupied in distant campaigns, but 'Īsā b. Mūsā was already in the Ḥijāz with the reserves when the revolt of Ibrāhīm b. 'Abdallāh began some two months after the initial uprising. The critical nature of the situation confronting al-Manṣūr should, therefore, have been readily apparent to anyone assessing these developments within the 'Abbāsid hierarchy.

One may go a step further and ask why 'Īsā b. Mūsā was sent to the Ḥijāz at all.[54] The choice of the Caliph's nephew to command this force seems quite logical, for he had considerable experience in the campaigns against the Umayyads. Nevertheless, the logistics of the entire operation would have been simplified had the government dispatched an army to the Ḥijāz from Syria. The possibility of employing Syrian troops against the 'Alids did not escape the attention of the Caliph. However, he apparently intended their use only for the protection of his capital, and, then, only after it was left exposed to attack from neighboring al-Kūfah when 'Īsā b. Mūsā and the reserves marched against the Ḥijāz.

The critical text describing the decision to utilize the Syrians is an extremely curious tradition preserved in the martyrology of Iṣfahānī.[55] Upon learning of the Shī'ite outbreak in al-Madīnah, al-Manṣūr is said to have discreetly consulted with his paternal uncle 'Abdallāh b. 'Alī. The former rebel, who was then incarcerated at al-Ḥīrah, is pictured as reluctant to volunteer any assistance without a compensatory release from his confinement. Nevertheless, he did eventually suggest that the Caliph guard the approaches to al-Kūfah and send to Khurāsān for the army contingents commanded by Salm b. Qutaybah. These troops were then to join reinforcements arriving posthaste from Syria (*mā yaḥmiluhu al-barīd*).[56]

It would perhaps take an act of faith to assume that the Caliph actually consulted his uncle in these circumstances. However, 'Abdallāh b. 'Alī had been governor of Syria and, of all the 'Abbāsid field commanders, he was closest to the indigenous army of that region. Moreover, according to Ṭabarī, Salm b. Qutaybah was eventually brought to Iraq with contingents of the imperial army. The time of this last event is recorded as occurring after the revolt of Ibrāhīm in al-Baṣrah, but before the return of 'Īsā b. Mūsā from his triumph in the Ḥijāz.[57] Although not explicitly stated, the necessity for the infusion of these new forces is apparent, as the chronicler immediately follows the arrival of the Khurāsānīs with a description of al-Manṣūr's beleaguered position at the capital vis-à-vis the neighboring Kūfans. There is no mention of Syria in this last account, but there are other sources that confirm the appearance of Syrian troops during the crisis in Iraq.

There is still another variant of that tradition in which al-Manṣūr was advised to strengthen the garrison at al-Baṣrah while the revolt was localized in the Ḥijāz.[58] This time, the Caliph solicited a Syrian shaykh whose ideas were highly valued (*shaykh min ahl al-Shām dhū ra'y*). He advised al-Manṣūr to reinforce al-Baṣrah with 4,000 Syrian troops (*min jund ahl al-Shām*). Because the situation in Iraq was then quiescent, the Caliph regarded this response as that of an old man touched with senility. However, when Ibrāhīm b. ʿAbdallāh brought the ʿAlid revolt to al-Baṣrah, the Caliph recalled the shaykh for consultation, and, once again, the shaykh repeated his suggestion to employ contingents from the Syrian army. When al-Manṣūr anxiously inquired how this was to be done, he was told to write to the governor of Syria requesting that ten be sent each day posthaste (*fī ḳull yawm ʿasharah fī al-barīd*).

The unique feature of this version is not that it introduces the Syrians as an element in the conflict, but that it recommends they be employed against Ibrāhīm at al-Baṣrah, rather than with the Caliph against the Kūfans. However, this divergence of detail from similar texts is not established through an "authentic" tradition, but apparently stems from the juxtaposition of two accounts involving the ubiquitous Jaʿfar b. Ḥanẓalah al-Bahrānī. Each depicts a different historical moment, with the composite story of the Syrian shaykh situated somewhere between them in Ṭabarī's presentation. The first account, which precedes the story of the Syrians in the narrative of the chronicler, describes an event taking place *before* the revolt of Ibrāhīm.[59] In that tradition, which has been previously cited, al-Bahrānī advises the Caliph to reinforce the garrison at al-Baṣrah and is dismissed, only to be recalled when Ibrāhīm emerges in Iraq. No mention is made, however, of Syrian forces. On the contrary, when news of the outbreak in al-Baṣrah is received, al-Manṣūr is reported to have dispatched two Khurāsānī commanders.

The second account, which immediately follows the incident of the shaykh, is chronologically fixed *after* the revolt in al-Baṣrah.[60] In effect, the Caliph is advised by al-Bahrānī to facilitate the transfer of a Syrian army to Iraq. This was done, not to combat Ibrāhīm b. ʿAbdallāh at al-Baṣrah, but to forestall an attack upon the capital from rebel sympathizers in the adjacent city of al-Kūfah. The extent of the Caliph's apprehension concerning the Kūfans is detailed in other accounts and requires no exposition here.[61] Although al-Bahrānī is concerned about al-Kūfah, and the anonymous Syrian shaykh about al-Baṣrah, there is nonetheless a similarity regarding the acquisition of Syrian manpower. Recalling the shaykh's advice that reinforcements be sent in groups of tens, the report of al-Bahrānī's consultations with the Caliph indicates that the Syrian army could not be quickly mobilized in an orderly fashion and consequently arrived in small units. In order to give the impression of larger numbers and thus serve as a deterrent against an attack from al-Kūfah, the Syrians reportedly left the Caliph's encampment by night and, retracing their steps, reentered the capital the following day.[62] As the account of the Syrian shaykh clearly has elements that are common to the traditions that both precede and follow it in the text of the chronicler, its composite structure is most likely suggested by them.

The significant point to be extrapolated from all these accounts is that the entry of the Syrians into the campaign appears to have been both haphazard and belated, with the historic moment fixed after the defeat of the rebels in al-Madīnah. The Syrians were thus utilized only as a last resort, after word of Ibrāhīm had reached the desperate Caliph in his unguarded capital. It would seem that military logic should have dictated that they be sent to the Ḥijāz when the revolt first broke out. 'Īsā b. Mūsā, who was governor of al-Kūfah, could then have remained behind with his full command and served as a strategic reserve in Iraq.

One may therefore conjecture that the failure to allow for such a course was dictated by a different set of circumstances. It was presumably not a military consideration that required the Caliph's nephew to lead the attack against the rebels in al-Madīnah, but, rather, a question of political priorities. Because the revolt provoked the Caliph's obsessive sensitivity with regard to the legitimacy of his regime, the entire episode took on a dramatic importance that bore little relation to military realities. Given al-Madīnah's status as a holy city, and given the impressive lineage of its rebel constituency, al-Manṣūr could do no less than send someone of equally distinguished credentials, no matter how trivial the direct military threat.

This may also explain, in part, the decision to rely almost exclusively on the ruling family in choosing subsequent governors for the *ḥaramayn*. Realism is, after all, often tempered by psychological perceptions derived from previously shared experiences. Regardless of the political divisions within the early Islamic community, the scions of the old guard commanded respect, if for no other reason than the contributions of their distinguished ancestors to the creation of the Islamic religion and state. Al-Manṣūr could no more send an army from Syria to remove Muḥammad b. 'Abdallāh than he could rule the holy cities by way of a governor chosen from among his client generals. The last Syrian invasion of this region was under the hated Umayyads, and their activities there gave rise to traditions of murder, rape, pillage, and the violation of holy territory.[63] Dealing with the Ḥijāz was at this stage still a family affair, to be conducted firmly but judiciously, with propriety, and, above all, with an eye to enhancing the image of an ʿAbbāsid regime whose claims to legitimacy were somewhat suspect, especially among its kinsmen from the aristocrats of Islam. Although the ʿAbbāsids could, no doubt, have held power with a good deal less circumspection with regard to their Ḥījazī relations, the psychological need of legitimizing their rule among the old Muslims should not be underestimated.

This perhaps explains the decision to enter into negotiations despite the weakness of the enemy, as well as the ideological tone of the overtures.[64] Every attempt was apparently made to avoid conflict within the holy city. Had the rebels chosen to capitulate and accept guarantees of safety rather than enter into combat, it not only would have spared the city and its populace, but, according to the text of the guarantee, it would have validated as well the claims of the ʿAbbāsid house. The Ḥijāzīs could hardly have been expected to enter into such delicate negotiations with anyone but a ranking member of the ʿAbbāsid family, in which case no better choice could be found than ʿĪsā b. Mūsā.[65] One may speculate that the coterie of friendly ʿAlids whom ʿĪsā b. Mūsā took with him on the campaign were more than casual bystanders. They were probably chosen to influence their relatives to accept the ʿAbbāsid demands. Given the realities of the situation, most of the Medinese abandoned the struggle before the Caliph's nephew entered the city. Muḥammad b. ʿAbdallāh, however, played out his role until the end, thereby adding still another ʿAlid martyr for veneration.

Such sensitivities required, by extension, future governors of acceptable background. In peace or in war, the *ḥaramayn* thus became the sinecure of the ʿAbbāsid family. This by no means suggests, however, that the Ḥijāz could serve as a base from which to challenge the central authorities. Whatever limitations geography imposed upon Muḥammad b. ʿAbdallāh held true as well for the relatives of the Caliph. Tradition may have generally reserved for Mecca and al-

Madīnah governors of impeccable genealogy, but their function was largely honorific and tied to local concerns.

C. The Ruling Family and the Iraqi Amṣār

Geography could very well explain the retention of royal governors in the Ḥijāz, but al-Baṣrah and al-Kūfah might seem, at first, to present a different problem, particularly in light of their turbulent history during the early Caliphate and under Umayyad rule. After the initial challenge within the 'Abbāsid family was repelled by al-Manṣūr, the sons of the discredited were allowed to occupy the sinecures of their fathers, an act of statesmanship which would seem to contradict the essence of 'Abbāsid policy. If the Caliph was willing to entrust provincial rule to the ruling family only in circumstances that could not threaten the centrality of his power, why should the government have assumed, especially in view of the recent revolt of Ibrāhīm b. 'Abdallāh, that al-Baṣrah and al-Kūfah could not serve as springboards for other attacks against the regime. A second reading of the economic and military potential of the *amṣār*, together with an analysis of the true character of the Shī'ite uprising, may clarify this seeming contradiction.

The troublesome nature of the *amṣār* derived essentially from their historic function as military camps. However, even before the Umayyads, the movement of large numbers of fighting men and their families for resettlement in Khurāsān had begun a process that weakened the independence of the Iraqi centers. This may or may not have been the result of a conscious government policy, but it was surely occasioned by the shift of the frontier far to the east, a salient geographical fact with vast political ramifications. The defeat of the Iraqi rebels during the period of the Marwānids in the latter part of the seventh century A.D. and the building of Wāsiṭ concurrent with the introduction of a large Syrian garrison (*ahl al-Shām*) into the general area further limited the military character and potential of al-Kūfah and al-Baṣrah. This is not to say that the old settlers did not retain some residual fighting skills, but their function as cohesive front-line units had passed, and their traditional role had been assumed by others.

When the Khurāsānī armies of the 'Abbāsids marched through Iraq, no significant military role can be detected for the populace of the *amṣār*, even though the major revolutionary apparatus of Abū Salamah was situated in al-Kūfah and the general sympathies of the local people were initially with the revolution. One could argue that this actually worked to the advantage of the 'Abbāsids, and that it was, perhaps, carefully calculated by them; however, such an analysis does not in any way alter the assessment of the military situation prevailing in the region.

There still remained a large and potentially subversive urban element. A successful revolt, however, one that had a measure of permanence leading either to the overthrow of the regime or to a more limited objective such as the de facto independence of a regional center, would have required military units of a highly professional nature. Ironically the 'Abbāsid revolution was itself occasioned by the availability of such forces in Khurāsān, rather than by a sense of ideological unity generated among its political adherents. The economic infrastructure of the *amṣār*, unlike the *ḥaramayn*, could perhaps have supported an independent military posture under favorable political conditions such as the presence of an 'Abbāsid pretender with an imperial garrison augmented by sizeable local levies. Such a local army would have required, however, initial organization and training, as well as active combat, to maintain its fighting capacity and incentive.

The shift of the frontier eastward left no natural opportunity for the development of an indigenous Iraqi force. Any unusual military organization on a large scale would immediately have caught the attention of the central authorities, who based their power on an imperial army created from those Khurāsānī contingents that had moved into Iraq with the revolutionary campaigns. Control of this army was, in fact, the key to the stabilization of the region and to 'Abbāsid rule in general. It comes as no surprise, then, that the integration of the Khurāsānīs into a special niche, geographically rooted in the region, became an urgent desideratum of the Caliph and resulted ultimately in the creation of a new and permanent capital at Baghdad.

The move to this hitherto inconspicuous but centrally located site was one with far-reaching consequences and could not help but leave its mark on the other urban centers of Iraq. Despite a continued cultural (and in the case of al-Baṣrah, commercial) importance, the *amṣār* were reduced to the status of provincial towns.[66] The sum effect of these factors precluded the emergence of any serious adversaries in the general area as long as the 'Abbāsid house at Baghdad was itself in order or, stated somewhat differently, as long as the Khurāsānī army garrisoned there remained loyal to the Caliph.

If there is no single dramatic event that gives vivid illustration to this change, it is because, unlike the Ḥijāz, the decline of the Irāqī *amṣār* was characterized by more gradual developments. Nevertheless, the year A.H. 145, which witnessed the revolt of Ibrāhīm b. 'Abdallāh and, concurrent with it, the beginning of construction at Baghdad, may be seen as the most convenient, if not most appropriate, watershed.

The critical impact of the 'Alid challenge, which reportedly came within a hair's breadth of success, may initially produce disquieting thoughts about the innocuous military posture of the *amṣār*. Underscoring the serious nature of the revolt is the gravity with which al-Manṣūr himself is reported to have viewed the events. The sources describe the Caliph as extremely tense and showing signs of somewhat erratic behavior. An eyewitness who stood over him with a flywhisk relates that al-Manṣūr took to a prayer platform (*muṣallā*), where, with the exception of public appearances, he remained for fifty days, sleeping and holding court in a grimy garment that he would not change. Even when appearing in public, he simply threw the black robes of the ruling house over his shabby attire.[67] Two elegant ladies, imported from the Ḥijāz to assist the Caliph in falling asleep, developed churlish dispositions because al-Manṣūr, displaying great rudeness, rejected them completely. In effect, he complained that there was no time for women, "until I know whether it is Ibrāhīm's head that I shall have, or he that will have mine."[68] An officer in his presence noticed that he did not return salutes, owing to his total preoccupation with the events unfolding around him, but displayed, instead, signs of highly irritable nervous behavior.[69] When a poet tried to console him with stirring verses, the Caliph was quick to offer in rejoinder a sober appraisal of the situation before him, to wit, Ibrāhīm perceived his weaknesses and was marching against him at the behest of the Kūfans. Only 'Īsā b. Mūsā stood between the Caliph and disaster; he might have added that 'Īsā was in no position to protect him from the Kūfans, because he had deployed his force in Ibrāhīm's path at Bākhamrā sixty miles away.[70] Even if one were to insist that these descriptions have been somewhat dramatized, it will be demonstrated that the difficulties confronting al-Manṣūr were real enough, and that the traditions, despite embellishments, all point to the same preoccupation.

The Caliph was surely aware that the initial advantage was held by the 'Alid rebel. However, Ibrāhīm b. 'Abdallāh did not capitalize on it, but, like his brother Muḥammad before him, succumbed to conflicting counsels, indecision, and peculiar notions about the etiquette of war. Having met with acclamation at al-Baṣrah, al-Ahwāz, Fārs, and Wāsiṭ, he rejected the sound advice that his army undertake a battle of attrition against al-Manṣūr, while he remained behind to strengthen the hold on those areas that had already declared for the 'Alids. His following at al-Kūfah, in the past, the graveyard of rebel pretensions, insisted that their support could be insured only through his personal appearance. Although the 'Alid pretender acknowledged their desires by taking the field himself, he nevertheless was reluctant to employ them for fear that an insurrection in the city, planned as a diversionary tactic, would bring massive retaliation against all its inhabitants including the aged and the young.[71] When it was pointed out that the Prophet himself made war in comparable circumstances, the reply was that the Prophet himself attacked only the polytheists; "these [Kūfans] are people of our religion and calling (*ahl millatinā, da'watinā, qiblatinā*)."[72] Ibrāhīm therefore compromised both plans that were put before him; he neither secured the areas under his control nor attacked when circumstances dictated bold action.

The impact of these and similar decisions on the campaign was critical. Al-Manṣūr, isolated with limited forces at his military camp opposite the city, was well aware of the danger implicit in residual Kūfan sympathies for the 'Alid cause. For him, al-Kūfah did not represent "people of our religion and calling," but 100,000 ambushers ready to pounce at a given moment.[73] Significantly, Ibrāhīm b. 'Abdallāh's peculiar sense of martial etiquette manifested itself in other situations as well. The 'Alid pretender on two occasions rejected night combat, causing one of his commanders to remark somewhat tartly that he sought rule yet disapproved of killing.[74]

Having squandered those opportunities when aggressive tactics were needed, Ibrāhīm b. 'Abdallāh threw caution to the wind. In certain respects the situation calls to attention his brother's decision to forego the advice of the Banū Sulaym, which was to fight a mobile war, and to choose instead a static defense of al-Madīnah.[75] With the rival armies ultimately arrayed against each other at Bākhamrā, Ibrāhīm, like his brother before him, was faced with the question whether or not to employ a tactical campaign. He could fight from behind a defensive enclave (a variation of the strategy employed in the Ḥijāz) or launch a full attack. During the discussion preliminary to the battle, it was pointed out that al-Manṣūr had already re-formed[76] his army. The implication is that the 'Alid had lost his initial edge. He no longer had to contend with a truncated fighting force standing in the shadow of a menacing urban population (the Kūfans), but was forced to fight with large enemy contingents in a distant field of combat. Included among these contingents was the command of 'Īsā b. Mūsā, finally arrived from the Ḥijāz, and positioned in Ibrāhīm's path some sixty miles from the unprotected capital. Although the circumstances might seem to have dictated a flexible response, the decision was carried by those advisors who sought a conclusive battle, "No, by God, we will not do this [set up a defensive enclave]. . . . Why not [go to meet him in battle]. He [al-Manṣūr] is in our hands any time we want him."[77] The conclusion of the contest proved otherwise, and with the subsequent death of Ibrāhīm, the rebellion disintegrated.

Despite the collapse of the insurrection, one cannot help but ask if, as it seems, Ibrāhīm b. 'Abdallāh came so close to overthrowing the regime from al-Baṣrah, what was to prevent others from avoiding the rather evident mistakes of his campaign and delivering a vital if not fatal blow to the central authorities? And, if the nature of the struggle evoked such disquieting thoughts, why did the Caliph persist in appointing his relatives to provincial posts in the *amṣār* of Iraq?

It may be argued that the circumstances of the rebellion were extraordinary and could not easily, if at all, be duplicated. This was not an internal struggle between various segments of the 'Abbāsid family, thereby confined to the ruling house and its military establishment. The uprising was that of the 'Alid Shī'ites, and so commanded wide allegiance derived from ideological positions that, though loosely defined, were of long duration.[78] There were historic grievances nursed by a considerable segment of the population, and, among these grievances, perhaps the most grating was the fashion in which the 'Abbāsids captured the revolution that brought the Umayyad dynasty to its end. Turned aside at what could have been the historic moment of their vindication, the ʿAlids were left to brood and plan a revolution of their own that was thirteen years in the making. No such popular sentiments were discernible among the backers of ʿAbdallāh b. ʿAlī, nor could one expect any other ʿAbbāsid rival of the Caliph to amass wide public support for a fratricidal struggle. Even when al-Ma'mūn challenged the authority of his brother, the Caliph al-Amīn, a half century later, the issue was clearly one of self-interest and not ideology.[79]

Moreover, the political and military lessons of the revolt have been obscured by painting the events in the broadest possible strokes. The historic indignation of the ʿAlids was never matched by revolutionary fervor or organizational acumen. Despite a show of revolutionary ideals, the initial response to being upstaged by the ʿAbbāsids betrayed a lack of cohesion and of political purpose. This is well-illustrated by a famous tradition that may be largely, if not entirely, an invention of later times. At best, it is probably marked by much tendentious shaping, but the account of Ibn Ṭabāṭabā nevertheless captures the general impotence of the ʿAlid actors as viewed by an author who was more than mildly sympathetic to their cause.[80]

It seems that Abū Salamah al-Khallāl, the first wazīr of the ʿAbbāsid house, turned against his patrons at the outset of their rule. He was prepared to join cause with any one of three ʿAlid contenders whose support he solicited in a series of secret letters; they were Jaʿfar al-Ṣādiq, ʿAbdallāh al-Mahd, and ʿUmar al-Ashraf. The first burnt his letter without replying, the prudent act of a cautious man. The second, ʿAbdallāh al-Mahd, was not given to political wisdom and was prepared to act, but unfortunately found no support from Jaʿfar al-Ṣādiq. On the contrary, Jaʿfar al-Ṣādiq asserted that he had also received such a communication and pointed out the weakness of the ʿAlid position among the Khurāsānīs, an indirect reference to the impotence of their military posture, for the Khurāsānīs represented the professional army of the state. The third, out of caution or, perhaps more likely, aristocratic bearing, returned his letter unopened, as he would not acknowledge a communication from someone with whom he had no direct familiarity. The ʿAbbāsid response to this somewhat less than dramatic challenge was to force Ibrāhīm and Muḥammad, the sons of ʿAbdallāh al-Mahd, into hiding for some years, after which they emerged in al-Baṣrah and in the Ḥijāz.[81]

Looking at these events in retrospect, one may well conclude that the general revolt of A.H. 145 was carried out largely by civilians and para-military forces against professionals, a confirmation, so to speak, of Ja'far al-Ṣādiq's penetrating comments. Were it not for extremely lax security at al-Baṣrah, it is unlikely that any serious threat would have been mounted against the Caliphate of al-Manṣūr. With Muḥammad already proclaiming his rights in the Ḥijāz, it is difficult to imagine why greater vigilance was not observed in the potential trouble spots of Iraq and easy to understand why the Caliph was reportedly indignant against the authorities who had allowed this to occur, particularly his cousins Muḥammad and Ja'far b. Sulaymān (b. 'Alī).[82] Be that as it may, the 'Alids, in seizing control of the administrative machinery in al-Baṣrah, were able to command the funds necessary to inscribe tens of thousands of names on a newly formed military roll.[83]

The registration of such an army on lists, however, is not necessarily commensurate with building an active and professional military force. Furthermore, the army that was assembled had to be dispersed for a campaign at Wāsiṭ.[84] An eyewitness, who had been pressed into service along with other men of his community, reckoned that, when Ibrāhīm encamped at Bākhamrā, the troops serving the 'Alid numbered less than 10,000 men.[85] This impression is more or less confirmed by a detailed text that, in describing the composition of the 'Alid force and its field officers gives the specific figure of 11,700, of which all but 700 were infantry.[86] Still another account indicates that the army reached the field of battle in a state of exhaustion.[87] Nevertheless, the first signs of fighting showed gains for the rebels.

'Īsā b. Mūsā reportedly had 18,000 well-trained professionals with him. How does one explain, then, the initial success of Ibrāhīm b. 'Abdallāh on the battlefield?[88] According to standard military organization, there were four divisions to the royalist command. It is clear that the brunt of the early battle was directed against one of these divisions, the three-thousand-man vanguard commanded by Ḥumayd b. Qaḥṭabah. The collapse of the front left the command post of 'Īsā b. Mūsā dangerously exposed and, with that, the battle in doubt, for the loss of the center and the necessary retreat of the commander in chief might have had a serious psychological impact on the remaining divisions.[89] However, the command held, and Ibrāhīm's army was soon enveloped by an action to the rear that swiftly signaled an end to his challenge. His army having fled, he was reportedly left with four or five hundred men and the end was inevitable. In all, the battle seems to have taken a little more than a day. Errors notwithstanding, the facts of the revolt would seem to indicate that Ibrāhīm b. 'Abdallāh was unable to marshall sufficient strength in al-Baṣrah and other areas to successfully challenge the regime.

There still remains the question of al-Manṣūr's troubled behavior. It would be simplistic to ascribe this to an emotional breakdown that had only passing relevance to the actual state of affairs. There was a real danger facing him, which was conditioned by two extraordinary factors: the proximity of his capital to al-Kūfah and the absence of a strategic reserve in Iraq. The danger implicit in having the machinery of government adjacent to al-Kūfah, with its strong Shī'ite sympathies, was not lost on the Caliph, and it is reported to have been a factor in his decision to seek a new capital. Al-Manṣūr had, in fact, already decided upon Baghdad and was at that site supervising construction when news of the initial revolt in the Ḥijāz was received.[90] He then returned to al-Hāshimīyah and dispatched 'Īsā b. Mūsā, who was governor of al-Kūfah, to the Ḥijāz.

By sending his nephew to al-Madīnah at the head of a sizeable force, the Caliph emptied Iraq of almost all the available military reserves, for it is reported that 30,000 men were with al-Mahdī in al-Rayy and 40,000 were on a campaign in North Africa under Muḥammad b. al-Ash'ath.[91] Therefore, when news of Ibrāhīm's emergence in al-Baṣrah reached him, the Caliph quickly perceived the potential disaster in the situation that was developing. It was not simple hysteria that compelled al-Manṣūr to act in an erratic fashion, but the realization that, should Ibrāhīm reach al-Kūfah before 'Īsā b. Mūsā returned, or should the Kūfans be induced to rebel, the Caliph would be left to face his adversaries with only token troops. Various ruses were therefore employed to dissimulate the actual numbers and give the impression of a much larger force. This included lighting numerous campfires and having the same troops leave under cover of night only to return the following day as if they were fresh contingents just arrived.[92] It is no wonder that al-Manṣūr swore that if he overcame this predicament, he would not so divide his army again (*wallāhi la'in salimtu min hādhihi la yufāraqu 'askarī thalāthūn alf*).

As luck had it, 'Īsā b. Mūsā returned in time to block Ibrāhīm's advance against the Caliph, and the rebel refused to enlist the Kūfans in a diversionary tactic.[93] The critical battle therefore took place, not in the vicinity of the capital, but sixty miles away at Bākhamrā.[94] Had the defenses of the 'Abbāsid troops been organized around al-Hāshimīyah and the battle fought there, the Kūfans, regardless of Ibrāhīm's intentions to keep them out of battle, could possibly have become the 100,000 ambushers envisioned by al-Manṣūr in his darkest thoughts.

For a fleeting moment, the possibility existed that a rebel backed by a hastily recruited army could topple the 'Abbāsid regime in Iraq. Even if Ibrāhīm had only succeeded in forcing the government to abandon the province and flee to Khurāsān,[95] the psychological impact would have been sufficient to raise grave doubts about the viability of al-Manṣūr's Caliphate. To be sure, the ultimate defeat of the 'Abbāsids would have depended on winning the support of the Khurāsānī army, and in Khurāsān itself. It would have been a difficult, but perhaps not altogether impossible task. The rebellion, however, with its unique opportunity for success, ended in failure.

Al-Manṣūr then abandoned al-Hāshimīyah, left the Shī'ites of al-Kūfah, and returned to Baghdad, where he completed construction of the city. An essential feature of the new capital's vast urban plan was the extensive military colonization to the north of the Round City in the area which generally came to be known as al-Ḥarbīyah. These colonies housed the strategic reserve of the imperial armies, just as the Round City contained the administrative agencies of the government and the Caliph's personal domain. The disposition of all these elements in a secure and geographically advantageous urban setting solidified the Caliph's hold on Iraq and on the empire as a whole.[96]

D. Additional Observations

Whatever misgivings al-Manṣūr may have harbored concerning the political influence of his immediate family, there was no question that they would continue to play some significant role in the affairs of state. It may be noteworthy that, in the quieter and perhaps less conspiratorial climate that followed, the sons of men discredited within the 'Abbāsid house rose to positions within the provincial administration—some occupying the very governorships that their fathers had been directly or indirectly forced to relinquish. In this fashion, Aḥmad b.

Ismā'īl b. 'Alī became governor of al-Mawṣil, Isḥāq b. Sulaymān b. 'Alī inherited his father's former sinecure at al-Baṣrah, and even Mūsā b. 'Īsā b. Mūsā received a variety of provincial assignments, including the post at al-Kūfah in which his father had served for thirteen years.[97]

Following the death of al-Manṣūr, al-Mahdī seems to have embarked upon a policy of reconciliation with various elements of the ruling house. Such a course would have been consistent with his return, earlier in his reign, of those properties that had been confiscated from members of the ruling family and others.[98] The change in the leadership of the community may have, in effect, wiped the slate clean and given the appearance of a different order. The humorless austerity that earned for Abū Ja'far the additional patronymic Abū al-Dawāniq (pl. *dāniq*, the lowest unit of monetary exchange even for theoretical purposes), as well as his obtrusive megalomania and suspicion, seemed to yield to a somewhat more leisurely style. Nevertheless, one should not assume that the political favors bestowed on the ruling family were not carefully regulated.

The distribution of these regional posts to his cousins does not necessarily imply that the Caliph was willing to share extensive power with them, for the number of positions assigned remained limited, and the critical posts to the east were kept from them. Moreover, it is not clear to what extent these notables could exercise independent action; it may well be that the Caliph retained considerable, if not full, control through trusted clients of lesser rank serving in the local bureaucracy. Unlike the 'Abbāsid Caliphs, and the Umayyads before them, the offspring of al-Manṣūr came to differentiate the functions of the provincial administrators. This division of labor among several servants of the state thus provided the necessary checks and balances to insure continued control by the central authorities.[99] In any event, until the reign of al-Rashīd, the governors of royal descent still represented only a fraction of the total number of local rulers serving in the provinces, including those in the holy cities and the former *amṣār* of Iraq.

In the time of al-Rashīd, there is a marked rise in the number of royal appointments from various branches of the house. Nevertheless, even this increase was essentially confined to the traditional royal sinecures. Tabular expression of the situation can be determined from the random lists of governors dispersed throughout the early medieval chronicles. The total number of provincial posts is juxtaposed against the royal appointments listed in parentheses.[100]

al-Saffāḥ		
Mecca	3	(1)
al-Baṣrah	2	(1)
al-Kūfah	2	(2)
al-Yaman	4	(1)
al-Jazīrah	2	(2)
al-Madīnah	3	(1)
al-Mawṣil	4	(3)

al-Manṣūr		
Mecca	6	(2)
al-Baṣrah	11	(3)[101]
al-Kūfah	3	(1)
al-Yaman	5	(0)
al-Jazīrah	7	(2)
al-Madīnah	7	(2)
al-Mawṣil	7	(2)[102]

al-Mahdī		
Mecca	3	(2)
al-Baṣrah	6	(3)
al-Kūfah	4	(2)[103]
al-Jazīrah	10	(3)
al-Madīnah	9	(5)
al-Mawṣil	6	(3)

al-Rashīd		
Mecca	15	(11)
al-Baṣrah	17	(13)
al-Kūfah	10	(9)
al-Yaman	10	(4)
al-Jazīrah	7	(2)
al-Madīnah	11	(7)
al-Mawṣil	9	(2)

Missing from the list are the governorships of Khurāsān and the eastern provinces, posts that, significantly, remained outside the orbit of the ruling family. These vast territories generated enormous sums of revenue for the Baghdad government, and the withholding of these monies might cause not only serious economic dislocation in the center of the empire, but, at the same time, the subversion of the standing army in Khurāsān. It can be assumed that the positioning of 30,000 troops there during the reign of al-Manṣūr was not an isolated action, but part of a general policy that required a formidable military presence for purposes of administration, and for the necessity of combat with the mixed Turco-Iranian population beyond the Oxus. Moreover, the continuing campaign in Transoxiana insured not only battle-tested troops, but a continuous supply of manpower as well to fill the ranks of the Khurāsān-based imperial contingents.[104] Long after Abū Muslim had been disposed of, the governorships in the east remained the most important of the provincial appointments, and Khurāsān itself was the one area from which a successful challenge could be launched against the authorities in Baghdad.

Al-Ghiṭrīf, the uncle of al-Rashīd, was, for all intents and purposes, the first ʿAbbāsid notable to receive a post in the east, and his relationship to the Caliph was limited to the maternal side of the family. It is of course true that al-Mahdī had been officially chosen by his father as governor of that region, but his exercise of power was more in name than in fact. Indeed, the appointment may have been occasioned by al-Manṣūr's overwhelming desire to establish the strongest possible claims to the Caliphate for his progeny vis-à-vis those of his nephew ʿĪsā b. Mūsā, then a legitimate heir to the throne. It is only with the appointment of al-Rashīd's son, al-Ma'mūn, as governor of Khurāsān that a real change may have been envisioned. The choice of al-Ma'mūn was apparently based on a complicated plan of succession in which the major provinces of the empire were divided into three parts, with each territorial bloc to be ruled by one of three designated successors.[105] Even then, the young al-Ma'mūn was put under the tutelage of the *mawlā*, al-Faḍl b. Sahl, just as his grandfather before him cut his administrative teeth in the same region under the watchful eyes of the future wazīr, Abū ʿUbaydallāh al-Ashʿarī.[106]

It is not easy to draw general conclusions even when this material has been well understood, for the last years of al-Rashīd's rule remain an enigma marked by the Caliph's disenchantment with politics at Baghdad, the unofficial move of the capital to Raqqah-Rāfiqah, the continued changes in provincial appointments, and curious arrangements to allow for an orderly succession upon his death. The tantalizing thought persists that this may all be related somehow to a larger scheme that gradually unfolded during his reign, though its significance is not at present clear. The boldest speculation may suggest that the Caliph conceived of nothing less than the decentralization of the empire concurrent with a greater presence for the ruling family in the administration of the state, a policy that, if ever formulated, collapsed in the wake of the civil war that followed his death.

IV

THE RULING FAMILY AND ITS CLIENTS (*MAWĀLĪ*): REFLECTIONS ON A CONVERSATION AMONG NOTABLES

Al-Manṣūr to al-Mahdī:

O my son . . . I have collected *mawālī* for you the likes of which have not been collected by any Caliph before me. . . . Show favor to them and increase their numbers, for indeed they are your reinforcements when difficult times overtake you.

Ṭabarī, 3/1: 444, 448.

'Abd al-Ṣamad to al-Mahdī:

O Commander of the Faithful. We are a family ['Abbāsids] whose hearts are filled with love for our *mawālī* and the desire to prefer them to others. But you yourself went to such extremes and entrusted them with all your affairs, making them your close associates by day or by night. I fear that this will cause your Khurāsānī army and commanders to change heart.

Ṭabarī, 3/1: 531.

The perplexing problems of early 'Abbāsid government reflect not only the interplay of forces within the ruling family, but also the relations between the 'Abbāsids and their numerous clients. According to a tradition preserved by both Ya'qūbī and Mas'ūdī, al-Manṣūr was the first of the dynasty to institutionalize the use of *mawālī* in the provincial administration and other critical areas, a practice then continued by the successive Caliphs of his line.[1] Concomitant with this development was an intended and perceptible decline in the status of the Arabs serving the regime (. . . *wa qadmihim* [*mawālī*] *'alā al-'arab . . . fasaqaṭat wa bādat al-'arab wa zāla ba'suhā wa dhahabat marātibuhā*). The general use of clients for delicate missions was, of course, well known long before the Caliphate of al-Manṣūr. What is of interest here is the way in which the 'Abbāsid institution of clientage is linked to the decline of Arab leadership and privilege.[2] In effect, the Caliphs increasingly preferred to conduct the business of government through agents tied exclusively to themselves rather than to rely on persons with well-established affiliations to tribal and other political units of importance. The consequences of this decision were bound to be felt by elements within the ruling family.

A. The Conversation between 'Abd al-Ṣamad and the Caliph al-Mahdī

A convenient point of departure in studying the effects of this policy on family politics is to turn once again to the *'umūmah* of the Caliph, and, in particular, to 'Abd al-Ṣamad b. 'Alī. Among the paternal uncles of al-Manṣūr, it was perhaps 'Abd al-Ṣamad who was most conspicuous. Although others may have had a more dramatic influence on given moments of history, none enjoyed so long and varied a career in the service of the state, and this, despite a temperament and flair for decision-making that were not always to his advantage and even earned for him a certain notoriety. He alone, among the *'umūmah*, rallied to the side of 'Abdallāh b. 'Alī and consequently enjoyed, for the short period of the revolt, recognition as his brother's designated successor.[3] Although defeated in battle, he was nevertheless granted a pardon that paved the way for reentering public service upon his recognition of al-Manṣūr's claims to rule. Having so fortuitously salvaged his political career, the defeated rebel might have been expected to act more cautiously. But 'Abd al-Ṣamad b. 'Alī was not one to allow discretion to overwhelm his need for frank talk and independent action.[4] Nevertheless, 'Abd al-Ṣamad continued to find a place in 'Abbāsid government and outlived not only al-Manṣūr, but the Caliph's son and grandson al-Hādī after him. He died of natural causes after a long and fruitful career that extended well into his eighties,[5] and he served, and in a variety of administrative capacities, no fewer than five Caliphs of the 'Abbāsid house.

With so little known of the inner workings of the 'Abbāsid family and its clients, 'Abd al-Ṣamad's participation through four generations of 'Abbāsid politics makes his career particularly important as a barometer of relations within the ruling house. It is instructive to recall, therefore, the remarkable account of a conversation between the venerable uncle and his brother's grandson, the Caliph al-Mahdī. In a unique tradition preserved by Ṭabarī, the elder statesman is reported to have warned al-Mahdī that, although the ruling house (*ahl al-bayt*)[6] was filled with love for its clients (*mawālī*), the Caliph's intimacy with them was excessive and might cause the Khurāsānī army and its commanders to waver in their allegiance to the 'Abbāsid house. Al-Mahdī, in reply, indicated that his clients deserved to be treated with trust and pointed out that he could rub knees with a *mawlā* one moment and have him groom his animal the next. The *mawlā* was satisfied with this relationship. The same, however, could not be said of others, that is, of certain members of the ruling family and elements of the Khurāsānī army. Unlike the *mawālī*, they would consider themselves beyond such menial tasks and would draw attention to their fathers' or their own past service to the 'Abbāsid cause (*da'wah*).[7]

That this paternal uncle should have been the vehicle for expressing sentiments against the house of al-Manṣūr and its dutiful clients is fitting. The veteran revolutionary personally had witnessed the political maneuverings of no fewer than five Caliphs, and it was his branch of the family that had been, at the outset, the most seriously compromised by the ambition of its rivals, the line of his brother Muḥammad b. 'Alī.[8] Given this political background, what may seem an innocuous reproach is actually a serious statement.

Although accounts of this sort are often marked by literary shaping, they are, nevertheless, at times revealing, for woven into the legendary fabric of these stories are often the strands of a significant historical incident. In this respect, the conversation between the Caliph and his great uncle is remarkable, for even if one were to invent a tradition out of wholly new cloth, it is doubtful that one could improve on this version, which conceptualizes with great clarity a central problem of early 'Abbāsid society. Reflected in these passages is the complex triangular relationship between the ruling house and its instruments of rule: the regular army, quartered, for the most part, in the northern suburbs of the capital, and key elements of the court and bureaucracy, represented largely by certain *mawālī*. The failure of the ruling family to keep its house in order, the propensity of the *mawālī* to stimulate rather than reduce tensions, and, above all, the decline of professionalism within the regular army all signaled the incipient decline of 'Abbāsid rule. This failure to rise above self- and group-interest was perhaps the most glaring weakness of state and society in early Islam, and, in time, it eroded the ability of the central authorities to respond to the periodic crises that beset the regime.

B. The Mawālī *of 'Abd al-Ṣamad: Some Speculations*

What was the great attraction that 'Abd al-Ṣamad's *mawālī* held for the 'Abbāsid rulers, that the Caliphs sometimes preferred them to their blood kin and felt free to entrust them with matters of the most delicate nature? One recollects that they were described by al-Mahdī, and in terms intended to be quite laudatory, as not being above grooming the Caliph's animal when required to do so. The metaphor, whether intentional or not, is well-taken, for the Arabic word for the grooming of animals became, in time, identical with that for training constituencies in political obedience, namely, *siyāsah*, the art of politics. Seen most superficially, what emerges then is a class tied by a special relationship to, and therefore dependent on, the very person of the ruler, a class that was brought into government and personal service because the complex machinery of state in the postrevolutionary period necessitated a search beyond the ruling family and its existing retainers for public servants and political confidants. However, it is the extent and nature of the *mawlā*'s involvement at the highest levels, the involvement so vividly alluded to by 'Abd al-Ṣamad, that is of primary interest here.

The Arabic legal sources of the middle ages contain extended discussions of clientage.[9] However, any attempt to understand the crux of 'Abd al-Ṣamad's concern with the *mawālī* exclusively on the basis of formal definitions derived from the legal literature is not likely to be very informative. What is particularly troublesome is the modus operandi of the 'Abbāsid house. Like any ruling order, it had a dynamic of its own that could circumvent the ordinary limits imposed by law and social convention. It is therefore prudent to record the important caveat that the actual function of clientage, insofar as it affected the ruling family, might have been rather different from the general picture obtained by way of the law books. A proper study of the *mawālī* entails a survey of the theoretical possibilities of association, based not only on the existing framework provided by the wide ranging legal literature, but, more particularly, on the needs of the early Caliphate, insofar as they can be historiographically defined.

The critical problem is to identify the type or types of clients referred to in the text under review, and to determine how they functioned within the general framework of 'Abbāsid government. Although the question is easily formulated, it eludes a convincing explanation, for even more difficult to understand than the attitude of ʿAbd al-Ṣamad is the nature of the institution itself. Early ʿAbbāsid historiography generally did not attempt to define or conceptualize social institutions but preferred to view the course of human events in narratives almost exclusively weighted by biographical considerations.[10] Moreover, even the material preserved in a highly structured biographical format was collected on a selective basis, thereby omitting tens if not hundreds of individuals of lesser rank, whose careers are nevertheless of great interest and significance. As a result, some of the most dramatic personalities among the *mawālī* are shadowy figures given the barest biographical entries or woven into the fabric of disjointed historical accounts. The contemporary historian is forced, therefore, to impose his own methodology on a highly resistant body of texts, which, allowing for a somewhat exaggerated metaphor, may perhaps be likened to the inmates of a conceptual prison awaiting their hour of liberation. Unfortunately, this task is so difficult that it discourages the creation of the detailed models preferred by modern social scientists; and although the scholar's desire to bring conceptual order to the study of human affairs is surely appreciated, it is with much forethought that the word speculation was used in the rubric of this very modest subsection. There is, to be sure, little hope that this caution will prove contagious, but, if nothing else, it indicates an attempt at a working hypothesis rather than the presentation of a definitive statement.

What is clear is that the institution of clientage, as expressed by the root *wly*, is both pre-Islamic in some of its forms and exceedingly complicated.[11] Given the type of association made possible by the medieval lawyers, it seems that the *mawlā* of whom ʿAbd al-Ṣamad speaks could have been tied to the ruling house by a complex series of relationships rather than by a single formula. These may have covered kinsmen, manumitted slaves, and freemen entering into voluntary agreement. That the *mawālī* referred to here were kinsmen of the Caliph can quite obviously be ruled out from the context of ʿAbd al-Ṣamad's remarks, in which the grand uncle of the Caliph is presented as the plaintiff for blood relatives of the house vis-à-vis encroaching outsiders.

It has been broadly suggested that the category of freemen (specifically, the *mawālī al-muwālāt*) represents a type of clientage that is important to the 'Abbāsid Caliph and the Muslim community as a whole during the second and third centuries A.H. One is therefore inclined to ask if 'Abd al-Ṣamad's *mawālī* might have specifically reflected this form of association.[12] Persons of this clientage were allies or confederates who had entered into voluntary agreement with their patrons for purposes of mutual assistance (*tanāṣur*) by a contractual arrangement that was both flexible and terminable. It is true that, among the major "schools" of legal thought, this arrangement was recognized only by the Ḥanafites; however, the Ḥanafite *madhhab* was generally predominant at Baghdad during the first 'Abbāsid century.[13] Granting the theoretical possibility that *muwālāt* clientage is implicit in the remarks of 'Abd al-Ṣamad, the critical question nevertheless persists as to how this type of association could have been of significant mutual benefit under the conditions of state and society at the outset of 'Abbāsid rule. This connection has not been made sufficiently clear by those who stress the importance of the *mawālī al-muwālāt*.

Mutual assistance may give the impression of an alliance based largely on military considerations, an attempt, to create larger units for purposes of self-defense and conquest. However, in such a case, there would seem to be theoretical limits within which *muwālāt* clientage could function effectively. If one considers the possibility of mutual military assistance, it is difficult to suppose that clients were widely recruited on an individual basis, for military service of freemen in early Islam was generally conceived of in terms of substantial social units arranged according to geographical or tribal affiliation. To be sure, one could enter into the army directly as a volunteer in the irregular infantry, but such individual enlistments neither required special status nor would have been considered noteworthy or leading immediately to great influence in ruling councils. Individual clients could also bring to the association various retainers of their own, that is, groups of fighting men responsible directly to them. There is no evidence, however, that this specific type of military clientage was practiced in the eighth century in contingents of the imperial army.

It is therefore likely that 'Abd al-Ṣamad's concern was derived, not from the *mawlā* specifically as soldier, but from a broader set of circumstances, especially that of client-confidant in relation to his patron. The general question of military service, then, is to be seen as a complicated matter that falls under a different rubric altogether. This is revealed not only by ʿAbd al-Ṣamad's particular grievance, but by the Caliph's response as well. One notes that al-Mahdī is admonished that he goes too far in deferring to his clients, for he entrusts the *mawālī* with all his affairs and makes them his close intimates by day and by night. Al-Mahdī replies that their personal allegiance to him is one of total commitment. To be sure, the personal service that is reflected in this statement could have been secured through *muwālāt* and related forms of clientage among freemen. However, a casual survey of the *mawālī* who served in high government circles early in the realm strongly suggests that they were recruited from a wider spectrum including manumitted slaves.

The freedman (*ʿātiq, muʿtaq*) generally enjoyed the same legal rights as the freeborn, but, unlike the latter, whose association was flexible and terminable, both he and his male descendants were attached by clientage to the family of his master-manumitter (*muʿtiq*) in perpetuity. The freedman has been described as a purely passive member of his new kin, considered by most lawyers as inferior to his patron for purposes of inheritance and marriage, in his exclusion from the *zakāt*, and in his eligibility to the Caliphate. In this sense, the client could hardly be described as enjoying equality of status with the *muʿtiq* and his blood kinsmen; rather, the manumitted slave is to be understood as a figure dependent on a patron whose position in the relationship was clearly preeminent.[14]

Although the sense of dependency generated by this form of clientage could have been very useful to the ʿAbbāsid house, there is reason to be wary of tying a complex historical institution to a formal legal text. One must keep in mind that the ʿAbbāsids did not come to power through a peaceful transition, but after a relatively short and decisive conflict that culminated a long clandestine struggle. Because the essential feature of clientage was self-interest, either through mutual assistance based on a contractual arrangement or by an outright grant of protection, the dismemberment of the Umayyad government could not help but bring about significant changes in the existing social order. Most seriously affected was the area of personal and group ties, for previous associations, especially those dependent on the political structures of the Umayyad state, were generally rendered void.[15]

The emergence of an ʿAbbāsid polity created new associations, some of which were perhaps variations of previous forms. As a result, manumitted slaves, whose ties to their patrons were torn apart by the change of dynasty, could have found themselves entering into the service of the 'Abbāsid house as de facto freemen. It is doubtful, however, that this distinction had any bearing at all on the actual function of clientage. The freemen and *mawālī* once removed from slavery who may have been received by the 'Abbāsids, as well as the *mawālī* directly manumitted by them, were all equally dependent on their patron. Regardless of his personal status as defined by the law then generally recognized, the *mawlā*'s ties to the ruling house were neither flexible nor terminable. The *mawlā* no more left the Caliph's service of his own volition than the soldier of the mafia voluntarily abandons his patron's family by invoking his constitutional rights. However, this is not to deny that there may have emerged a wide variety of associations by different formulae. Although these made little difference as regards ties to the Caliph, they were perhaps of importance in understanding the relationships of the various types of *mawālī* to one another. This, however, awaits further study.

C. Function of the Mawālī *and the Ruling Family*

Seen in the context of a highly dependent form of clientage and given what is known of state and society under the early 'Abbāsids, a paradigm, however incomplete, may be conjectured as to the structure and function of 'Abd al-Ṣamad's *mawālī*.

Aside from a generally understood legal status, the clients are not easily defined as a group within the 'Abbāsid hierarchy. They may have eventually included servants of the ruling household, as well as generals in the army, the royal executioner, and the powerful wazīrial interests, though the full force of 'Abd al-Ṣamad's comments was no doubt reserved for al-Mahdī's closest intimates from among this group. The reference here was presumably intended for the circle of the wazīrs and their apparatchiks, whose status as part of a separate institution with special functions was initially developed during the career of al-Mahdī, at first, to tutor young princes in the affairs of government and later, to remain as their confidential advisers.[16] Nevertheless, the client, because of his dependent status, had no recognizable constituency of his own. Whatever powers he accrued were not derived from, and were not generally transferable to, his social class as a whole. The system was, therefore, theoretically suited to the conspiratorial outlook of the 'Abbāsid rulers, for the vulnerable *mawlā* could be treated in a more isolated fashion than a member of the ruling family or of some other recognizable political structure. On the other hand, because the *mawlā* and his progeny were in fact tied to his master's house, either by law or by circumstance, there was the possibility in certain cases such as that of the Barmakids, of perpetuating meaningful service on behalf of a patron, thereby creating structures of powerful client families within the administration of the state. These mini-constituencies and individual sinecures were, however, highly sensitive to changes within the ruling house.

The Barmakids, lacking sustained ties to the military, were disposed of without complications despite their vast influence in the affairs of government. Khālid b. Barmak, the patriarch of the family, was nominally attached to the military during the 'Abbāsid revolution; however, his function seems to have been essentially political. His primary responsibility was the distribution of booty, a trusted position, but one that did not require the capacity to lead large armies in the field. Although Khālid's subsequent career included participation in a number of campaigns, his value to the state was largely that of an administrator in the capital and, occasionally, in the provinces.[17] Of all the Barmakids, only his grandson al-Faḍl b. Yaḥyā had any sustained tie to a large military organization. It therefore may not be a coincidence that al-Faḍl's powers were severely curtailed before the Caliph, Hārūn al-Rashīd, struck hard against the entire family. As it was, four years elapsed between al-Faḍl's fall from grace and the mysterious events that precipitated the imprisonment of the entire family.[18]

Once the Caliph decided on resolute action, even so formidable a figure as Abū Muslim, the "commissar" of the revolutionary armies, could be removed with no more than moderate difficulty—this, in contradistinction to al-Manṣūr's more prolonged dealings with the paternal uncles and his nephew 'Īsā b. Mūsā. One recalls that 'Abdallāh b. 'Alī, a declared rebel against the regime, could hardly have been characterized as a quixotic figure. When defeated, he commanded a sizeable army of veteran front-line troops; yet, after being officially apprehended, it took years to create the preconditions necessary for his death, and even then, his demise was far less dramatic than tradition would lead one to believe. The execution of Abū Muslim, on the other hand, required only that he be lured away from his army contingents; once his death was a fait accompli, it was an easy matter to calm the passions of key personnel through the distribution of favors. The various revolts reportedly invoked in his name appear to be relatively minor affairs greatly embellished with the passing of time.[19]

The *mawlā* realistically assessing his circumstances, understood only too well the limits of his political power and promoted his career accordingly. He aligned his ambitions with the needs of his patron, to their mutual benefit. Al-Jāḥiẓ was quick to emphasize the trustworthiness of the client in delicate matters of state, thereby explaining the preference for *mawālī* that incurred the jealousy of others.[20] It also seems that such critical positions as the directorships of the security forces (*ḥaras*) and security police (*shurṭah*) tended to become the sinecures of old and trusted families, a pattern that had already taken shape with the emergence of the revolution.[21] This is not to say the ʿAbbāsid royalty regarded the *mawālī*, no matter how well-placed, as social equals. Perhaps the best illustration of the formal gap between them is al-Rashīd's proviso that the marriage of convenience arranged by him between Jaʿfar, the Barmakid, and the Caliph's sister ʿAbbāsah must never be consummated.

A late medieval author could not bring himself to believe that the Caliph might have gone even that far:

> This story is irreconcilable with ʿAbbāsah's position, her religiousness, her parentage, and her exalted rank. . . . How could she link her pedigree with that of Jaʿfar b. Yaḥyā and stain her Arab nobility with a Persian client? His ancestor had been acquired as a slave, or taken as a client, by one of her ancestors, an uncle of the Prophet and noble Qurayshite. . . . How could it be that al-Rashīd . . . would permit himself to become related by marriage to Persian clients![22]

The utility of the *mawālī* was nevertheless self-evident and their companionship was often sought. Although particularly influential in affairs of the court, some participated as well in military service. They were generally not, however, in large elite units of their own, unlike the Khurāsānī imperial army alluded to by ʿAbd al-Ṣamad.[23] Still, the activities of the *mawālī* in handling the affairs of state had an enormous influence on the development of military organization, a point that is crucial to an understanding not only of ʿAbd al-Ṣamad's remarks, but of early ʿAbbāsid society as well. Beginning with circumstances following the death of the Caliph al-Mahdī, the most influential clients serving in high councils of government could not be isolated from intrigues within the innermost circles of the ruling family. On the contrary, when internal dissensions bordered on civil strife, they were compelled by the nature of their position to take sides and to become provocateurs acting in the best interest of their royal patrons. Immature in years, disinclined to rule, or simply overburdened, the ʿAbbāsid dignitaries increasingly turned the functions of state over to their confidants. Whereas in the past, the *mawālī* may have vied with one another to serve a single master, they now began to manipulate the affairs of state for several interests, a fact reflected in the creation of shadow governments for the young ʿAbbāsid princes being considered for rule.[24] Nonetheless, real freedom of movement for the *mawālī* was ultimately restricted by their lack of a strong military connection and cohesive political structure. One has the impression that they were quite resilient in their political careers, despite occasional indiscretions. If this was indeed true, their resiliency may have been a function more of their inability to act independently than of any external resources that they may or may not have commanded.

The political intrigues of the government functionaries helped ultimately to create the preconditions for the intervention of a still more powerful group that was to diminish not only the limited influence of the *mawālī*, but that of their patron, the Caliph, as well. Unlike the *mawlā* in government service who, once discarded, could simply be relegated to political obscurity, the regular, or professional, army found the means of effecting significant action when it felt compelled to do so. Concomitant with the growing economic and political instability that led eventually to the erosion of Caliphal authority, the military emerged more and more as a factor in internal government affairs. Difficulties that could not be resolved in localized court intrigues, and thus isolated from the society at large, required the direct intervention of the imperial army. These developments added a new and volatile dimension to the existing structure of ʿAbbāsid society and brought to the forefront those clients whose function in the service of the state was defined primarily by its military character, although the distinction between military and administrative functions was not always clearly drawn.

Generally, those *mawālī* who commanded the support of large armies retained considerable power, while others, whose influence was derived more directly from their role in the governmental bureaucracy, appear to have lost ground. This was the situation apparently envisioned by ʿAbd al-Ṣamad when he warned that the Khurāsānī army and its commanders would change heart. Once the exclusive agents of the Caliph, they became, amid growing political instability, and, more particularly, economic uncertainty, a vested interest group available to the highest bidder with the prerequisite credentials to rule. Having entered directly into the affairs of state at the time of the great civil war between the sons of al-Rashīd, the army proved to be a disruptive, rather than a unifying, factor at a time of political instability, thus bringing about the fulfillment of ʿAbd al-Ṣamad's prophetic pronouncement.

D. Additional Thoughts: Clientage and the Army of al-Manṣūr

Is it possible that al-Manṣūr conceived of his Khurāsānī military forces as he did elements of the civilian bureaucracy and court, that is to say, tied by special status to the ruling house? Could circumstances have permitted the growth of an ʿAbbāsid military organization totally responsive to the central authorities? If so, a complex and extended system of military service could then have developed along professional lines, resulting in a fighting force free from the debilitating effects of the group interest (*ʿaṣabīyah*) that had weakened the tribal armies of their predecessors and prevented the creation of a distinctive and lasting polity.

The ʿAbbāsid army, like all other institutions of government, would then have been based on intricate personal relationships ultimately traceable to the ruling family. It was the dynamic of the client-patron relationship, even more than the formal structure of institutions, that bound ʿAbbāsid ruling society together and gave it cohesion during the formative years of the regime. The Caliph's policies toward the imperial army and his policies concerning the court and civilian bureaucracy were functions of the desire to bind all the instruments of rule to himself by special ties of clientage. If this assessment of his intentions is correct, clientage, in the broadest sense, and the system of patronage that it engendered, provided the structure for all 'Abbāsid government, while the 'Abbāsid theoreticians supplied, in turn, the ideological cement that held the ruling institution together. In this fashion the geographically uprooted Khurāsānīs who came to Iraq with the advance of the revolution, as well as the politically rootless *mawālī* serving in the government and at court, were to have been the personal agents of the Caliph in opposing any external or internal challenges to his rule. The *mawālī*, who were isolated in society and were, therefore, fully dependent on their patron, adapted quite easily to this role. The task of molding the army into the image of client must have been quite another matter.[25]

The successful conclusion of the revolution left the 'Abbāsids with a disjointed military apparatus, brought together in common cause for divergent reasons reflecting ideological, political, and pecuniary interests.[26] During the formative period of the revolution, an army was recruited by Abū Muslim from among the old Arab settlers and their Iranian clients in the villages of Khurāsān. Despite an impressive political commitment to the cause, this army was one of limited fighting potential and would have been hard pressed to protect its own regional enclaves, let alone challenge the professional Syrian armies of the incumbent Umayyad regime. Much larger and better trained contingents would be necessary to sustain a lengthy campaign against men like Nubātah b. Ḥanẓalah and 'Āmir b. Ḍubārah.

Skillful political maneuvers in time added the fragmented and disaffected Arab tribal armies of Khurāsān, specifically those of the Yaman and Rabī'ah. Although they initially embraced the 'Abbāsid cause for reasons of political self-interest, and not ideological conviction, the tribal armies were eventually subsumed, along with the assimilated villagers and their clients, within what became known as "the people of Khurāsān" (*ahl Khurāsān*). This regional identification gave rise to some feeling of cohesion, particularly in opposition to the Umayyad army of Syrian designation (*ahl al-Shām*), with which the *ahl Khurāsān* is often contrasted. Nevertheless, the tribal armies were highly independent in outlook and suffered from all the traditional effects of *'aṣabīyah*. Later, in the cantonments of Baghdad, the descendants of the *ahl Khurāsān* would develop into a unified army of great esprit de corps without divisive tribal sensitivities. However, at the outset, any long-range guarantee of loyalty from the Arab tribesmen had to be regarded as a rather risky expectation. Still less reliable were the Syrian units, who defected to the 'Abbāsids following the defeat of their patrons and who would later serve as the backbone of 'Abdallāh b. 'Alī's revolt against al-Manṣūr.[27]

The 'Abbāsids, who began as a family in search of a revolution, were therefore compelled to look for a means of controlling the forces that Abū Muslim had unleashed on their behalf. This problem was attacked through several converging strategies. Although forced to rely on the tribal armies, the 'Abbāsids found it convenient, indeed imperative, to retain control of the command structure through agents of their own choosing. The supreme military command was initially entrusted to Qaḥṭabah b. Shabīb al-Ṭā'ī,[28] whose associations with the 'Abbāsid cause can be traced back to the clandestine activities of the *da'wah* in Khurāsān. To their good fortune, the 'Abbāsids found in Qaḥṭabah the rare combination of qualities they required. His impeccable credentials as a revolutionary agent were matched by his tactical skills as a brilliant field commander, and although he was himself an assimilated Arab of the villages, these earned for him the allegiance of the recently recruited tribal armies. Following Qaḥṭabah's premature death in battle the 'Abbāsids retained command of the military through his able sons, al-Ḥasan and Ḥumayd, and through 'Abdallāh b. 'Alī and other paternal uncles, who emerged from political concealment once the 'Abbāsid Caliphate had been proclaimed.

The unbroken string of military victories compiled by Qaḥṭabah and his successors accounted, in no small way, for the continuing loyalty of the volatile tribal armies. Of equal importance, however, was the firm control that the 'Abbāsids exercised over the internal administration of the military. The critical role here fell to trusted clients of the 'Abbāsid family such as Abū Muslim, Khālid b. Barmak, and Jahm b. 'Aṭīyah. These men were not professional field commanders but were, in effect, the political commissars of the burgeoning military apparatus. They were responsible for recruitment, payroll, the intelligence services, the security forces, and later, the palace guard. There is no doubt that their responsibilities also extended beyond the technical administration of the army. This leads to speculation concerning still another possible strategy employed by the ruling family to control its newly acquired fighting units. It has been suggested that the distribution of regular service pay and bonuses was augmented by an intensive campaign of propaganda within the military, so that, in time, the diverse elements of the tribal armies would be united in their enthusiastic support for the ruling family on ideological, as well as pragmatic, grounds. The evidence for such a program, however, seems rather scant. Although there is no reason to deny that the ʿAbbāsids launched an intensive campaign of indoctrination within the army, the successes claimed because of it should be regarded with caution.[29]

The text most often cited with regard to military propaganda is the *Risālah fī al-ṣaḥābah*, a treatise attributed to the client-littérateur Ibn al-Muqaffaʿ.[30] A late convert to Islam, the author attached himself as a secretary to the Umayyad ruling establishment in Kirmān. With the change of dynasty, he prudently shifted political associations and became the client of the new Caliph's paternal uncles ʿĪsā and Sulaymān b. ʿAlī. However, ʿAbbāsid family politics in the wake of ʿAbdallāh b. ʿAlī's unsuccessful rebellion left Ibn al-Muqaffaʿ on the horns of a dilemma. His patrons had succumbed to pressures from the Caliph al-Manṣūr to terminate the protective custody that ʿAbdallāh b. ʿAlī enjoyed in Sulaymān's household. Fearful of what might befall their brother, Sulaymān and ʿĪsā b. ʿAlī finally agreed to hand him over to the central authorities, but only under conditions carefully delineated in a document guaranteeing the rebel's safety.

Because his command of Arabic was superb, Ibn al-Muqaffaʿ was called upon to draft the delicate letter of pardon issued by al-Manṣūr to his rebellious uncle. The text of the document contained protective clauses that allowed the Caliph little room to maneuver, and it is alleged that the author fell victim for having exercised his charge with excessive zeal. Stated somewhat differently, it would appear that Ibn al-Muqaffaʿ's close connections with the *ʿumūmah,* whose political fortunes were in full decline, compounded by personal grievances held against him in high circles, left the author isolated against hostile intrigues. Despite meritorious service to his patrons in the earthly kingdom, the dutiful client was soon dispatched to the realm of the spirits. In a sense, his career is a striking illustration of the manner in which the politically rootless *mawālī* gained and lost position within powerful circles. The facts also establish that Ibn al-Muqaffaʿ was an eye witness to the inner workings of the government and the ʿAbbāsid family, so that any observations he may have made about the ruling institution should be treated with great interest.

Seen against this background, the *Risālah fī al-ṣaḥābah* is a truly remarkable document. Its date can be fixed some time after the revolt of ʿAbdallāh b. ʿAlī and the subsequent murder of Abū Muslim, as these events are obliquely referred to in the text.[31] The content is not filtered through the lenses of subsequent chronicles, and, thus, might very well reflect conditions concurrent with the formative years of al-Manṣūr's reign. The Caliph is not mentioned by name, but it is evident that the treatise is addressed to him. One can indeed speculate that it was Ibn al-Muqaffaʿ's intention to ingratiate himself with al-Manṣūr when the author's connection with the *ʿumūmah* took on the appearance of a potential, if not actual, liability.

Although written in the general style of the Arabic *Fürstenspiegel* literature, the *Risālah* actually contains concrete proposals for establishing an enduring ʿAbbāsid state.[32] The basic thesis is that all the institutions of government, whether secular or religious, should be subordinated to the direct authority of the Caliph.[33] Implicit in this notion is the marriage of religion to political authority, an idea bandied about by early ʿAbbāsid propagandists. Theoretically, the acceptance of this proposition would have enabled the Caliph to obtain a firm grasp over the army through special ties of religious obedience.[34] Actually, the defeat of ʿAbdallāh b. ʿAlī and the Syrian army, together with the subsequent execution of Abū Muslim, who was the major political influence on the Khurāsānī units, had already paved the way for al-Manṣūr to assume direct control of the military apparatus. Ibn al-Muqaffaʿ was well aware of the possibilities created by these events, and some of his most interesting comments concern the function of the army in relation to its sovereign. The author implies that al-Manṣūr had a unique opportunity. If he would only follow the program outlined in the *Risālah*, the military would, in turn, follow him blindly, and, with that, his role would no doubt be firmly secured.

Not all the military contingents could, however, be regarded as receptive to a centralized authority on religious, or, for that matter, any, grounds. The Arab tribal armies of Syria were originally the instrument of the Umayyad Caliphs and only later became the backbone of 'Abdallāh b. 'Alī's rebellion. Moreover, they were the most susceptible to effects of tribal xenophobia. It is no surprise that Ibn al-Muqaffa' suggests caution with regard to the Syrians; this judgment is echoed in numerous accounts from the early 'Abbāsid period.[35] A Baghdadi poet, extolling the virtues of the dynastic capital, points to the tranquility of the city and declares in contrast, "you will not see a stranger coveting sleep in the land of Syria."[36] The factors underlying these sentiments are reflected in al-Azdī's history of al-Mawṣil, which is replete with accounts of localized tribal warfare. It will be recalled that, when the hard pressed al-Amīn later attempted to co-opt the Arab tribesmen of Syria in the war of the brothers, his plans were subverted from the beginning by tribal sensitivities aroused by a petty argument over a stolen horse.[37]

Perhaps the most pointed illustration of this lingering distaste for the Syrians is an account preserved by Ṭabarī concerning the Caliph al-Ma'mūn.[38] A man persistently appeals to the Caliph to consider the Arabs of Syria as he considers the *'ajam* of *ahl Khurāsān*. Al-Ma'mūn responds, "By God, I only dismounted the Qays from the backs of their horses because I discovered there was not even a single dirham left in my [public] treasury.[39] As for the Yaman, I did not love them and they did not love me at all. As for the Quḍā'ah, its chiefs are waiting in anticipation of the Sufyānid [that is, the Umayyad pretender] and his rebellion so they can become his partisans. As for the Rabī'ah, they are angry with God ever since he sent his Prophet [Muḥammad] from the Muḍar. Of every two Khārijites who revolt, one is from the Rabī'ah. . . ." Then, in terms that are not found in the conventional Arabic vocabulary for hospitality, the Caliph told him to be off.

In contrast with the Syrians, the Khurāsānīs come in for high praise from Ibn al-Muqaffa'. He regards their qualities as unmatched by any army of Islam.[40] They are tractable, steadfast in service, and incapable of corruption. Their devotion to the Caliph is indeed staggering. There are officers among them who believe that, if the Caliph ordered the mountains to move, they would move, and, if he ordered turning ones' back to the Ka'bah during prayer, one would comply. This license against the natural order and religious law is, no doubt, presumed because these Khurāsānī officers are imbued with the messianic fervor of the time and the radical views that it fostered. They recognize no authority, save God, that transcends the Caliph himself. For Ibn al-Muqaffaʿ, views such as these reflect the excessive zeal of the Khurāsānīs, and the army thus requires strict control, lest the Caliph appear, as he put it "like the rider of a lion who terrifies those who see him, but is himself the most terrified of all." If the qualities of the Khurāsānīs are to be harnessed, their responsibilities must be carefully defined and their activities closely regulated.

The author prescribes a text. It has been suggested that a catechism is intended here,[41] but it appears more likely to be a manual or code of military procedure that covers all conceivable situations (*āmān maʿrūf balīgh wājiz muḥīṭ bikull shay yajibu an yaʿmilū fīhi aw yakuffū ʿanhu*). It is to be learned by the leadership of the army so that they may lead the lower ranks according to its provisions. Elsewhere, the author stresses the need for a religious education among the troops.[42] Men in the ranks (who exhibited qualities of leadership) should be given instruction in Qur'ān, *sunnah*, and in basic religious beliefs (in order to take full advantage of their inner capabilities)[43] and to emulate the humble life style of the Commander of the Faithful.

However devoted to the Caliph, the Khurāsānīs are still not to be exposed to worldly temptations. They should be denied the primary responsibility for collecting taxes, for that leads to the corruption of warriors. In any event, military service is a noble calling that should be sufficiently rewarding in itself (*wa innamā manzilat al-muqātil manzilat al-karāmah wa al-luṭf*).[44] The primary concern here is to deny the army a direct source of revenue and, with it, a capacity for independent action. Nevertheless, the army is not without practical concerns. It is desired that it be religiously obedient, but this does not imply that it should or will be ascetic. The Commander of the Faithful may have been humble in his life style, but he was not self-denying. On the contrary, the needs of the military are to be cared for according to a regular schedule of service pay and by a specific payroll. Every three or four months or the like, the troops registered in the dīwān will receive their allotments, so as to forestall any dissatisfaction in the ranks. Furthermore, since it is known that fluctuations in the market may have a bearing on the price-wage factor, it is recommended that the distribution of foodstuffs and fodder be regulated in order to keep the army without cause for complaint.[45] The author's strategy seems clear. An army relieved of the responsibility for its own sustenance becomes increasingly dependent on its provider; the mouth filled with nourishment is also more likely to be muted in its criticism.

There is, in this military program of Ibn al-Muqaffaʿ, a marriage of the ideological to the practical. As articulated by the author, the overall objective is to "set in proper order (*taqwīm*)[46] the hands, thoughts, and words" of the Khurāsānīs. To be sure, the program, as it is depicted here, is not exactly based on any conventional model of clientage previously described. However, the operative force of these measures was intended to bind the Khurāsānī army to the Caliph with ties as close as any between patron and client. The existing military establishment had already trusted veterans of the revolution in the command structure of the fighting units, as well as in the security forces and the administrative branch of the army.[47] The stipulation concerning education for men in the ranks may be derived from a wish to maximize the fighting potential of the ʿAbbāsid regiments, but it presumably reflects as well the need to establish a continuing form of patronage within the military. The "ignorant" troopers, whose qualities exceed those of some officers (*minhum min al-majhūlīn man huwa afḍal min baʿḍ qādatihim*), would be extremely grateful for this opportunity to rise in the ranks. Given the circumstances of this advance, one would have to assume that they conceived of their future in political as well as military terms.

In the absence of more definitive data, one may theorize endlessly from these few scraps of information. Yet, the picture of the army program obtained from a first reading of Ibn al-Muqaffaʿ's *Risālah* seems consistent with ʿAbbāsid needs. There are, to be sure, unanswered questions. Are the qualities of the Khurāsānīs listed by the author an accurate reflection of existing conditions or an idealized picture of the relationship between the imperial army and its sovereign? Were any of these measures actually carried out? Or, for that matter, could any of them have been put into effect?

For those who stress the efficacy of ʿAbbāsid indoctrination, such questions inevitably lead to the accounts of the Rāwandīyah revolt, an event of uncertain date that is reported alternatively for the years A.H. 136, 137, 141 and 142.[48] It is possible to link the various branches of the Rāwandīyah with the broad spectrum of eighth century proto-Shīʿite groups, but, given the confusing state of Arabic heresiography, one is then left with explaining the obscure by that which is equally obscure. Although this methodology retains a certain compelling attraction, it does not make for an easy analysis of the event in question. The details, such as there are, indicate that the Rāwandīyah of the aforementioned disturbance were a group of Khurāsānī origin that may have had some vague connection with Abū Muslim. It is neither clear whether they are to be identified with any specific ethnic group or geographic location, nor whether their ideological position was broadly based or confined to a limited following.[49] It seems that they were drawn to the doctrine of metempsychosis, which had a particular appeal among the contemporary proto-Shī'ites, and that they eventually linked this concept to an 'Abbāsid eschatology. The Rāwandīyah thus believed that the transmigration of souls (*tanāsukh al-arwāḥ*) specifically defined the 'Abbāsid claims to rule. A propagandist called al-Ablaq (as fate may have it, a leper, who spoke in hyperbole) maintained that the spirit (*rūḥ*) attached to 'Īsā b. Maryam passed on to 'Alī b. Abī Ṭālib and then, successively, to each of the divine imāms (*wakānū ālihah*), until it came to rest with Ibrāhīm b. Muḥammad, the brother of Abū al-'Abbās and Abū Ja'far.[50] Like other radical Shī'ite groups, the Rāwandīyah espoused extreme libertine views and thus felt free to indulge in acts that were not permissible (*istaḥallū al-ḥuramāt*). As if to reinforce this last point, al-Ablaq combined the new religious sentiments with traditional Near Eastern hospitality and invited his colleagues to partake of his food, his drink, and his wife. The local authorities who were charged with the defense of public morality and order were, however, more conventionally inclined, and the Rāwandī and his followers were killed and crucified.[51]

The lamentable fate that befell this group did not, however, write an end to the saga of the Rāwandīyah. With the rise of the 'Abbāsids, a branch of the sect turned its attention to the new order, and Abū Ja'far al-Manṣūr eventually took his turn as the object of their veneration (*fa 'abadū Abā Ja'far*). It was perhaps inevitable that the Rāwandīyah should have come to visit their lord (*rabbihim*) in order to receive food and drink at his court in al-Hāshimīyah. Although there is no indication that they wished also to partake of his women, their public acclaim of al-Manṣūr's divinity (*anta, anta*), which was quite heretical, and their general behavior, which was quite unruly, led to a serious altercation. Between leaping from the Caliph's palace (possibly with the expectation of a good transmigration) and liberating the prison in which their leaders had been quickly incarcerated, the overzealous Khurāsānīs forced the entry of the security forces and the ensuing slaughter of their group.[52]

To be sure, the Rāwandīyah incident is reminiscent of Ibn al-Muqaffaʿ's description of the intense views held by some Khurāsānīs with respect to the Caliph (a man who could move mountains or turn his back to the Kaʿbah during prayer). It is perhaps no accident that the central event of this description is reported by the chronicler under the year A.H. 141, the same year in which the *Risālah fī al-ṣaḥābah* was most likely presented to al-Manṣūr.[53] This being the case, one must ask whether the event reflects broadly held sentiments, or whether it is, in fact, the particular model on which Ibn al-Muqaffaʿ based his remarks in the treatise. Were the Rāwandīyah a small extremist segment that was, at most, marginal, or were sentiments approaching their blind devotion to the Caliph and the ruling house widely spread throughout the Khurāsānī army?

The references to extreme communalism, which appear in accounts of the Rāwandīyah, seem to suggest the kind of radical propaganda spread by the ʿAbbāsid *dāʿī* Khidāsh among the villagers of Khurāsān. The circumstances of his career are, however, shrouded in mystery and confused by contradictory traditions. In the end, ʿAbbāsid historiography made a point of discrediting the early director of revolutionary activity in Khurāsān. The bill of particulars against him included, among other things, certain extremist tendencies that he endorsed in the name of the hidden imām without seeking the latter's approval. For his efforts on behalf of the revolution, Khidāsh was seized by the local authorities and, after being brutally tortured, was killed and crucified. Other reports state that the ʿAbbāsids themselves killed him, presumably because of his independent, if not heretical, actions.[54]

There is, nevertheless, reason to suspect that Khidāsh may have been the victim of politics rather than ideology.[55] There was nothing to prevent ʿAbbāsid propagandists from assuming a multitude of poses during the period of clandestine operations, especially during its formative stages; they could then appear as all things to all people. Moreover, the marriage of a radical outlook to an ʿAbbāsid eschatology was not without advantages in an age of messianic expectations. From this perspective, the extreme views held by certain sectarian groups regarding the violability of the inviolable cannot be understood as a simple manifestation of libertinism. They may, indeed, refer to a much more pervasive concept, that of "redemption through sin," in preparation for the messianic age.[56]

One could, then, perhaps claim some success for the extremist line among certain villagers, but the Arab tribal armies who later formed the backbone of 'Abbāsid military strength were attracted initially by more practical considerations. Hopelessly divided among themselves, they succumbed to the skillful political (and financial) manipulations of Abū Muslim that drew them together against common enemies. In the same fashion, Qaḥṭabah b. Shabīb gave the diverse contingents of the *ahl Khurāsān* a sense of unity and direction in the field of battle. Their early and sustained military successes are more likely to have enhanced the esprit de corps of the tribal units than any ideological pronouncements of the *du'āt*. This is not to say that the 'Abbāsids passed up a subsequent opportunity for political indoctrination among the tribal forces, or that such a program was ineffective; it simply implies that caution should be exercised before issuing extravagant claims for the success of a policy that is, in any event, very difficult to document.[57] The one point that seems certain is that no 'Abbāsid Caliph, least of all al-Manṣūr, would have encouraged views of permissiveness at a time when he was responsible for public order. Such excesses may have been acceptable in anticipation of the millennium, but the 'Abbāsids came and the millennium did not.

Contrary to the view of those who would see the Khurāsānī army as thoroughly indoctrinated and religiously committed to the 'Abbāsid Caliph, one can argue that the professional soldiers of the *ahl Khurāsān* were less likely to have been impressed by ideology than by the pragmatic elements of Ibn al-Muqaffa''s program: regular service pay and the measures taken to protect the army against the effects of fluctuating prices. The evidence, such as it is, suggests that the military payroll was a matter of top priority, and that some of the author's suggestions actually reflect government procedures.[58] Following this line of reasoning, it appears that the Caliph's strong sense of fiscal responsibility, rather than his religious attributes, won him the full backing of the imperial troops.[59] This does not imply that powerful personal ties did not exist between the Commander of the Faithful and key elements of the military establishment, or that patronage was not dispensed within the army. It was, of course, desirable to control the army through a network of strategically placed clients and trusted officers; this is quite different, however, from making the entire army the *mawlā* of its sovereign.

The system of clientage was successful because the politically rootless *mawlā* could exercise influence only through his patron, the Caliph. With respect to the army, the situation was quite the reverse, for it was only through the direct support of the military that the Caliph could hope to establish his authority effectively. To be sure, the army would not betray the Caliph on behalf of a non-Muslim enemy, but its primary responsibility was the preservation of order within the boundaries of Islam. Here the issues of loyalty and authority could become exceedingly complex. There were occasions when the Caliphate itself was contested by more than one party that carried bona fide credentials to rule. Such occasions served only to complicate relations between the government and the military, and the response of the army came to be governed by strong attitudes of self-interest. This sentiment is summed up best by Ṭabarī in a postscript to the great civil war between the brothers, the war that marked a tragic watershed in the history of the Islamic state.[60] Sandwiched between the details surrounding the death of al-Amīn (the act that effectively ended the war) is the wry comment of a contemporary. Al-Ḥasan b. Abī Sa'īd is credited with observing that, "both armies [*jund*], that of Ṭāhir [b. al-Ḥusayn] and the *ahl Baghdād*, regretted the murder of Muḥammad [al-Amīn] because of the wealth that they were accumulating." The statement clearly implies that, in at least one respect, the opposing forces stood to gain from the continuation of the conflict. Thus, the agencies of government whose primary charge it was to preserve public order had developed a vested interest in continuing chaos.

Difficulties within the military led ultimately to the introduction of the Turks into the imperial army. Although the further subjugation of Transoxiana under al-Ma'mūn had brought significant numbers of Turkish slaves to the center of the Islamic empire, it was al-Ma'mūn's successor, al-Mu'taṣim, who is credited with the actual formation of elite Turkish regiments. The latter's interest in establishing such units apparently predated his accession to the Caliphate. The geographer Ya'qūbī, who lived at the time of the Turkish ascendency, reports a tradition to that effect on the authority of a Ja'far al-Khushshakī.[61] Al-Khushshakī indicates that, in the days of al-Ma'mūn, al-Mu'taṣim sent him to Nūḥ. b. Asad in Samarqand to purchase slaves on a yearly basis, and that he thus acquired some 3,000 Turks for the future Caliph. Other sources indicate that, when al-Mu'taṣim was governor of Egypt, 4,000 Turkish troops participated in his campaign against the Arabs of the Ḥawf.[62] Upon assuming rule, the new Caliph extended the search, purchasing, as well, various slaves who had earlier been brought to Baghdad, including, it is said, Ashnās, Itākh, Waṣīf, and Simā al-Dimashqī. All were then the property of 'Abbāsid notables, and all were later destined to become generals and powers behind the throne.

It should be made clear that the Turks were not recruited exclusively to guard the Caliph, but were brought in relatively large numbers to serve as active fighting units. As such, they did not replace, but supplemented, the contingents of the regular army. The attractive features of these new units were their absolute ties to the Caliph, as a result of their servile status, and their well-known military prowess, particularly as armed cavalry. During a military disturbance in the year A.H. 251, Turkish units of the imperial army were referred to specifically as *mawālī*.[63] The term, as applied in this context, would seem to indicate a general rather than technical meaning. It does not necessarily suggest that a particular contractual arrangement existed between the Turks and the Caliph, but implies that their allegiance to the ruling house was thought of as transcending their ties to local concerns. Because they were brought as slaves forcibly removed from their native regions in Transoxiana (Eastern Khurāsān), the bonds between the Turks and the Caliph superseded all previous loyalties. They became, in effect, his personal contingents within the broader structure of the army, thereby explaining the use of the term *mawālī*. Although it is true that the *mamlūk*, or slave institution, started almost simultaneously with the birth of Islam and has deep roots in the pre-Islamic period as well, it awaited the reign of al-Mu'taṣim to serve as a central factor in the formation of an Islamic military society.

One may view the conception of a praetorian guard tied exclusively to the ruler as the logical outgrowth of earlier efforts to professionalize the army. However, unlike the free Khurāsānī forces, who could exercise some measure of independence, the servile Turks were presumed to be nothing less than the clients of the Caliph, and were thus completely dependent on their patron. Moreover, in a series of unprecedented measures,[64] the Caliph sought to assure both the safety and the personal loyalty of his Turkish regiments by isolating them completely from society at large. It is not clear to what extent such a policy was, or could have been, enforced, but it is evident that, left on their own, the Turks could develop a sense of cohesion among themselves. They were, therefore, very different from the *mawālī* in government circles, who lacked identification within a well-defined group and who were, above all, without a viable military presence.

It was perhaps inevitable that the Turkish commanders came to define their loyalty to the regime in terms of self-interest, and that the slave army of the Caliphs intervened directly in the affairs of the state, just as the free Khurāsānīs had done before them. Whatever personal ties existed between the Caliph and his clients were lessened by the general malaise within the ruling society. The successors of al-Muʿtaṣim were not his equal, but beyond that, the empire itself had undergone serious dislocation. The reign of al-Rashīd may be likened to a flashy veneer overlying rotting wood. It was noted for its brilliance, but it was characterized also by the loss of key provinces. The civil war following its end accelerated the incipient decay. In time, wealthy regions became the hereditary fiefs of provincial governors who perpetuated family rule and, in effect, created petty dynasties. Although loyal in their allegiance to the central authorities according to established formulae of protocol, the governors withheld tax revenues for their own purposes, thereby exacerbating the economic strains on the central authorities. The allegiance of an army, professional or otherwise, is bought with substantial monies. The declining state revenues only forced the army to intervene still further in affairs normally falling to the civilian administration. The Turkish generals went so far as to exercise veto power on the succession to rule and to eliminate Caliphs not to their liking. Internal bickering among the Turkish officers aggravated further the already chaotic situation. The Caliphate nevertheless retained a certain vitality, and when conditions allowed room for political maneuver, the Commander of the Faithful managed to reassert his position. The process begun with the great civil war, however, was degenerative; the Caliphate never fully recovered, and the military dimension became awesome in the affairs of government.

V

THE REGIMENTS OF THE IMPERIAL ARMY: NOTES ON AL-JĀḤIẒ'S EPISTLE TO AL-FATḤ B. KHĀQĀN

Al-Ma'mūn, al Mu'taṣim, and an officer whose name is not mentioned, disagreed as to the bravest among the officers [*quwwād*], troops [*jund*], and clients [*mawālī*]. Al-Ma'mūn maintained that there were none braver than the non-Arabs among the people of Khurāsān [*ajam ahl Khurāsān*, that is, the Transoxanians who brought him to power]. Al-Mu'taṣim, in turn, favored the Turks [that were the backbone of his support], but the officers held out for the *abnā'*. They were the ones that shackled the Turks [that is, lead them to Islam], just as their forefathers led the ['Abbāsid] revolution [*dawlah*]. They fought the Commander of the Faithful [during the civil war] but now pay him obeisance, and it is through them that his rule is secured.

Based on Ibn Ṭayfūr (Cairo), 80.

The professional army of the 'Abbāsid state came to include a variety of ethnic groups from diverse regional backgrounds and social strata. The first century of the dynasty began with an army composed of vestiges of somewhat independent Arab tribal forces and concluded with the formation of a slave corps recruited primarily from among Turkish and Iranian peoples taken prisoner in Transoxiana. Although this military organization must be regarded as among the most salient and important institutions of the government, the precise identification of various fighting constituencies and their specific functions remains problematic. Much of the confusion is no doubt derived from the haphazard presentation of the medieval chroniclers. However, in contrast with the untidy state of Arabic historiography, a work of belles lettres by a well-known literary figure provides a concise and cogent statement about the general composition of the early 'Abbāsid armies.

A. The Text

The important text, *On the Virtues* [*Manāqib*] *of the Turk*, is an interesting essay (*risālah*) by the ninth century theologian and littérateur al-Jāḥiẓ.[1] In what may be succinctly described as an ornate prose style, the qualities of the recently recruited Turkish fighting units are compared to four other groups in the army of the Caliphate: the Arabs, clients (*mawālī*), *abnā'*, and Khurāsānīs. The treatise seems to call for the full acceptance of the Turks and to imply that the reconciliation of all these elements would promote an integrated and more stable society.

From the outset, al-Jāḥiẓ performs rather intricate intellectual gymnastics to demonstrate that the distinctions between the Turks and other elements of the Caliph's army are more apparent than real, but it is strongly suggested that diversity and unity are not necessarily antithetical conditions. Geography, which determines cultural values, not only divides societies, but unites them as well, for, the author contends, diverse groups inhabiting the same, or contiguous, regions may come to share common characteristics. It is not possible to tell the difference between Baṣran and Kūfan (Iraq), Meccan and Medinese (the Ḥijāz), Jabalite and Khurāsānī (Iran), or Jazarite and Syrian. Moreover, there were Arabs and bedouins who settled in Khurāsān, and "one cannot distinguish between the man who settled in Farghānā [a district of Transoxiana] and the indigenous inhabitant of that country."[2]

This last and rather casual insertion concerning the Arab of Khurāsān belies a second significant formulation. The conventional wisdom of medieval Arabic geographers not only divided the world into various inhabited climes, but it also described the ethnic composition and social behavior characteristic of each. What is implied in al-Jāḥiẓ's remarks is that the inherent cultural traits of a particular region can be transferred to a settler population. The Arab transplanted in Khurāsān thereby becomes a native of that region. In this fashion, the *abnā'* can be considered as both Khurāsānīs and Iraqis, and the Turks, who originate from the far reaches of eastern Khurāsān, can be legitimately counted as equal to the indigenous inhabitants of the western districts. A common bond is thus created for the entire army by linking its diverse elements to Khurāsān, the breeding ground of the 'Abbāsid revolution. Given a single geographical setting, the points of agreement in 'Abbāsid military society could come to predominate over the points of difference and thus serve as a basis for unity.

The legitimacy of the Turks is also reflected by their client relationship with the ruling house, a status they shared with others among the military. The author, who was himself a client of the Banū Kinānah, observes that, from ancient times, the Arab tribes, while scrupulously guarding their genealogies, acquired clients as a matter of course. As clientage bestowed a recognizable status on both parties of the association, dissimilar groups may be found sharing a common bond. It was general knowledge that the Caliph al-Mu'taṣim first acquired large numbers of Turkish slaves in order to fashion them into a regular regiment of the imperial army. By virtue of their personal ties to the ruling family, certain Turks became clients of 'Abd Manāf and Hāshim and were therefore linked to the Arabs in general and to Qurayshite nobility in particular.[3] Nevertheless, if there is any doubt that clientage and geographical contiguity could effect the assimilation of the Turks within 'Abbāsid society, the author provides additional evidence to argue his case.

Al-Jāḥiẓ also seeks to strengthen the ties between the Turks and the Caliphate (that is, the Arabs) by claiming an ancient blood relationship. It is stated that the Commanders of the Faithful are descended from Ismā'īl, the son of Ibrāhīm. The example of Ismā'īl demonstrates the extent to which integration can be achieved despite one's ethnic origins. The son of Ibrāhīm was counted among the Arabs, although he was born of foreigners, for God adapted his uvula to the correct pronunciation of Arabic without instruction or practice and then bestowed great eloquence upon him without formal education or training. He thereby removed those features foreign to Ismā'īl and transplanted him into the Arab nation as an equal to those born of Arab stock. This fact would indicate that the most noble of contemporary Arabs are themselves the descendants of a client, or, if one were to insist on putting it more delicately, they stem from a distant ancestor who was adopted by the Arabs through a creative act of God's will.[4] Be that as it may, in addition to Isḥāq and Ismā'īl, the respective sons of Sarah the (north) Syrian (*Suryānī*) and Ḥajar the Copt, Ibrāhīm had also six children by Qaṭūrā the Arab woman. Four of these offspring were fortuitously situated in Khurāsān, where, tradition has it, they became the progenitors of the Turks. Therefore, should an Arab boast of his noble descent, the Turk can always offer as a rejoinder, "But Ibrāhīm is my [grand]father and Ismā'īl is my uncle."[5]

Both in his preliminary remarks and in the main body of his presentation, which details the relative merits of each group, the author relentlessly pursues the same theme. He constantly reaffirms the mutual ties that exist between all the units and, hence, the legitimacy of the Turks within the ʿAbbāsid military and within society at large.

B. The Problem of Historicity

There is, to begin with, the critical issue of whether the *Manāqib* can be considered a historical document that actually sheds light on the structure of the ʿAbbāsid military. There is, in addition, the related question of the author's motivation in preparing the essay. Although the treatise is often cited, it remains elusive, for, lacking a systematic explication of the text, either by historians or literary scholars, no clear judgment of the historicity of the author's remarks can be made. The present chapter can best be described as a series of preliminary observations. The intention is to identify some of the many historical allusions to groups and events found throughout the treatise and to illustrate how they serve al-Jāḥiẓ's overall strategy for legitimizing the presence of the Turks within the imperial army.

Turkish officials and their patrons within government circles would, no doubt, have favored such a line, for the introduction of Turkish contingents in large numbers, beginning with the Caliphate of al-Muʿtaṣim, created great tensions within the army and society at large. Given the highly charged political atmosphere, one is obliged to ask if the picture of the ʿAbbāsid regiments drawn by the author and cited by modern historians is an accurate reflection of contemporary military organization, or if it represents the idealized creation of a highly inventive literary mind. Even if al-Jāḥiẓ's need for literary license, to say nothing of diplomatic discretion, overwhelmed his sense of historical accuracy, there are at least vestiges of an historical truth that can be distinguished here.

Although he achieved fame as the greatest prose writer of his time, al-Jāḥiẓ's literary interest in horses, slaves, misers, and various ladies of pleasure might cause one to suspect the acuity of his observations on so technical a subject as the ʿAbbāsid army. Nevertheless, the author's credentials for observing the government and military were impeccable. He was an eyewitness to events at the twin capitals,

Baghdad and Sāmarrā, and he served for a brief time as court tutor to the young children of the Caliph al-Mutawakkil (d. A.H. 247). Although not really a courtier, his views were nevertheless sought by high ranking officials, and the *Manāqib* is in fact addressed to al-Fatḥ b. Khāqān, the Turkish wazīr of the Caliph. The author therefore had a practical as well as scholarly acquaintance with the development of the imperial army. He may have chosen to bend history in order to suit his purposes as well as those of his patrons, but his text is nevertheless rich in allusions to historical events and personalities.[6]

Be that as it may, one critical approach might argue that al-Jāḥiẓ's facile portrayal of the military melting pot should be met with considerable skepticism. Political expediency is often the mother of rather dubious genealogies. For example, the realities of assorted alliances led the Arabs to claim descent from fictitious ancestors, thereby promoting the division of their society into tribal units of north and south Arabian origin. The author's analysis is similarly not above suspicion. The Turkish wazīr of the Caliph, to whom the essay is addressed, was more than a public functionary. He was widely recognized as a great patron of the literary establishment and had artistic pretensions of his own (although with only thirteen surviving lines of verse, it is not quite possible to establish his position as a man of letters). In addition to al-Jāḥiẓ, he was familiar with the poet al-Buḥturī and the polyhistor al-Tha'ālibī.[7] It is therefore possible to regard al-Jāḥiẓ, who was an occasional figure at court, as still another littérateur attempting to curry favor with an important official of state by giving literary expression to that which was certain to please his patron. The author's complimentary remarks concerning the superior martial skills of the Turks and, more particularly, his effort to integrate them into an 'Abbāsid society resentful of their position can, then, be regarded as self-serving political fictions. Seen in this light, the *Manāqib* may be the creation of a cynical and extremely clever man, and, like other works of this genre, it would therefore be interesting only for reasons of language and not for historical content. This, however, is not the case.

The central message of the text may also reflect the ambiguities of the author's self-identification. Al-Jāḥiẓ, who was a *mawlā*, was also part black, and the search for compatibility between disparate elements of society is one that finds ambivalent expression elsewhere in his literary endeavors. With a writer of al-Jāḥiẓ's skill and subtle sense of humor, the problem of establishing his real attitude toward race and color is likely to be difficult. One has the impression that the interests of individuals on the lower end of client-patron relationships were best served by their masking their intentions. This was true even for those of marginal background who gave every indication of being fully adapted to the society of their patrons. Moreover, it is not always clear, in these delicate relationships, whether the author is himself emotionally prepared to declare in favor of a specific reality. Al-Jāḥiẓ can thus devote a treatise to praise of the blacks, while he elegantly pokes fun at them. Who is to say what the author's true intentions are —perhaps not even the author himself.

Nevertheless, one is struck by his remarks concerning Ismā'īl. His interest in the rejected son of Ibrāhīm may be more than a literary device and tempts the reader, whether intentionally or otherwise, to draw obvious comparisons. With or without God's intervention, al-Jāḥiẓ, like Ismā'īl before him, was living proof that the literate client could overcome his ethnic origins by excelling in the language of his acquired patrons. Seen from this perspective, *The Virtues of the Turk* is not only an artistic creation and means of entry into courtly circles, it is a reflection of the author's search as well for an integrated society and his personal niche within it. Such a view suggests that the composition of the army described by al-Jāḥiẓ may have existed largely in his imagination and is, in reality, a metaphor for a much wider polity, namely, the sum of Islamic society.[8]

There may be a good deal of truth to all of this, but it should not lead us to dismiss the *Manāqib* out of hand. When writing on historical themes, medieval Arabic littérateurs tended to embellish rather than invent, and the embellishment was often fashioned from raw data of historical interest. The methodology of the modern historian is directed toward distinguishing the residue of historical truth from the literary shaping of the medieval author—a task easily proclaimed, but often difficult to accomplish.

Although the basic thematic lines are clear enough, the text of the *Manāqib* does not readily lend itself to a thorough explication. The catalogue of virtues that is ascribed to each of the five regiments is the key to the author's design. However, the allusions to historic movements and personalities are presented with particular care, so that, given an imprecise knowledge of early 'Abbāsid history, the fine detail of the work is at times complex and elusive. Moreover, the specific setting is difficult to fix. The author begins his lengthy section on the Turks by indicating that it was originally composed as a letter to the Caliph al-Mu'taṣim, but, for reasons not specified, it was never delivered.[9] On the other hand, the introduction to the work *in toto* indicates that it was addressed to al-Fatḥ b. Khāqān, the Turkish wazīr of al-Mu'taṣim's son, al-Mutawakkil.[10] Elements of the *Manāqib* could have been composed, therefore, over a stretch of time encompassing almost three decades. Because this was, by and large, a turbulent period characterized by many changes, there is a serious problem of chronology that must be resolved. A close reading of the text seems to suggest that the basic lines of the *Manāqib* could have been formulated as early as the reign of al-Mu'taṣim and that the text indeed reflects even earlier conditions. For, with the exception of the Turks, who are the subject of the treatise, it is not al-Mutawakkil's or even al-Mu'taṣim's Sāmarrā-based army that is being described, but that of the Baghdad Caliphate of an earlier time.

C. The Composition of the Army

The formative years of the dynasty at Baghdad saw the evolution of a professional fighting force based almost exclusively on the revolutionary armies from Khurāsān. Recent "revisionist" histories have stressed the mixed character of the troops that brought the 'Abbāsids to power. Contrary to earlier assumptions of a grass roots uprising among the indigenous Iranians, the backbone of the 'Abbāsid military was the Arab tribal army stationed in the region. These Arab units identified themselves according to their tribal origins and initially suffered from the damaging effects of xenophobia. There is, however, reason to believe that they may have also felt a sense of regional loyalty and identified themselves not only as Arabs, but also as Khurāsānīs.[11]

Another component of this army were the descendants of the old Arab settlers in Khurāsān. Transplanted into the villages of the region, they too retained their tribal identification, but intermarriage and assimilation with the indigenous Iranian population had eroded tribal sensibilities. These Arab settlers may have lost their facility with their native language. In any event, they spoke Persian among themselves.[12]

When the formal structure of the 'Abbāsid army was first established during the revolution, the settlers received their service pay according to a military roll (*dīwān*) arranged by village rather than by tribal affiliation.[13] They probably retained some martial skills, but could not be relied upon as first-rate soldiers, for, unlike the Arab tribal army, they had long ceased to function as cohesive military units in the employ of the state. Nevertheless, the old settlers produced a disproportionately high number of field commanders and political agents (*naqīb*)—a fact no doubt related to their early and sustained ideological commitment to the 'Abbāsid house.[14]

The last, and surely least significant, element of the early 'Abbāsid army were the local *mawālī*. Although their military contributions were no doubt negligible, various clients, nevertheless, did assume extremely important positions within the political apparatus and in the financial administration of the army.[15] From almost the outset of the open revolution, all of these groups, the tribal army, the villagers, and the *mawālī*, were subsumed within the single military force known as the *ahl Khurāsān*. As a result, the 'Abbāsid army, despite its varied Arab and Iranian components, had a distinctive Khurāsānī identity.[16]

This military force is clearly distinguished from other regional armies, tribal auxiliaries, irregular troops, and local militia. In addition to the customary distribution of bonuses before and after battle, it received subsistence pay according to a carefully regulated schedule, a measure that presumably reinforced its sense of ideological commitment.[17] Moreover, the professional army had specific ties to the Caliph and his newly established capital city. Having swept into Iraq with the advance of the revolution, the Khurāsānīs were eventually concentrated at the recently constructed administrative center in Baghdad. Their resettlement in a new regional environment no doubt strengthened their common ties based on old geographic associations and gave rise in time to new feelings of group unity. In an ambitious and unprecedented scheme of social engineering, the general area of al-Ḥarbīyah, the northern suburb of Baghdad, was reserved for the exclusive settlement of the 'Abbāsid, that is, Khurāsānī, military.[18] From their cantonments at al-Ḥarbīyah, the army was sent on distant campaigns to serve as the main battle contingent of the state. However, even in these circumstances, it was sufficiently large to allow for a standing reserve at the capital, so that at no time was the Caliph's domain without the services of his trusted Khurāsānīs. There is reason to believe that, in time, this army, or, at least, significant elements within it, was transformed into a still more cohesive grouping, the enigmatic contingent known as the *abnā'*. The composition of this last regiment will be discussed later.

It is evident, from the catalogue of virtues ascribed to each group, that al-Jāḥiẓ's army is not the imperial force that existed when the *Manāqib* was submitted to al-Fatḥ b. Khāqān, but this earlier army of the Baghdad-based Caliphate. There is the exception of the Turks, and a lingering influence can be detected for the *abnā'*, but the Khurāsānīs described in the *Manāqib* were apparently those subsumed within the *abnā'* and bear little relationship to the Transoxanians who served al-Mutawakkil and his predecessors at Sāmarrā. Moreover, the Arab tribal units, which retained their identity, are said to have been removed from the military roll in the time of al-Mu'taṣim (probably in the central provinces of the empire).[19] They would hardly be mentioned, therefore, in any discussion of his son's Sāmarrā army. Finally, although individual *mawālī* were prominently involved in military and political service, it is very unlikely that they would have been considered a distinct contingent of the professional forces after the early stages of the open revolution. This is borne out by the text of the *Manāqib*, for, in enumerating the qualities of the clients, the author has nothing to say of their military activities, but draws attention, instead, to their trustworthiness in serving the political interests of the regime.[20]

The detailed proof of these assertions is derived from an analysis of the virtues credited to each group. Moreover, an examination of this particular material suggests also the basic strategy employed by al-Jāḥiẓ in order to legitimize the Turks. It is more subtle than a contrived argument based on geography, clientage, and alleged blood ties. The Turks are seen as the last in a line of Khurāsānīs who served the 'Abbāsid family—an unbroken connection that goes back to the revolution that brought the regime to power. There is apparently no point in describing the virtues of the Turks in relation to the other contingents in the army of al-Mutawakkil. The non-Arab Khurāsānīs from Transoxiana, the Farāghinah, the Ushrūsanīyah, the Shāshīs, the Maghāribah, and the Shākirīyah possessed credentials that were no better than those of the Turks.

Al-Jāḥiẓ is seeking an earlier model, when the imperial army represented the integrated fighting force of a relatively stable and unified empire. The legitimization of the Turks is, in a sense, the call for a return to the earlier age. In this respect, it mirrors the messianic propaganda of the 'Abbāsid revolution, which proclaimed a spiritual return to the era of the Prophet Muḥammad and the birth hour of Islam. The pagan Turks, who were brought in shackles during the campaigns in eastern Khurāsān, were thus accorded a status equal to that of the old 'Abbāsid revolutionaries and, by extension, to that of the earliest Muslims as well.

D. *The Catalogue of Virtues*

If Khurāsān is the geographical linchpin of al-Jāḥiẓ's armies, the revolution is the predominant historical event that links them together. Al-Jāḥiẓ begins his list of virtues with the case for the Khurāsānīs and immediately invokes the memories of the 'Abbāsid revolution.[21] These are not the Transoxanians, who, for al-Mu'taṣim's brother, the pretender al-Ma'mūn, laid siege to and conquered Baghdad amid great devastation. These are the early Khurāsānīs who brought the regime to power. The Khurāsānī boasts: "We are [revolutionary] agents [*naqīb*] and the sons [*abnā'*] of agents, nobles [*najīb*] and the sons of the nobles. . . . The twelve agents are from us as are the seventy nobles. We are the men of the moat and the sons [*abnā'*] of the men of the moat. . . . We are the men [*aṣḥāb*] of this revolution [*dawlah*] and this ['Abbāsid] propaganda [*da'wah*], the root of this tree, from which blows this wind. We are the men of the [revolutionary] black standards . . . who destroy the cities of tyrants and take away rule [*mulk*] from the hands of the oppressors, the Umayyads."[22]

There then follows a list of major military campaigns, beginning with the fortification of the villages in Khurāsān, which signified the declaration of the open revolution, and ending with an allusion to the siege of Wāsiṭ (*naḥnu . . . aṣḥāb Ibn Hubayrah*), the Umayyad capital of Iraq and the last stronghold offering armed resistance. The Khurāsānī proclaims, "Ours is the old and the new, the beginning and the end of the 'Abbāsid revolution."[23] It was no accident that the Khurāsānīs came to play this role. The author cites a variant of the famous tradition in which Muḥammad b. 'Alī, the father of the revolution, considered where to send his propagandists (*du'āt*). Various regions were considered but were found lacking. To be sure, there were a few 'Abbāsid partisans in al-Baṣrah, but the city and its environs were clearly pro-'Uthmānid. The loyalty of the Syrians, on the other hand, was with the family of Abū Sufyān and the Marwānids. Finally, there was al-Jazīrah, but the inhabitants there displayed distinct Khārijite sympathies. Only Khurāsān was adequate to 'Abbāsid needs. The Khurāsānī therefore boasts, "We are the best contingent for the best imām. We vindicated his [original] opinion, confirmed [the wisdom of] his idea, and proved the accuracy of his insight."[24]

There are allusions throughout the discourse to the messianic propaganda of the revolution. This was a radical line that was tempered fairly early by the 'Abbāsid Caliphs and thus suggests, once again, that al-Jāḥiẓ's description is not contemporary with his own era. When the Khurāsānī says, "Ours is the old and the new, the beginning and the end," he speaks not only of the political revolution, but of heralding a new age. This was to be a period that marked a return to the pristine society of early Islam. The events that brought the 'Abbāsids to power did not merely signify the exchange of one dynasty for another, but the return to the ethos of an earlier age when moral authority was vested with the true believers, whose interests were now properly represented by the 'Abbāsid family.

Al-Jāḥiẓ indicates that there are, in reality, two groups known as the helpers (*al-anṣār anṣārān*). He points out, through his Khurāsānī interlocutor, that the Aws and Khazraj supported the Prophet in the early days (*fī awwal al-zamān*) and the people of Khurāsān (*ahl Khurāsān*) will support his inheritors on the last day (*fī ākhir al-zamān*).[25] When the Khurāsānī claims, "The twelve agents are from us," he is referring, as well, to the twelve *nuqabā'* from the Aws and Khazraj. These were agents established by the Prophet Muḥammad at al-Madīnah in order to facilitate his acceptance in that community, an act that paved the way for the future success of his mission. Similarly, in the time of Muḥammad b. 'Alī, twelve agents of the 'Abbāsids fanned out into the various regions of Khurāsān to lay the groundwork for the uprising that was to bring the latter-day Muḥammad to power.[26] When the Khurāsānī boasts, "We are the people of the moat and the sons of the people of the moat," he refers to two events. The first is rooted in the age of the Prophet, when Salmān al-Fārisī, the original Islamic hero of Iranian origin, saved the faithful by suggesting that Muhammad dig a moat or trench (*khandaq*) around the oasis of al-Madīnah. He thereby befuddled the opposing Meccan cavalry, who had never seen such a strategy before. This was a critical moment in the series of great victories that led to the capitulation of Mecca itself. In the same fashion, the Arab settlers and *mawālī* later fortified their villages in Khurāsān by digging a moat around the defensive perimeter. This act, together with the unfurling of the messianic black banners, signified the beginning of revolutionary warfare and heralded the new era about to come.[27] It is no wonder that the Khurāsānī can proudly say, "We were thus nurtured by our ancestors and we thus nurture our sons (*abnā'*)."[28] Al-Jāḥiẓ completes the case for the Khurāsānīs with a description of their cultural background, fighting qualities, and armor. These are not people to be taken lightly. Even if the men of Tibet and Zabaj, the cavalry of India, and the horsemen of Byzantium were to attack the Khurāsānīs in concert, they would be forced to throw down their arms and flee. Is it any wonder that pregnant women give birth prematurely upon hearing the battle cry of Khurāsān?[29]

If these are the virtues of the Khurāsānīs, who are the Arabs and what are their claims? Al-Jāḥiẓ's description of the Arabs is tersely presented. There is no indication how pregnant women reacted in their presence, but it is clear that their claim similarly invokes Khurāsān and the ʿAbbāsid revolution. What is more, it is the very same claim as that of the Khurāsānīs. The Arab boasts, "Who are most of the agents (*naqīb*), if not, in essence, Arabs (*min ṣamīm al-ʿarab*)."[30] The phrase, "in essence, Arabs," is carefully chosen, for the author indicates that, as a group, the Arabs have great respect for genealogy. As it happens, the Arabs listed by al-Jāḥiẓ among the *nuqabā'* may not all have been of pure blood, for they were descended from the old settlers who took local women while partially assimilating to native life in the villages of Khurāsān. Listed among them are some of the most prominent names of the revolution: Qaḥṭabah b. Shabīb al-Ṭā'ī, the legendary commander of the army until his mysterious and untimely death, Mālik b. al-Haytham al-Khuzāʿī, the director of the security forces, and Sulaymān b. Kathīr, an early political operative of importance.[31]

A description of their military exploits is the same as that of the

Khurāsānīs. They also defeated Ibn Hubayrah and killed Ibn Ḍubarah and Nubātah b. Ḥanẓalah. There is, perhaps, one difference: whereas a Khurāsānī is credited with killing the last Umayyad Caliph, it was an Arab who spread the good news. If there are any other subtle differences between the so-called Arabs and Khurāsānīs of al-Jāḥiẓ, it is not clear from a reading of the text.[32] There were, to be sure, Arab tribal armies in the early years of the 'Abbāsid regime, but these represented regional forces and were not counted as part of the imperial army at Baghdad. The Khurāsānī, in trumpeting his own praise, has a few unkind words for these Arab tribesmen, "We are not like the army of Syria who attack women and violate all that is sacred"—a not so veiled reference to the rape and pillage that marked a Syrian campaign against the holy cities in Umayyad times. When al-Ma'mūn declared against the central authorities, with a Transoxanian army at his back, an effort was made to enlist the Arab tribes of Syria in support of the Baghdad regime. However, they could not overcome their susceptibility to *'aṣabīyah*, and proved a greater danger than a help. An incident at the initial muster involving a stolen horse gave rise to a debilitating tribal conflict within the greater conflict.[33]

The smallest section of the *Manāqib* is reserved for the *mawālī*.[34] This comes as no surprise for, as mentioned earlier, their role as a distinct division of the army was limited. There were units under the name of *mawālī* that fought in campaigns subsequent to the revolution, but these were relatively small and the occasions on which they served were extremely rare.[35] It is also true that, in certain instances, the Turks are called *mawālī*; however those references are to the client-patron relationship that existed between them and the Caliphate, and not to a specific element of 'Abbāsid military organization.[36]

According to al-Jāḥiẓ, the forte of the client is personal service to his patron. His value is measured here, not in terms of military prowess, but in terms of those qualities that are highly valued in government servants: good advice, trustworthiness, patience, the ability to keep secrets, and so forth. The references to specific personalities in the text clearly indicate, once again, a link between Khurāsān, the revolution, and the unsullied early era of "primitive" Islam. The Prophet himself appointed his adopted son and client Zayd b. Ḥārithah to be the commander of the Muslim forces at Mu'tah and governor of every region that he subdued. He showed the same preference to Zayd's son

Usāmah by appointing him over the chiefs of the *muhājirūn* and the great men of the *anṣār*.[37] Al-Jāḥiẓ stresses the continuation of this tradition in 'Abbāsid times. The *mawlā* proclaims, "Our service [to our patron] is like that of sons [*abnā'*] to fathers, and fathers to grandfathers."[38] Emulating the example of the Prophet in an earlier age, the 'Abbāsid family treated its clients with trust and generosity. Even the black (client) was not despised because of his color. . . . The Caliphs entrusted (the political education of) their older children to clients and assigned to them special ceremonial functions, preferring clients (at times) to members of the ruling family (*wa dhālika biḥaḍrah min al-'umūmah wa banī al-a'mām wa al-ikhwah*).[39]

The ties of the clients to Khurāsān and the revolution are reflected in the boast of the *mawlā*. He invokes the names of Abū Muslim al-Khurāsānī and Abū Salamah, the two most prominent political operatives in the revolutionary leadership outside the ruling family.[40] He states that the *mawālī* are found as well among the chiefs of the revolutionary agents (*nuqabā'*) and cites several by name.[41] The *mawlā* can therefore assert that he shares the virtues (*manāqib*) of the clients of the 'Abbāsid propaganda (*da'wah*) and those of the Khurāsānīs (*wa naḥnu minhum wa ilayhim wa min anfusihim*). This is something that no Muslim, no true believer can deny. The Arab may stress genealogy, but the *mawlā* can also claim (through his clientage) a genealogy that is both correct for the Arab, and worth boasting about by the non-Arab. He has earned this right by sharing the pride of the Arab, the bravery of the Khurāsānī, and the excellence of the *banawī* (sing. of *abnā'*).[42] In short, the client, despite some distinctive features, is a man of no particular group, because he is a man of all groups and, indeed, all times. As such, he has partaken in the glories of early Islam, as well as those of the revolution and the 'Abbāsid triumph that followed.

E. *The* Abnā'

Among the early contingents of the army, only the enigmatic *abnā'* remain to be discussed.[43] Who, indeed, are the *abnā'* and what is their excellence that is shared by the client? The conventional wisdom concerning this group is confined essentially to several paragraphs in the new edition of the *Encyclopedia of Islam* (*EI*^{2}). The relevant passages indicate two pre-Islamic designations and one that is contemporary with the early ʿAbbāsids. The latter falls under the rubric *abnāʾ al-dawla* (sons of the revolution or dynasty). It is indicated that this term "applied in the early centuries of the ʿAbbāsid Caliphate to members of the ʿAbbāsid house and by extension to the Khurāsānī and other *mawālī* who entered its service and became adoptive members of it. They survived as a privileged group until the 3rd/9th century, after which they were eclipsed by the growing power of Turkish and other troops." There is no indication what is meant by "members of the ʿAbbāsid house" nor how they are to be distinguished from the *mawālī* who "became adoptive members of it." Similarly, although there is the suggestion of a military presence for the *abnāʾ* in relation to the Turks and others, there is no clear picture of their place within the wider framework of the ʿAbbāsid army.

The brief bibliography appended to the last entry includes the *Manāqib* (listed by its other title, the *Faḍāʾil al-Atrāk*) and two secondary sources.[44] A careful reading of the references fails to bear out the claim in *EI*² regarding membership and adoption into the ruling house. Only the *Manāqib* speaks of a distinct social unit called the *abnāʾ*, and al-Jāḥiẓ links them, as a group, to service in the army. One cannot deny that an individual *banawī* or client may have become an adoptive member of the ʿAbbāsid house (whatever that implies); however, in the sources that are cited, there is not the slightest hint of any specific group bearing the name *abnāʾ* outside the military context.

In addition to the bibliography cited in *EI*², the author also relied on the "cryptic remarks of L. Massignon's *Salmān Pāk*."[45] A subsequent investigation of the pertinent material in that work failed to uncover anything that resembled an institution to which one can affix the name *abnāʾ*. Massignon does write of adoption. He attempts to show that Salmān al-Fārisī, the client of the Prophet, and Abū Muslim al-Khurāsānī, the client of the ʿAbbāsids, were both accepted into the ruling house (*ahl al-bayt*) according to the same formula (*wa anta minna ahl al-bayt*).[46] However, the evidence presented by Massignon speaks to that end and bears no relationship to the subject under review. The one reference to *abnāʾ* apparently cited by him is found in a late medieval source, where it is reported that Abū Jaʿfar al-Manṣūr established "the sons of Fārs as leading men of their [ʿAbbāsid] dynasty (*wa ja'ala abnā' Fārs rijālāt dawlatihim*)." Specifically mentioned are two well-known client families, the Barmakids and the Banū Nawbakht.[47] Even the most casual reading reveals that *abnā' Fārs rijālāt dawlatihim* cannot be confused with a military institution known as the *abnā' al-dawlah*. There is a tendency among other modern scholars to use various expressions containing the words *abnā'*, *da'wah*, and *dawlah* loosely, and even interchangeably. Such a practice only adds to the confusion surrounding the identity of this particular contingent.[48]

The text of al-Jāḥiẓ is a convenient point of departure from which to sort out the facts. The term *abnā'* literally means "sons." One is impressed by the frequent repetition of references to family in the *Manāqib* and, in particular, to fathers and sons. The Khurāsānī proclaims, "We are agents and sons of agents . . . we are the men of the moat and the sons of the men of the moat. . . . Ours is the old and the new, the beginning and the end." The *mawlā* serves his patron as a son serves his father, and a father, his father. Zayd b. Ḥārithah, the client of the Prophet, is his adopted son. Ismā'īl, the son of Ibrāhīm, is the "father" of the Caliphs. The sons of Qaṭūrā bt. Mafṭūn are the progenitors of the Turks. The point in these and every other example of this sort is to stress the inherent sense of unity and continuity in 'Abbāsid society and the debt that it owes to the legacy of the past.

This theme is continued by al-Jāḥiẓ in his description of the *abnā'*, hence, the explanation of the name. He notes that the *banawī*, like the Turk, is also considered a Khurāsānī. Because the identity of the *abnā'* has never been firmly established in any published work, the author's remark that "the *banawī* is a Khurāsānī" may not, at first, seem informative.[49] By way of explication, al-Jāḥiẓ simply asserts, "the genealogy of the sons is that of the fathers, and the deeds of the fathers and grandfathers before them are reckoned to the account of the sons (*abnā'*)."[50] Although the statement has a sermonic quality and a morally edifying tone, it is, in itself, hardly revealing. Nevertheless, when it is juxtaposed against al-Jāḥiẓ's detailed description of the qualities of these regiments and considered together with incidental information obtained from the chroniclers, the author's vague observation takes on a specific meaning.

It is possible to establish a clear relationship between the *abnā'* and Khurāsān and, hence, a link between the *abnā'* and the Turks. It is also possible to show that the *abnā'* are designated as sons of the dynasty (*dawlah*) and the 'Abbāsid propaganda (*da'wah*), not because they have been adopted into the ruling house, but because they are, in fact, the second generation of the revolutionaries that brought the 'Abbāsids to power. Of the early contingents listed by al-Jāḥiẓ, only the *abnā'* do not invoke the events and personalities of the revolution in establishing their claims. That is because the *abnā'* are the Baghdad-based regiments of the imperial army, which were fashioned from descendants of the older revolutionary forces. They are mindful, indeed, boastful, of their origins as well as of their ties to both Khurāsān and the revolution, but it is the new capital, Baghdad, and a subsequent martial history in which they glory.

The *banawī* proclaims that the root of his lineage (*aṣl*) is Khurāsān, the same region from which the 'Abbāsid revolution (*dawlah*) and propaganda (*da'wah*) burst forth to bring about a new age. This reference to a new age is both explicitly stated and clearly imbued with messianic allusions.[51] However, if Khurāsān is the root, then Baghdad is the branch (*far'*) and is therefore called the Khurāsān of Iraq. It is the (new) seat of the Caliphate, and houses the remaining veterans (*baqīyah*) of the ('Abbāsid) propaganda and the sons (*abnā'*) of the 'Abbāsid faction (*shī'ah*).[52] If the *banawī*'s fate is inextricably linked to the new Khurāsān, it is justifiably so. He considers himself more rooted to the dynasty than his father, and more a part of it than his grandfather. He presumes to make this claim though the *Manāqib* specifically mentions his ancestors (*ābā'*) as leading the revolution. The expression "more rooted" (*a'raqu*) appears to be a play on words to indicate more Iraqi, that is, Baghdadi, for it is the tie to the capital that gives the *banawī* his distinction.[53]

The *abnā'* can thus be described as the foster sons of the Caliphs and the neighbors of the wazīrs. They are born in the court of their kings and under the wings of their Caliphs. They follow in their rulers' footsteps and imitate their example. The *banawī* declares, "We recognize only them and will not be recognized except by them. . . ."[54] In a sense, the passage reaffirms the ties between the *abnā'* and the seat of the Caliphate at Baghdad, but the words surely lend themselves to a still wider interpretation, namely, the personal relationship between the *banawī* and his sovereign.

A tradition preserved by the historian Ṭabarī, under the year A.H.

163, immediately comes to mind in this connection. It is, coincidentally, the earliest evidence I have encountered that may refer to the *abnā'* as a specific group. The chronicler reports that the Caliph al-Mahdī, anxious for his son, al-Rashīd, to cut his teeth in a provincial campaign, is about to send him off against the Byzantines. The young prince, however, is seen in need of some mature advice. To that end, the Caliph ordered the secretaries (*kuttāb*) of the *abnā' al-da'wah*[55] to appear before him so that he might choose his son's companion from among them. The choice ultimately fell upon Yaḥyā, the son of Khālid b. Barmak, the old revolutionary. Yaḥyā was given far-reaching powers and, along with his father and two close relatives, accompanied the heir apparent.

Examining this account in relation to the passage from al-Jāḥiẓ describing the *banawī* as an intimate of the Caliph, P. Crone attempts to identify the *abnā'* and establish their relationship to the ruling family.[56] There can be no argument that al-Jāḥiẓ's *banawī* stresses his loyalty and close association with the 'Abbāsid house. For some, depicting the *banawī* as foster brother to the Caliph may be a mere figure of speech, but for Crone, it is nothing less than evidence of an institution. She argues that there were two groups drawn from the ranks of the old Khurāsānī army and their descendants. The first was the *ahl-al-dawlah*. The second, a smaller circle, were the *abnā' al-dawlah* or *abnā' al-da'wah*. Thus, the concept of *dawlah* provided two hierarchical ranks, which were in turn subdivided, according to Crone, thereby resulting in a still smaller group belonging to the circle of the ruling family itself.

It cannot be denied that various individuals and family groups who were the descendants of the old revolutionaries maintained close contacts with the 'Abbāsid house and were to be numbered as members of the *ahl al-bayt* in its widest sense.[57] The example of the Barmakids perhaps stands out above all others. Indeed, al-Rashīd and al-Faḍl b. Yaḥyā suckled at the same breast, and the latter entered into marriage with the Caliph's sister, 'Abbāsah, however calamitous the result.[58] Nevertheless, the isolated reference by the chronicler to the "scribes of the *abnā' al-da'wah*," even when bolstered by the rather vague passage in al-Jāḥiẓ, is hardly reason to assume the existence of three well-defined institutions: *ahl al-dawlah, abnā' al-dawlah*, and the *ahl al-bayt*.

The only certain claim that can be made for the *abnā'*, before the great civil war between the brothers, is that they are Baghdadis descended from the Khurāsānīs who come to Iraq with the advance of the revolution. The first specific indication of this is a report that dates from the reign of the Caliph al-Rashīd, under the year A.H. 187. An informer reporting the whereabouts of the Caliph's enemy Yaḥyā b. 'Abdallāh is interrogated by none other than al-Rashīd himself. When asked his identity, the informer replies, "a descendant [grandson?] of the *abnā'* of this dynasty (*rajul min a'qāb abnā' hādhihi al-dawlah*). My place of origin [*aṣl*] is Marw [the revolutionary capital of Khurāsān], but my place of birth is Baghdad [*Madīnat al-Salām*, the capital of the established dynasty]." When the Caliph asked, "Is your domicile there [that is, at Madīnat al-Salām]?" the man answered affirmatively.[59]

Abnā', as a generic term signifying military units, does not appear with any frequency until the outbreak of the conflict between the pretender al-Ma'mūn and his brother al-Amīn (A.H. 195).[60] They are then described as the dominant force in the army of the deposed al-Amīn and were designated by the expression, "people of Baghdad" (*ahl Baghdād*).[61] In connection with this loyalist army, the following expressions are found: the people (*ahl*) of al-Ḥarbīyah,[62] the *abnā'* of the suburbs (*arbāḍ*),[63] the *abnā'* of the Khurāsānī faction,[64] and the *abnā'* of Khurāsān who have become "Arabicized" (*muwallad*),[65] that is to say, born in Baghdad and raised among Arabic speakers (one recalls that the Khurāsānīs of Arab descent spoke Persian perhaps better than Arabic).

This does not imply that the *abnā'* were the only element in the *ahl Baghdād*, but it appears clear, from a review of the conflict, that they were the dominant force in the Caliph's contingents—certainly they were the professional backbone of the army.[66] This was a role for which they were well suited, because they now represented the standing army of the dynasty, which was originally recruited in Khurāsān during the revolution and was then transplanted to the military cantonments of al-Ḥarbīyah, the northern suburb of the capital. The positioning of the army in what were intended to be exclusive military colonies to the north of the city administrative center explains some of the expressions connecting the *abnā'* with the suburbs.[67]

The initial successes of al-Ma'mūn's Transoxanian army portended serious changes in 'Abbāsid military society, particularly in the distribution of payments (*'aṭā'*). Baghdadis no doubt suspected that a victory for the pretender would enhance the position of the new Khurāsānī forces from Transoxiana that supported him.[68] It is no small wonder that the *abnā'* fought with great tenacity during the early siege of Baghdad and continued to resist a change in status long after. This is strikingly reflected in al-Jāḥiẓ's description of the military skills of the *banawī*.[69] He is an expert at close quarter combat. When weapons are exhausted, the *banawī* grabs the neck of his foe. He knows how to stab with the knife and fend off the dagger. When surrounded, he and his comrades have the ability to respond and are therefore called the sons of difficult, that is, close combat in confined places (*abnā' al-maḍā'iq*). The *banawī* boasts, "We know how to fight at the entrances to protective moats [*khandaq*] and at the bridge heads [a reference to the many masonry structures, *qanṭarah*, that bridged the canals of the western city, giving access to various quarters].[70] Bloody death confronts [those who oppose] us at the breaches in the protective wall [*wa naḥnu al-mawt al-aḥmar 'ind abwāb al-nuqab*] and exhaustion in the narrow lanes [*aziqqah*]. . . . We are masters of night fighting and kill openly in the markets and the roads. . . . We fight in the water as well as on land [a possible reference to the flotillas of al-Ma'mūn that bombarded the city from the Tigris river]."

Other images of the *banawī* during the siege of Baghdad reappear in al-Jāḥiẓ's description of the qualities of the Turks. Unlike the Turks, who are cavalry, the *abnā'* are infantry, whose lances are for protecting the entrances to moats and narrowly confined places (*maḍā'iq*). Their skills are suited to fighting in side streets (*sikak*) and trenches (?*sujūn*). These are all vivid references to the grim battle for Baghdad, when the defensive lines of al-Amīn's forces were established along the natural barriers protecting the approaches to the Round City. The administrative complex was the last bastion of the beleaguered Caliph and his weary defenders.[71]

After the fall of Baghdad, the *abnā'* remained a highly volatile element with considerable military skill, so that the *banawī* of al-Jāḥiẓ claims, "All of Baghdad is ours. It is quiescent when we are quiescent, it is in turmoil when we are in turmoil."[72] Although prudence dictated that the new authorities continue to pay their salaries (with all that this implied for the financial condition of the government), the *abnā'* were not fully committed to the current regime. It would be some years before al-Ma'mūn would set foot in Baghdad. His successor, al-

Mu'taṣim, was forced to abandon the city altogether and built a second capital sixty miles to the north at Sāmarrā.[73] There he garrisoned a new imperial army with Farāghinah, Khurāsānīs and Turks from Transoxiana, Maghāribah from the west, and an enigmatic elite corps known as the Shākirīyah. This army, however, never attained the sense of unity of the old Baghdad regiments, and the history of the Caliphate at Sāmarrā, following al-Mu'taṣim, was one of increasing turmoil.

By describing the Baghdad army, al-Jāḥiẓ recalls an earlier age, before the cumulative effects of the great civil war, and before the move to Sāmarrā, for the imperial army that served the early Baghdad Caliphs represented, by and large, the integrated fighting force of a relatively stable and unified empire. This early 'Abbāsid state made for a very attractive model in contrast to the turbulent reign of al-Mutawakkil, which was to end with the Caliph's assassination, the murder of al-Fatḥ b. Khāqān, and, shortly thereafter, the eruption of still another civil conflict between elements favoring Baghdad and the partisans of the new capital. Had 'Abbāsid society chosen to emulate this earlier model, it might have been spared the political chaos reflected in contemporary events. The Turks, because of their central political and military role, were the key element to any reconciliation within society. Although devoid of the messianic overtones that characterized early 'Abbāsid propaganda, al-Jāḥiẓ's appeal for the acceptance of the Turks and the creation of a united society also called for a new era, one whose values were to be rooted in the early years of the 'Abbāsid regime. One recalls that the 'Abbāsids themselves originally established their legitimacy on the legacy of a still earlier time, the unadulterated Islamic age contemporary with the birth of Islam. The author's vision of a new society was, however, not destined to be realized.

PART TWO

The Physical Setting

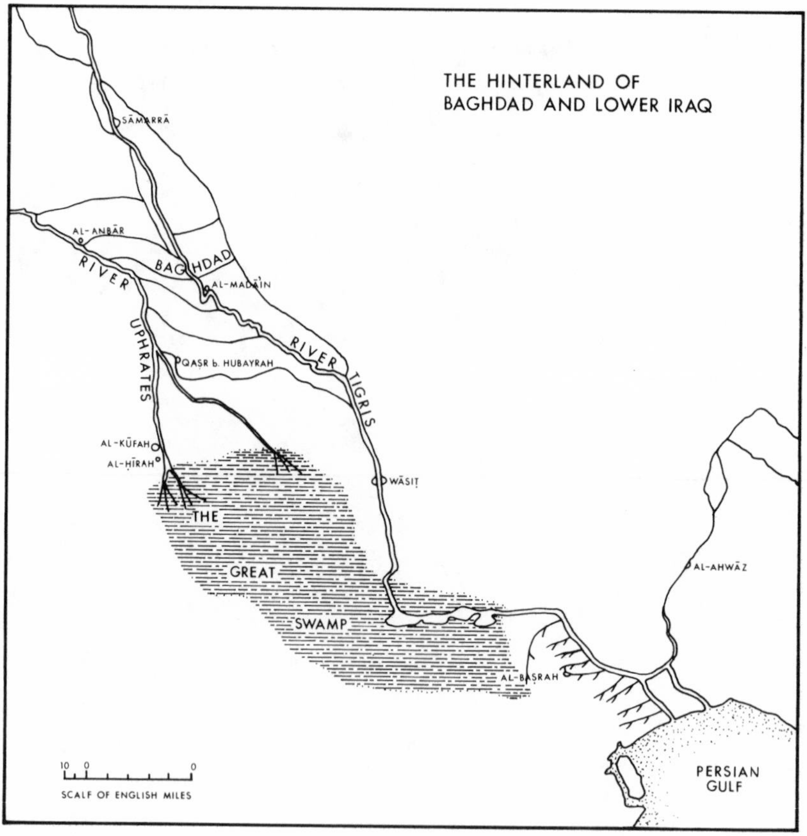

THE HINTERLAND OF
BAGHDAD AND LOWER IRAQ
SĀMARRĀ
AL-ANBĀR
BAGHDAD
AL-MADĀ'IN
RIVER
UPHRATES
RIVER
TIGRIS
QAṢR b. HUBAYRAH
AL-KŪFAH
AL-ḤĪRAH
WĀSIṬ
THE
GREAT
SWAMP
AL-BAṢRAH
AL-AHWĀZ
PERSIAN
GULF
SCALF OF ENGLISH MILES

VI

BEFORE BAGHDAD: THE EARLY 'ABBĀSID CENTERS OF GOVERNMENT IN IRAQ

"When the Commander of the Faithful, Abū al-'Abbās took office, he established himself at that city [*tilka al-madīnah*], completing various [unfinished] chambers [*maqāṣir*] and initiating construction of his own. He named it al-Hāshimīyah, but the populace persisted in calling it by the name of Ibn Hubayrah. The Caliph said, 'I do not see that it will cease to be called after Ibn Hubayrah,' whereupon he left the site and built al-Madīnah al-Hāshimīyah opposite it [*biḥiyālihā*]. He established himself there [that is, in the new al-Hāshimīyah] but then chose to settle at al-Anbār where he built his famous city. When he died, he was buried in the capital at al-Anbār. Abū Ja'far al-Manṣūr now became Caliph. He established himself at al-Madīnah al-Hāshimīyah in [the vicinity of] al-Kūfah [*bi-l-Kūfah*], completing whatever [structures] were left to be built and adding new construction according to an arrangement [*hayya'a*] of his own choosing. Then he transferred to Baghdad where he built *his* city."

Balādhurī, *Futūḥ*, 287

A. The Political Background

Although Khurāsān gave birth to the 'Abbāsid Revolution, Iraq was chosen by the new regime to serve as the center of the imperial administration. There was, no doubt, a calculated risk in this choice, for the province had been the focal point of Shī'ite political interests ever since 'Alī b. Abī Ṭālib, the last of the righteous Caliphs, was assassinated in al-Kūfah. Throughout the course of 'Alī's campaigns against the Syrians, the Iraqi garrison town had served as the unofficial capital of the Islamic state; however, his unexpected death hastened the inevitable collapse of the 'Alid position, and the Caliphate was then formally transferred to Damascus. The local people responded to the ascendancy of the Syrians with a combination of residual sympathy for Shī'ite causes and a desire for de facto autonomy in the affairs of the region. As a result, Iraq emerged as a turbulent province, the center of frequent intrigues and occasional insurrections based on varied and complex political alignments.[1]

The Umayyad authorities attempted to stabilize the situation by neutralizing the unruly *amṣār*. To that end, they established the provincial capital of Wāsiṭ equidistant from al-Kūfah and al-Baṣrah and settled the new city with a formidable Syrian garrison to augment the troops already stationed in the region. The introduction of large numbers of Syrians into Iraq and the continued movement of Arab tribesmen from the province to a new frontier in Khurāsān altered the nature of military and, thus, political realities.[2] Nevertheless, the settlers who continued to occupy the former garrison towns remained sufficiently skilled militarily as to constitute a real concern for the central administration.[3]

The ʿAbbāsids, for reasons well known, took a guarded view of the situation in Iraq. Although the original formulation of their claims and the composition of their early adherents placed them within the broad spectrum of the proto-Shīʿite groups, there was no guarantee that ʿAbbāsid claims could win universal backing from among the various Shīʿite constituencies.[4] Moreover, the Iraqis tended, as a rule, to be somewhat fickle in their long-standing flirtation with Shīʿite causes. They encouraged marriage but abandoned the liaison when objective realities threatened to overtake their own interests. There can be no doubt that the ʿAbbāsids were quite aware of the risks inherent in any Kūfan venture, and although this did not dissuade them from maintaining an active revolutionary station in Iraq, it did force them to focus the major thrust of their effort elsewhere.[5] For reasons previously discussed, their choice ultimately narrowed to the eastern districts known collectively as Khurāsān.

The various traditions that deal with Muḥammad b. ʿAlī's decision to cultivate the eastern connection all point to the unreliable nature of the Iraqis. A late medieval account, reflecting the views of a strongly partisan Shīʿite author, stresses that the Kūfans and Baṣrans shared the responsibility for the death of ʿAlī b. Alī Ṭālib and the murders of his sons al-Ḥasan and al-Ḥusayn.[6] There is, to be sure, no direct accusation that they were the active agents in these tragic events, but their passive betrayal of the ʿAlid cause was sufficient to discredit them as potential allies. This particular assessment apparently coincides with views that reflect 'Abbāsid thinking. When Zayd b. 'Alī, the grandson of al-Ḥusayn, was encouraged by the Kūfans to revolt in A.H. 121, Dāwūd b. 'Alī, the patriarch of the '*umūmah*, is reported to have cautioned him, pointing out in graphic terms that the Kūfans had betrayed 'Alī and 'Alī's sons, al-Ḥasan and al-Ḥusayn, after him.[7]

Success for Zayd b. 'Alī would have been a crippling blow to 'Abbāsid ambitions. Yet, it cannot be said the 'Abbāsid notable gratuitously offered this advice in order to prevent the 'Alid from seizing power. Quite the opposite—his apprehension resulted from the almost certain failure of the insurrection and the possible consequences of that failure for local 'Abbāsid agents. When it appeared that it might be too late to head off the revolt, the coterie of 'Abbāsid revolutionaries stationed in al-Kūfah left the city for neighboring al-Ḥīrah, lest they become publicly enmeshed in a rebellion quite obviously destined for failure. This carefully measured decision, against the weight of public opinion, illustrates the astuteness with which the 'Abbāsids recognized political realities and promoted their as yet undeclared claims to the Caliphate.[8]

The current heir to Shī'ite martyrdom, however, did not choose to follow the prudent course suggested by his kinsman, but opted instead to accept the urging of the Kūfans in what turned out to be still another premature and disastrous adventure. Dismayed, but undaunted, the lamented imām's followers then espoused the cause of 'Abdallāh b. Mu'āwiyah, a descendant of 'Alī b. Abī Ṭālib's brother Ja'far. This last revolt, which took place in the waning years of the Umayyad Caliphate, attracted broad support including (for unspecified reasons) that of various members of the 'Abbāsid family; however, the Kūfans, true to form, abandoned the Shī'ite leadership whom they had encouraged to rebel, and, in the end, only the Zaydīs stood firm with their Ja'farid relatives.[9] This is not to say that the Iraqis were totally cynical in their support of Shī'ite causes and aligned themselves with various 'Alid pretenders only to serve their own narrowly defined regional interests. There is, however, the inescapable conclusion that they preferred to have others assume the major risks when they perceived that success was in doubt, and these doubts came all too early in the rebellions that the local people helped to proclaim.

Furthermore, one may suppose that, even after the collapse of Umayyad rule, Iraqi politics reflected some desire for a measure of regional autonomy. This being the case, the inhabitants of the *amṣār* would have welcomed a change of dynasty, but only in circumstances that did not compromise their ambitions or curtail their limited power. For the Iraqis, the emergence of the ʿAbbāsids may have had the chilling effect of substituting one authority for another. Although it is not certain to what extent the Iraqis still felt the need for some measure of regional control, they clearly understood that the instrument that destroyed the Syrian hold on the province was forged not locally, but in Khurāsān. An ʿAbbāsid decision to locate the central administration of the new regime in Iraq was probably acceptable, and even desirable, but the concurrent settlement of the Khurāsānī army in the region was quite another matter. Thus, one of the factors that had led to the Iraqi-ʿAlid symbiosis in Umayyad times was recreated by the development of a highly centralized ʿAbbāsid government in the same province.

The provincial objectors did not have to look far for a candidate who would indirectly champion their cause. There were ʿAlid elements who refused, from the outset, to acknowledge the legality of ʿAbbāsid claims. The Ḥusaynid family, in particular, felt a sense of dismay and betrayal over the course of events that left them empty-handed, while those bearing lesser credentials assumed power.[10] The frustration of the Ḥusaynids and their partisans thus established the second precondition for a new Iraqi-ʿAlid alliance. Even under the most favorable circumstances, the new rulers had entered a political cul-de-sac. If ʿAbbāsid claims were denied, the local people could be expected to re-establish ties with an ʿAlid pretender who was willing to declare against the ruling house. On the other hand, even if the ʿAbbāsids won recognition as the legitimate political heirs of ʿAlī's grandson, Abū Hāshim b. Muḥammad b. al-Ḥanafīyah, there was no guarantee that they would enjoy the continued support of the Iraqis, particularly if this had the effect of severely limiting regional authority. The Shīʿite writer cited earlier (who was himself a descendant of al-Ḥasan b. ʿAlī) saw the ʿAbbāsids preferring Khurāsān because the perfidious nature of the Iraqis was demonstrated in their previous betrayals of the ʿAlid cause; however, other less partisan accounts stress the opposite, that is, that Muḥammad b. ʿAlī sent his missionaries to the east, because the Kūfans could be expected to support the claims of ʿAlī b. Abī Ṭālib's family, and not those of ʿAlī's ʿAbbāsid kinsmen.[11]

There is some truth to both these assessments, but the factors that led the 'Abbāsids to propagandize in Khurāsān included other important considerations as well.[12] What is particularly interesting is that, despite their long-standing contacts to the east, and in full cognizance of the potential for local intrigue in the *amṣār*, the new rulers decided to designate Iraq as the central province of their imperial administration. There is no text that specifically argues the case for Iraq, but, examined realistically, the 'Abbāsid options appear to have been quite limited. The factors that made Khurāsān an ideal base for revolutionary activity made it unacceptable as a center for administrative rule. The remoteness of the vast eastern region can be contrasted with the unique accessibility of Iraq to the key provinces of the realm.[13] There may also have been a mystique about Iraq due to its long history of revolutionary efforts. The earth drenched with the blood of Shī'ite martyrs could have been an image with potent emotional and political appeal for those who saw themselves restoring the *ahl al-bayt* to its rightful place in ruling society. In any event, historical circumstances conspired to bring the 'Abbāsids to al-Kūfah and to keep them in Iraq until the last vestiges of Umayyad rule were eradicated and the internal contradictions of their own political apparatus were resolved.[14] Once rooted in the province, the 'Abbāsid regime continued there until the end of the dynasty.

B. The Ḥīrah-Kūfah Region

Although the move to al-Kūfah was initially stimulated by a sudden concern for personal safety, it marked a significant departure in 'Abbāsid tactics. The previous claimants to rule had been extremely circumspect in testing the treacherous political waters of the *amṣār*; however, that was before circumstances threatened to overwhelm the principal figures of the 'Abbāsid family. The unexpected incarceration of Ibrāhīm al-Imām, on the heels of revolutionary triumphs to the east, created great apprehension in family circles.[15] Fearful of remaining in Syria, Abū al-'Abbās, the newly designated leader of the 'Abbāsid house, decided to join the clandestine political apparatus centered in al-Kūfah.[16] A source reflecting the official 'Abbāsid position on these events indicates that Abū al-'Abbās was determined to declare for the Caliphate in Iraq, despite the obvious dangers inherent in such a move. When confronted by his paternal uncle, Dāwūd b. 'Alī, regarding the wisdom of so rash an undertaking, he reportedly answered that excessive caution breeds submissiveness (*yā 'ammī man yuḥibbu al-ḥayāt dhalla*).[17] Because a variant of this expression is also applied to the unfortunate Zayd b. 'Alī, the bravura attributed to Abū al-'Abbās may well be the invention of later dynastic apologists, who required of their first Caliph a willingness to risk martyrdom as had the lamented 'Alids before him.[18] There is surely nothing in the career of Abū al-'Abbās to suggest that he was one to act indiscreetly, let alone rashly.

Given the nature of Iraqi politics and the presence of large Umayyad forces in the region, it is probable that the future Caliph would have been willing to remain inconspicuous until such time as caution was no longer necessary. The likely circumstances would have been the conquest of the *amṣār* and the pacification of the area. It seems that Dāwūd b. 'Alī's concern was not so much the strategy of declaring for the Caliphate in al-Kūfah as the timing of such a move. He was worried about the continued presence of powerful Syrian forces in the region (*yā Abā al-'Abbās takhruju bi-l-Kūfah wa shaykh Banī Umayyah Marwān muṭill 'alā al-'Irāq fī ahl al-Shām wa al-Jazīrah wa shaykh al-'Arab Ibn Hubayrah fī jillat al-'Arab bi-l-'Irāq*). It is therefore not surprising that the journey to al-Kūfah was arranged, from the outset, amid great secrecy. In the end, the trek to Iraq connected Abū al-'Abbās and his family with the Khurāsānī armies that had advanced boldly from the east. With their military triumphs, the proclamation of 'Abbāsid rule in al-Kūfah was not simply a possibility, but a foregone conclusion.

One would suppose that the new regime might then have established al-Kūfah as the first center of its administration, but this was not to be the case. The family leadership had not moved so deliberately during the revolution to throw caution to the winds once they actually seized power. Despite their choice of Iraq, the 'Abbāsids had no intention of ruling from the troublesome *amṣār*. Instead, they established a series of provisional administrative centers that were to serve them until the construction of al-Manṣūr's Round City at Baghdad. In deciding upon the geographical locations for each of these centers, the new rulers succumbed to the attractions of an established urban environment; however, their political concerns required that the actual administrative complex be situated some distance from an existing city. The new precincts apparently contained the residence of the Caliph and his retinue, as well as the administrative machinery of the government. Also situated in the immediate vicinity were the Khurāsānī armies that had entered Iraq with the advance of the revolution. The position of the military cantonments, like that of the government complex, was presumably fixed by an overwhelming concern with security.

The preference for this type of arrangement was evident from the time Abū al-'Abbās was openly proclaimed Caliph, an event that marked the end to a rather confused and trying stay for the 'Abbāsid family in al-Kūfah. Although the 'Abbāsids were secretly en route to the city, the revolutionary forces had continued to make significant gains against the Umayyads in Iraq. When the leading members of the family ultimately arrived, al-Kūfah was firmly in the hands of the rebels. Nevertheless, Abū Salamah, the regional director of 'Abbāsid interests, kept news of their arrival from the Khurāsānī commanders encamped nearby. In utmost secrecy, he arranged for Abū al-'Abbās and his retinue to be billeted at the house of al-Walīd b. Sa'd where they remained incommunicado for a period in excess of a month. Ostensibly, this was done for reasons of security, but the real motive behind Abū Salamah's action may have derived from considerations far more complex.[19] Be that as it may, once they learned of the army's desire for them to appear publicly, the 'Abbāsids are described as annoyed and impatient with the long sojourn arranged for them by their trusted client. When contact was finally made with the Khurāsānīs, arrangements were quickly set into motion to secure the Caliphate for Abū al-'Abbās in a formal public ceremony.

The Caliph was not destined to remain in the city. Immediately after his investiture, he left to join Abū Salamah and elements of the Khurāsānī army that had arrived in Iraq. They were then positioned some distance from al-Kūfah in a camp that Abū Salamah had set up for himself at Ḥammām A'yan.[20] In view of what has been written about the Kūfans, it is not difficult to understand why Abū Salamah abandoned the city and chose instead to direct the nascent revolutionary government from a regional center nearby. Similarly, the Khurāsānī army was not about to encamp amid a large civilian population with mixed political sentiments. After a parade for the benefit of the local inhabitants, the triumphant Khurāsānīs withdrew and attached themselves to Abū Salamah at his recently established command post.[21]

Because this military force was the single most important prop supporting the emergent regime, the Caliph also left al-Kūfah, where the question of support was rather problematic, and took up residence at Ḥammām A'yan with the others.[22]

Abū al-'Abbās now took full advantage of the opportunity before him. With the period of clandestine operations formally ended, he and his relatives moved boldly and decisively to solidify their tenuous hold on the revolutionary apparatus.[23] Locally in al-Kūfah, the Umayyad governor, who had defected to the cause, was replaced by Dāwūd b. 'Alī, the most venerated of the Caliph's paternal uncles. Various clients and members of the new ruling house were also attached to the Khurāsānī commanders operating throughout the province. These steps were clearly efforts to take over direct control of the functioning government from Abū Salamah, whose activities, beginning with the prolonged 'Abbāsid stay in al-Kūfah, brought him under increasing suspicion. As a result, Ḥammām A'yan, a hitherto inconspicuous place, became, initially, the nerve center of revolutionary rule in Iraq and, later, the first administrative complex of the 'Abbāsid regime.

The exact location of the Caliph's administrative center is, nevertheless, difficult to indentify because specific references to Ḥammām A'yan are rare. Yāqūt's compendious geographical dictionary of the Middle Ages contains only a brief entry, in which he indicates the derivation of the name and establishes that it was situated "in al-Kūfah" (*bi-l-Kūfah*).[24] This statement may, however, refer to the greater urban area rather than to al-Kūfah itself. Even the early Arabic authors had difficulty in distinguishing between the city and its neighboring environs. By the time of Yāqūt (d. A.D. 1225), much of the surrounding area had fallen into disuse, and the historic memory of individual sites had grown dim. Indeed, another source places Ḥammām A'yan approximately three *farsakh* (eleven miles) from the city, thereby suggesting a separate development somewhere in the general vicinity.[25] The most likely choice would seem to be the ancient Christian town of al-Ḥīrah, which was in fact separated from the newer Islamic city (al-Kūfah) by that very distance.[26] This would explain why Ḥammām A'yan appears in Balādhurī's chapter on the toponymy and topography of al-Kūfah but is actually listed in the text among places of interest situated in al-Ḥīrah.[27] Unfortunately it is impossible to be more specific, because al-Ḥīrah itself was not a unified city, but a sprawling urban area with diverse settlements and abandoned structures of uncertain location.[28] What is important is that Abū Salamah's camp should be fixed in the immediate vicinity of al-Ḥīrah and not in the larger Islamic city nearby.

One recalls that the 'Abbāsid agents who fled al-Kūfah on the eve of Zayd b. 'Alī's unsuccessful revolt took up residence in al-Ḥīrah until it was deemed safe to return. At the time, their caution was dictated by suspicions that the local political leadership would be unwilling to pursue its stated objectives, thereby endangering the 'Abbāsid effort as well. The most salient reason for the Caliph's later move to al-Ḥīrah was, similarly, the unreliable nature of the Kūfans. This does not explain, however, Abū al-'Abbās's specific choice of location. That is, perhaps, best understood in light of al-Ḥīrah's historical development, particularly with respect to the changing fortunes of the town as an administrative center.

The area surrounding al-Ḥīrah formed the southern flank of a frontier that was traversed by periodic tribal migrations from the Arabian Peninsula. Medieval Islamic authors, who speak of ancient Arab settlements in the region, attribute to the town a history that can be traced back to the reign of Nebuchadnezzar (*Bukht-Naṣar*). The city, however, did not reach great importance until the third century before the rise of Islam, when the Lakhmid princes were entrusted by the Persian Emperor with protecting southern Iraq from the further incursions of Arab tribesmen. The town then became the capital of the Lakhmid principality and the administrative center of the region; however, in a subsequent reversal of policy (A.D. 602), the Lakhmid state was deliberately weakened by the imperial authorities. The consequences of this shortsighted policy were severe. The garrison was rendered ineffective, the overall security of the border zone declined, and the influence of al-Ḥīrah waned.[29]

Three decades later, following the Arab conquest of Iraq, the ancient city was officially displaced as the regional center of government. In keeping with a familiar pattern, the Arabs chose to garrison their tribal armies in an exclusive settlement of their own, which was established, in this instance, at a nearby site adjacent to the Euphrates. Al-Kūfah thus became one of the twin capitals of Iraq (the other being al-Baṣrah). Although it lost this preeminence after the construction of Wāsiṭ, it continued to function as the principal city for the surrounding area until late Umayyad times, when Yūsuf b. 'Umar al-Thaqafī was entrusted with the provincial administration. The new governor returned the seat of local rule to al-Ḥīrah, which now became a base for contingents of the Syrian army (*ahl al-Shām*).[30]

The medieval sources provide no commentary concerning the resurgence of the old Lakhmid capital, but the introduction of a strong Syrian garrison in a politically sensitive area was, no doubt, the decisive factor. A modern observer has suggested that al-Ḥīrah was "apparently better suited for a garrison than the populous neighboring Muslim town," and also that "Hishām [b. 'Abd al-Malik, the Caliph] had expressly forbidden Yūsuf to quarter the Syrian soldiers with the Kufaites."[31] I can find no textual evidence for this last statement, but political as well as military considerations would have made such an assessment inevitable. Control of the troublesome Iraqis required stationing troops within easy access of al-Kūfah, but security demanded as well that they be kept from mingling with the local inhabitants. The old Christian town, with its docile populace, its legendary credentials, and, above all, its widely dispersed palace areas, was ideally suited for conversion into a Syrian military camp and administrative center. The choice was immediately justified by Zayd b. 'Alī's abortive insurrection. When the 'Alid rebel prepared to declare his Caliphate, 2,000 Syrian troops were available in al-Ḥīrah to advance against him.[32]

There is some evidence to suggest that al-Ḥīrah not only displaced the newer Islamic city as the seat of local rule, but it probably also became the de facto capital of Umayyad Iraq. If true, the unofficial move may have been partially dictated by the circumstances of Yūsuf b. 'Umar's succession. The Thaqafite did not assume the governorship through a peaceful transition. At the Caliph's behest, he marched secretly from the Yaman and deposed the established provincial leadership at Wāsiṭ. There does not seem to have been much, if any, sentiment for the political order that had been overturned; nevertheless, prudence may have required a disassociation with the previous administrative capital. Be that as it may, the two subsequent Umayyad governors of Iraq, Manṣūr b. Jumhūr and 'Abdallāh b. 'Umar, both established their residences at al-Ḥīrah.[33]

The positioning of large foreign forces so close to al-Kūfah must have been distasteful to the local inhabitants, accustomed as they were to periodic demonstrations for regional autonomy. Moreover, the internal breakdown of the Umayyad administration, which was then well advanced in several regions, had the potential for tempting the local people to defiant gestures and, perhaps, to more serious action.[34] An attempt by 'Abdallāh b. 'Umar to restore the Iraqis to the military roll (*wa a'ṭā al-nās arzaqāhum wa a'ṭiyatahum*) was no doubt undertaken to buy their compliance, and even support, in politically troubled times.[35] However, this served only to antagonize the Syrian commanders, causing them to complain, "You divide our booty [*fay'*] among those who are our enemies." With a difficult situation at hand, the governor vacillated. He declared to the Kūfans that he had acted in good faith but was facing strong opposition within the Syrian ranks. The Kūfans, not mollified by such a confession, took to the public meeting grounds (*jabbānah*), where an ugly confrontation between hotheads (*ghawghā'*) of both parties ensued. Although injuries were restricted to a small number of persons, tensions continued. The local people now wanted to dislodge the Umayyad prefect of al-Kūfah from his citadel (*qaṣr*), an act that would have signaled the open defiance of established authority. Fortunately, their passions were calmed through the intervention of a skilled diplomat, who apparently bought peace with a promise to distribute bonuses.[36] The affair underscored not only the propensity of the Kūfans for causing trouble, but also the inherent wisdom of placing the main contingents of the Syrian army outside the city. Throughout the incident, 'Abdallāh b. 'Umar remained in al-Ḥīrah, where his forces were concentrated. When, shortly thereafter, the Kūfans supported the cause of the Ja'farid, 'Abdallāh b. Mu'āwiyah, they were compelled to take the conflict to the Syrians in al-Ḥīrah, with all too predictable results.

It is true that the historian Ṭabarī reports, under the year A.H. 127, that a sizable Syrian force was stationed in al-Kūfah.[37] However, this was due to the extraordinary conflict that was developing within the fragmented Umayyad regime, and not to any policy change by the regional authorities. Throughout the Islamic state, the Muḍarī and Yamanī elements of the Umayyad army had aligned themselves with rival factions of the ruling house. Upon assuming the Caliphate, the Sufyānid, Marwān II, sought to replace 'Abdallāh b. 'Umar with an officer serving under his command. Although there were no guarantees of extended tenure in the provincial administration, the political implications of 'Abdallāh's replacement must have been obvious to all concerned. This could hardly have been construed as the innocuous rotation of provincial administrators. The incumbent governor was the son of the late Umayyad Caliph, 'Umar II, and was therefore descended from the rival Marwānid branch of the ruling family. He was, in fact, originally chosen for this post by the previous Marwānid Caliphs, because it was felt that the Iraqis, who had been sympathetic to his father, would be inclined to favor him as well.[38]

When he first arrived in al-Ḥīrah, 'Abdallāh expected resistance from his predecessor, Manṣūr b. Jumhūr, but the latter exited gracefully after handing over the reins of government. Now that it was his turn to step aside, 'Abdallāh b. 'Umar was anything but compliant. The incumbent governor was not about to relinquish control of the provincial administration to a Sufāynid appointee. Instead, he fortified himself at his capital in al-Ḥīrah, together with the Yamanī faction of the Syrian army that had rallied to his side. His former subordinate, the governor-designate al-Naḍr b. Sa'īd, gathered the Muḍarī troops of the regional army and established a base of operations nearby at al-Kūfah. Throughout the next four months, an indecisive battle continued in the area that lay between the two neighboring urban centers.[39] Then, the sudden appearance of a Khārijite army caused the Syrians to close ranks and establish joint defensive fortifications around al-Kūfah.[40] Despite well-equipped forces estimated at some 30,000 troops (*naḥwa min thalāthīn alf wa lahum quwwah wa 'uddah . . . wa ma'ahum qā'id . . . fī alf fāris*), the Syrians suffered a humiliating defeat and were forced to abandon the region. What began as an internal struggle between rival factions of the ruling family ended with the temporary collapse of Umayyad rule in southern Iraq.

Two conclusions are clear from the account of these events. First, the stationing of a large Syrian contingent at al-Kūfah was necessitated by the intransigence of the former governor, and not by a change of heart on the part of the regional authorities towards the Iraqis and their city. And second, aside from 1,000 horsemen who had been sent from Qinnasrīn to reinforce al-Naḍr b. Sa'īd, the entire Syrian garrison facing the Khārijites consisted of troops originally quartered in al-Ḥīrah and its environs. Even if the figure of 30,000 men is somewhat exaggerated, it reveals the extent of the Umayyad investment in a regional base at the ancient Christian town.

When the Khārijite menace subsided in A.H. 129, Yazīd b. 'Umar b. Hubayrah became the Umayyad ruler of Iraq. The new governor is generally associated with Wāsiṭ, because he staunchly defended the besieged city after all of the province had fallen to the 'Abbāsids. Nevertheless, Wāsiṭ was not his initial choice for the provincial capital. Ibn Hubayrah's first inclination was to establish an administrative center along the Euphrates in the general vicinity of al-Kūfah (*bi-l-Kūfah 'alā al-Furāt*). It is not stated why the governor did not return the seat of provincial rule to al-Ḥīrah, or why this particular site was chosen instead. Perhaps the recent discord in the regional army created the impetus to seek a new location in the general vicinity. In that case, he still could have enjoyed the commercial advantages of al-Kūfah as well as the facilities existing in the surrounding area. The new capital was quite appropriately named the "city" of (Madīnat) b. Hubayrah and was settled even before construction was completed. The Caliph, however, was not enthusiastic about this development. Marwān II was fearful that the most recent palace precinct would bring his governor too close to the Kūfans. Although the objections to the Kūfans are not explicitly stated, one can well imagine the source of his concern. Upon receiving an official letter stating these objections, Ibn Hubayrah felt compelled to abandon the partially built structures named after him. The governor not only left Madīnat b. Hubayrah, but, despite the existing facilities, he forsook the Ḥīrah-Kūfah region altogether in order to build another government complex (Qaṣr b. Hubayrah) near Jisr Sūrā, midway between al-Kūfah and Baghdad.[41] Nevertheless, the abandoned area contained many advantageous features, and these quite understandably attracted the attention of the early 'Abbāsid Caliphs when in search of a site for their own capital.

C. *Al-Hāshimīyah*

Ḥammām A'yan may have been suitable for the transplanted Khurāsānī army, but it was only a temporary residence for Abū al-'Abbas. He was apparently the house guest of Abū Salamah; both Caliph and client reportedly shared the same quarters, with only a curtain separating them.[42] Under no circumstances could this have been considered desirable. Quite aside from the difficult living conditions, there may have been political implications to this particular arrangement. It appears that it was the client, and not the patron, who had both privacy and freedom of movement. Furthermore, Abū al-'Abbās had cause to suspect the political sentiments, if not the activities, of his provincial governor—a suspicion that led to Abū Salamah's assassination a short time later.[43] Consequently, after a stay that lasted several months, the Caliph left Ḥammām A'yan and established al-Hāshimīyah, the first official capital of the 'Abbāsid regime. The name was subsequently applied to several other administrative centers, as each, in turn, became the focal point of 'Abbāsid rule. The continued application of this name was surely not accidental. In the broader sense, it may have referred to Hāshim, the ancient ancestor, whose descendants included Muḥammad, 'Alī, al-'Abbās, and the members of the *ahl al-bayt*. It thus would have commemorated the end of the usurpative Umayyad interregnum and the return of rule in Islam to those rightfully destined for it. This was a sentiment entirely consistent with the 'Abbāsid revolutionary propaganda that heralded a new era built on the foundations of an earlier age. On the other hand, it could also have been derived from the proto-Shī'ite group of that name inherited by the 'Abbāsids, along with the right to rule, from Abū Hāshim b. Muḥammad b. al-Ḥanafīyah. In that case, the name al-Hāshimīyah would have focused attention on the legitimacy of 'Abbāsid claims vis-à-vis those of their disgruntled Ḥusaynid kinsmen. To be sure, all this is conjecture, as the Arabic sources are silent on this matter. It may very well be that this silence is intentional. The ambiguity attached to the name of the 'Abbāsid capitals undoubtedly served the ruling family insofar as it enabled them to attract the widest possible following without risk of directly offending any particular constituency.

In addition to the problem of the derivation of al-Hāshimīyah, there is some difficulty in specifying the geographical location of the administrative centers. This is already evident in the Arabic texts of the early middle ages. Not only does the use of al-Hāshimīyah for several places lead to obvious confusion, but some of the sites at which the capitals were built also display earlier names that are identical or easily confused.[44]

The chronicler Ṭabarī, in what appears to be a broken text, suggests that, after leaving the camp of Abū Salamah, the Caliph settled at the citadel of al-Kūfah (*thumma irtaḥala fanazala al-madīnah al-Hāshimīyah fī qaṣr al-Kūfah*).[45] It is, however, difficult to believe that Abū al-'Abbās would have chosen to establish his government in the city itself, particularly when, under similar circumstances, he had abandoned the Kūfans at the first opportunity. Moreover, such a choice would have run counter to the long-established trend of government settlement in the area. If the Caliph was determined to rule from the Ḥīrah-Kūfah region, there were certainly other places that were eminently more suitable than a city known for its troublesome inhabitants and pretension to self-rule. Indeed, the apparatus of the text proposes a possible reading of *qrb* "near" instead of *qṣr* "citadel," perhaps suggesting a place in the general vicinity, rather than al-Kūfah itself.

One should keep in mind that Ṭabarī's report on the first al-Hāshimīyah is limited to a single concise statement. The most complete account of the early 'Abbāsid capitals is found in Balādhurī's chapter on the toponymy and topography of al-Kūfah.[46] Balādhurī begins with a description of Ibn Hubayrah's attempts at establishing an administrative center for the provincial government: "Yazīd b. 'Umar b. Hubayrah built a city [*madīnah*] along the Euphrates in the vicinity of al-Kūfah [*bi-l-Kūfah*]. Although there was still some construction left to be completed, he established himself there. But he then received a communication from the Caliph ordering him to avoid settling near the Kūfans. As a result, he left it [Madīnat b. Hubayrah] and built the palace complex [*qaṣr*] known as Qaṣr b. Hubayrah near Jisr Sūrā."[47] The author then points to the relationship between these late Umayyad palace areas and those of the early 'Abbāsids who followed:

> When the Commander of the Faithful, Abū al-'Abbās, took office, he established himself at that city [*tilka al-madīnah*], completing various [unfinished] chambers [*maqāṣīr*] and initiating construction of his own. He named it al-Hāshimīyah; but the populace persisted in calling it by the name of Ibn Hubayrah. The Caliph said, "I do not see that it will cease to be called after Ibn Hubayrah," whereupon he left the site and built al-Madīnah al-Hāshimīyah opposite it [*biḥiyālihā*]. He established himself there [at the new al-Hāshimīyah] but then chose to settle at al-Anbār where he built

> his famous city. When he died, he was buried in the capital at al-Anbār." Abū Ja'far al-Manṣūr now became Caliph. He established himself at al-Madīnah al-Hāshimīyah in [the vicinity of] al-Kūfah [*bi-l-Kūfah*], completing whatever [structures] were left to be built and adding new construction according to an arrangement [*hayya'a*] of his own choosing. Then he transferred to Baghdad where he built *his* city.

Although the author does not specify the site of the first capital by name, the language of the text seems clear and the meaning fairly obvious. The expression, "that city," (*tilka al-Madīnah*) though it follows a statement concerning the center at Jisr Sūrā, undoubtedly refers to Madīnat b. Hubayrah. The reader is therefore informed that the first 'Abbāsid Caliph completed and enlarged the partially built palace complex that originally housed the Umayyad governor of Iraq. This is partially confirmed by other sources, which report that Abū al-'Abbās moved from the Ḥīrah-Kūfah region when he transferred the Caliphate to al-Anbār in A.H. 134.[48]

The geographer Yāqūt (6th century A.H.) nevertheless found sufficient ambiguity in this text to relate two confused and contradictory accounts, and these have in turn led to still further confusion among modern scholars. In his entry on Qaṣr b. Hubayrah, he echoes the earlier author on the matter of the Umayyad administrative centers; however, after reporting on the move to Qaṣr b. Hubayrah, he proceeds with the following description of subsequent events:

> When [Abū al-'Abbās] al-Saffāḥ assumed rule, he established himself there [at Qaṣr b. Hubayrah], completing the roofs of various chambers [*maqāṣīr*] and adding new construction. He named it al-Hāshimīyah, but the populace persisted in calling it by its original name, Qaṣr b. Hubayrah. The Caliph said, "I do not see that it will cease to be called after Ibn Hubayrah," whereupon he left the site and built a city opposite it [*ḥiyālahu*]. He established himself there completing whatever [structures] were left to be built, and adding new elements according to an arrangement [*ja'ala*] of his own choosing. Then he transferred to Baghdad.[49]

In this last passage, Yāqūt apparently paraphrases the text of Balādhurī; however, in doing so, he completely alters the meaning of the original version. He not only mistakes Qaṣr b. Hubayrah for Madīnat

b. Hubayrah, but, as the text stands, he also attributes to Abū al-'Abbās the founding of Baghdad. This last statement, which runs counter to all other sources, is clearly due to a copyist's error. The identification of al-Hāsimīyah with Qaṣr b. Hubayrah is, on the other hand, a more serious problem reflecting a basic misconception on the part of the author. This is graphically illustrated in a second entry concerning al-Hāshimīyah:

> Al-Hāshimīyah is also a city [*madīnah*] built by [Abū al-'Abbās] al-Saffāḥ in [the vicinity of] al-Kūfah [*bi-l-Kūfah*]. That is, when he [Abū al-'Abbās] assumed the Caliphate, he established himself at Qaṣr b. Hubayrah. He finished building it [*istatamma binā'ahu*], made it an administrative center [*ja'alahu madīnah*],[50] and named it al-Hāshimīyah. The populace, however, persisted in calling it by the name of Ibn Hubayrah. The Caliph said "I do not see that it will cease to be called after Ibn Hubayrah," whereupon he left the site and built a "city" [*madīnah*] opposite it [*ḥiyālahu*], which he named al-Hāshimīyah. He established himself there, but then chose to settle at al-Anbār. Abū Ja'far al-Manṣūr now became Caliph and he also established himself there [at al-Anbār], completing whatever [structures] were left to be built, and adding new construction of his own choosing. Then he transferred from it and built Madīnat Baghdād.[51]

It is evident that Yāqūt has succeeded only in substituting one confusion for another. In this entry, he successfully identifies the Ḥīra-Kūfah region as the site of the first al-Hāshimīyah, but he confuses Madīnat b. Hubayrah with the Umayyad capital at Jisr Sūrā. The author correctly reports that it was al-Manṣūr who built Baghdad; however, he indicates that this move was initiated from al-Anbār, and not from the original al-Hāshimīyah to which he had returned. The actual sequence of events is clear. Abū al-'Abbās first settled at Madīnat b. Hubayrah and the site opposite it. He then moved to al-Anbār, which remained the capital of 'Abbāsid rule until the time of his death. When al-Manṣūr succeeded his brother as Caliph, he continued to reside at the city,[52] but then returned (for unspecified reasons) to the original capital near al-Kūfah. It was from al-Kūfah that al-Manṣūr undertook his search for still another administrative center, thereby beginning the quest that ended with the building of Baghdad.

There are, nonetheless, unanswered and perplexing questions. Why did Abū al-'Abbās decide to move his administrative center to al-Anbār after residing two years at Madīnat b. Hubayrah? Conversely why did his successor, al-Manṣūr, abandon al-Anbār only to return to the original capital of the regime? The sources offer no direct explanation for the rather frequent and puzzling moves; however, this need not discourage careful speculation. If Marwān II thought Madīnat b. Hubayrah too close to al-Kūfah, his 'Abbāsid successor may have eventually arrived at the same conclusion. After all, the loyalty of the Kūfans was no less problematic for Abū al-'Abbās than it had been for the Umayyad governors of Iraq. The long association of the local populace with 'Alid causes was not a matter to be taken lightly. To be sure, the revolution that carried the 'Abbāsids to power was to have ushered in a new era. This was to be an age forged in the unity that had characterized the early Islamic community; however, certain elements of the *ahl al-bayt* were not reconciled to the emergent dynasty. One should not confuse the initial passivity of the 'Alids with an open endorsement of the first 'Abbāsid regime. Political realities may have dictated public acquiescence to the new order, but there was no recognizing the legitimacy of 'Abbāsid claims. This was no doubt a source of great disappointment to the ruling family, but more significant, it was a political fact that could not be dismissed. Given the inclination of the Kūfans, Abū al-'Abbās had ample reason to be wary of remaining at Madīnat b. Hubayrah.

The decision to leave Madīnat b. Hubayrah is more easily understood than the move to al-Anbār. What could have led the Caliph to choose that particular site from among the various urban centers of Iraq? Although al-Anbār also traced its history back to the reign of Nebuchadnezzar, the first strong impressions of the Jisr Sūrā area appear only with the emergence of the Sassanid dynasty, when Shāpūr I (A.D. 241-272) built the garrison town of Fīrūz Sābūr.[53] This name later gave way to al-Anbār, "the granary," because the food allotments (*rizq*) of the local soldiery and artisans were kept in the storehouses of the town citadel. In time, al-Anbār became a large and prosperous city. Its strategic importance was derived from its position along the western limits of the 'Īsā Canal, a man-made water channel that connected the river systems of the Tigris and the Euphrates.[54] Following the Arab conquest, Sa'd b. Abī Waqqāṣ considered the city as the possible site for an Islamic settlement (*dār hijrah*), but he reportedly lost interest because of the prevalence of disease and the overabundance of flies.[55] Al-Anbār then seems to have declined as a center of political importance, for little is written about it until Abū al-'Abbās established his capital on the outskirts of the city.

When completed, the Caliph's administrative complex consisted of a palace situated between sections (*khiṭaṭ*) that were allotted to his Khurāsānī army.[56] The exact position of the new center in relation to the established urban area is uncertain. Although the author of the article on al-Anbār in *EI*[2] indicates that Abū al-'Abbās built a city for his Khurāsānī troops half a *farsakh* (2 miles) above the town, none of the sources that he cites justifies such a conclusion.[57] Only Dīnawarī specifies the location of the new capital, and he simply reports that, after leaving al-Ḥīrah, the Caliph built a great administrative center in the region of al-Anbār somewhere in the upper reaches of the city (*bia'lā al-madīnah*).[58] In any case, it is almost certain that Abū al-'Abbās would have preferred to leave some distance between himself and the quarters inhabited by the local populace, for this had been the pattern consistently followed by the 'Abbāsid Caliph and the later Umayyad governors who had preceded him in the province.

There is, at present, no way to expand on this rather skimpy review of the Jisr Sūrā region with only vague clues to help in explaining why the Caliph moved there. However, if one were inclined to speculate, it would be useful to focus on two interrelated sets of facts. First, al-Kūfah was potentially volatile, but al-Anbār was docile. There is no evidence that the populace actively participated in the various revolutionary outbreaks that plagued the later years of the Umayyad regime. Nor is it clear that the Anbārīs possessed the necessary fighting skills to pose a serious threat to the new order had they desired to do so. Unlike the Iraqi cities previously mentioned, al-Anbār did not become a major political or military center in early Islamic times. Second, the city, nevertheless, apparently remained an important commercial hub, conveniently situated along a major canal. The later 'Abbāsid move to a permanent capital at Baghdad was based in large part on strategic and economic considerations. It may well be that Abū al-'Abbās was similarly inclined to weigh the merits of geography in relocating the government that had been situated at Madīnat b. Hubayrah. By moving to al-Anbār, the first 'Abbāsid Caliph could thus have enjoyed the advantages of an established urban area without the security problems posed by a politically unreliable populace nearby. Although the old capital was actually some undisclosed distance from al-Kūfah, it was still too close to suit the Caliph's purposes. The reservations held by Marwān II concerning Madīnat b. Hubayrah were certainly no less applicable to his successor.

D. Al-Manṣūr

Why, then, did al-Manṣūr return to the Ḥīrah-Kūfah region shortly after taking power? By every indication, the second 'Abbāsid sovereign was an extremely cautious individual, given to exaggerated suspicions of friend and enemy alike. He was surely aware that the nearby Kūfans, with their political inclinations, represented a potential danger to the newly established regime. According to Ṭabarī, this was a major factor in the Caliph's later decision to abandon Madīnat b. Hubayrah in favor of a new capital (*qurb jiwārihi min al-Kūfah wa lam ya'man ahlahā 'alā nafsihi faarāda an yab uda min jiwārihim*).[59] A later sourçe goes a step further and indicates that the neighboring Kūfans had already subverted al-Manṣūr's army (*wa ḳānū qad afsadū jundahu*) when he undertook the journey that resulted in the construction of Madīnat al-Salām.[60] Yet, despite the obvious dangers inherent in the area, the Caliph not only reoccupied the old administrative center at Madīnat b. Hubayrah, he also built a second complex behind (*biẓahr*) al-Kūfah, which he named al-Ruṣāfah.[61]

Because al-Manṣūr was neither foolhardy nor given to bravura, one should perhaps look for the particular circumstances that might explain this strange turn of events. Although there is no proof, it is possible that the Caliph's decision to return to the Ḥīrah-Kūfah region was determined by the political situation within the ruling family. It will be remembered that al-Manṣūr's claims to the Caliphate were contested from the outset by his paternal uncle 'Abdallāh b. 'Alī. The Caliph's uncle, though he was then governor of Syria, commanded a large army consisting not only of local troops, but of elements from Khurāsān, al-Jazīrah and al-Mawṣil as well. Furthermore, 'Abdallāh b. 'Alī also controlled the former treasuries of the Umayyad house, which gave him the potential leverage to gain wide backing from among these diverse contingents.[62]

Al-Manṣūr lacked a strong regional base from which to press his claim. He had been governor of al-Jazīrah, but his tenure there was marked by difficulties with the *'umūmah*.[63] Moreover, his paternal uncle enjoyed a great reputation in the province owing to his past military triumphs.[64] By any objective standard, 'Abdallāh b. 'Alī would have been predicted as the likely winner in this internal struggle. The factors that favored the new Caliph were few indeed. At the outset of his succession, al-Manṣūr had only two allies, and one of these, Abū Muslim, is presented as a very reluctant supporter.[65] Only the Caliph's nephew 'Īsā b. Mūsā, who stood second in the line of succession, was firmly committed to his cause. This was a significant commitment, however, for 'Īsā b. Mūsā was not only a compelling figure within the ruling family, he was also the governor of al-Kūfah and thus commanded the large network of palaces and military bases within the area. The continued support of 'Īsā b. Mūsā and the large local garrison were, no doubt, critical to al-Manṣūr's future plans. These included eliminating Abū Muslim, weakening the power base of the *'umūmah*, and consolidating the military commanders firmly behind the central authority. To be sure, the Kūfans remained a potential threat to his regime, but Abū Ja'far al-Manṣūr had more pressing business to attend to at the outset of his reign. In these circumstances, he seems to have preferred to remain with his loyal nephew in the Ḥīrah-Kūfah region despite the risks represented by the neighboring populace. The risks, however, remained.

The Caliph's ultimate decision to leave his capital in search of a new administrative center was arrived at slowly and was, according to the medieval sources, conditioned by two factors.[66] In addition to the omnipresent threat of a Kūfan uprising, there was the inadequate security arrangement within the confines of his own palace area. This last point was emphasized rather dramatically by the Rāwandīyah incident, when al-Manṣūr came perilously close to losing his life. The significance of this event has already been discussed.[67] To recapitulate briefly: the Caliph was visited at al-Hāshimīyah by a group of Khurāsānīs belonging to an extremist proto-Shī'ite sect known as the Rāwandīyah. They had come to proclaim their sovereign God (*rabb*) and to partake of his food and drink. The expression of this heretical idea was apparently more than al-Manṣūr could tolerate. He therefore gave orders to imprison two hundred of the Rāwandī leaders and forbade the others to congregate; however, they were not to be denied. They stormed the prison, liberating their brethren, and then set out for al-Manṣūr in his palace.[68] Although the disturbance was ultimately crushed, the fact that several hundred armed rioters[69] could have penetrated an area designated for maximum security indicated a serious shortcoming in the current administrative center. The Rāwandīyah were, after all, a mob and could therefore be suppressed, albeit after some hair-raising moments. The Kūfans, on the other hand, were a flood tide of humanity that would be very difficult to contain. One may thus suppose that, from this moment, the Caliph regarded the transfer of the government as inevitable. Nevertheless, it was four years before al-Manṣūr determined the site of a new capital and began the construction of its major buildings. Not until A.H. 145 did he lay the foundations of the Round City at Baghdad.

Ironically, the wisdom of leaving the Ḥīrah-Kūfah region was dramatically confirmed by a Shīʿite revolt that took place that very year. Although this critical event has been previously analyzed in detail,[70] it may be instructive to focus again on several important developments. One recalls that the Caliph was supervising the early construction of a new administrative center at Baghdad when word was received of an ʿAlid insurrection in the Ḥijāz. Al-Manṣūr returned immediately to al-Hāshimīyah and dispatched ʿĪsā b. Mūsā with the regional garrison to deal with the disturbance. This last move, though entirely justified by existing circumstances, depleted Iraq of its strategic reserve, because the major forces of the imperial army were already committed to extensive campaigns in Khurāsān and the west. But the worst was yet to come. Al-Manṣūr's difficulties were seriously compounded by the outbreak of a second insurrection in southern Iraq. A highly agitated Caliph now found himself closeted at his capital with meager defense forces. Approaching him from al-Baṣrah was a large Shīʿite army led by the Ḥusaynid, Ibrāhīm b. ʿAbdallāh. To his rear were the Kūfans, "one hundred thousand swords lying in ambush for him."[71]

The Kūfans, as always, were somewhat coy. As a rule, they withheld support until assured of success, and withdrew if the prospect of failure seemed remotely possible. In this case, they made a commitment from the Ḥusaynid to march against the neighboring capital a precondition to their active participation in Ibrāhīm's cause. Al-Manṣūr's perception of the local danger was shared by his enemies. If the rebel command had some misgivings about marching against the beleaguered Caliph in al-Hāshimīyah, it was because they preferred to consolidate their newly acquired influence before attacking him frontally. They were not entirely aware of the desperate situation facing al-Manṣūr, for he had managed to conceal his weakness through a series of clever ruses. Nevertheless, once prodded by Ibrāhīm b. 'Abdallāh into taking the initiative, they suggested using the Kūfans for a diversionary attack against the nearby capital. Such an attack, if successful, might very well have had a catastrophic effect on 'Abbāsid rule in Iraq. At the least, the Caliph would have been forced to retire, probably eastward to Khurāsān, in order to link up with the imperial army stationed there. It was only a stroke of luck that Ibrāhīm b. Abdallāh did not follow the sound counsel of his advisors and that he decided, on religious and humanitarian grounds, not to use his willing Kūfan supporters.

Al-Manṣūr realized both the error of his adversary and his own good fortune. Despite its varied advantages, the Kūfah-Ḥīrah region had outlived its usefulness. Once al-Manṣūr had defeated the rebels, he returned to Baghdad, where construction had been delayed since the outbreak of the fighting. In A.H. 146, he transferred his household and the agencies of government from al-Hāshimīyah to the new capital, which he named Madīnat al-Salām.[72] Three years later, he had completed the outer fortifications and various other structures that had been unfinished.

It may be said that this most recent development was the continuation of a policy begun at the outset of the regime. Anxious to preserve a delicate balance between security and the advantages of an established urban area, the first 'Abbāsid Caliphs had shifted their centers of rule from place to place. Between Abū al-'Abbās and his successor, the capital was moved no fewer than four times: from Madīnat b. Hubayrah to an adjacent site, from there to al-Anbār, and from al-Anbār back to the original complex. Seen in this light, Baghdad was not a creation ex nihilo, but the last and most grandiose of the early 'Abbāsid settlements in Iraq. Somewhat more cautiously, one could claim that the new administrative complex was only a significant variation on a well-known theme.

There is something to be said for this point of view, but it does not adequately explain the phenomenon of Baghdad. Although Madīnat al-Salām may have been derived from earlier ideas and experiences, in many respects it represented a new conception—as if dropping the name al-Hāshimīyah, which was generic to all the early ʿAbbāsid centers, signified a decisive break with the recent past. In architectural scope and execution, to say nothing of general planning and urban development, there had never been anything quite like Baghdad in the Islamic world. The essayist al-Jāḥiẓ perhaps put it best when he wrote, "It is as though it were poured into a mold and cast."[73] Al-Manṣūr's creation was a unique achievement. It is only from this perspective that the subsequent topographical growth of the city can be properly understood.

VII

BAGHDAD: LEGENDARY ORIGINS AND HISTORIC REALITIES

O Commander of the Faithful! You will be situated along the Ṣarāt [Canal] between the Tigris and the Euphrates. If anyone should attack you, the Tigris and the Euphrates will serve as water barrier for your city. . . . Your enemies will only be able to reach you by way of pontoon [*jisr*] and masonry bridges [*qanṭarah*]. If you cut the *jisr* and destroy the *qanṭarah* they will not be able to reach you. You are situated amid al-Baṣrah, al-Kūfah, Wāsiṭ, al-Mawṣil and the Sawād. You are near the land and water [routes] and the mountains.

Ibn Ṭabāṭabā (Beirut), 162

A. Choosing the Site

The Arabic accounts that discuss al-Manṣūr's decision to build a city at Baghdad are an interlacing of various lengthy reports from which two distinct traditions emerge: the first, which reflects the geographical advantages of the site, is evidently factual, the second, which establishes the legitimacy of the Caliph's decision, is largely apocryphal.[1]

Several historical facts would seem to be self-evident. For al-Manṣūr, the central location of Baghdad made it eminently suitable as the site for an administrative center from which to rule his far-flung empire.[2] Its geographic location gave access to overland routes of trade and pilgrimage, as well as to the major inland water carriers. Its canals not only allowed for the easy transport of materials, but also provided natural barriers against assault from without. Having been persuaded by the obvious advantages of the site, al-Manṣūr began to erect an elaborate series of structures throughout the area. To the north, in the suburb that came to be called al-Ḥarbīyah, he established large military cantonments for his Khurāsānī army. To the south, in an area that had been a small local market, he developed large commercial districts to serve the rapidly growing urban center. Sandwiched between the military and the markets was the magnificent Round City, comprising the Caliph's palace and the center of his administration. Protected behind imposing fortifications, which gave eloquent testimony to the efficacy of his regime, the Caliph was able to survey the perfection of his design and the orderly nature of his domain. The Caliph had reason to be satisfied, for the city was in every respect a fitting monument to the legitimacy of his reign. Even when Baghdad fell victim to indiscriminate urban expansion,[3] it continued to enjoy, in history, and particularly in legend, a reputation as the quintessential model of urban planning.

There are certain areas where the line between legend and historical reality is not clearly drawn, and these are the concern here. Although the topographical data for the early development of Baghdad stands in bold historical relief, the entertaining tales of the city's origins and early growth are complex and elusive. The foundation lore, by its very nature, obscures the subtle line between fact and fiction; such accounts nevertheless remain among the most important sources for the early history of Baghdad and, more generally, for the period of al-Manṣūr's Caliphate. It is no wonder that they continue to fascinate, as well as charm, the scholar interested in the Caliph and his city.

Of particular interest are those accounts that shed light on the relationship between architectural development and al-Manṣūr's quest to authenticate the foundations of his rule.[4] A text discussed earlier serves once again as a useful point of departure, for it illustrates clearly the relationship between al-Manṣūr's city and the legitimization of his political authority. The historian Ṭabarī, in describing the events of the year A.H. 145, preserves an interesting account that refers to the major events of that time. The story, which is told elsewhere with some variation,[5] is concerned with al-Manṣūr's search for a new capital to serve his personal needs as well as those of the ruling house and the army. While traveling in the general vicinity of al-Madā'in, that is Ctesiphon, the ruined capital of the defunct Sassanian empire, one of the Caliph's entourage was forced to remain behind to be treated for an inflammation of his eyes. When asked by the local physician about his master's intentions, al-Manṣūr's companion informed the doctor of the Caliph's desire to find a site suitable for a new capital. The doctor, perhaps with a hint of skepticism, pointed to a prophecy that is recorded in an ancient book sacred to his own tradition.

In this prophecy, it is said that a man called Miqlāṣ[6] will build a city called al-Zawrā' between the Tigris and the Ṣarāt Canal. When he has laid the foundation and constructed part of the enclosure wall, there will be a breach from the Ḥijāz interrupting construction. He will undertake to repair the damage of this breach, but, when he is at the point of repairing it, there will be another breach from al-Baṣrāh causing a greater degree of damage than before. However, it will not be long before he repairs the breaches and returns to building the city. Upon completing it, he will take up residence there. It will thrive for generations to come and will be a continuous seat of rule. The literary play is to indicate that al-Manṣūr would be wasting his time there, unless, of course, his name was really Miqlāṣ.

When the Caliph was informed of this conversation, he was apparently not in the least dissuaded, because he recalled that, in his youth, he was indeed called Miqlāṣ. Al-Manṣūr then related the story of how he had acquired that name. It appears that, when al-Manṣūr was a mere lad, it was once his turn to entertain a circle of young friends; however, the future Caliph, much to his embarrassment, was without funds to reciprocate their previous hospitality. It seems that, even then, al-Manṣūr displayed the resourcefulness that would stand him in good stead throughout his political career. He stole a ball of yarn from a servant and exchanged it for the much needed items. After the theft was discovered, he was upbraided and given the nickname Miqlāṣ after a well-known thief in the vicinity. The name stuck for a while but was then forgotten—until this propitious moment. Armed with an ancient prophecy awaiting fulfillment, al-Manṣūr did not hesitate to choose exactly that spot indicated by the doctor in which to build his new capital—coincidentally the location of an ancient hamlet called Baghdad.

One may choose not to believe this account in all its particulars, but neither should one dismiss it altogether. A more cautious examination of the text clearly reveals that, although employing language that is deliberately vague and prophetic, the author is alluding quite clearly to the central events of the year A.H. 145, that is, the building of Baghdad and the 'Alid revolts of Muḥammad b. 'Abdallāh in al-Madīnah and, somewhat later, of his brother Ibrāhīm in al-Baṣrah. These last events have been dealt with earlier in great detail.[7] It is sufficient to recall here that the first armed resistance was a tragicomic affair, but the second confrontation was a serious challenge to the Caliph's authority.

In the words of the prophecy, it was a "breach causing a greater degree of damage than before."

The particular use of language in these passages is critical to an understanding of their broader meaning. The rather odd term describing the vague breaches in the wall denotes "to tear" or "to split" (*ftq*), but it connotes even more clearly and directly a disunion within the community of believers. Similarly, the expression that indicates the repair of the damaged wall (*iṣlāḥ*) may also mean religious reconstruction. The double entendre is intended and is integral to the structure of the account. According to the text, the mysterious breaches will cause work on the wall to be temporarily suspended. The allusion here is once again to an actual incident, for Ṭabarī reports elsewhere that construction at Baghdad had already begun when work of the 'Alid uprising was received.[8] With the main contingents of the imperial army away in Khurāsān and North Africa, the hard pressed Caliph was forced to scavenge for manpower. As a result, the military forces at the construction site were removed, some building material was destroyed, and construction was completely halted until the rebels had been subdued.

If this is insufficient it can be shown that the name al-Zawrā', given to the city in this purportedly ancient manuscript is also an indication that the doctor's sacred vision is actually based on contemporary events. Admittedly, this is not the view of G. LeStrange, whose book on medieval Baghdad remains in many respects the classic work on the subject. Basing his opinion on a fourteenth-century Persian text, LeStrange could not resist speculating, "that while the Arabs spoke of Baghdad or Madīnat al-Salām, it was in preference called al-Zawrā' by the Persians, which almost looks as though this Arabic word al-Zawrā' 'crooked' may have stood for some ancient Iranian name long forgotten."[9] This conclusion is once again an indication of that resilient methodology that explains the obscure by that which is still more obscure. For some reason never fully explained, the unknown seems always to look more attractive in Persian garb. Although such attributions are often made carelessly, and even whimsically, it can at least be said on behalf of LeStrange that his mysterious Persian origin for al-Zawrā' does not seem to have been proposed with much conviction.

The medieval Arabic authors are themselves divided with regard to the subject of the name's origin. Several theories are advanced that play with the obvious meaning "the crooked." The Tigris, which meandered through the city, took the undulating course that is expected of an ancient waterway and was thus called al-Zawrā' (*wa bihi summiyat Dijlat Baghdād al-Zawrā'*).[10] For LeStrange, this casual observation of the Arabic geographer meant that "Baghdad took the name al-Zawrā' from the river Tigris. . . ."[11] One may wish to argue this case, but it certainly is not the contention of the medieval author, who draws a clear distinction between al-Zawrā', the waterway, and Madīnat al-Zawrā', the Round City of Abū Ja'far al-Manṣūr (*al-Zawrā' madīnat Abī Ja'far al-Manṣūr wa hiya fī al-jānib al-gharbī . . .*).

The identification of al-Zawrā' with the Round City is in fact echoed in several texts and leaves no doubt that this association was well understood. Yāqūt, in his entry on Baghdad, discusses the various names for the city and states: "As for [the name] al-Zawrā', it refers specifically to the [Round] City of al-Manṣūr [*faammā al-Zawrā' faMadīnat al-Manṣūr khāṣṣah*]."[12] The great historian of Baghdad, Aḥmad b. Thābit, is even more explicit in quoting an account on the authority of al-Jāḥiẓ: "I have seen the great cities including those noted for their durable construction. I have seen such cities in the districts of Syria, in Bilād al-Rūm and in other provinces, but I have never seen a city of greater height, more perfect circularity, more endowed with superior merits or possessing more spacious gates or more perfect *faṣīls* than al-Zawrā', that is to say, the city of Abū Ja'far al-Manṣūr. . . ."[13]

How, then, did this consummate effort of architectural planning assume the graceless name "the crooked"? Several sources suggest that this is a reference to the skewed orientation of the principal mosque, which lay adjacent to the Caliph's palace in the Round City. In order to preserve the perfect symmetry of the total plan, it was necessary to compromise on this structure.[14] The most plausible explanation, however, is the one that indicates that the name is derived from the system of bent entrances built into the outer gateways of the famous wall system. These were erected by al-Manṣūr himself and are described in considerable detail in several medieval sources.[15] Al-Zawrā' thus does not represent anything mysterious and Iranian that is long forgotten. The attribution is Manṣūrid; it is contemporary with the other events alluded to in the prophetic document, and it is consistent with the central metaphor of that text, namely, the enclosure wall. The author employed an ancient literary technique to promote the authenticity of his account and to enhance the Caliph's stature. He projected a recent historical event back into the remote past and presented it through a narrator offering a tale deliberately vague and prophetic. The fulfillment of the prophecy, therefore, not only satisfied ancient expectations but also offered the current proof of al-Manṣūr's legitimacy to rule. The building of Baghdad was, in this sense, the symbolic act that gave visual expression to al-Manṣūr's claims and to those of the 'Abbāsid family.

Although little, if anything, is known of the earlier 'Abbāsid settlements in Iraq, it would be safe to say that nothing quite like the Round City had ever been conceived by a Muslim ruler. The Caliph himself is pictured as being very much involved in planning the details of construction.[16] To some, this may seem evidence of his legendary parsimony—this is even suggested in the medieval sources—but the issue of al-Manṣūr's participation is more complicated. The new capital was not merely the choice of a new city; it carried with it the prestige and authority of the Caliphate itself.

It is therefore pertinent to ask if the imposing architectural arrangement of al-Manṣūr's administrative complex could have been a conscious attempt to physically recapture the grandeur of his imperial predecessors. Although there are no existing remains of the Round City, detailed descriptions are preserved in the literary sources.[17] The picture obtained from the medieval texts is that of a perfectly circular city with two concentric defending walls separated by an *intervallum* (*faṣīl*) and surrounded by a water trench. Extending from the outer fortifications, which are entered through a bent entrance, are four elaborate gate complexes and arcades, each equidistant from one another and forming the residential and administrative quadrants of the city. The center of the circle is formed by a large enclosed court that surrounds the principal mosque and the adjoining residence of the Caliph. In back of his palace is an audience hall surmounted by an enormous green dome visible from the outskirts of the city.

There is considerable discussion among scholars about the ways in which symbols of authority are expressed through architectural forms and decorative motifs. This is a complicated problem, and, in the case of Baghdad, it is further compounded by the presence of a varied labor force drawn from different regions.[18] It is not altogether clear whether this organization of labor implies the use of concurrent, diverse artistic traditions. Certain architectural patterns were no doubt determined by the general taste of the great patron, and the overall plan of the Round City seems to have been drawn according to al-Manṣūr's personal preference. But to what extent did the Caliph, in building his city, consciously consider such matters as aesthetics, architectural function, and political symbolism?

These questions are difficult to answer, for they are not explicitly addressed in the Arabic sources. The medieval author viewed the creation of al-Manṣūr's city with a sense of immediacy and wonder that excluded such discussions of style, taste, and political symbolism as might interest his modern counterpart. Despite evidence to the contrary, Aḥmad b. Thābit went so far as to echo the claim that "no other round city is known in all the regions of the world."[19] The famous preacher of Baghdad thus considered the city unique, and if it was not, then he was still disposed to declare it so. On the other hand, some modern scholars have been no less modest working from the opposite perspective. They are inclined to attribute to the Islamic world in general, and to the 'Abbāsids in particular, all sorts of cultural borrowings that the men of the time never consciously acknowledged, if they thought about them at all. This is not to say that contemporaries of al-Manṣūr had no eclectic tastes of their own—far from it. Nevertheless, the argument in favor of a direct cultural borrowing must be sustained by a plausible connection rooted in history rather than by the presumption of a shared cosmic experience. This kind of methodological restraint remains, however, the exception and not the rule.

B. Theories of Cosmology and City Planning

In a far-ranging book, the distinguished art historian H. P. L'Orange described Baghdad as "the most famous of all the cosmic 'round cities' of the east [by east he meant western Asia]."[20] The author considered these to be unlike the Roman rectangular camps, in that cosmic reflection is clear in the royal cities that are round:

> The kingdom in the Ancient Near East mirrored the rule of the sun in the heavens. The king amongst his vassals and satraps was a reflection of the heavenly hierarchy. *Traced back to Babylonian times*,[22] the king was the "axis and pole of the world . . ." "the king of the universe," "the king of the Four Quadrants of the World,"

> and these titles were repeated in ever new adaptations right up to the Sassanian period when the king was "Frater Solis et Lunae."

The author then asks:

> Is there not a striking correspondence between these cosmic titles of the king and his place in the cosmic city? Wall and fosse are traced mathematically with the compass, as an image of the heavens, a projection of the upper hemisphere on earth. Two axis streets, one running north-south and the other east-west, divide the city into four quadrants which reflect the four quarters of the world. At the very point of intersection, in the very axis of the world in which the palace is situated, here sits the king, "The axis and Pole of the World," "The King of the Four Quadrants of the World," here resides "The King of the Universe," as the very moving universal power.[21]

For L'Orange, al-Manṣūr's Baghdad is the "unsurpassable incarnation" of this ancient tradition of the king's cosmic city, "the greatest and most splendid urban center of the early Middle Ages, the focus of world trade and intellectual life. . . ." Surely there is no wish to argue against the centrality of Baghdad's position in the history of the early Middle Ages. Moreover, the author's remarks concerning the ancient Near East may be partly true. Of what use is all this, however, in understanding the fact of al-Manṣūr's Round City. There is the overwhelming temptation to register a rather fatuous observation. Here are the Roman legions, the worshippers of the sky God, Jupiter, confined, as fate would have it, to their rectangular enclosures, while Abū Ja'far al-Manṣūr, whose authority and regnal titles derived from history, and not nature, is left to enjoy the symbolic advantages of a cosmic city.

In the course of events there may be an infinite variety of human responses to any given situation, but from these limitless choices certain ill-defined models of behavior always seem to reappear. It is the historian's craft to record and evaluate the human condition, and to this end he may of course employ any stratagem that seems fitting. One should keep in mind, however, that vague similarities in cultural response to certain types of situations may be more than offset by profound differences. The Caliph's engineers had no need for the heavenly hierarchy in order to understand the mathematical advantages of the circle. The jurist Wakīʿ makes it clear that, "Abū Jaʿfar fashioned his city out of a circle because it had certain advantages over the city formed from a square." As the author put it, "If the monarch were to be in the center of a square, some parts would be closer to him than others; however, regardless of the divisions, the sections of the Round City are equidistant from him when he is positioned at the center."[23] Implicit in the last statement is an appreciation for the economy of construction made possible by a particular geometric form, but even more important is the notion of a highly centralized authority. It is the intense desire to establish such an authority in appropriate physical surroundings that seems to be the underlying reason for the choice of the city plan.

There can be no question that, in both design and function, the Round City was a most dramatic expression of centralized rule and was thus well suited to al-Manṣūr's particular needs. The Caliph was very sensitive to the unsettled conditions that existed when the ʿAbbāsids came to power, and he perceived only too well the limitation of his own appeal. What was required was an assertive posture that would enhance the Caliph's stature and project his authority. Certainly, this realization must have served as a direct stimulus to the development of his remarkable edifice and to the development, in general, of the institutional framework that came to be recognized as the ʿAbbāsid style of rule.

The Commander of the Faithful did not require the example of his pre-Islamic predecessors to appreciate the significance of highly centralized power. Besides, the earlier conceptions of authority were derived from a world view of a rather different order. Al-Manṣūr was not the earthly counterpart of a divine being destined to play out the countless seasons of cosmic dramas in a terrestrial setting. His mission was fixed in time and based on vivid historical memories. The authority vested in him was inherited from the Prophet Muḥammad. The Caliph's charge was to restore the society of the Faithful to the unequivocal religious standards of early Islam. This did not, by any means, imply a return to all the cultural values of the past. Baghdad was not Mecca, and governing the vast domains and populations of the ʿAbbāsid empire was not to be compared with political maneuvering among the Arab tribesmen of the Arabian Peninsula. The new dynasty obviously required a much more intricate mechanism of rule. Its immediate predecessor had developed a royal presence based in part on Iranian and Byzantine models, but the internal contradictions of the Umayyad regime had prevented the evolution of an orderly government.[24] There was, nevertheless, much to learn from the past about statecraft and its practice in the domain of the ruler.

There is reason to believe that the imperial style, of the early 'Abbāsids may also reflect the world of the Sassanians. That this was due to a conscious cultural borrowing is not at all clear, for little is known of the residual effects of Sassanian institutions on the Islamic world of the eighth century. Still, like many subjects about which much is said and little is known, there is ample room for conjecture. Might the Round City, which was the most dramatic visual expression of the imperial style, have thus reflected eastern influences in a general, or perhaps even specific way? This is a question that is explored with great enthusiasm and considerable learning by C. Wendell.[25] Unlike L'Orange, who posits the origins of al-Manṣūr's "cosmic city" in Western Asia, Wendell is inclined to search farther to the east in what he describes as "the unshattered Indo-Iranian world preceding the great migrations of the second millennium B.C."[26] He contends that, in the course of time, the sacral image of the world held in common by Buddhists, Hindus, and Zoroastrians was translated visually into the curious architectural arrangement of the great 'Abbāsid capital. The data brought in support of this far-reaching conclusion are highly diverse and bound by very wide parameters of geography and chronology. There are citations of technical studies about the early casting of iron, a reference to examples of "center-symbolism" and the "sacralization" of space, a brief discussion of the Hindu "world-picture" as it was transmitted through Buddhism, and reflections about the universal "world-plan" of Zoroastrian scripture, which, the author states, is "essentially the same as that of Buddhism, if we strip the latter of its wealth of demons, divinities, humans, and subhumans and their pictorial representation."[27] One could add to this, quotations from ancient Egyptian literature, references to astrology, a prayer attributed to Assur-Nasir Pal II (883-859 B.C.) and evidence of a similar sort.[28] For all the diligent research and fascinating data, what can one say about this tour de force?

There can be, in the case of Baghdad, no quarrel with a modest claim for a general cultural borrowing. Discussions of style are often elusive, but it does not require much daring to assume that "in any society organized into a hierarchy of classes under an autocracy, symmetry and axial plans predominate not only in the design of individual buildings but in the arrangement of groups of buildings, and finally in the layout of the inclusive group, in the city."[29] It is Reuther's description of Sassanian city planning, but it could easily describe 'Abbāsid Baghdad. In fact, many general features of the Round City are prominently displayed at several known pre-Islamic sites in western Iran and Mesopotamia, namely, in Hatra, Darābjird, Gūr, and Ctesiphon; however, the available archeological and literary evidence does not suggest any direct prototype for the Round City, let alone the sweeping conclusions advanced by those enamored of cosmological explanations. As for the cosmological view, it is perhaps best articulated by the following quotations from Wendell's study:[30]

> The plan of Baghdad is really nothing less than an Islamic *mandala* worked out on a huge scale of urban architecture. It is certainly a schematic representation of the world—essentially that of the Sassanian monarchs—in purely formal aniconic terms. All the elements are there: the four (median) directions; the circumambient mountain wall that separates the "formal" universe from chaos; the "world-navel" supporting the mosque and throne, the latter sheltered by a celestial dome which recalls the ancient divinity of kings and is the visible sign of heaven's approval. . . . Possibly [al-Manṣūr] thought of [Baghdad] as the imperial version of an "army-camp" as one of the narratives in Ṭabarī would seem to suggest,[31] but . . . this model must be attributable to Iranian and not Arabian prototypes, and may represent a shadowy survival of the moving camp and court of the ancient Indo-Iranian conquerors who would "recreate" the world at each stage of their progress across Asia.

If the conclusion appears familiar, it is entirely coincidental, for nowhere does the author quote the earlier work of L'Orange. Whether one begins in the East or in the West, however, the proposed cosmic origins of the Round City seem at best a rationalization after the fact. This is especially clear when the "cosmologist" turns to the Islamic sources in support of his argument.

Attention is focused on the walls of Baghdad, particularly on the gate complex, which consisted of four symmetrically arranged structures, each named after the major city or region that it faced. Thus, the northeast quadrant of the city was entered through the Khurāsān Gate and the northwest quadrant through the Damascus Gate. Similarly, the southeast gate opened onto the road to al-Baṣrah, while the southwest gate faced the direction of al-Kūfah. To most scholars, the orientation of the city gates would seem to be eminently sensible. It is a practiced plan that has been effectively used throughout the course of urban history and in many regions of the world. However, there is apparently more here than meets the eye. We are informed that "the particular orientation of the city's gates united the 'symbolic' world-center of Baghdad with the 'actual' world-center of Mecca since the Kūfa-Gate . . . functioned as a *trait d'union* between the two."[32] The author considers this the only strikingly Islamic note in what is otherwise an eastern conception.

The last point is reinforced by a philological note of sorts. Once divested of its obvious significance, the orientation of the city gates is used to explain that elusive name given to Baghdad in several texts, that is, al-Zawrā'. The new interpretation is derived from a Persian perspective and is preferred to the explanations of the medieval Arabic authors. Thus the name, which means "the crooked," does not stem from the skewed orientation of the city mosque or the bent entrances of al-Manṣūr's wall system. It is, instead, based on the position of the gateways as they would appear on the compass (southeast, southwest, northeast, northwest). In the author's words, "Since the normal orientation of four gates in a Sassanian foundation would have been toward the cardinal points [that is, due south, north, east, and west], this feature of the Baghdad plan may be the most likely reason of all for the name al-Zawrā' looking at the city from a purely 'Persian' viewpoint."[33]

The basic thrust of the cosmological argument can be succinctly summarized. Those espousing this point of view assert that the grand design of al-Manṣūr's city, and especially its domed elements, was not casually conceived through a marriage of architectural concepts and aesthetic principles. On the contrary, they maintain that the Round City was a conscious imitation of earlier models, and, what is more, that it gave full expression to the cultural associations inherent in these models. This imitative borrowing would most likely have been motivated by political considerations. Certainly, the Caliph was a political animal able to appreciate what is described as "the visible sign of heaven's approval." We are informed that "By utilizing . . . 'the visual language' of the Baghdad plan, al-Manṣūr presented himself to the world as the successor to the great emperors of the past."[34] One could argue on behalf of this viewpoint that perhaps no Caliph in the early history of Islam so intensely felt the need to establish his legitimacy as did Abū Ja'far al-Manṣūr. The Iranian images supposedly conveyed by the Round City would therefore have been ideally suited to the historic needs of its founder.

C. The Argument against Cosmological Origins

The search for eastern origins is, however, not without difficulty. If there was indeed a pure (or even distinct) Persian viewpoint, why is it suddenly reflected in Iraq some hundred and twenty years after the ultimate destruction of the Sassanian dynasty? There is surely no reason to deny a lingering interest for things Sassanian, but the structure under review was designed expressly for an Arab Caliph brought to power largely by Arab tribal armies. Moreover, it was built by a labor force from the outlying districts of Syria and Iraq rather than by one recruited in the provinces to the east. Under the circumstances, it would have been quite a feat to engineer the conscious revival of an Iranian world view in this particular Islamic foundation.

Despite the Caliph's concern for the legitimization of his rule, Wendell is unwilling to attribute so grand a scheme to al-Manṣūr. "One somehow cannot connect [the Caliph] with a project which depended for its success . . . on aesthetic vision and the ability to wield symbols. . . . Everything about the scheme points to advisors of Persian origin and [a] deeper inherited culture than he [al-Manṣūr] could lay claim to."[35] There is even a plausible candidate to have acted as advisor: Khālid b. Barmak, who reportedly traced the city plan and otherwise served as a consultant in the development of the city (*khaṭṭa Madīnat Abī Ja'far lahu wa ashāra bihā 'alayhi*).[36]

Although the evidence is admittedly thin, the pre-Islamic background of the Barmakids as custodians of Buddhist religious shrines is next called to attention. Their original homeland in Transoxiana is described as "the meeting ground of a number of major cultural, religious, and linguistic traditions, and was a *macédoine* of ethnic diversity." In addition, the mixture of the local Iranian artistic styles "was characteristic *mutatis mutandis* for all aspects of Central Asian culture." All that remains to complete the circle is for the author to cite the tradition preserved in Ṭabarī that the Caliph accused his trusted advisor of non-Arab sentiments (*yā Khālid abayta illā al-mayl ilā aṣḥābika al-'ajam*)[37] after Khālid b. Barmak advised against dismantling the ruins of Īwān Kisrā, the palace of the Sassanian monarchs in al-Madā'in. On the whole, this lengthy and learned presentation presents a rather elegant argument, but the discourse is characterized by a certain preciosity.

Even if it can be assumed that Khālid b. Barmak represents a genuine historical link with the world of Central Asia, his role in building Baghdad is anything but certain. A careful analysis of the various traditions describing construction at the administrative complex does not support Wendell's conjecture that the Caliph's advisor was in a position to decisively influence the overall plan of the city. The most basic methodological restraint requires that every account be carefully weighed in relation to existing parallels. The text previously cited may credit Khālid b. Barmak with serving as a consultant and actually tracing the city plan, but it in no way specifies that he was responsible for its conception. In fact, the line immediately preceding this tradition indicates that the Barmakid was only one of several consultants (*lammā arāda al-Manṣūr binā' madīnat Baghdād shāwara aṣḥābahu fīhā wa kāna mimman shāwarahu fīhā Khālid b. Barmak*).[38] The tracing of the city plan appears to have been a routine technical task that was shared, according to the sources, by a number of individuals, including al-Ḥajjāj b. Arṭāt and a group of men from al-Kūfah.[39]

As to the grand design of the administrative complex, the impression is conveyed elsewhere that it was the Caliph himself who formulated the basic concept (*famaththala . . . ṣifatahā allatī fī nafsihi*).[40] Then, in order to visualize the form of the structure, he ordered that the lines be traced with ashes. When this was done, he gave the site his personal inspection, walking about and picturing in his mind the intended architectural elements: the *faṣīls*, gates, arcades, courtyards, and the protective wall. Apparently pleased with what he saw, the Caliph ordered cotton seeds, which were subsequently placed along the ash marks, doused with naphtha, and set aflame. After viewing the spectacle of the fiery outline, al-Manṣūr commanded that the foundations be laid according to these tracings.[41] The plan of the Round City therefore seems to have been created personally by the Caliph, as one would indeed expect with an individual of al-Manṣūr's character. It seems inconceivable that this obsessive figure could have been maneuvered into anything as dramatic as the construction of a new capital without first investigating every facet of the undertaking. The Barmakid may have had considerable influence at the court, but al-Manṣūr was in every respect his own man, and no one has claimed that the Caliph himself thought in terms of cosmic symbols.

Doubts may also be raised concerning the tradition of Khālid b. Barmak's non-Arab sentiments—the residual effect, no doubt, of his family background. To put it briefly, al-Manṣūr was anxious to utilize the building materials of the ruined Sassanian palace at nearby al-Madā'in (Ctesiphon).[42] To that effect, he ordered the demolition of the ancient structure, over the objections of Khālid b. Barmak, who argued that, as long as the shell of the building remained in situ, it represented a monument to the great Islamic triumph over the Iranian dynasty and should therefore be preserved. The Caliph thought otherwise and accused his advisor of pro-Iranian sentiments. The venture, however, proved to be uneconomical, as the salvage costs exceeded all expectations. Renowned for his stinginess, al-Manṣūr had no recourse but to order a halt to the undertaking. Once again, this was done over the objections of Khālid b. Barmak. Reversing himself, al-Manṣūr's advisor now argued that terminating the project would be an admission of the Caliph's inability to destroy this vestige of Sassanian rule, an implication that this would reduce the Caliph's stature in the eyes of his subjects. The tradition therefore indicates, contrary to Wendell, that the Barmakid's intentions were not pro-Iranian and anti-Arab, but were in the Caliph's best interests after all.

For Wendell, "The wilful destruction of a predecessor's works was a long-established Eastern custom, with many precedents going back as far as ancient Egypt and Assyria."[43] He then wonders "if al-Manṣūr did not have it in mind to illustrate his dominion by a device which was to be used quite consciously by a descendant of his, [the Caliph] al-Muktafī, in the tenth century." Al-Muktafī is said to have demolished two remaining Sassanian structures at al-Madā'in and utilized the materials salvaged from them in his Tāj Palace at

Baghdad.[44] Having previously dismissed al-Manṣūr as the source of inspiration for the cosmic symbols employed at Baghdad, Wendell is at least willing to grant that al-Manṣūr may have understood the political significance attached to a symbolic transfer of power.

But can it accurately be said that al-Muktafī was consciously attempting to proclaim himself as heir to the kingdoms of the past? According to the geographical dictionary of Yāqūt, the manner in which the ancient architectural members were redeployed at al-Tāj created quite a stir. For, what originally served the Sassanian Khusraw as a battlement was deposited at the base of a new retaining wall, and what had been a foundation deposit was now used to create a battlement.[45] The symbolic meaning of this fact was apparently clear and is reflected in several verses attributed to the poet al-Buḥturī which the geographer appended to his account.[46] Wendell, endorsing the view of M. Streck, understands the report of Yāqūt to mean that the reverse use of the architectural members signified, in a symbolic way, the full disintegration of Sassanian rule. This may indeed be true, but the poet, who died before al-Muktafī came to rule and hence could not have had the dismantling of al-Tāj in mind, seems to be reflecting more generally on the frailty of earthly power in a world turned upside down.

Al-Muktafī and his contemporaries were no doubt struck by the irony of the situation and may have drawn obvious conclusions about the transfer of power, but there is no reason to believe that the transfer of the building materials resulted from a conscious political decision. The nature of the salvage operation can be more easily explained in practical terms. The demolition of a building still intact begins at the highest point of its surviving structures; new construction begins at the foundations. The Caliph could thus have removed the battlements of the Sassanian palaces to begin the walls of al-Tāj[47] while fashioning his own battlements out of brick work obtained from the foundations at al-Madā'in. There is a still more plausible explanation. It is almost certain that after two and one half centuries of neglect, various elements atop the Sassanian wall would have collapsed. For simple reasons of economy it would have been convenient to collect the fallen battlements first and ship them to Baghdad. Only at a later time, after construction was advanced at the new palace, would it have been necessary to demolish the shell of the older building, exposing the foundations and making the material contained therein available for use.

One may recall that al-Manṣūr was interested in reducing expenditures, and scavenging from the dilapidated or ruined buildings of an earlier era was a time-honored procedure for cutting costs. It is not the Caliph, but Khālid b. Barmak, who is described as concerned with the symbolic connotations of Īwān Kisrā. If there is any historicity to this tradition, it is in al-Manṣūr's businesslike approach to the problem of construction. The role of his client-advisor might very well have been a later embellishment suggested by the subsequent history of the Barmakids, when those jealous of their influence impugned them with hints of impiety.

There is, in short, no way of tying the architectural arrangement of the Round City to conceptions of astral symbolism, and even if one were grudgingly to admit the existence of a vague connection with the remote world of the East, it would hardly imply a recognition, let alone an acceptance, of all the cultural baggage from pre-Islamic times. Moreover, if there were a deliberate cultural borrowing, it should be possible to identify the objective, even if not fully articulated. The suggestion has been put forth that al-Manṣūr wished to present himself as the "successor to the great emperors of the past," but, among the subjects whose loyalty he coveted, who was likely to be impressed by representations derived from Iranian cosmology?

In an earlier study of mine dealing with this problem, the rebellious Khurāsānī followers of the murdered Abū Muslim were proposed as the most logical candidates to be influenced by things Iranian. Given the flimsy nature of the evidence, this view was very cautiously advanced, to say the least. In retrospect, the disclaimers appear more convincing than the original contention, for, in the end, I can find no data that suggest "the Caliph was anxious to promote himself as heir to the defunct Sassanian Empire *in order to* claim the allegiance of those subjects who dwelled on its former territories. . . ."[48] What would have been the purpose of such a deliberate pose? As a serious challenge to the Caliph's authority, the power and the attraction of Abū Muslim's dissident following was more apparent than real, and the basis of their grievance remains elusive at best.[49] In any event, such groups from the east were hardly al-Manṣūr's primary concern. The most likely breeding grounds for a challenge to the Caliph's authority were among the 'Alids and within the ruling family itself. There was, in addition, the more remote possibility of a Sufyānid pretender who might raise Messianic expectations among the defeated followers of the Umayyads.

Here, among these political groupings, could be found individuals whose claims al-Manṣūr could understand and fear. They would not propose themselves as heirs to the great Khusraw, but of the Prophet Muḥammad. This right to rule, derived from the earliest Islamic experience, was the only ideological position that the Caliph consciously understood and promoted on his own behalf. Furthermore, it was the only ideological position understood by the potential allies of those who might contest his claims to rule: the tribal armies of Syria, the local populace of Iraq, and, particularly, the imperial army recruited in Khurāsān. Even though these Khurāsānīs were partly assimilated to Iranian ways, their identity was completely rooted in the history of Islam, and their mission could only be comprehended in Islamic terms: to overthrow the Umayyads and restore the faith to its proper position in the lives of the faithful. There were also the obvious self-serving considerations that linked the Arab tribesmen of Khurāsān with the 'Abbāsids, but these were not at all affected by notions of cosmology. The quest for power and material gain had a universal meaning of its own.

This is not to say al-Manṣūr did not appreciate the political significance of monumental architecture or that he was oblivious to such notions as the symbolic transfer of power. There is, however, no reason to search for vague prototypes from a dimly understood past when the examples of recent history will do better. It is reported that, after conquering Ctesiphon, Sa'd b. Abī Waqqāṣ settled at al-Kūfah, modeled his palace after the Īwān Kisrā, and removed the iron gates from that building for his own use.[50] Similarly, when al-Ḥajjāj b. Yūsuf built Wāsiṭ, he brought the gates of his city from nearby al-Zandaward, a town that tradition ascribed to King Solomon.[51] Four of the five iron gates from Wāsiṭ were later transported to Baghdad and set into the main gateways of the Round City. The fifth was positioned in the entrance to al-Manṣūr's palace.[52] In addition, the Caliph erected a gate from Pharaonic times in the (outer) gateway of the Khurāsān complex; and, in the Kūfah Gateway (outer), he erected a gate constructed by (Khālid) al-Qasrī, the former Umayyad governor of Iraq. The gate of the Damascus complex was of local manufacture, but, lacking the legendary credentials of the others, it was considered the weakest of the lot.

In the medieval Near East, the transfer of gates from one city to another may have had a certain practical significance, but it was also a symbolic act expressive of authority. One may recall that Iraq had the reputation of being a turbulent province—one that required a strong administrative hand. As a result, the governors of Iraq, who were ordinarily retained at their positions for extended periods of time, became synonymous with Umayyad rule. This was a trend that continued to the end of the dynasty, when Ibn Hubayrah was chosen to bring order out of the mounting chaos.

Hence, Umayyad Iraq was most often governed by dominant personalities. Of these, none created a greater impression than the legendary al-Ḥajjāj b. Yūsuf.[53] It was al-Ḥajjāj who suppressed the anarchic tendencies of the Arab tribesmen and pacified the area. He improved the lands of the region by digging new canals and repairing the old, and he was granted the great honor of issuing coinage. From the Syrian army camp that he established at Wāsiṭ, he subjugated the rebellious Iraqis of al-Baṣrah and al-Kūfah, thus solidifying the Umayyad hold on the province. Wāsiṭ thereby became the Umayyad capital of Iraq, a preeminence it enjoyed throughout most of the period in question. In fact, its inhabitants continued to resist the ʿAbbāsids even after the fall of the dynasty. The reputations of al-Ḥajjāj and Wāsiṭ were not distant memories, but living symbols of the recent historic past. Any great similarity between the structures of al-Ḥajjāj at Wāsiṭ and those of al-Manṣūr at Baghdad, is, therefore, critical to the questions raised here.

In addition to the transfer of the gates, there is the remarkable likeness between the palace-mosques of the two cities. The significance of this fact was discussed in earlier publications, but it is instructive to examine the data once again.[54] Both buildings are described in the literary sources of the Middle Ages. Quite remarkably, the dimensions of the palace and mosque at Wāsiṭ, as indicated by Yāqūt, coincide with those given by the Khaṭīb for al-Manṣūr's structure within the great central court of the Round City. At both complexes the palace was four hundred cubits square and the adjoining mosque, two hundred cubits. Moreover, it is reported that both palaces were surmounted by a green dome (*qubbah khaḍrāʾ*) of remarkable height that could be seen at a great distance from the city and that served as a characteristic landmark for the surrounding region.[55]

The thought immediately comes to mind that Yāqūt may have confused the two structures, writing as he did four hundred years after the construction of Baghdad; however, archeological evidence from Wāsiṭ, though still incomplete, tends to confirm his data on the dimensions of the buildings.[56] It is almost certain, therefore, that the medieval author is also correct in ascribing to al-Ḥajjāj the large green dome that served as his audience hall. It has been observed that such a cupola was featured at Ruṣāfat al-Shām, the functioning capital of the Umayyads during the reign of Hishām b. ʿAbd al-Malik (A.D. 724-743), and that Muʿāwiyah, the founder of the dynasty, is reported to have given receptions under the *khaḍrāʾ* of his palace in Damascus.[57] The question raised by O. Grabar in his treatment of this material is therefore incisive: "Is there a Syrian Umayyad tradition of such domes, perhaps going back to Muʿāwiyah's *khaḍrāʾ* in Damascus [the official capital of the dynasty], that would have been imitated by al-Ḥajjāj and then subsequently by al-Manṣūr?"[58]

Another art historian has suggested that, even if true, this tradition may represent nothing more than a curiosity, for the green color of the dome was most likely the result of oxidized copper, rather than the product of human design.[59] The circumstantial evidence is, however, overwhelming. In addition to the reported transfer of the gates from Wāsiṭ and the data on the dimensions of the palace-mosques from both cities, there is Ṭabarī's account of the Rāwandīyah disturbance. The event is described as taking place at the Caliph's former palace in al-Hāshimīyah, where several of the rioters ascended the *khaḍrāʾ* and jumped off as if to fly.[60] If the chronicler has not confused the palaces of al-Manṣūr, the Caliph was apparently quite conscious of the symbolic meaning of the green dome, for he twice used this architectural form in a building that served as his residence. Thus, Baghdad might possibly have enjoyed the symbolic trappings of authority that had previously accrued to Wāsiṭ and the official capitals of the Umayyad Caliphs.

In time, al-Manṣūr's cupola came to be regarded as the most prominent architectural symbol of ʿAbbāsid rule. Surmounted by a mechanical device that acquired its own legendary credentials,[61] the entire structure was remembered long after it had fallen into disuse. The Khaṭīb, writing in the eleventh century, recalls: "Indeed that dome was the crown of Baghdad, a guidepost for the region, and one of the memorable things that one associates with the 'Abbāsids."[62] On the night of Tuesday, the seventh of Jumādā II, A.H. 329, the top of the green dome collapsed during a night of torrential rain, awesome thunder, and terrible lightning.[63]

VIII

THE TOPOGRAPHY OF BAGHDAD IN RETROSPECT: THE GOVERNMENT SECTOR AND URBAN DEVELOPMENT

> O Commander of the Faithful, indeed you have erected an edifice such as no one before you; yet it has three shortcomings. . . . The first is the distance of the palace from water, which is necessary for the lips of the populace. As for the second shortcoming, indeed the eye is green and yearns for green foliage, yet there is no garden in this palace of yours. Now, as for the third shortcoming, your subjects are with you at your palace, and when subjects are with the ruler in his palace, his secrets are disclosed. . . . The Caliph then understood what had to be done; he sent for Shamīs and Khallād . . . and said, "Dig two canals leading from the Tigris, landscape al-'Abbāsīyah, and transfer the populace to al-Karkh."
>
> Khaṭīb (Cairo), 1: 78-79

A. The Palace Complex: Plan and Function

It is universally accepted that the specific location of the Round City was dictated by both economic and defensive considerations. To the east, the Caliph was protected by the Tigris, a wide, winding river that could not be forded. As a result, throughout the history of Baghdad, movement across the ancient carrier of international trade was generally funneled through a series of pontoon bridges (*jisr*).[1] These structures rose with flooding, were easily repaired, and could be relocated at more desirable crossing points when necessary; but above all, the pontoon bridge could be easily cut from its moorings, thus safeguarding the Caliph from a flanking action. Similarly, the intricate system of canals situated directly south of the Round City served a double purpose. On the one hand, they functioned as conduits for material and supplies being shipped along the Euphrates route via the Ṣarāt and 'Īsā Canals, thereby explaining the commercial importance of al-Karkh, the southern suburb; on the other, they provided a natural barrier against an attacking army, so that an adversary marching on the city would be forced to canalize his troops in a predictable line of attack. Finally, the western and northern approaches were shielded by Khandaq Ṭāhir, a man-made waterway, which bifurcated from the ʿĪsā west of the Round City and emptied into the Tigris to the north of it. This arm of the ʿĪsā Canal also framed the military cantonments of the northern suburbs, thus affording the Caliph a double line of protection against any incursions from that direction. These considerations are reported with some variation in a number of medieval Arabic sources—among them, Yaʿqūbī, who credits al-Manṣūr with describing Madīnat al-Salām as "this island between the Tigris to the east and the [canals extending from the] Euphrates to the west."[2]

Had the enemy broken through the difficult barriers at the perimeter, there would still have remained the Round City with its impressive outer fortifications: a moat sixty feet wide and two protective walls. The second of these walls was a massive formation with numerous and elaborate defensive arrangements.[3] The original round structure, delicately balanced in the center of the geographical setting, was not a city in the conventional sense. Like the earlier ʿAbbāsid capitals, it was an enormous palace complex, which, in this case, combined the administrative agencies of the government with the residence of the Caliph. This design reflected a desire to provide adequate security for the household of the sovereign and the machinery of his rule. To this end, al-Manṣūr confined the markets to the southern suburb of al-Karkh and established large and accessible military cantonments in the suburban districts north of the Ṣarāt. Within the walls, the Caliph excluded all commercial and industrial establishments and limited access to the residential as well as administrative areas.

As a result, two zones of security were established within the Round City. The first consisted of the residential quadrants housing the government functionaries. This formed the outer ring of the city, and was comprised of a living area of four segments framed by two encircling *intervalla* (*faṣīl*) and the large arcades (*ṭāqāt al-kubrā*) of the gate complexes.[4] Entrance to the outer ring was obtained by crossing the wide moat (*khandaq*) surrounding the outer wall and then passing through an elaborate series of gateways and courts before

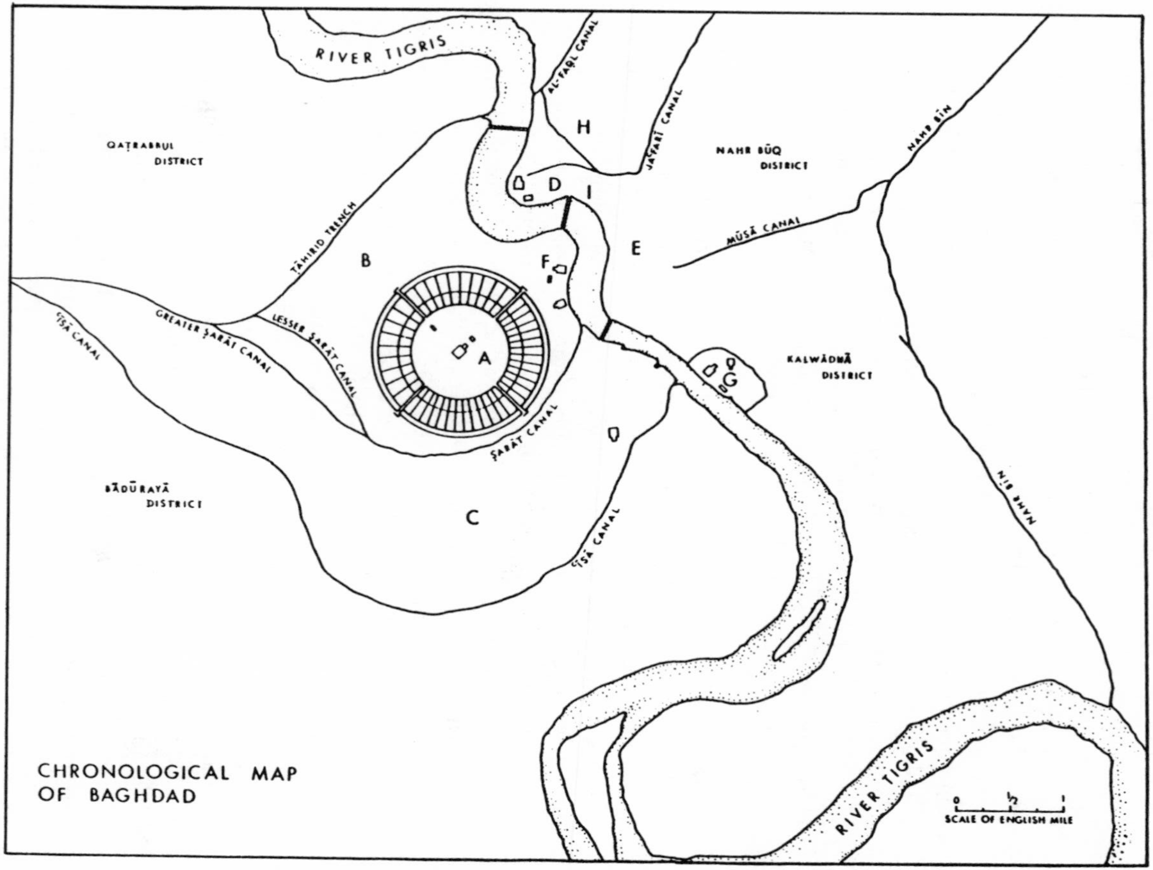

CHRONOLOGICAL MAP
OF BAGHDAD

LEGEND

A. The Round City, also known as Madīnat al-Manṣūr. The first palace complex of the ʿAbbāsid Capital, it contained the palace-mosque of the Caliph, the administrative agencies of the government, and the residences of various public officials. Construction began in A.H. 145 and was completed in A.H. 149.

B. Al-Ḥarbīyah. A suburban area north of the Round City, it contained the military cantonments of the Khurāsānī army stationed at Baghdad. Its development was concurrent with the construction of the Round City, with its major growth in A.H. 151 and 157.

C. Al-Karkh. The great market suburb of the greater urban area, it was occupied in Pre-Islamic times, with large-scale development concurrent with the construction of the Round City. It was redeveloped in the suburban expansion of A.H. 157.

D. Al-Ruṣāfah. The Palace complex of the Caliph al-Mahdī, it contained his residence and a second principal mosque. Construction began in A.H. 151 and was completed in A.H. 159.

E. Al-Mukharrim. A residential district, it was possibly occupied as early as A.H. 151, with significant development after A.H. 159.

F. Al-Khuld. Al-Manṣūr's second residential palace, it was built in A.H. 157 and later occupied by Hārūn al-Rashīd and Muḥammad al-Amīn.

G. Dār al-Khilāfah. The third palace complex, it was built by the ʿAbbāsid Caliphs in stages, subsequent to their return from Sāmarrā in A.H. 279.

H. Al-Shammāsīyah. Originally a staging ground for military reviews and a camping ground, it was developed as a palace area by the Būyid amīrs in the tenth century.

I. Bāb al-Ṭāq. Contained the commercial section serving al-Ruṣāfah and the upper reaches of al-Mukharrim. The general area probably underwent some development as early as A.H. 151 with great expansion after A.H. 159.

reaching the exits of the second *intervallum*.[5] This winding boulevard, which was situated directly behind the inner wall of the city, gave access to the portals of the forty-five streets of the residential quadrants. A third *intervallum* was entered by passing through a similar exit beyond the large arcades and gave access to a second series of portals situated at the opposite end of the quadrants. The critical feature of this arrangement was that movement in and out of the residential area was possible only by passing through fortified gateways leading to the exits of the *intervalla*, thereby allowing the Caliph to carefully regulate the traffic flowing to and from the outer ring.

The second zone, which reflected a desire for even greater security, consisted of three elements: the actual gate complexes, an inner ring framed by the small arcades (*ṭāqāt al-ṣughrā*), and the great circular plaza (*raḥbah*), which formed the core of the structure.[6] Situated within this great inner court was the residence of the Caliph (Qaṣr al-Dhahab) and the adjoining principal mosque, as well as two other buildings. One of these, adjacent to the Damascus Gate, housed the chief of military security forces (*ḥaras*) and his troops; the other, the location of which is not indicated, contained the quarters of the chief of the security police (*shurṭah*) and presumably rooms for some of his men, thereby providing maximum safety for the area of the Caliph's personal domain.[7] These structures, the only buildings other than the palace-mosque in the plaza, were probably intended for those men actually on duty in the central courtyard. The remainder of the contingent was no doubt quartered in those streets situated in the residential quandrants flanking the arcades of the Baṣrah Gate and designated for the security forces of the military and police.[8]

Surrounding the inner court (*ḥawla al-raḥbah ḳamā tadūrū*) were the residences of al-Manṣūr's younger children,[9] his servants in attendance, his slaves, and, in addition, the public treasury, the arsenal (*ḳhizānat al-silāḥ*), the bureau of palace personnel (*dīwān al-aḥshām*), the public kitchen, and various other government agencies.[10] These buildings were contained within four quadrants framed by the small arcades, thus forming a second inner ring within the Round City. This area was also designated for maximum security, and one can assume that the various forces attached to the central plaza bore responsibility for the inner ring as well.

Various safeguards were built into the architectural conception. The buildings of the inner ring were accessible only through entrances facing upon the great central plaza, so that individuals or groups negotiating government business were compelled to pass through a series of well-guarded structures running the length of the gate complexes. The massive iron gates of the outer fortifications were specifically installed to seal off the complexes in time of emergency.[11] Similarly, each of the covered arcade systems was provided with flanking rooms that originally served 1,000 men and a handpicked commander.[12] Because the lengthy arteries that led from the massive protective wall to the inner court were not directly accessible from the residential quadrants, all the approaches to the Caliph's residence and the agencies of government could be hermetically sealed at various strategic checkpoints.

It should be noted that neither the inner ring nor the type of small arcades that flanked it are found in the reconstructions of the Round City provided by modern architectural historians.[13] They assume that the agencies of government were located on the streets of a single set of quadrants and that the round structure built by al-Manṣūr was in effect an integrated city containing a diverse population and a full range of urban institutions. Thus, the Round City is thought to have included a full complement of merchants and craftsmen, as well as their commercial establishments. The descriptions preserved by various chroniclers of suburban development toward the end of al-Manṣūr's reign are seen by them as evidence that the Round City was bursting with an excess population from all walks of life. This view is quite misleading, as detailed arguments have shown. It is sufficient to recall here that the palace complex functioned as a center of imperial administration, and not as a fully developed city.[14]

From the moment a visitor entered the gate complex, he was aware that this was the personal domain of the sovereign. The gates, arcades, and the inner ring that housed the machinery of government and elements of the Caliph's household, comprised, along with al-Manṣūr's palace and mosque, a single unit. According to the original architectural plan, the gate complexes were extensions of the Caliph's residence, though his actual living quarters were in the great Gold Palace (*Qaṣr al-Dhahab*) in the central plaza. It is clear, then, why various ceremonial functionaries were permanently attached to each of the gate complexes,[15] and although the troops assigned duty in the

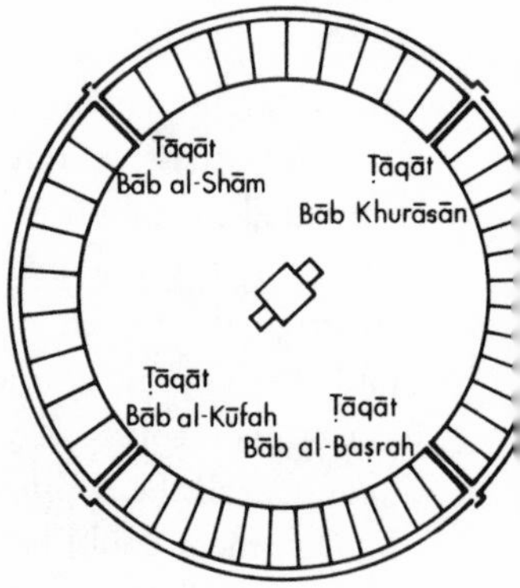

Figure 1. The Round City
(After Herzfeld and Creswell)

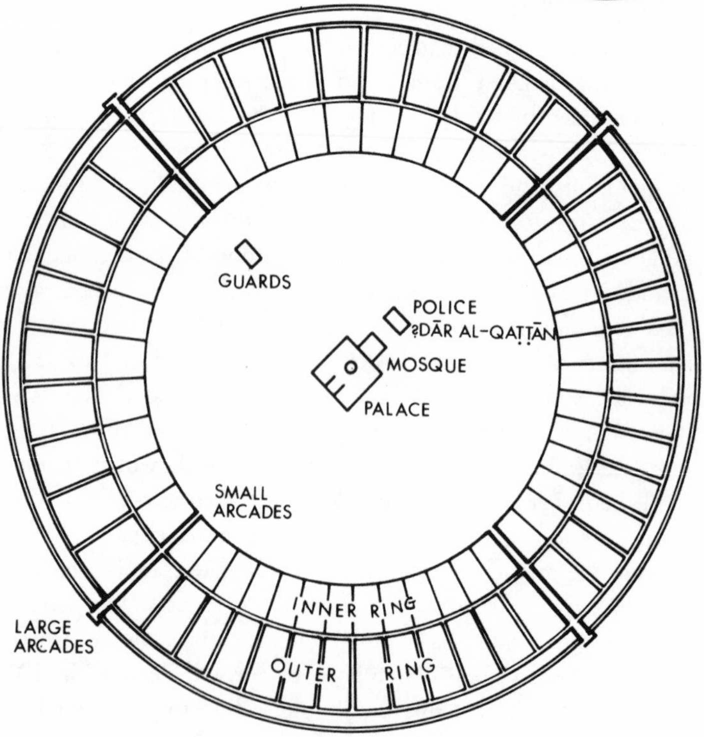

Figure 2. The Round City

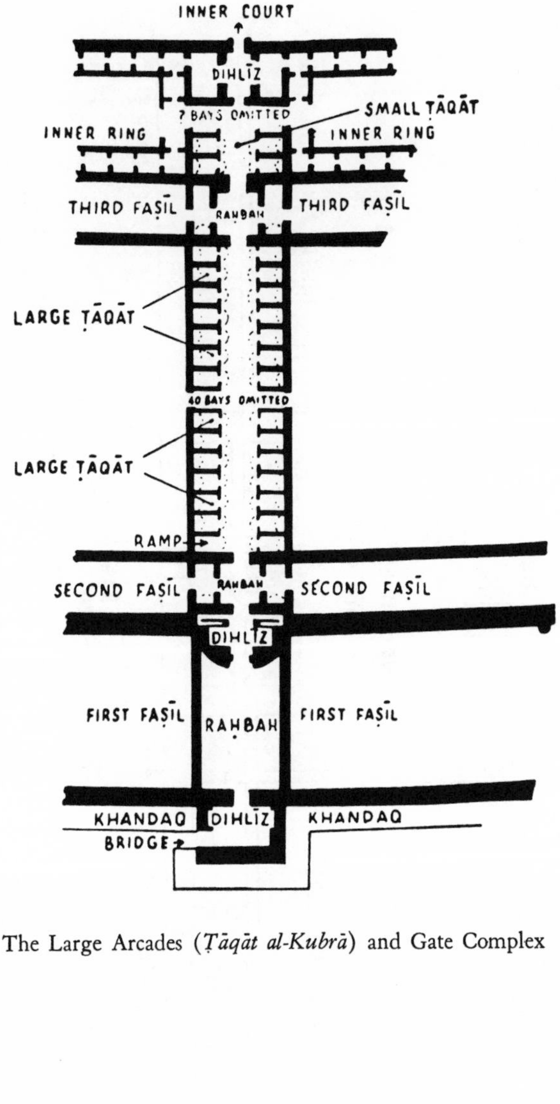

Figure 3. The Large Arcades (*Ṭāqāt al-Kubrā*) and Gate Complex

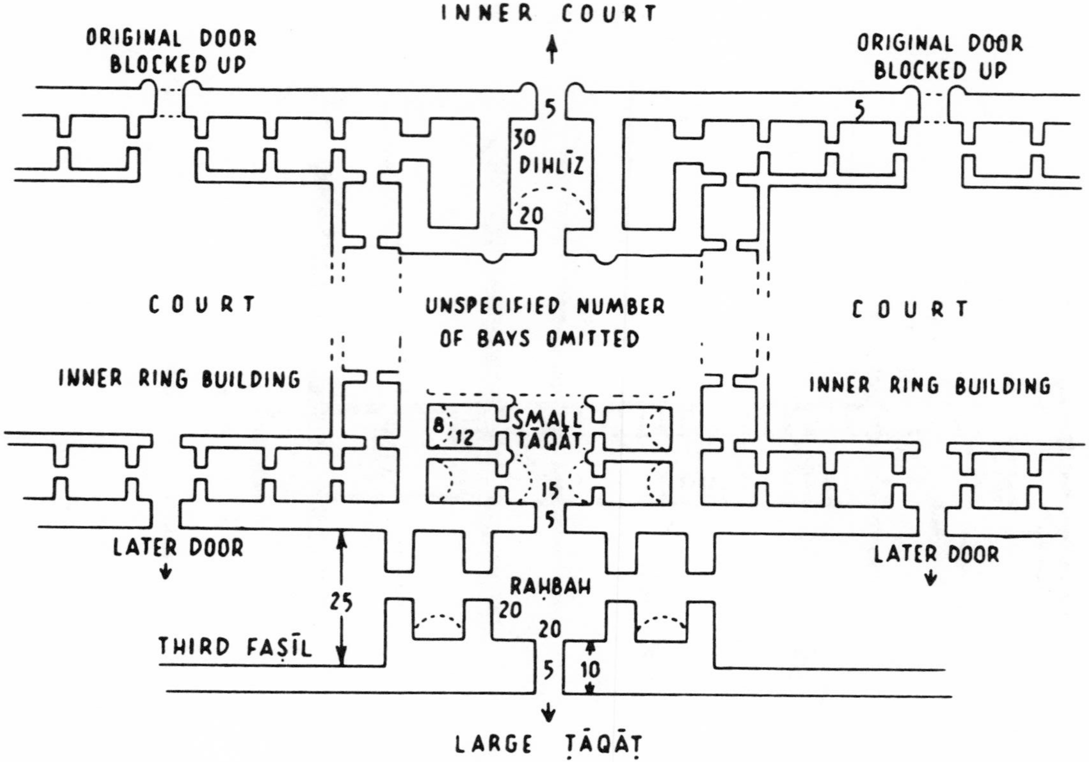

Figure 4. The Small Arcades (*Ṭāqāt al-Ṣughrā*) and Government Agencies

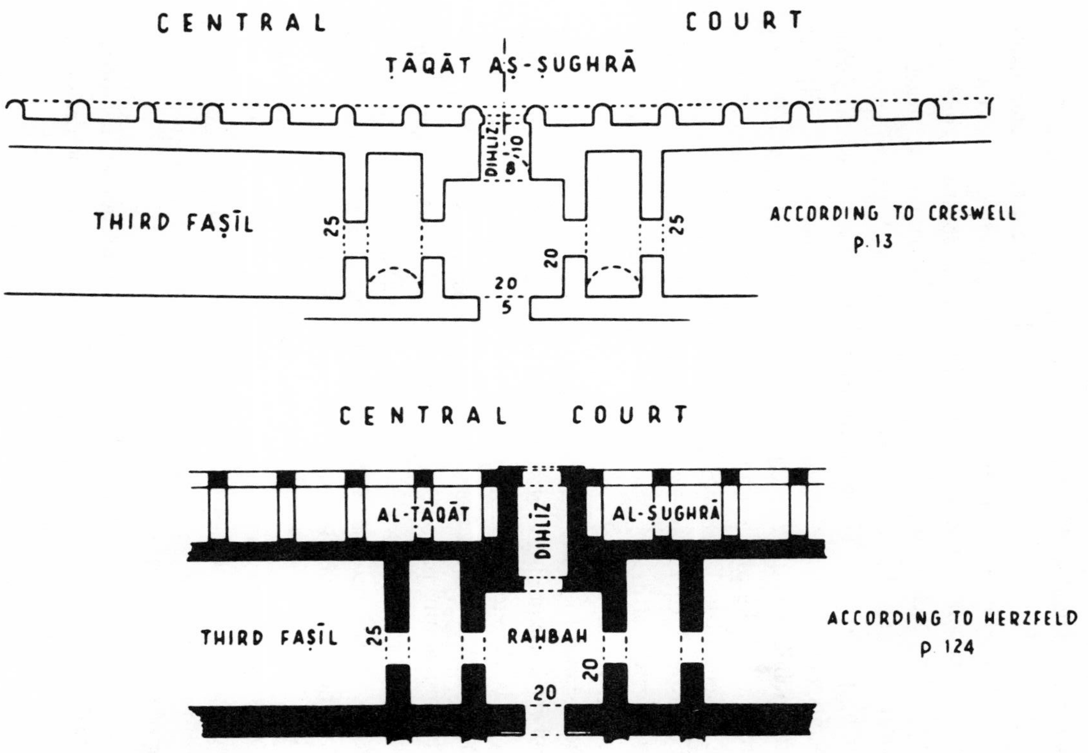

Figure 5. The Small Arcades (according to Herzfeld and Creswell)

arcades acted primarily as a security force, they were presumably called upon, when required, to serve in ceremonial reviews as well. However, the most compelling evidence that the Caliph's palace extended to the outer fortification walls was, no doubt, the existence of a Caliphal audience hall (*majlis*) surmounting each of the city's outer gates. These rooms, covered with magnificent domes, were modeled after the legendary cupola that crowned the Qaṣr al-Dhahab in the great inner court.[16] The architectural and symbolic function of these structures is clear: to enter the gateway of the protective wall was to enter the Caliph's palace itself. The residential quadrants that housed the public servants were a separate segment of the city, but they were hardly part of the public domain. For only those who served al-Manṣūr directly were granted the privilege of permanent residence within the walls, and fewer still had access to him at his residence.

The Round City was a tremendously ambitious project, but the very enormity of its scope compromised the delicately balanced factors of security and supply. An administrative center must function at some distance from the general populace, which is a potential source of subversion, but always close enough to be provided with basic services. It is therefore understandable that al-Manṣūr's city was built adjacent to, but distinct from, the market areas of al-Karkh. The great population of the palace complex created a demand for goods and services that required extensive reliance on outside markets and craftsmen; however, the distances, as well as the security arrangements within the palace complex, made the supply process unwieldy. Accepting the statistics attributed to Rabāḥ, the architect of the city walls, one obtains a surface area of approximately 450 hectares.[17] With the exception of Ctesiphon (540 hectares), the palace complex alone was larger than any known urban center in upper Iraq since the beginning of recorded history.[18]

It is reasonable to assume that the first compromises regarding security procedures within the Round City were pragmatic decisions, and not the result of official action. The central court, which contained the Caliph's quarters and the entrances to the government buildings of the inner ring, was unquestionably subjected to the most stringent security precautions, and yet it became necessary to allow pack animals carrying water (and perhaps other sorts of commercial traffic) to enter the area. The historian Ṭabarī cites an account[19] in which a fatigued ʻĪsā b. ʻAlī complained about having to walk (the great distance) from the gate of the court (*bāb al-raḥbah*)[20] to the palace. When al-Manṣūr suggested that his uncle might wish to make the trip in a litter, ʻĪsā b. ʻAlī refused for fear of being embarrassed and suggested instead that he hitch a ride on one of the pack animals. Although the Caliph was stunned to discover that pack animals or riders might be entering his personal domain, he clearly understood the circumstances that gave rise to this breach of security. The architectural arrangement so brilliantly designed to protect the ʻAbbāsid sovereign and his government simply did not allow for normal daily functions within the residential and working areas of the city.

As a result, the Caliph yielded and gave orders for the people (in the inner ring) to shift the portals (that opened onto the great plaza), so that they now faced the *intervalla* of the (small) arcades.[21] No one was permitted to enter the inner court except on foot. Markets were then transferred to each of the four (large) arcades (previously occupied by the guards),[22] where they remained until the danger posed by their proximity to the Caliph was allegedly brought to his attention by a visiting Byzantine ambassador. Al-Manṣūr then removed them from the Round City.[23]

These changes redefined the function of the palace complex. When the Caliph shifted the portals of the inner ring so that they opened onto the third *intervallum*, he connected the administrative agencies that were formerly in the maximum zone of security with the residential streets of the quadrants, a somewhat less sensitive area.[24] The Caliph's personal domain was thus limited to the small arcades, which presumably remained guarded, and the structures actually situated in the great central court: his residence, the mosque, and the security buildings. This area, as before, was accessible only by passing through stringent security checks within the small arcades. The rest of the palace complex was, however, more or less open. It was now possible to move various markets and shops into the rooms flanking the large arcades, for the gate complex was no longer an integral element of the palace precinct and therefore did not require the presence of the guard. The new markets made it possible for the residents of the Round City to receive their provisions and other items without leaving the walled area.

This does not imply, however, that the economic hub of greater

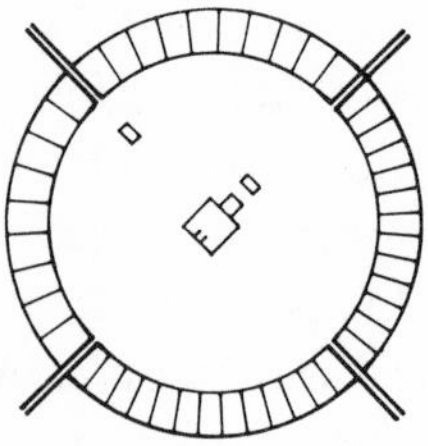

Figure 6. The Caliph's Personal Domain, Stage One

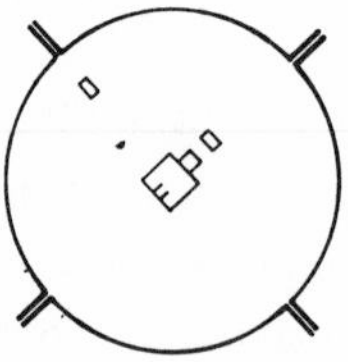

Figure 7. The Caliph's Personal Domain, Stage Two

Baghdad was relocated within the walls of the Round City, or that merchants and artisans now joined the government functionaries in occupying the residential quadrants. The space made available by the architectural arrangement of the palace complex was much too limited for that.[25] Moreover, it was, at this time, the Caliph's intention to adjust his original concept, not abandon it altogether. The key commercial center of the area remained, as it had since pre-Islamic times, in the suburb of al-Karkh, where the intricate system of canals provided superb arrangements for market facilities. The potentially hostile general populace therefore continued to reside at some distance from its ruler. When the Caliph later decided to redevelop the suburbs and, for security reasons, to remove the recently installed markets from the large arcades, he understandably chose to relocate them in the general area of al-Karkh.[26]

In the end the Caliph's compromise proved unmanageable. Even the original arrangement had had its limitations, for if one discounts as legend the secret passage that extended some eight miles beyond the city,[27] once the outer walls were breached, the Caliph was trapped in an architectural cul-de-sac. As difficult as it was to reach him, it was equally difficult for him to reach safety should the need arise. Moreover, the position of the principal mosque adjoining his palace meant that the very heart of the Caliph's personal domain was inundated by a populace from beyond the walls every Friday during the time of prayers. The weakening of security along the gate complex, subsequent to the introduction of the markets, only served to intensify the danger. Ultimately the Caliph was forced to abandon the new scheme in favor of a much more dramatic change, in which he first removed the markets and then forsook the Round City altogether.

B. Leaving the Round City

The circumstances leading to the departure from the Round City are described in several traditions. The setting is usually an audience that the Caliph has granted to a visiting Byzantine Patrikios. In each instance, the guest is either requested to give, or voluntarily gives, an assessment of the palace complex. His comments prove shocking to the proud Caliph, for the structure that al-Manṣūr considered the quintessence of architectural planning and execution is found to have serious shortcomings.

The Khaṭīb[28] reports that the royal audience was interrupted by a series of sudden shrieks. It appears that a cow, which was about to be slaughtered, broke free from the butcher and was running about the markets (in the arcades) amid considerable tumult. When informed of the facts, the visiting dignitary offered the Caliph some gratuitous advice. "O, Commander of the Faithful, indeed you have erected an edifice such as no one before you; yet it has three shortcomings." At the Caliph's request he listed them as: the lack of an internal water supply, the lack of garden areas, and more serious yet, "Your subjects [that is, the market people] are with you at your palace and when subjects are with the ruler in his palace, his secrets are disclosed."

Given his temperament and character, the Commander of the Faithful was not about to accept such comments graciously, and from a Greek. He replied stiffly, "As for your statement concerning water, we have calculated the amount necessary to moisten our lips; with regard to the second shortcoming, we were not created for frivolity and play; and, as to your remarks concerning my secrets, I hold no secrets from my subjects [as if to imply that security was a problem restricted to rulers like the Byzantine Emperor]." Nevertheless, in a private moment, the Caliph was able to digest the import of the Patrikios' remarks. "He sent for Shamīs and Khallād, the grandfather of Abū al-'Aynā', and said: Extend two water channels leading to me [that is, to my palace] from the Dujayl, which is a tributary of the Tigris, and another from the Karkhāyā, which is a tributary of the Euphrates."

In its present form, this tradition, like the other variants, shows evidence of literary embellishment; it does not accurately recall the specific details of a particular ambassadorial visit. An analysis of the text suggests that its basic design was to explain the widespread expansion in the suburban areas that was concurrent with the transfer of the markets from the arcades and the Caliph's subsequent move from the Round City.

As to the ambassador's first criticism, the lack of a direct water supply, it is curious that the description of his visit is directly preceded by a variant of the aforementioned tradition found in Ṭabarī, in which the Caliph's paternal uncle seeks entry to the city by way of a pack animal carrying water.[29] In the account of the Khaṭīb, the Caliph reacts by ordering that a teakwood conduit be extended from the Khurāsān Gate.[30] The author thus suggests—no doubt intentionally—a link between the original arrangement of the Round City and the Patrikios' later observations of its shortcomings. There is, however, an apparent inconsistency here; for if the provision for a direct water supply was a consequence of 'Īsā b. 'Alī's public disclosure and preceded the establishment of markets in the Round City, how could the Byzantine miss the water channel in his subsequent appraisal of the palace complex? And if the ambassador was simply in error, why did the Caliph feel constrained to act upon his criticism?

Despite the Patrikios' remarks, the weight of the evidence would seem to indicate that the palace complex was provided from the outset with a direct supply of water. The trench (*khandaq*) that surrounded the outer walls would have required some sort of feeder channel, from either the Tigris or the major canals nearby. Under the circumstances, it would have been a rather simple arrangement to extend a conduit into the palace complex itself. That the trench was in fact a water barrier can be ascertained from the design of the structure and the nature of the materials utilized. Ya'qūbī reports[31] that the base of the city wall (fronting the trench) was lined with a quay (*musannāh*) of burnt brick (*ājurr*) cemented with quicklime (*ṣārūj*).[32] Although burnt bricks were more porous then than now, their strength improved considerably when combined with quicklime. They were therefore frequently used in foundations, at the bases of retaining walls, wherever good insulation was necessary, and in tunnel vaults and domes.[33] The conduits that al-Manṣūr had built to bring drinking water from the Dujayl and the Karkhāyā were reportedly vaulted structures composed of these materials.[34] Finally, Ya'qūbī is quite explicit in indicating that the area of the palace complex received water even as construction was begun, for he reports that conduits leading from the Karkhāyā entered the city to provide for the personal needs of the laborers and for the construction of bricks and clay cement.[35]

On every level of accountability, Ya'qūbī's report seems the more authentic of the two, yet, the account of the Khaṭīb is rooted in a concrete set of circumstances. One may argue that the tradition introduced by the latter is not so much a reflection of the Caliph's needs within the Round City, as an explanation of the numerous hydraulic engineering projects undertaken at the time al-Manṣūr decided to develop the suburban districts. The historian of Baghdad makes it quite clear that the two new conduits built by the Caliph were intended for the entire urban area and not just the palace complex. "Both entered the city [that is, Madīnat al-Salām] and passed through the streets [*shāri'*], side streets [*darb*], and suburbs [*rabaḍ*], flowing without interruption in summer or winter."[36] In addition, he notes that al-Manṣūr expanded the already extensive system of water routes in al-Karkh by digging several new canals, including Nahr al-Dajāj, Nahr al-Qallā'īn, Nahr Ṭābaq, Nahr al-Bazzāzīn, and an unnamed canal in the Anbārite Mosque Quarter.[37] The reason for this intensive activity was presumably the unprecedented expansion of the urban area in its first decade of growth.

A similar assessment can be made with regard to the ambassador's second observation. Although the Patrikios' next criticism, the lack of a green belt, is perhaps compelling on aesthetic grounds, there is no reason to believe that such remarks would have had any visible effect upon the Caliph. Al-Manṣūr was, by nature, an austere man, and this component of his character was celebrated in history and in legend. The disdain for frivolity that is the essence of his reply could have been suggested by any one of numerous accounts and is perfectly consistent with the reader's expectations. What is puzzling about this segment of the tradition is al-Manṣūr's later command to develop al-'Abbāsiyah in response to the second uncharitable statement concerning the palace complex. For al-'Abbāsiyah was not situated within the walls of the Round City, but was a nearby island formed between the Lesser and Greater Ṣarāt.[38] Moreover, the circumstances by which al-'Abbāsiyah came to be cultivated are detailed in an extremely important entry that will be treated later.[39] Suffice it to say, there were no considerations of aesthetics or leisure. The development of the island was an ambitious commercial venture that reflected opportunities for capital investment at a time of widespread expansion in the suburban districts.

Even the incident of the escaped cow, which gave rise to the entire sequence of events, may have been suggested by developments beyond the city walls. Another account preserved by the Khaṭīb[40] describes the organization of a market area that was developed during the expansion of the suburbs. The new commercial zone was designed to supplement or replace some of the existing facilities in al-Karkh. Of all the craftsmen and merchants, only the butchers are singled out by name and notoriety. It is reported that al-Manṣūr called for a wide garment and traced the plan of the markets on it, arranging each type of establishment in its proper place. The butchers were positioned at the outer extremity because they reportedly bore the frightening combination of dull wits and sharp knives.

There is nonetheless an obvious element of truth to the story of the runaway animal. The episode of the cow is clearly intended to describe the problem of security within the walls of the palace complex, a theme forcefully argued, not only in this account, but also in another variant describing the Patrikios' visit. The second text is that of Ṭabarī.[41] It begins with the familiar account of al-Manṣūr's uncle attempting to ride one of the pack animals entering the great plaza and the Caliph's reaction, which was to redefine the architectural arrangement of his personal domain by introducing markets into various arcades formerly staffed by security forces. The chronicler then goes on to indicate that the new arrangement remained in effect until the visit of an ambassador from the court of the Byzantines.

As a matter of course, the visiting dignitary was escorted by al-Rabīʿ b. Yūnus, the Caliph's wazīr, on a tour of the Round City and its environs. The Patrikios had an excellent opportunity to survey the entire structure in detail, for he ascended (the walkway along) the great protective wall that encircled the city and also reached the domed audience rooms that looked out upon the palace complex and the surrounding environment. Upon returning, he was asked by al-Manṣūr to give an assessment of what he had seen. The ambassador diplomatically replied, "a superior structure [*binā' ḥasan*];" but he then added the caveat, "However, I saw that your enemies are with you in your palace."[42] When the Caliph inquired who they might be, he answered, "the market people [*al-sūqah*]." Al-Manṣūr controlled himself, but when the Byzantine departed, he ordered the markets removed from the Round City. He then summoned Ibrāhīm b. Ḥubaysh al-Kūfī and Jawwās b. al-Musayyab al-Yamanī and entrusted them with the construction of a new market complex in the vicinity of al-Karkh. They arranged for rows (*ṣufūf*) of shops and houses according to each type of establishment (*ṣanf*).[43]

A slight variation regarding the danger of markets in the arcades is seen in the next account. The author reports that al-Manṣūr transferred the markets from the Round City to al-Karkh because it was called to his attention that strangers and other suspicious people (*ghurabā' wa ghayrahum*) were spending the night there.[44] One could not be assured that there were not spies among them, or that the nearby security gates would not be opened while the city slept. Al-Manṣūr then removed the markets (from the arcades) and replaced them with the (original) security forces, the *shurṭah* and the *ḥaras*.

The tradition of the visiting Byzantine Patrikios may or may not be factual, but there is still further reason to believe that the Caliph was disturbed by the presence of a potentially troublesome element in the arcades of the Round City. Both Ṭabarī and the Khaṭīb preserve yet another explanation for the transfer of the city markets.[45] It is reported that, in the year A.H. 157, Abū Zakariyā' Yaḥyā b. 'Abdallāh, the supervisor of the city markets and defender of public morality, was in collusion with Shī'ite followers of the martyred rebels, Muḥammad and Ibrāhīm b. 'Abdallāh.[46] The result seems to have been a relatively minor affair, in which Abū Zakariyā' induced the rabble (*suflah*) to cause a disturbance, the implication being that he used his sensitive position to carry on subversive activities against the state. The Caliph sent his personal emissary, Abū al-'Abbās al-Ṭūsī, who succeeded in quieting matters. The abortive insurrection ended when the seditious *muḥtasib* was executed and his body hung, for all to see, on the palace gate in the great central plaza. The presumption was that the general populace, in attending Friday prayers, would be witness to this public demonstration of the Caliph's authority and would note his swift and efficient method of dispensing justice. Al-Manṣūr then transferred the city markets to the expanded suburb of al-Karkh.

Concurrent with this new development, the Caliph also established a second principal mosque for the inhabitants of the suburb.[47] The existence of a second building not only would have relieved the congestion at the mosque of the central plaza, but, by making it unnecessary for the people of the markets to enter the walled city for their prayers, would also have further tightened the security of the Caliph's domain. In later times, al-Karkh, which was heavily populated by Shī'ites, was the scene of frequent religious disturbances.[48] The historian al-Wāqidī (d. A.H. 207), a Shī'ite of modest persuasion, is credited with having said that al-Karkh was infested with the lowest rabble, to which the Khaṭīb added by way of clarification: al-Wāqidī meant by this statement certain sections . . . inhabited only by the Rāfiḍites (that is, Shī'ites).[49]

The building of the new mosque, the transfer of the arcade markets to redevelop districts outside the walled city, and the return of security forces to the flanking rooms, seem to have served two purposes: they relieved the increasing pressures of urban growth while providing for increased security in the palace complex housing the machinery of the state. Although the Caliph now returned to what was basically the original concept of the palace precinct, he was still faced with the insurmountable problem of supplying the Round City. At the request of Abān b. Ṣadaqah, al-Manṣūr relented slightly and allowed a greengrocer to be posted in each of the four quadrants;[50] however, shortly thereafter, the Caliph felt constrained to abandon the Round City altogether, and he then moved to the newly built residence of al-Khuld, situated along the Tigris shore above the Khurāsān Gate.[51]

C. The Subsequent Compromise: Widening the Administrative Center

The Caliph's decision to leave the Round City greatly changed the existing concept of the administrative center. Whereas the functioning government had been confined essentially within the walls of the original palace complex, it now extended to a wide tract of land on both sides of the Tigris and included, in addition to the Round City, numerous official residences, the military cantonments of the northern suburbs, and an entirely new palace complex across the river. Together, these areas represented the government sector, as distinct from those areas of the city occupied by the general populace. There is reason to believe the location of the Khuld Palace was deliberately chosen with this topographical pattern in mind.

The Caliph's new residence, one of several 'Abbāsid family estates located in the area, was strategically linked with construction that had been underway for some time on the east bank of the Tigris in the section that came to be called al-Ruṣāfah.[52] When the Caliph's son and heir apparent Muḥammad al-Mahdī triumphantly returned from Khurāsān in A.H. 151, al-Manṣūr began to build him a palace complex across the river directly opposite the future location of al-Khuld.[53] As it happens, this was a departure from the original plans, which apparently called for al-Mahdī's residence to be situated at a place called al-Sharqīyah. It would seem that there was some confusion about these two residences, for Yāqūt feels compelled to point out that al-Sharqīyah (meaning "eastern") does not signify a place on the left bank, but a location to the east (actually southeast) of the Round City.[54] A more precise fix would place it somewhere in the general vicinity of al-Karkh, where the suburb was bounded by the Ṣarāt Canal as it flowed past the Baṣrah Gate toward the Tigris.[55] Moving eastward from al-Sharqīyah, one reportedly came upon the fief of Ja'far b. al-Manṣūr, which formed the southern flank of the 'Abbāsid family estates along the river.[56]

One could perhaps assume that al-Mahdī's West Side palace was intended to be part of this series of residences, and possibly the original linchpin. Yāqūt (d. A.D. 1225), who wrote at a later period, described al-Sharqīyah as a neighborhood (*maḥallah*),[57] but the early texts refer to it as a *madīnah*, which, in this case, most likely implies some sort of administrative center. This is only a supposition; however, it may be noted that, when the Caliph transferred the markets from the Round City in order to strengthen security within the palace complex, he initiated a similar policy with regard to al-Sharqīyah.[58] No specific reason is given for the decision to abandon this site in favor of a new location on the East Side, but, if it was intended that al-Sharqīyah function as a second administrative center, its proximity to the market populace of al-Karkh may have been regarded as a serious shortcoming. With al-Mahdī's new residence nearing completion, provisions for security no doubt deteriorated. The original estate of the heir apparent ultimately became part of the public domain, as the principal mosque serving the populace of al-Karkh came to be situated there, along with the presiding judicial authority (*qāḍī*) of the area.[59]

In any event, the site of al-Khuld was most likely chosen with all these topographical developments in mind. The caliphal palace was not simply a new residence, but part of a delicate compromise by which the Caliph hoped to retain some of the outward features of the old palace complex, though he himself was now formally detached from the government agencies. There was surely no attempt here to duplicate the facilities of the Round City. The original palace complex therefore continued to function as a place of government administration with security precautions similar to those of the past. Indeed, one could argue that, in certain respects, security was even tighter than before, because the market people no longer required access to the principal mosque, which lay contiguous to the Caliph's original palace. Although there is no indication that al-Manṣūr's new residence was protected by massive and complex fortifications, the position of al-Khuld in relation to the development on the East Side nevertheless allowed for an ingenious defensive arrangement.

The palace construction at al-Ruṣāfah, which took eight years to complete, was an undertaking of enormous magnitude. It was surrounded by a protective wall and moat, and perhaps contained a military review ground in addition to various garden areas. As was true in the Round City, the palace was situated adjoining a principal mosque that Yāqūt reports was even larger and more splendid than that of al-Manṣūr. Unfortunately, there is no information about al-

Ruṣāfah that is comparable to the descriptions of the Round City. It is, however, evident that the entire complex covered a considerable area, and was somewhat similar in function to the original administrative center across the Tigris.[60]

An integral element of the expanded administrative center was the military settlement north of the Ṣarāt, where the main contingents of the imperial army resided in specifically designated cantonments. It is significant that similar facilities could be found across the river as well. Various authorities report that al-Ruṣāfah was originally called 'Askar (the military encampment of) al-Mahdī, and was so named because the Caliph-to-be camped (*'askara*) there while journeying to al-Rayy.[61] More persuasive, however, is the explanation of Ṭabarī, who indicates that, at the suggestion of Qutham b. al-'Abbās, the Caliph divided his troops according to regional and tribal groupings. One detachment then encamped on the East Side; the other remained where it had been, so that the Caliph could now play one faction against the other. Should an insurrection break out on the left side of the river, the Caliph would still have access to military support and provisions on the opposite shore; the reverse would of course be true for the right bank. Al-Mahdī then took charge of the eastern area, settling in the palace that was built expressly for him.[62]

An analysis of this enigmatic and very important tradition will be undertaken shortly. It is sufficient to point out here that the later construction of al-Khuld is directly related to these developments. The new caliphal residence on the West Side bisected the entire northern section of the city and was therefore strategically situated directly between the two major areas of military settlement. The eastern extremities of the Caliph's estate gave access to the bridges leading to al-Ruṣāfah; the western limits gave access to the military cantonments, the royal stables, and the administrative agencies of the Round City. Although al-Manṣūr no longer enjoyed the security of an elaborate protective wall, he was still situated near the pulse of government, at some distance from the general populace, and he had large and accessible security forces nearby in al-Ḥarbīyah and across the river. The Caliph's new residence may have been more vulnerable to frontal assault, but it afforded him better protection against the more subtle danger of a possible coup. In any event, he still had access to the walled fortress of the Round City and to al-Mahdī's palace at al-Ruṣāfah.

When al-Manṣūr moved from the original palace complex closer to the Tigris shore, he connected the lower East Side with al-Karkh (Bāb al-Shaʻīr) by spanning the river with a pontoon bridge that subsequently became a major artery of traffic.[63] The Khaṭīb indicates that the Caliph had also ordered the erection of three additional bridges: one for women, and two others at Bāb al-Bustān (that is, Gate of the Garden) for his personal use and the use of his household retinue.[64] The reference here is either to the magnificent gardens (*bustān*) of al-Khuld, from which the palace allegedly derived its name, or to Bustān al-Zāhir, which was located on the East Side where the main bridge later connected al-Ruṣāfah with the right bank.[65] Thus, these last bridges represented a private and rapid means by which the Caliph could pass from one palace complex to another. When the main public bridge (al-Jisr) was built—probably soon thereafter—its eastern end faced the fief of Khuzaymah b. Khāzim, the director of the security police (*shurṭah*) under al-Mahdī. The same man also received a fief on the West Side, which is listed by the Khaṭīb together with various locations along the Tigris bank. It may of course, be coincidental that the highest ranking security officer in the ʻAbbāsid state had residences on both sides of the bridgehead. It seems more likely, however, that the district headquarters and men of his command were stationed there to insure the general security of this sensitive area despite the encroachment of public use.[66]

The idea of combining the administrative agencies and the Caliphal residence within a self-contained unit nevertheless remained a desideratum. Upon assuming rule in A.H. 159, al-Mahdī formally moved into the palace at al-Ruṣāfah, thereby signifying that it had become the official residence of the Commander of the Faithful. The new Caliph may have attempted to recreate the equilibrium of the original administrative center, but the conditions of growth that had compromised the Round City also affected al-Ruṣāfah, for large markets began to develop around the area of the bridgehead in order to serve the burgeoning population of the upper East Side. One such place, the famous market subsequently called Sūq al-ʻAṭash, contained every conceivable commercial and industrial enterprise, and so was likened to al-Karkh, the great market area of the West Bank.[67] The creation of a major commercial district close to the new palace complex could not fail to leave its mark. In the end, al-Ruṣāfah could not fully satisfy the Caliph's needs. Although for official purposes it continued as the cen-

AL-RUṢĀFAH AND THE NORTHERN SUBURBS

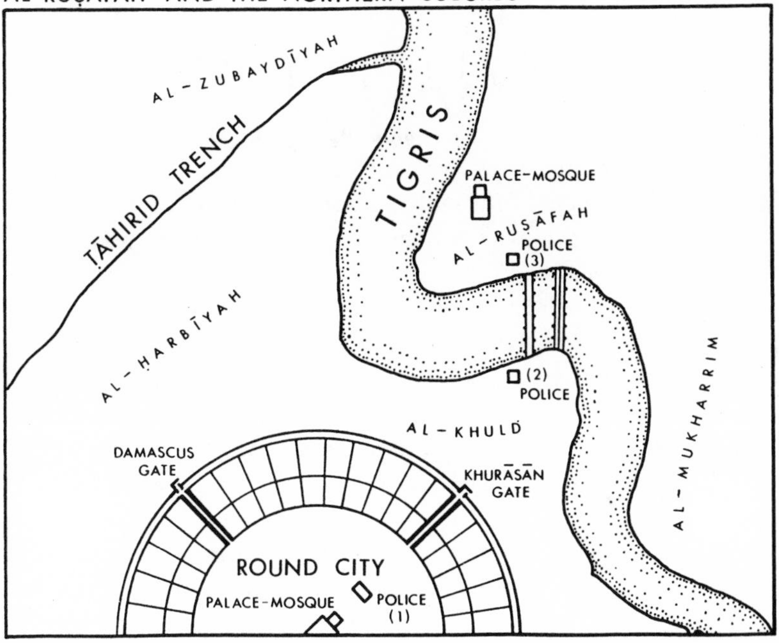

ter of his rule, al-Mahdī spent a good deal of time, toward the end of his reign, at his pleasure palace (*mustaqirrah*) in ʿĪsābādh, a place located somewhere on the East Side of the city.[68]

Al-Hādī lived at ʿĪsābādh until he was assassinated in the first year of his Caliphate, but al-Rashīd returned to al-Khuld, where his son al-Amīn also came to reside. It is remarkable that al-Rashīd, whose reign reportedly marked the apogee of construction in Baghdad, never saw fit to establish an administrative center of his own in the urban area.[69] On the contrary, he grew restive and disenchanted with the great city, preferring to pass his later years at a second palace complex in the regional center of al-Rāfiqah.[70] Perhaps he understood, only too well, the inherent contradictions of life in an imperial city. The Caliph's other two sons emulated their father's later preference by choosing residences outside the capital. Al-Ma'mūn, following the great civil war, remained distant from the hostile populace, spending most of his reign away from Baghdad, and his successor al-Muʿtaṣim made the break completely by transferring the capital of the realm sixty miles up the Tigris to Sāmarrā.

D. The Pattern of Military Settlement

An essential element of urban planning at Baghdad was the necessity of providing for large and diverse military forces. Unlike the garrisons in the smaller capitals of the outlying districts, which in times of peace were entrusted largely with regional security, the military resources of the 'Abbāsid administrative center were instruments for the expansion, as well as the consolidation, of imperial power. In addition, the very presence of the Caliphal precinct created unique security problems that required extraordinary precautions and demands on manpower. Sufficiently large forces were thus required to handle a variety of objectives, including external challenges, without depleting the reserves at the capital. The need for a flexible response by the central authorities explains the complex differentiation of military personnel that came to be found at Baghdad. In addition to the regular army, there were the personal contingents of the Caliph, the various divisions of security forces and police, and the paramilitary troops of the city garrison—altogether, a military presence of staggering variety and dimensions.[71]

Descriptions of an ambassadorial visit in the time of al-Muqtadir (under the year A.H. 307)[72] indicate that the Caliph had his troops lined up from the Palace of Ṣā'id to the Dār al-Khilāfah; that is to say, they were positioned along almost the entire length of the East Side.[73] The review troops alone are said to have comprised 160,000 cavalry and infantry, a figure obviously exaggerated, but nevertheless indicative of the forces available locally. Moreover, this did not include the Ḥujarite guard and the various classes of armed attendants attached to the palace complex. It is safe to assume that the earliest 'Abbāsid armies at Baghdad were less formally conceived, but the troops serving al-Manṣūr and his offspring were also broken down into a variety of functioning units representing a formidable military organization. One recalls the Caliph's reaction when he was left with only a token number of troops at his previous capital, al-Hāshimīyah,[74] during the widespread 'Alid revolt of A.H. 145. Isolated from the main contingents of the imperial army, which were off on a variety of campaigns, al-Manṣūr surveyed his predicament and vowed that he would never again be left without a standing reserve of 30,000 men.[75] It is probable that the Caliph was entirely serious about this matter, and that his continuing concern, even after the rebels were ultimately defeated, led to the unique arrangements at Baghdad.

Providing for the military was not an easy matter for al-Manṣūr. In choosing a new site, he had to be sure that the logistics were favorable, the surface area ample, and the lay of the ground suitable for defensive purposes. Although there is unanimity among the medieval sources that the site of Madīnat al-Salām satisfied all of these requirements,[76] the settlement of a large military force in an urban environment creates problems of its own. This is particularly true when the army contingents are not indigenous to the area, as was the case of the Khurāsānīs in Iraq.

Even before the 'Alid revolt, the Caliph understood only too well that al-Hāshimīyah was not suitable as an administrative center because of its close proximity to the hostile populace of al-Kūfah.[77] The Kūfan proclivity toward adventurist Shī'ite pretenders, linked with a past history of regional ambitions, should have been sufficient to cause a Caliph of al-Manṣūr's temperament much concern. From this point of view, Baghdad was a definite improvement, because the local inhabitants were essentially imported along with the army, though, unlike the military, which was composed entirely of Khurāsānīs, the civilian population represented widely diverse geographic groups from the surrounding regions of northern Syria and Iraq.[78] Although, in the course of time, the great 'Abbāsid capital would give them all a new sense of regional identity and a pride they would share in being Baghdadis, the need for security should have dictated, from the outset, a division between the military and civilian sectors. The function of the administrative center always required that the regular army be separated from the general populace and, in particular, from the people of the markets. This was almost certainly a requirement once the Caliph occupied his new palace complex, but it is likely that the pattern had already been invoked, in response to a rapid buildup of population, even before the Round City was completed.

Unlike the garrison towns (*amṣār*), the 'Abbāsid administrative center was not a prefabricated military camp given permanence by the haphazard growth of a sedentary settlement. It was a major undertaking built according to a plan of the Caliph's own choosing.[79] The successful completion of so vast a project required not only a predetermined architectural design, but a highly organized and efficient set of work procedures as well. Because the local environment lacked the human resources to carry the effort through to conclusion, a complex method of recruitment was set into motion. The essential purpose of the public works program was to supply skilled and unskilled laborers from the outlying regions of Syria and Iraq. Salaries were fixed according to the division of labor and were apparently paid out at set intervals. A rare text preserving a comparative analysis of prices and wages gives the impression that Baghdad was an emerging boom town,[80] thereby explaining the many thousands of skilled and unskilled laborers that were attracted to the site.[81] So large a labor force would have soon required an area of housing close to the sites of construction, as well as access to established services. It is safe to assume that the imported laborers and their dependents first settled about the original market areas of al-Karkh and soon extended beyond that into the vast reaches of the southern suburb, which remained, even subsequently, the major commercial entrepôt of the city.

Although the actual construction of the Round City was entrusted to technical experts, the overall responsibility was apparently that of the army (*wallā ḳull rubʿ min al-madīnah qāʾid yatawallā al-istiḥthāth ʿalā al-farāgh min bināʾ dhạliḳa al-rubʿ*).[82] Given the heterogeneous composition of the labor force, the army's primary objective was, no doubt, to keep order. This could have been a formidable task. In any event, when the ʿAlid revolt broke out in A.H. 145, the Caliph was compelled to use every force available, and the troops were therefore withdrawn from the building site. As a result of their absence, it was necessary to suspend construction. The army was also involved in the subsequent development of the suburbs.[83] The entire West Side was divided into quarters (*rubʿ*) according to the position of the city gates, and each was under the supervision of a military commander assisted by one of the Caliph's *mawālī* and an engineer (*muhandis*). It was presumably the confidant's duty to keep the Caliph informed of developments and, above all, to accept responsibility for expenditures, for this was an area of concern best left outside the control of the military.[84] In effect, al-Manṣūr seems to have used a system of checks and balances that found prominence in the provincial administration, that is, the system of dividing fiscal and military responsibilities.

With the formal transfer of the government from al-Hāshimīyah in A.H. 146, the Khurāsānī military presence at the capital grew enormous. Following the model of civilian settlement in al-Karkh, one would expect the arriving contingents to have settled in the general area originally occupied by the forces overseeing the construction of the city. There is, however, no direct indication where this area might have been. One supposes that, if the civilian, or private, sector was essentially confined to the area south of the Ṣarāt (the boundary of al-Karkh), the military cantonments may well have been situated north of the waterway in the general vicinity of the Round City. The advantage of such an arrangement is that it would have kept the general populace at some distance from the sensitive areas of the emerging administrative center. This supposition is supported by incidental evidence gathered from all the sources containing descriptions of the city based on contemporary accounts.

The geographer-historian Ya'qūbī, whose material about the suburban districts of Baghdad is perhaps the most detailed and systematic of the sources, does not list a single place in al-Karkh that can be construed as a military camp.[85] Nor, for that matter, do any of the other collectors of topographical information. On the other hand, these sources do indicate that the northwest suburbs were heavily settled by military personnel. They list the estates of numerous 'Abbāsid commanders and the quarters of their men, each arranged according to geographic origins. The critical problem here is, first, to establish a sense of chronology, so that one may link the growth of these various military cantonments with specific moments in the development of the city and, second, to formulate an organizational profile of the early imperial armies. Unfortunately, the information about the early period that is preserved in descriptive accounts such as that of Ya'qūbī and the Khaṭīb is often confusing. For the most part, this residual material represents a listing of various localities appearing sequentially along the major arteries of traffic. The language tends to be terse and the syntax loose. One cannot always know if and where the original account breaks off and resumes, particularly if the sequence is interrupted by the interpolations of later authors. Moreover, the list of localities that can be assembled from the combined texts is not all-inclusive, for incidental reading in the more general literature turns up place names that cannot be elsewhere identified.[86] The topographical accounts are, nevertheless, absolutely indispensable for understanding the nature of military settlement and for establishing a coherent general model for the growth of Baghdad.

Invariably, one begins with al-Ḥarbīyah. The reference here is not to the specific location of that name, but to a vast area north of the Round City. This was the section developed by Ḥarb. b. ʿAbdallāh, one of al-Manṣūr's generals, during the initial expansion of the suburban districts.[87] The tract, which was bounded by the Ṭāhirid Trench, encompassed all the lands north of the palace complex extending from the Damascus gate to the river. Among the various authorities describing al-Ḥarbīyah and the other suburbs, Yaʿqūbī (d. A.H. 284) is the most detailed and systematic. More important yet, he consistently relies on information that is contemporary with the early growth of the city. The author himself testifies that his description is based on a pattern of settlement originally established by al-Manṣūr (*wa hādhihi al-qaṭāʾiʿ wa al-shawāriʿ wa al-durūb wa al-sikak allatī dhakartuhā ʿalā mā rusimat ayyām al-Manṣūr wa waqt ibtidāʾihā*).[88]

A close reading of the text, particularly the extended description of the East Side, would seem to indicate that the author is being overly modest, and that his account also reflects conditions appropriate to the time of al-Mahdī—although certainly no later.[89] For, conspicuously missing from the catalogue of locations are ʿĪsābādh, the pleasure palace occupied by al-Mahdī towards the end of his reign,[90] the great Ḥasanī Palace built originally by the Barmakids,[91] the princely residences of al-Maʾmūn and al-Muʿtaṣim,[92] and the Qarār Palace occupied by Zubaydah, the widow of Hārūn al-Rashīd.[93] One could perhaps claim a simple oversight if one of the locations were omitted; however, the absence of all five is evidence that the author most likely relied on materials composed in an earlier period, before these structures were erected.

Having thus obtained a sense of chronology, one can turn to the actual description of the northern suburbs and the composition of the groups contained therein. Yaʿqūbī's account of the various localities leaves a vivid impression of the military settlement.[94] According to him, the northwest side was heavily, if not exclusively, populated by contingents of eastern origins arranged according to geographic grouping.[95] Southward from the Damascus Gate, in the direction of the Ṣarāt, the area of military occupation seems to grow somewhat more diffuse, and the eastern character of the settlement is less pronounced.[96] There are, nevertheless, frequent references to estates of military commanders, including those of some of the most prominent Khurāsānīs serving the dynasty. Among the leaders mentioned are the descendants of Qaḥṭabah b. Shabīb, the legendary commander of the revolutionary armies.

In the suburb of Ḥarb itself, the representative units are said to have been from Balkh, Marw, al-Khuttal, Bukhārā, Asbījāb(?), Istīkhān(?),[97] Kābūl, and Khuwārizm. Each contingent was jointly under the command of an army officer (*qā'id*) and a second official (*ra'īs*) who was in charge of affairs of a nontechnical military nature.[98] Because the author's material is generally set in the earliest period of the city's history, it may, at first glance, be surprising to see the inclusion of complete units from beyond the Oxus. Conventional wisdom has it that the Transoxanian regiments, which were important to the formation of the later 'Abbāsid armies, were first introduced in large numbers during the Caliphate of al-Ma'mūn (A.H. 198-218). Indeed, the earliest reference that I have obtained concerning the possible recruitment of Transoxanian contingents for Baghdad stems from the reign of Hārūn al-Rashīd. The chronicler reports, under the year A.H. 176, that al-Faḍl b. Yaḥyā (al-Barmakī) campaigned vigorously beyond the Oxus and adds, in the very next account, that the Barmakid assembled an enormous client army in Khurāsān drawn from the indigenous population (*jund min al-'ajam*). This army, which is said to have numbered 500,000 men (a figure obviously exaggerated), was known as al-'Abbāsiyah. Of these, 20,000 troops were sent to Baghdad (where they presumably settled) and were subsequently called al-Karanbīyah.[99] Even if this terse report reflects the recruitment of an army beyond the Oxus, the event most likely occurred after Ya'qūbī's material on Baghdad had been compiled, so that the reference to Transoxanians in his account still requires an explanation.

It is perhaps not coincidental that the description of the ethnic composition of this particular suburb called Rabaḍ Ḥarb b. 'Abdallāh is immediately preceded by a parenthetical statement representing a later interpolation by the author. The question is then raised whether or not the description of the suburb is actually an extension of this statement (the grammar is ambiguous) and thus reflects the topographical pattern of a later period in which the presence of Transoxanians in large numbers could be assumed. The text would then read, ". . . to the suburb of Ḥarb b. 'Abdallāh al-Balkhī. There is at present [*fī al-ḥāl*; that is, third century A.H.] no suburb [*rabaḍ*] in Baghdad that is more spacious or more magnificent. None has more streets or markets. Its populace [*wa ahluhu*] is drawn from the people of Balkh, Marw, al-Khuttal. . . ."[100] Even if this reading is correct, the account of the northern suburbs immediately returns, so it would seem, to older material. The next location mentioned is the Estate (*Qaṭī'ah*) of al-Ḥakam b. Yūsuf al-Balkhī, an important officer who served under al-Manṣūr and al-Mahdī. The description then continues with the catalogue of military settlements and includes various groups of eastern origin from such diverse regions as Kirmān, Ṣāmghān, Jurjān, and Badhgīs. There is also reference to areas beyond the Oxus, that is, Ṣughd and Farghānah.[101] When taken as a whole, the picture seems to indicate the wide geographical distribution of the early Baghdad armies. Moreover, it may suggest that the Khurāsānī forces were being augmented by other eastern units not long after the new administrative center came into being—perhaps already during the lifetime of its founder. In any event, the military colonies of the northern suburbs undoubtedly originated with the development of this administrative center. One may note that the Khaṭīb adds to the locations of this general area a Suburb (*Rabaḍ*) and Square (*Murabba'ah*) of the Persians and indicates that it consisted of land grants (*qaṭī'ah*) distributed to them in the reign of al-Manṣūr.[102] Similarly, al-Khuwārizmīyah, which was situated adjacent to the Suburb of Ḥarb, was listed by the author as one of the Caliph's military colonies (*jund min jund al-Manṣūr*).[103]

It is remarkable that, among the many references to military cantonments (to say nothing of the more general locations), there is absolutely no mention in all the topographical literature of a specific area of tribal settlement. The possibility exists that various tribal units were further subdivided along regional lines, but this in itself would represent a significant departure from the past. The absence of any reference to tribal cantonments is all the more surprising because it has been assumed that the Khurāsānī armies of the 'Abbāsid revolution were originally registered according to two separate rolls: the first, that of the old settlers, was established on the basis of geographical origin; the second, that of the disaffected Arab armies of Khurāsān, was drawn according to tribal affiliation.[104] If this was indeed the case, one is forced to conclude that the ʿAbbāsids had already destroyed the residual tribal structure of the Khurāsānī military units within the first decade or so of the dynasty. The most obvious advantage of this development was that it would help to neutralize the rivalries engendered by tribal xenophobia. The Caliphs continued to make military use of Arab tribal groups, but not as part of the regular imperial army stationed at Baghdad. They were, rather, provincial forces, presumably the remnants of the old Umayyad military apparatus in Syria and the regions adjacent to it.[105] It is not clear that there was any specific incident that gave rise to this historic shift in military organization; in all likelihood, the tribal units were assimilated into regional cantonments over a period of time. Judging from the topographical accounts, the process was probably completed with the expansion of the suburban districts at the end of al-Manṣūr's reign (as A.H. 157) and, perhaps even earlier, during the construction of the palace complex.

Those seeking to argue against this early date will find relevant, if not critical, a particular text dealing with the developmental pattern of military settlement. The details are preserved by Ṭabarī in a previously mentioned historical tradition.[106] The account reports, under the year A.H. 151, that al-Manṣūr divided his Baghdad armies according to regional and tribal groupings while developing a palace complex for his son and successor, al-Mahdī, on the east side of the river. A section of the army remained with the Caliph on the West Side, while their traditional rivals among the tribesmen were stationed under his son's command in the vicinity of al-Ruṣāfah. If taken at face value, this tradition clearly reveals that the Khurāsānī tribal armies of the ʿAbbāsids were still operative at this time and, what is more, they fully retained their sense of group identity and cohesion, with all that this implied for the destabilization of public order. When examined in detail, however, this unique account appears to be marked by several serious inconsistencies.

The chronicler[107] indicates that Qutham b. al-ʿAbbās, one of the leading figures at court, approached the Caliph at the time of the Rāwandīyah disturbance. The ʿAbbāsid dignitary expressed great concern lest the army unite against the regime and topple it. When asked for his advice, he persuaded the Caliph to allow him carte blanche in working out a secret scheme to insure that this fear would not be realized. In the morning, Qutham b. al-'Abbās approached the palace of the Caliph (*dār amīr al-mu'minīn*) mounted on a mule (*baghlah*) in full view of the ranking courtiers (*aṣḥāb al-marātib*). According to a prearranged plan, one of Qutham's slaves (*ghulām*) engaged him in a feigned conversation after grabbing the bridle of the animal, thereby preventing his master from moving on. The slave insisted that Qutham answer his question, but, still more important, before asking it he forced him to invoke the names of the Prophet, the progenitor of the ruling family, and the Commander of the Faithful. Upon hearing the question, the 'Abbāsid nobleman grew angry and responded accordingly; however, the slave, following his instructions, continued to insist on an answer, even when cursed and whipped. The reason for his master's reticence became evident once the slave blurted out his query in full voice. "Which of the tribes is more noble (*ashraf*), the Yaman or the Muḍar?" In view of the long and tragic history of intertribal warfare—conflicts often sparked by seemingly trivial incidents—the diplomatic response would have been to remain silent; but Qutham b. al-'Abbās was already sworn to answer truthfully: "The Muḍar," he responded. "It produced the Messenger of God, it received the sacred Book of Almighty God, its [territory] is the place of God's House, and the Caliph is chosen from it." The slave then loosened the bridle, and, for his indispensable part in this charade (which entailed a certain amount of discomfort, if not danger), he was eventually set free.

The underlying strategy is clear. It was Qutham's intention to kindle the traditional enmity between the tribal factions without involving the government directly, and in this he succeeded. One of the Yamanī commanders, reflecting the mood of his compatriots, was greatly offended by the unequivocal tone of the remarks. He wondered why nothing positive could be said of his tribal group; then, in anger, he ordered his servant to grab the bridle, forcing the animal to give way and fall on its forelegs. The insult could not go unnoticed, and it was now the Muḍar's turn to react, "Can this be done to one of our shaykhs?" they asked. Lest there by any doubt as to the answer, a man of the Muḍar instructed his servant to sever the hand of the presumptuous Yamanī slave as the game of the proxies continued. The tribesmen eventually dispersed amid mutual antagonism (*nafara al-ḥayyān*); the mule, having served its purpose, was dispatched, and

Qutham b. al-'Abbās went to see the Caliph. Without formal sanction, let alone official action, Qutham had, in effect, divided the imperial army into various contingents. According to the text, the break was along tribal and regional lines representing, first, the Muḍar and Yaman, but also the Rabī'ah, and the Khurāsānīs that is, the old settlers and perhaps some newer groups from the east that may have augmented the revolutionary armies.[108]

The Caliph's confidant informed him of his success. "I have already divided your army [*jund*] according to factions [*ḥizb*]. Each will fear to initiate action against you, lest you employ the other factions against them. There remains, however, an administrative act that is incumbent upon you [*wa qad baqiya 'alaykа fī al-tadbīr baqīyah*]." When al-Manṣūr asked what that was, Qutham b. al-'Abbās suggested that he transfer the heir apparent, al-Mahdī, to a palace complex (*qaṣr*) built expressly for him on the East Side, along with various contingents of the imperial army. The rest of the troops would remain with the Caliph on the West Side, with both sections becoming well-defined urban areas (*fayasīru dhālika balad wa hādhā balad*). Should an insurrection break out on one side of the river, the army from the other side could be called into action to quell it. That is to say, should the Muḍar attempt to subvert the regime, the Yaman, Rabī'ah and Khurāsānīs remained to deal with them; and should the Yaman need controlling, the Caliph could call upon his following from the Muḍar and others.

The account informs us that al-Manṣūr accepted the advice and divided the agencies of his rule (*fa istawā lahu mulkuhu*), thereby explaining the new construction on the East Side as well as the distribution of land grants to military commanders in that area. Ṣāliḥ Ṣāḥib al-Muṣallā, who was a Khurāsānī, was entrusted with the task of distributing these grants, just as Abū al-'Abbās al-Ṭūsī was responsible for the West Side. The specific areas under Ṣāliḥ's charge were the Gate of the Bridge (Bāb al-Jisr), Sūq Yaḥyā, Masjid Khuḍayr, and various places that were reserved for his Khurāsānī compatriots in al-Ruṣāfah and along the Road of the Skiffs (*Ṭarīq al-Zawāriq*).[109]

The essential truth contained in this tradition seems clear. The efforts of Qutham b. al-'Abbās are intended to explain the disposition of large military forces on the East Side as well as the settlement of the major palace complex at al-Ruṣāfah. The account also offers an indirect, and indeed plausible, explanation of how this area across the

Tigris came to be called ʿAskar al-Mahdī, that is, the military encampment of al-Manṣūr's son and heir apparent. The critical issue concerning the tribal armies is, however, much more difficult to evaluate on the evidence currently available. Detailed references with regard to a large-scale military presence on the East Side are unfortunately lacking. The topographical literature does show considerable evidence of an official settlement around al-Ruṣāfah, for there are numerous references to Khurāsānī officers and clients of the Caliph al-Mahdī. There is, however, no mention of particular military cantonments outside the brief references to Khurāsānīs in Ṭabarī.[110] Yaʿqūbī, whose regional breakdown of army groups in the northwest suburbs is detailed and informative, offers only the most casual observations on the pattern of military settlement across the river. He simply points out that the commanders and notables received land grants there just as they had on the West Side, and that the army colonies were situated amid those holdings (*wa bayna al-qaṭāʾiʿ manāzil al-jund*).[111]

The specific details of the tradition under review simply cannot be confirmed by the material now available; quite the opposite, for the internal inconsistencies of the account, which will be studied shortly, suggest a text that seemingly contains more embellishment than hard fact. As a result, several questions immediately come to mind: Did the Khurāsānī tribal armies still exist at this moment of history? If they did, did the policies reportedly outlined by Qutham b. al-ʿAbbās have any basis in fact? Or, is the tradition preserved by Ṭabarī largely a fiction based on the lingering echo of the great tribal rifts that plagued the Khurāsānī armies during the later years of a disintegrating Umayyad authority? The answers to these questions are at best problematic.

The text in its present form is a juxtaposition of several different moments. Although the chronological setting is fixed by Ṭabarī as A.H. 151 (the year in which construction began at al-Ruṣāfah), we are informed that Qutham b. al-ʿAbbās set his plan in motion following the disturbance of the Rāwandīyah. As reported, this was an event of such apparent magnitude that it caused the ʿAbbāsid notable to immediately seek the Caliph's tacit approval in dividing the imperial army to prevent it from uniting against the ruling house (*qad khiftu an tajtimaʿ kalimatuhum fayakhruju hādhā al-amr min aydīna*). The actions of the Rāwandī extremists, to the extent that they are known, are discussed in an earlier chapter;[112] it is sufficient to recall here that a somewhat confused chronicler lists the aforementioned disturbance under the years A.H. 136, 137, 141, and 142. That is to say, it actually took place prior to the original Manṣūrid construction at Baghdad, ten to fifteen years before the Caliph's kinsman allegedly undertook his complex scheme. Furthermore, there is nothing in the known descriptions of this event that would have caused al-Manṣūr to suspect the loyalty of his imperial regiments. On the contrary, when the Rāwandīyah became overly rambunctious, he did not hesitate to call out the security forces and, after a few harrowing moments, the riot was crushed. It cannot even be said that the Rāwandīyah were disloyal; if anything, they suffered their cruel fortune because of their excessive zeal for the Caliph, declaring, as they did, his divinity and wishing to be nurtured by his food and drink. The riot itself was of passing importance. If it had any bearing on the course of history, it was to demonstrate the inadequate security arrangements at al-Hāshimīyah, which were one of the factors that led, several years later, to the founding of a new capital at Baghdad. Even then, the particular concern was not the army as such, but the heavy concentration of 'Alid sympathizers in the adjacent city of al-Kūfah.[113] The rioters from among the Rāwandīyah numbered only several hundred; the Kūfans, whom the Caliph described as 100,000 potential ambushers, were a problem of greater dimensions.

If the specific words credited to al-Manṣūr's kinsman echo any historic truth, it is to describe a situation that existed at the outset of the 'Abbāsid regime some twenty years before the Caliph divided his forces and undertook the development of the East Side. When the 'Abbāsid family emerged from the long period of clandestine operations in A.H. 132, it discovered that the real levers of power were in the hands of its clients: Abū Muslim, the creator of the revolutionary army in Khurāsān, and Abū Salamah the director of the political station in al-Kūfah.[114] Between them, the two servants of the 'Abbāsid house controlled not only the entire political and military apparatus, but also the accumulated wealth necessary for the regime to function.

Moreover, given the secretive nature of the early movement, the greater 'Abbāsid political constituency knew neither the inner leadership of the family nor the theoretical basis for their rule. Under the circumstances, Abū al-'Abbās and his circle could hardly have been sure of receiving universal acclaim. The defeat of the Umayyads may have paved the way for 'Abbāsid rule, but only the full support of the Khurāsānī armies could make it a reality.

Whatever potential there was for mounting an internal challenge to the ruling family apparently dissipated with the onset of al-Manṣūr's Caliphate in A.H. 136. 'Abdallāh b. 'Alī's decision to use the vestigial Umayyad tribal armies from Syria in contesting his nephew's right to rule only served to rally the Khurāsānīs and a reluctant Abū Muslim to the side of the new Caliph. The subsequent (A.H. 137) murder of Abū Muslim (who may have had a vague connection with the Rāwandīyah) removed the last obstacle to the consolidation of the Khurāsānī armies behind al-Manṣūr. Contrary to the expectations of various notables, the assassination of the second most powerful figure in the 'Abbāsid state was carried out; the political repercussions were essentially mild and confined to the periphery of 'Abbāsid rule. When Qutham b. al-'Abbās expressed great concern lest the military at Baghdad unite and overthrow the regime, there had not been the slightest indication of any difficulties with the imperial army in Iraq for fifteen years.

The method and solution proposed by Qutham for al-Manṣūr's nonexistent dilemma are incongruous at best. There is no denying, however, that the tradition is artfully conceived and the narrative strategy is carefully worked out. One can easily imagine how the dramatic incident between the reluctant notable and his persistent servant was designed to capture the attention of the assembled courtiers and, hence, the reader. The pledge extracted from Qutham b. al-'Abbās, even before the question was put to him, was a clever and indispensable artifice that compelled him to abandon discretion for bluntness. His continued and painful silence and the physical abuse that he heaped upon his trusted servant were presumably indications that he sought to hold his tongue. But having sworn by no less than the Prophet, by al-'Abbās, and by Abū Ja'far al-Manṣūr to reveal his innermost thoughts, he was unwittingly forced to precipitate the divisive incident that followed. Because Qutham certainly intended no insult to the Yaman, the 'Abbāsid could not be blamed for the subsequent events leading to the breakdown of relations within the army. Similarly no accusations could be leveled against his kinsman, the most famous Muḍarī of them all, for Qutham b. al-'Abbās had been scrupulously careful to shield the Caliph from any direct involvement in this complex web of intrigue. The internal strain was thus confined to the regiments of the imperial army.

If this was indeed the case, the initial incident should have ended with Qutham's remarks and nothing more than injured feelings. As it was, the tribal units did not enter into conflict with one another; they simply dispersed amid mutual antagonism. The tradition has, therefore, to explain the delicate situation that emerged, in which there was sufficient bitterness to separate the army, but not enough to cause a breakdown in authority. The response of the Yaman to their ruffled sensitivities and the subsequent reply of the Muḍar are deftly constructed. One recalls that a Yamanī page is ordered to grab the mount by its bridle, forcing it and its rider to give way; because of this grievous insult, his Muḍarī counterpart orders that he suffer the loss of a hand. There is no mistaking that the metaphor used in this passage is chosen to signify a struggle for preeminence in government, for he who controls the bridle (*'inān* also means reins) has a firm grip on rule itself. Quite appropriately, the term *siyāsah*, which in Arabic signifies the handling of animals, applies equally to the art of politics, that is, the training of human consituencies to be obedient.[115] Although there is no violence in the first action, the symbolism proclaimed by the gesture clearly implied the submission of the Muḍar to the Yaman. The Muḍarī response, though at first glance excessive, was actually quite measured; the loss of a hand, although serious enough, is hardly the same as the loss of a life, particularly because the blow was sustained by a mere slave and inflicted by the same.

For the contemporary scholar, the literary merits of the tradition are, in a sense, incidental to the larger concern of its historicity. One therefore notes, with a certain surprise, that Qutham b. al-'Abbās set his plot into motion by riding conspicuously amid the courtiers assembled before al-Manṣūr's palace. This incident, which allegedly occurred in the year A.H. 151, recalls a familiar account reported by Ṭabarī and the Khaṭīb, wherein al-Manṣūr's paternal uncle complained about having to walk the long distance to the Caliphal residence.[116] Al-Manṣūr offered him a litter, but the proud 'Abbāsid would have nothing of it and suggested instead that he ride one of the pack animals used for transporting water into this area of the palace complex. This was, no doubt, a daring suggestion, for it was explicitly understood that no one entered the court mounted except the Caliph's son and heir apparent, Muḥammad al-Mahdī. It appears that al-Manṣūr was totally unaware that precautions had been so relaxed as to allow animals (even without riders) into the area of the great central court.

There is no sure indication how al-Manṣūr would have finally responded to his uncle's plight had he not been distracted by this last revelation. For the Caliph was apparently so distraught about the breakdown in security that, instead of attending to his discomfited relative, he gave explicit orders to alter the architectural design of the palace complex. When completed, the new arrangement restricted pack animals and any similar traffic from encroaching upon his personal domain. The full significance of this last tradition has been described earlier. One need only emphasize here that the incident of the gout-ridden uncle reportedly took place in A.H. 157. That is to say, there were still no riders officially permitted entry at the gates leading to the Caliph's palace a full six years after Qutham b. al-ʿAbbās supposedly appeared in the great central court mounted on a mule.

Although it can be argued that this last analysis plays one tendentious account against another, there is still further reason to suspect Ṭabarī's report on the division of the imperial army. Perhaps the most unaccountable aspect of the tradition under review is the rationale behind Qutham b. al-ʿAbbās's solution. One is asked to believe that an important dignitary of the ruling house wished to rekindle tribal enmity at a time when the great tribal wars in Khurāsān and elsewhere were still vividly etched in historic memory. This would have been, at the least, an invitation to recreate the disasters that eventually sealed the fate of the Umayyad dynasty. Such a deliberate act would have run counter to the general policy of the regime, which was to establish a highly centralized form of government, with the key personnel of each particular institution strongly linked to the ruling family by absolute bonds of clientage. Thus, the breakdown of the military into mutually antagonistic units could hardly have been a policy designed to further ʿAbbāsid interests as they perceived them. Qutham b. al-ʿAbbās notwithstanding, the presumptive evidence indicates that it was the intention of the early Caliphs to dissolve the structure of the tribal regiments and to re-form them as quickly as possible into a professional army divided along regional lines. The total absence of references to tribal settlements in the topographical accounts is the most compelling proof of this policy.

E. Defining the Government Sector

An additional problem, which is perhaps best discussed at this juncture, is that of identifying particular locations and larger patterns of settlement. There are not always equivalent terms in Arabic to convey the specific sense of various abstract conceptions. As they are used here, such terms as "palace complex," "administrative center," and "government sector," are not based on a direct translation of the medieval text; they are derived from what is perceived as its implicit meaning. On the reverse side of the coin, Arabic topographical terms are often ambiguous: a *shāri'*, for example, may simply connote a road or thoroughfare, but it may also indicate the surrounding quarter. Similarly, it frequently happens that the name of a particular place will, in time, extend to a wider area, for example, Bāb al-Ṭāq (the Gate of the Archway), which refers not only to a given monument, but to an entire section of the East Side.[117] It is generally wise, in such cases, to retain and transliterate the Arabic topographical terms and names, so as to avoid a potentially misleading translation. This may be more of a convenience for the author than the reader, however, for it allows the former to pass on the ambiguity of the original text without a hard analysis of its meaning. In most instances, the confusion is without great consequence, but occasionally the lack of precise language affects a basic understanding of the city and its function. This is particularly true in distinguishing between the original government-related areas of the 'Abbāsid capital and the adjacent districts housing the civilian populace. Without a clear picture of this pattern, it is difficult to chart the subsequent physical development of the city and to relate topographical changes to more broadly defined problems of historical interest.

The sprawling urban complex, which rapidly engulfed the administrative center and then spread to the neighboring environs, was generally known as Baghdad. That is to say, this vast urban expanse retained the name of a Persian hamlet that had previously occupied only a small part of the overall site. The frequent, and sometimes indiscriminate, use of the name, Baghdad—a practice found already in the medieval sources—creates an ambiguity when it is necessary to distinguish between well-defined locations,[118] for earlier studies indicate that the great ʿAbbāsid capital was not so much a city as a city of cities or, at least, a city of semiautonomous localities.[119]

The critical problem here is to define the greater administrative center, that is, those public areas designated for essentially governmental and military functions, as opposed to the private sector occupied by the general populace. The task is complicated because there is no explicit statement in the literature that divides greater Baghdad into government and private sectors, even though such a pattern is suggested in the accounts of the medieval geographers. It may be assumed, however, that this division was part of the original comprehensive urban plan, and that it had important significance for the future development of the city. According to the topographical evidence surveyed earlier in this chapter, it would seem that the original dividing line was the Ṣarāt Canal. Situated north of the waterway was the palace complex and the adjacent suburbs that housed the cantonments of the imperial army; below was the market suburb of al-Karkh, the major commercial center of the city, if not of the entire empire.

No less distinguished an authority than the legal scholar Aḥmad b. Ḥanbal (d. A.H. 241) is credited with a (juridical ?) statement that has direct bearing on this pattern of settlement. His terse comment, when considered with the accompanying explanation of a later author, gives the impression of having been part of a responsum defining the boundaries of Baghdad. As reported by the Khaṭīb: "Baghdad [according to Ibn Ḥanbal] comprises everything from the Ṣarāt to Bāb al-Tibn."[120] By way of clarification, the Khaṭīb adds: "Aḥmad, in that statement, refers specifically to Madīnat al-Manṣūr [the Round City] and what is adjacent to it, for the upper part of the greater urban area [*aʿlā al-balad*] is the Fief of Umm Jaʿfar [= al-Zubaydīyah],[121] below which is the trench canal [Khandaq Ṭāhir] that divides this fief from the built-up area that is part of the city [proper].[122] Similarly, the lower part of the greater urban area, consisting of al-Karkh and what is adjacent to it, is separated from the city [proper] by the Ṣārāt Canal. That is the city [proper] according to width. As to length, it extends from the Tigris shore to the place called al-Kabsh wa al-Asad. . . ."[123]

If I understand this passage correctly, and if the Khaṭīb accurately reflects the meaning of Ibn Ḥanbal's statement, it would seem that a distinction is to be drawn between a city proper, which in this case is called Baghdad, and various suburbs of the West Side. The city proper would then consist of the original palace complex (the superstructure was very much intact in the lifetime of Ibn Ḥanbal)[124] and the adjoining localities north of the Ṣarāt Canal. The reference here is to the general area that presumably made up the government sector. It included the original agencies of the government and the residences of the Caliph and various notables of the 'Abbāsid house, as well as the military cantonments of al-Ḥarbīyah and the adjacent settlements. The suburbs not covered in Ibn Ḥanbal's city proper were the Fief of Umm Ja'far (which must have been relatively small) and the great southern suburb of al-Karkh, which comprised the land between the Ṣarāt, its northern limits, and Nahr 'Īsā,[125] its boundary to the south. The suburbs west of al-Karkh were also excluded from Ibn Ḥanbal's city. They were, in fact, areas that more accurately conveyed the impression of real suburbs, that is, gardens, parks, estates, and the like. The East Side was not mentioned, but it was considered a separate urban area for administrative purposes.

The impression is therefore conveyed that the great capital of the 'Abbāsid Caliphs was not a unified city, but a complex municipal composite. There was, above all, the greater urban area, which, despite Ibn Ḥanbal's specific usage, was generally known as Baghdad; but, within that enormous sprawling complex covering 7,000 hectares—the largest in the medieval Near East[126]—there were other municipal components, each retaining a specific identity of its own. The Round City and its adjoining settlements above the Ṣarāt comprised one of these elements. It is the supposition here that this geographic area was intentionally designed as a government sector; the commercial suburb of al-Karkh, in turn, comprised the private sector. Given the testimony of the topographcial sources, this pattern of mutually exclusive settlements was, in all probability, established by the time al-Manṣūr's palace complex was completed, or shortly thereafter.

There may be those who wish to contest the notion of a government sector between the Ṣarāt and the Ṭāhirid Trench, or who, at the least, will see little reason to link the early development of the city with Aḥmad b. Ḥanbal's dictum. The statement attributed to the great legal scholar is far too terse to be informative, and the explanatory note that accompanies it is, after all, the commentary of an eleventh-century author. Far from explaining what Ibn Ḥanbal had in mind, the Khaṭīb may be reflecting a division of the urban environment that is three centuries removed from the original period of settlement. Moreover, the conception of public and private sectors is not implicit in the Khaṭīb's formulation. The division of the West Side is based, rather, on a juridical principle centered on water boundaries: When a river, or similar body of water, bisects a city, creating two distinct areas, each may be considered a separate municipal entity for certain legal purposes, such as the establishment of a second principal mosque (*masjid al-jāmiʿ*).[127]

This last connection is confirmed by a somewhat bizarre tale found in the Khaṭīb's chapter on places of worship in Baghdad.[128] It seems there was a mosque at the Fief of Umm Jaʿfar (= al-Zubaydīyah)[129] that could not legally be used for Friday prayers. Then, in Dhū al-Ḥijjah in A.H. 379, a woman of the East Side dreamed she saw the Prophet at this mosque. He informed her (in sadness, no doubt) that she would die the following day at the time of her *ʿaṣr* prayer, then placed his palm on the orientation wall. Upon awakening, she went to the West Side mosque and discovered (to her horror, one would imagine) the imprint of a palm. It is understandable that all this proved overwhelming, and the woman confirmed her vision by dying at the designated time. The incident created quite a stir among the local inhabitants, who, having repaired and enlarged the mosque, sent petitions to the Caliph to establish it as a *masjid al-jāmiʿ*.[130]

It should be noted, however, that it was not the convenient miracle that formed the legal basis of the plea; the request simply asserted that the mosque was situated beyond the (Ṭāhirid) trench that divided it (that is, the Fief of Umm Jaʿfar) from the city proper (*balad*), thus making the area in which the mosque was situated a town in its own right. Faced with the logic of the argument and the legal principle from which it was derived, the Caliph granted his permission. To some the story may seem a bit fanciful, but the historicity of the woman's dream and her timely death is not the issue here. The significance of the account is that it confirms the Khaṭīb's earlier statement that the Fief of Umm Jaʿfar was a separate municipal entity because it was below the Ṭāhirid trench, which divided the fief from the built-up area of the city proper. Thus, the territorial integrity of the city proper (the area lying between the Ṣarāt and Khandaq Ṭāhir) is also confirmed. Additional evidence that al-Karkh was a distinct urban unit has been dealt with elsewhere.[131]

Although there is nothing in these accounts that even remotely suggests the notion of a government sector, the weight of the topographical evidence previously examined, combined with the proof of a separate municipal entity between the Ṣarāt and the Ṭāhirid Trench, makes a strong argument in favor of the existence of such an area in Manṣūrid times. As to the contention that the Khaṭīb is an eleventh-century authority commenting on an earlier text, there is not the slightest reason to assume that, in this passage, he is describing Baghdad as he saw it. On the contrary, in his topographical introduction, he generally relied on earlier materials, and, what is more, he seldom analyzed this data in light of subsequent changes. For example, the Khaṭīb preserves an entire chapter on the canals of Baghdad, most of which had silted up long before he set pen to ink, a fact that he indeed reflects upon in a casual observation elsewhere.[132]

Incidental remarks such as the Khaṭīb's mention of these silted canals are extremely valuable in sifting out the chronological layers of the text. It will be recalled that the author ends his explication of Ibn Ḥanbal's dictum by setting the western limit of Baghdad as al-Kabsh wa al-Asad, "The Ram and Lion Quarter," but he then adds, "All of these places were completely built up with palaces and dwellings. Today, the Kabsh wa al-Asad is a sown field some distance from the city. I once saw that place while visiting the grave of Ibrāhīm al-Ḥarbī,[133] who is buried there, and I noticed houses, which gave it the appearance of a village in which farmers and woodcutters dwell. Later I returned to that place and saw no trace of any dwellings."[134] He also mentions that, three generations earlier, Abū al-Ḥasan Bishr b. 'Alī b. 'Ubayd al-Naṣrānī had recalled that he used to pass through the Kabsh wa al-Asad with his father and could not free himself of the surging crowds in the markets.[135] This total decline of a once vibrant neighborhood was not an isolated incident, but one instance of a widespread pattern that had reached grave proportions by the lifetime of the Khaṭīb. When the author writes, "all of these places were built up with palaces and dwellings," he is referring to an earlier age when his comments on the division of the West Side were applicable. He is certainly not describing the city of his contemporaries, because eleventh-century Baghdad, though it still covered a large area, consisted of many truncated quarters separated from one another by vacant lands.[136]

This changing situation clearly affected long-established topographical patterns, even within the city proper. One notes that the people of al-Ḥarbīyah were petitioning for a principal mosque as early as the reign of the Caliph al-Muṭī' (A.H. 334-363) and were finally granted their request by al-Qādir in A.H. 383.[137] This was not a simple matter, for the number of principal mosques in any given location was generally limited by law and practice to a single structure. According to the Ḥanafite school, which was predominant at Baghdad, Caliphal permission was required for a second mosque; the Shāfi'ites took an even stricter position, and required a valid reason as well. The need of a *masjid al-jāmi'* for al-Ḥarbīyah actually was decided in consultation with the jurists, and, although no indication is given of their reasoning, the decision was presumably based on the distance between al-Ḥarbīyah and what had been the original Caliphal mosque. What had at one time been an integrated area of continuous occupation was now marked by an incipient decay that created open space between the various populated centers. Al-Ḥarbīyah would therefore have become, de facto, a separate municipal entity, even though it originally had been part of the city proper. Yāqūt, writing two centuries later, reported that, in his time, al-Ḥarbīyah was confined to the area of Bāb Ḥarb about two *mīl* (four kilometers) distant from the city, and that it gave the appearance of a separate town, with markets of all kinds, a principal mosque, and an enclosure wall.[138] Even the original palace complex was affected by the ravages of time. The arcades of the Round City were partially destroyed by flooding in the 330s Hijrī,[139] and the great cupola that crowned the former Caliphal palace collapsed in A.H. 329, a symbolic event that formally marked the passing of an era for both the city and the empire that sustained it.[140]

The Khaṭīb did not invent the aforementioned juridical principle; he simply explained Aḥmad b. Ḥanbal's statement by combining a well-known legal concept with a few well-known geographical facts. Because the canals that framed the Round City and its environs predated the Manṣūrid construction, there is no reason to doubt that the earliest generation of scholars at Baghdad could have drawn the same conclusion as the Khaṭīb—that the area encompassed by the proposed government sector was, from the outset, a distinct municipal entity.[141] Conveniently enough, the existence of such a government sector during the formative years at ʿAbbāsid Baghdad, can provide the most suitable starting point for understanding the city's subsequent growth. Although there is no clear indication when this commercial district began to develop, the need for a local market in the north must have been felt from the onset of settlement in that area. One may then suppose that provision was made for the early introduction of distributive outlets, a scheme later adopted by the Caliph's great-grandson al-Muʿtaṣim during the construction of Sāmarrā in the third century A.H.[143]

Like his ancestor before him, the Caliph al-Muʿtaṣim was much concerned with problems of security, particularly as they related to his newly formed Turkish regiments. Improvising on a pattern previously established at Baghdad, the Caliph settled these units far from the general populace and even separated them from the other military contingents at Sāmarrā. The Turkish cantonments, in their splendid isolation, nevertheless required basic services and supplies, so that a *suwayqah* (pl. *suwayqāt*) was established at each locality. The term *suwayqah* is the diminutive of *sūq*, which, in Arabic, literally means "market"; however, in this case the basic difference between the two is one, not of size, but of function. This is clear from the explicit description of the *suwayqāt* at Sāmarrā, each of which reportedly "contained several shops (*ḥānūt*) for men such as foodsellers (*fāmiyīn*), butchers (*qaṣṣābīn*), and dealers in other indispensable commodities and services."[144]

As described by Yaʿqūbī, the markets of the Damascus Gate were far more substantial than a distributive outlet (*sūq aẓīmah fīhā jamīʿ al-tijārāt wa al-biyāʿāt*),[145] but he is apparently portraying a later moment in the history of the city, namely, the great expansion of the suburbs in A.H. 157, when measures were taken to provide each well-defined suburban district (*rubʿ*) with its own market facilities.[146]

F. The Dynamics of Urban Expansion: Preliminary Thoughts

In the end, the history of urban planning at Baghdad was one of conspicuous failure. This does not imply that the various schemes to partition the greater urban area into governmental and private sectors were not thoughtfully conceived or efficiently executed. The rapid and unprecedented growth of the new capital simply overwhelmed the authorities and compromised the most meticulously planned developmental patterns. For those who believed in the signs of the stars, this should have come as no great surprise. As Madīnat al-Salām was completed, the Caliph sent for Nawbakht, the astrologer, who cast the horoscope of the city and discovered that Jupiter was in Sagittarius. The signs (needless to say, all favorable) spoke of the "city's long life and of the greatness of its civilization and predicted that the world would gravitate to it in order to enjoy what it had to offer."[142] These were regarded, to be sure, as "good tidings . . . a gift indicated by the stars"; but the horoscope ultimately signified a mixed blessing, for the rapid growth of this vast urban area and the accompanying prosperity of the recently established imperial center undermined the initial urban design by setting into motion disruptive economic forces.

The very factors that caused the Caliph to abandon the Round City were soon in evidence in the areas adjoining the military cantonments to the north. The Khurāsānī regiments, like the inhabitants of the palace complex, could not function effectively without more direct access to services and supplies. Ya'qūbī, in describing the northwest suburbs, indicates the existence of a market area in the vicinity of the Damascus Gate. Although it is not likely that the commercial section of the Damascus Gate was comparable to al-Karkh or the new markets of the East Side, the area, with its large government sector caught between the demands of security and supply, seems appropriate for the kind of suburban development previously suggested. Thus, the original *suwayqāt* would have grown into a more extensive network of establishments, though presumably it still would have lacked the comprehensive infrastructure of artisans that characterized the great commercial districts of the city.

The placement alone of a substantial market facility in an area otherwise designated as a government sector, would have affected the delicate function of the northern suburbs. However, given the dynamics of urban growth, the development caused by the presence of the market was far more complex than simply the pernicious encroachment of the public domain into an area hitherto restricted for official use. The authorities themselves developed a vested economic interest in the general expansion of the greater urban area, for, aside from direct extortion and perhaps long-distance trade, investment in landed property remained the best means of raising substantial private and public sources of revenue. Thus, in addition to the very important topographical changes resulting from the development of the suburban districts, the manner in which the building program was carried out by the early ʿAbbāsid Caliphs reflected some rather sophisticated notions on the use of state and private capital and ultimately led to the direct involvement of the government in a wide variety of commercial and industrial enterprises.

An apt illustration of the process is found in a tradition preserved by the Khaṭīb and others concerning the Caliph al-Mahdī and a visiting Byzantine Patrikios.[147] It appears that, when al-Mahdī became Caliph, an ambassador was sent from Byzantium to offer his congratulations. Upon being received by the new Caliph, the Patrikios remarked, "I have not come to the Commander of the Faithful for the sake of wealth or any ulterior motive, but have come yearning to meet him and thereby see his face, for, indeed, we have found written in our books that the third person from the house of this community's Prophet (*ahl bayt nabī hādhihi al-ummah*) will fill the earth with justice, just as in the past it has been filled with tyranny." Al-Mahdī was pleased by these words and promised the Patrikios that he would fulfill any wish the ambassador might have. The Patrikios was then led to his quarters and honored with a variety of gifts. After having remained there for a while, he was treated to a tour of the urban area and passed by a particular location that he thought suitable for a commercial investment. Mindful of the Caliph's offer, he requested that al-Rabīʿ, the wazīr, arrange for a loan of 500,000 dirhams, "so that I may build a commercial establishment (*mustaghallā*) that will return the initial investment within a single year." An undertaking of such magnitude required the attention of al-Mahdī himself. When informed of the Patrikios' plan, the Caliph did not hesitate, but replied, "Give him 500,000 dirhams and 500,000 better; also pay him whatever income the property may yield, and, should he return to his native land, send him the money in yearly installments." Al-Rabīʿ acted accordingly and the great Mills of the Patrikios (*Riḥā al-Baṭrīq*) were built at the confluence of the Lesser and Greater Ṣarāt. When the ambassador returned to Byzantium, the income from the venture was forwarded to him until the time of his death, at which point the Caliph ordered the mills annexed to his own property (*an yuḍamma ilā mustaghallihi*). This is, to be sure, a tradition that is understood on several levels. The flattering words of the Byzantine to indicate that this was not an ordinary diplomatic exchange between a head of state and a foreign dignitary. The ambassador's greetings commemorated al-Mahdī's election to supreme rule among the Muslims and set the tone for future relations between the Byzantine Emperor and the new ruler of the Islamic realm. Thus, the Patrikios is presented as having chosen his words carefully in order to elicit a favorable response from the Commander of the Faithful.

On the face of it, al-Mahdī had reason to be pleased with a statement identifying him as the third person from the house of the Prophet; that is, the one who "will fill the earth with justice just as, in the past, it has been filled with tyranny." The contemporary reader (or listener) attuned to the subtle nuances of the tradition realized only too well how pleased the Caliph should have been, because the prophetic expectations reflected in the Patrikios' remarks were derived from a familiar eschatological conception. That is to say, the arrival of such a person from the house of the Prophet signaled the coming of the Messiah, when the body politic would be cleansed of impurities and replaced with the justice of a pristine age. In Arabic, the most appropriate technical term for the Messiah is al-Mahdī, literally, "he who is rightly guided." The informed reader clearly understood the literary play here and was well aware that the account signified, on the one hand, the advent of a messianic era long heralded by 'Abbāsid propagandists and, on the other, the emergence of a new Caliph bearing a regnal title commensurate with their expectations.[148]

One supposes that, in modern times, the Byzantine diplomat might have been accused of meddling in the internal affairs of a sovereign and independent nation, for his congratulatory message was not as innocuous as it might at first seem. The Patrikios, through his deliberate choice of language, was supporting the claims of the Manṣūrid branch of the ruling family against both external and internal challengers. As recorded in the text, the third person from the house of the Prophet (*ahl al-bayt*) specifically denotes the third Caliph of the 'Abbāsid line. The text therefore argues against the 'Alid house, which understood *ahl al-bayt* to mean the descendants of 'Alī b. Abī Ṭālib.

The ambassador's formulation thus undermined an ideological conception that had been central to 'Alid claims since the rebellion of al-Mukhtār in the previous century.[149] Were this not enough, the account also supports the legitimization of al-Manṣūr's son in opposition to the deposed heir apparent 'Īsā b. Mūsā and other potential contenders from within the ruling family, for, without saying so explicitly, it affirms that al-Manṣūr's successor was destined to be called al-Mahdī (that is, the Messiah), the very title assumed by Muḥammad upon taking office.

Because the tradition is perfectly consistent with other commissioned efforts to promote the Manṣūrid line, it is questionable that these words were ever uttered by the Byzantine ambassador.[150] Be that as it may, the historicity of the mills is above suspicion.[151] A close reading of the text leads one to believe that, if there is anything authentic in this tradition, it is the incidental economic data gathered from the words and actions of al-Mahdī. The first and most obvious impression conveyed by the account is that of the new Caliph's largesse. Although the ambassador's specific request was for 500,000 dirhams (an enormous sum), the Caliph doubled the amount and added other benefits as well.[152] The story thus portrays a generous al-Mahdī—a sharp contrast to his lamented father whose frugal, indeed austere, nature was widely known. However, the account is not only an exemplar of the Caliph's generosity, as it was no doubt intended to be, it also describes his ability to determine a good investment. For, according to the original stipulation of the grant, the income from the mills accrued to the Caliph's personal fortune following the death of the Patrikios. In time, the mills yielded a full twelfth of the entire property tax collected at Baghdad.[153]

The sources speak less favorably of al-Mahdī's father and predecessor, al-Manṣūr, whose reputation for parsimony was well-known. There is, however, another dimension to al-Manṣūr's legendary frugality, one that reveals him to have been familiar with highly sophisticated techniques of raising revenues. It should be recalled that the great development of the suburbs in A.H. 157 was financed from the Caliph's personal funds according to a complex plan that he had himself conceived.[154] The picture of al-Manṣūr's generosity during this moment of urban expansion seems, at first glance, incongruous in comparison with other accounts portraying him doling out salaries in small coins and cutting down on expenditures for various government projects. It becomes somewhat less difficult to understand al-Manṣūr's actions, however, if one assumes that the Caliph's primary concern during this period of building activity was not with expenditures, but with revenues.

His decision to develop various areas beyond the walled city can hardly be regarded as a spontaneous act of largesse, for, prior to their development, there were apparently no special taxes levied on market properties. Subsequent to the development of the suburbs, however, a special tax (*ghallah* and *ujrah*) was fixed, its amount reportedly based on the size of the business establishment.[155] In the favorable economic climate generated by the growing imperial center, the desire to participate in the Caliph's program was very great. The market areas underwritten by al-Manṣūr could not provide facilities sufficient to satisfy all who were interested in expanding the existing commercial enterprises. The energetic entrepreneurs were not to be denied, however; they financed the development of their own establishments, but, significantly, because no capital was provided for them by the Caliph, they petitioned for, and were granted, preferential treatment in the tax structure (*faulzimū min al-ghallah aqall mimmā ulzima alladhīna nazalū fī binā' al-sulṭān*). The government thus provided both direct and indirect incentives to increase commerce and industrial production in order to supply the needs of a burgeoning urban population. At the same time, the state generated an additional and continuous source of revenue, for the original investment was presumably returned many times over in tax receipts.

Other reports indicate that it was not until the reign of al-Mahdī that taxes were levied on the market areas.[156] However, this conflict in testimony, which is already recognized by the medieval authorities, may refer specifically to specific markets of the East Side that were not developed until the transfer of the government across the river, or to a change in the tax structure itself, or to both. Perhaps favoring this second interpretation is the report that al-Mahdī's tax program was undertaken on the advice of his wazīr, Mu'āwiyah b. 'Ubaydallāh b. Yāsar.[157] An expert in such matters, Ibn Yāsar had previously reformed the fiscal structure of the Sawād by basing the tax formula on a percentage of the yield (*muqāsamah*) rather than on a fixed sum (*misāḥah*), although the latter system was not entirely abandoned.

In theory, the net effect would have been to make the tax structure more flexible, allowing for a maximum of revenue while minimizing the distress of the agriculturists. Implicit in this policy was the realization that set taxes, accompanied by agricultural decline, would, in the long run, be counterproductive and result in a shortage of revenues as well as serious social dislocation.

Could the Caliph's wazīr have instituted a similar system to cover specific types of urban levies? Or put somewhat differently, could the principle of progressive taxation have been applied to the entrepreneurs in order to provide the state with a steady source of revenue? The practice would have been only a partial innovation, for, despite the confusion of the medieval sources regarding special property taxes, there is no compelling reason to doubt that a liberal tax program was not already in effect during the reign of al-Manṣūr. It will be remembered that his agent reportedly gave preferential treatment to those venturesome merchants and artisans whose building activities were not covered by government grants. These urban taxes are said to have been collected according to the size of the establishment (*'alā qadr al-dhirā'*),[158] but another source indicates that the Caliph assessed them relative to the wealth of the craft (*'alā qadr al-ṣinā'ah*).[159] If this last expression does not confuse the two methods, it may very well indicate that the fixed levy (size of establishment) was supplemented (or replaced?) by a second assessment adjusted to the income of the more lucrative enterprises. In this fashion, the burden of taxation would theoretically have fallen on those able to sustain it. A silk or spice merchant dealing with expensive items operating from a relatively small establishment was most assuredly a better source of revenue than, say, a large producer of household pottery. The rationale is similar in principle to the reforms in agricultural taxation, causing one to speculate that the levy (*'alā qadr al-ṣinā'ah*) attributed incidentally to al-Manṣūr by a late (twelfth century A.D.) source was in fact an innovation of al-Mahdī, thereby reconciling the confusion surrounding the origins of the special property tax. In either case, the total yearly income derived from this initial investment was reported to be 12,000,000 dirhams.[160]

There is reason to believe that the Caliphs were not alone in seeking such investments. Once the possibility existed of acquiring enormous and continuous revenues from landed property (and, indeed, from other commercial ventures), many lesser government officials are likely to have emulated the initiative of the ruling family, particularly after the expansion of the markets. They were governed in these matters by the Ḥanafite jurists who were predominant at Baghdad, and thus could have benefited from the most flexible legal approach to commercial arrangements allowed by Islamic law.[161] Short of direct participation in trade and industrial production, what possibilities were there for public servants to augment their fixed salaries and thus guard against an inflationary spiral?

During al-Manṣūr's Caliphate, the West Side of Baghdad quickly filled up, with areas of occupation becoming contiguous. The crowding became so apparent that various building regulations were enforced in the exclusive new areas across the river in order to prevent the same congestion there.[162] Nevertheless, the excessive demands on space created excellent prospects for investment, particularly in the market areas of the crowded West Side. The commercial and industrial development of the city and the resulting dislocation were likely to have created heavy speculation based on rising land values, so that, generally speaking, the enterprising land broker stood to profit handsomely. This was apparently true during the construction of Sāmarrā, an imperial city whose growth was comparable, in many respects, to that of Baghdad. That is to say, a feverish building program of enormous magnitude created a critical need there for services, supplies and *Lebensraum*. Although it is well to remember that suburban expansion in Baghdad called for settling lands that had been previously unoccupied, the new urban plan meant that various populated areas as well were scheduled for redevelopment. A more efficient series of roads was required to handle the increased flow of traffic. As a result, the thoroughfares were broadened to forty cubits (approximately sixty feet), and those dwellings that projected out onto the roads scheduled for widening were demolished by right of eminent domain.[163] The creation of various new canals between the 'Īsā and the Ṣarāt no doubt created similar problems.[164]

There was, in addition, a rather different type of dislocation, one that is somewhat analogous to the transfer of the modern business executive. In this instance, the individual was not displaced from his dwelling because the land was needed for urban development. On the contrary, he retained the original property but was forced to relocate his residence for reasons of a more discreet nature, namely the transfer of the palace complex. The Caliphs periodically shifted their residences and the administrative agencies of the government, causing certain elements of the court and the bureaucracy to move along with them. Thus, various courtiers, officers and public officials found themselves possessing several land grants simultaneously. For the grantee who was willing to convert some of his property into a commercial investment, the situation presented unusual opportunities for economic gain. It may have also led, however, to further civilian encroachment in the area originally designated as the government sector. The full extent of this pattern is probably not reflected in the topographical sources, for they are incomplete and describe only the major holdings. Moreover, pertinent information on the subsequent history of the original grants is limited essentially to the estates of the wazīr al-Rabīʿ b. Yūnus and al-Manṣūr's brother al-ʿAbbās. Nevertheless, some speculative remarks based on this highly restricted sample are very much in order.

When al-Mahdī established his palace complex at al-Ruṣāfah, al-Rabīʿ b. Yūnus, like many other important notables, was compelled to take up residence on the East Side.[165] This left the wazīr with two other estates reportedly granted him by al-Manṣūr across the river. These were a so-called inner fief (*al-dākhilah*), and an outer fief (*al-khārijah*) that some authorities credit to the beneficence of al-Mahdī.[166] The exact location of these land grants is unclear. According to the Khaṭīb, the inner estate was *bayn al-sūrayn ẓahr Darb Jamīl*, literally "between the walls in back of the Street of Jamīl." G. Salmon, the original editor and translator of the text, seems to suggest that the inner fief was actually located in the Round City *entre les deux murailles* (presumably an attempt to explain the designation inner).[167] Salmon's reading is not without logic, but the expression *bayn al-sūrayn*, if it applies to the architecture of the palace complex, can only refer to the *intervalla* between the double protective walls, and the Khaṭīb is quite explicit in pointing out that no building was permitted in this space. [168] Moreover, it is difficult to imagine what kind of grant could have been issued for such an area: an open avenue between two walls, approximately one hundred twenty-five feet wide and anywhere from one to four miles long.

It is far more plausible to emend the text and read "[at] Bayn al-Sūrayn," thus designating an actual place of that name.[169] The second reading is based on an entry of Yāqūt that indicates that, although the name Bayn al-Sūrayn is derived from the double walls of the city (*tathniyat sūr al-madīnah*), it had been, in fact, a large neighborhood (*maḥallah*) of al-Karkh until its destruction during the Saljūqid conquest (A.D. 1055).[170] This account seems to agree with Ya'qūbī, who fixes the Fief of al-Rabī' (unspecified as to inner or outer) somewhere in the vicinity of the Karkh Gateway (*Bāb al-Karkh*), a place that commanded the western approaches to the suburb.[171] Furthermore, Darb Jamīl, which reportedly backed onto the fief, was set in the Anbārite Mosque Quarter, a neighborhood that was, according to the topographical sources, also situated near Bāb al-Karkh.[172]

The Khaṭīb and Ṭabarī, citing the same account, report that the Fief of al-Rabī' (unspecified) was located on lands originally cultivated by the inhabitants of a village called Banāwarī. The village itself was in a subdistrict (*rustāq*) of Bādūrayā, the major administrative unit (*ṭassūj*) of southwest Baghdad.[173] As such, Bādūrayā encompassed all the territory between the Ṣarāt and Nahr 'Īsā, the legal boundaries of the greater area that came to be known as al-Karkh.[174]

Although the Khaṭīb continues with his discussion of the fief, Ṭabarī is compelled to interject a wry story concerning an official (*dihqān*) from Bādūrayā.[175] It seems the dihqān visited a colleague, dressed in a torn garment. This immediately caught the attention of the host, who inquired about his careless attire—the dihqāns wore distinctive uniforms that were representative of their office.[176] The visitor explained that his garment had been torn by the crowds of people seeking Bāb al-Karkh—this, in a place where, for a long time, rabbits and fawns had to be driven away. The implication is clear: the dihqān, in describing the enormous changes brought about by urbanization, is specifically referring to the farm land around Bāb al-Karkh that was incorporated into the inner fief of the Caliph's wazīr.

However, these accounts, which place the Fief of al-Rabī' near Bāb al-Karkh, are seemingly contradicted by still another statement. According to the Khaṭīb, the land occupied by Suwayqat Ghālib and the Fief of al-Rabī' (again unspecified as to inner or outer) was originally called Warthāl.[177] The geographer Yāqūt reports that, before the development of Baghdad, the land occupied by the Nahr al-Qallā'īn Quarter was a village called Warthāl, thus forcing the inescapable conclusion that the Fief of al-Rabīʿ was located in Nahr al-Qallāʾīn.[178] The latter was, however, situated in the eastern part of the great southern suburb (*maḥallah kabīrah fī Baghdād fī sharqī al-Karkh*). It therefore cannot be placed near Bāb al-Karkh, which was at the western extremity. In fact, the Sunnite population of Nahr al-Qallāʾīn came to consider itself as distinct from the Shīʿites of al-Karkh, with whom they had numerous and well-documented altercations (*ahluhā sunnah kānat baynahum qadīman wa liahl al-Karkh ḥurūb dhukirat fī al-tawārīkh*).[179]

The contradiction found by contrasting the two series of accounts is, nevertheless, more apparent than real. Indeed, the data resolves a long-standing problem, that is, the position of the inner and outer fiefs and the origin of their designations. For, if al-Rabīʿ actually held land in Nahr al-Qallāʾīn, the reference here is most assuredly to a second estate, the so-called outer fief of the wazīr. One recalls that the development of the Nahr al-Qallāʾīn Quarter belongs to a second stage in the growth of the city, after the Caliph al-Manṣūr left the palace complex for a new residence at al-Khuld.[180] Because the new palace was situated east of the Round City, the wazīr's second estate would have brought him closer to his patron and the adjoining residences of the ruling family. This conclusion also explains the designations "inner" and "outer." The inner fief was considered part of al-Karkh, as it was situated just inside the gateway that signaled the approaches to the market suburb from the west. The outer fief, though it was technically part of the greater southwest suburb, was a newer area that apparently attained some identity of its own and thus remained, in some respects, outside a more narrowly defined al-Karkh.

The purpose of this rather lengthy digression is to indicate that the western land grants of al-Rabīʿ b. Yūnus were situated on prime lands in the most vibrant commercial district of the city. It is not surprising, therefore, that, upon moving to the East Side, the wazīr converted his estates into commercial property (*aswāq wa mustaghallāt*), from which he presumably realized a healthy source of income.[181] The occupants of the inner fief were various clothing merchants from Khurāsān, including some who dealt with exclusive wares (the commercial uses of the outer fief are not specified).[182] Al-Rabīʿ and his son after him continued as absentee landlords until the occupants gained possession of their establishments from the family.[183]

A similar story concerning investment in real estate is told of al-'Abbās, the youngest brother of Abū Ja'far al-Manṣūr. When al-Mahdī established his residence on the East Side, the 'Abbāsid notable moved to an estate somewhere in the vicinity of the bridgehead and converted his western land grant into a "garden" (*ja'ala qaṭī'atahu fī al-jānib al-gharbī bustān*).[184] The acquisition and conversion of this western property is described in some detail by Yāqūt.

It appears that al-'Abbās was visiting with Mūsā b. Ka'b (some say 'Umārah b. Ḥamzah), one of the most prominent generals serving the state. During the course of the conversation, the Caliph's brother commented about the limited space in Mūsā's residence, which was situated near an expanse of land (*raḥbah*) opposite the walls of the Round City. The general replied that he was planning to correct the situation. Because the Commander of the Faithful had already begun to distribute land grants (during the suburban development of A.H. 159), Mūsā had decided to ask the Caliph for the nearby property in order to facilitate the necessary expansion. Al-'Abbās remained silent, but, after concluding his visit, he went to the Caliph and preempted Mūsā's bid, thereby acquiring the property for himself. It was subsequently called al-'Abbāsīyah.

The text of Yāqūt preserves the deed (*sijill*) to this estate: "You requested that the Commander of the Faithful grant you the open space [*sāḥah*] that was previously utilized as a brick yard during the construction of Madīnat al-Salām. The Commander of the Faithful hereby grants it to you per your request. The responsibility for the property is thus yours [*ḍaminta*]."[185] The author then adds a puzzling comment. The language is somewhat difficult, but it seems to indicate that al-Manṣūr was responsible for transmitting the tax revenue from this holding to Egypt (*wa kāna taḍammana lahu an yu'addiya kharājahā biMiṣr*). If this interpretation is correct, the purpose underlying this curious arrangement becomes clear in light of a variant reading preserved in the Mashhad manuscript of Ibn al-Faqīh.[186] Here the text reads: *wa ja'ala yu'addī kharājahā biMiṣr faittakhadha bihā al-'Abbās zanj kānū yunsabūna ilayhī fayuqālū zanj al-'Abbās*. That is to say, "and he [al-Manṣūr] took responsibility for transmitting tax revenue from the property to Egypt, where al-'Abbās acquired the slaves that were known by his name, that is, the slaves [*zanj*] of al-'Abbās."[187] The presumption is that the fief, which lay between the Lesser and Greater Ṣarāt, was subsequently cultivated with this imported labor; its crops grew throughout the year, were harvested in all seasons, and enjoyed a wide reputation as fine produce.[188] Although the initial planting was in a type of bean (*baqillā'*) that was a diet staple, there is the impression that al-'Abbās may have diversified his farming to include other crops, such as those later seen at Sāmarrā, and possibly plants that could be used for industrial purposes, for example, in the production of resins and dyes.[189]

In the account of Yāqūt, the story of al-'Abbās's crafty acquisition is first introduced in a shortened version: the author simply indicates that al-'Abbās acquired the fief by snatching it from one of the army commanders by devious means (*fasabaqahu ilayhā al-'Abbās za'ūj*). There is no condemnation implied by this; perhaps there is even a grudging admiration for his resourcefulness. After all, Mūsā b. Ka'b was interested only in expanding an estate that was too small for his purposes, whereas the Caliph's brother seemed to have a clear vision of the island's business potential.

One need not assume, however, that all the army officers were innocent in matters concerning investment and real estate. It is reasonable to suppose that steps similar to al-'Abbās's development of his fief were taken by other government functionaries who moved across the Tigris. They would therefore have been able to establish residences in the fashionable new sections of the East Side, while retaining financially attractive holdings in the older quarters—particularly in al-Karkh, but also north of the Round City, in the newly expanded commercial area that had originally been the government sector. The movement of many army contingents across the river could not have helped but stimulate such a development. For the public functionary or military officer who otherwise was limited to a fixed salary and occasional bonuses, the opportunity to augment his income through investment in real estate must have been compelling. In any event, he had the Caliph and the ruling family to serve as his models.

Although these developments were largely a result of self-interest, they facilitated, in the short run, economic expansion and general prosperity. Who could have foreseen the clouded long-term prognosis? In the end, the expansion of the city could not be controlled, and the unsatiable appetite for private wealth and influence created the precondition for the salient decline of the 'Abbāsid capital and the empire as well.

POSTSCRIPT

> Then know—and you will know it well—that this dynasty ['Abbāsid] was one of the greatest. It ruled the world through a political program that was coupled to both the spiritual and the temporal. The best and most pious obeyed it out of religious considerations, the rest out of fear or self-interest.
>
> Then know that the 'Abbāsid dynasty was one marked by deceitful maneuvers and trickery. The elements of subterfuge and deceit were more in evidence than those of power and strength, especially in its later days . . . Nevertheless it was [until later times] a dynasty of many praiseworthy qualities and virtues.
>
> Ibn Ṭabāṭabā (Beirut), 140, 149-50: reflecting on the rise and fall of the 'Abbāsids

There are perhaps few civilizations that can boast of a family dynasty possessing the longevity of the 'Abbāsids. They ruled, as it were, for five hundred years, a tribute, to precedents established by the founding Caliphs and to a later resilience in the face of changing circumstances. Given the turbulent history of government in early Islam, it is doubtful that an astute observer would have predicted so long a tenure. It is true that, when Hulākū's Mongol forces conquered Baghdad in A.D. 1258, the power that had been vested in the early 'Abbāsid Caliphs had long since passed on to others outside the ruling family. And yet, although the Caliph was no longer de facto ruler, it was held inconceivable that the body politic could exist without his formal presence.

Tradition has it that, when Hulākū considered executing the Caliph al-Musta'ṣim, thereby signifying an end to the dynasty, he was initially dissuaded from doing so, for an act of such magnitude might very well tamper with the cosmic order of the universe. The sun might be veiled, the rains might cease to fall, and the earth might fail to give rise to vegetation.[1] Whether or not the Mongol Sulṭān actually experienced feelings of dread is very much beside the point. Until this tragic moment of history, the presence of an 'Abbāsid Caliph, no matter how chosen or how legitimate, had long been recognized as a prerequisite for established order.[2]

Ibn Ṭabāṭabā, undoubtedly viewed the end of the 'Abbāsid polity with mixed feelings. He was, after all, an 'Alid, the direct descendant and namesake of a ninth-century member of the Ḥasanid branch who, like other members of his family, had been martyred in an attempt to overthrow 'Abbāsid rule and restore the family of 'Alī b. Abī Ṭālib to its rightful place at the head of the Faithful. On the other hand, the 'Abbāsids, like their 'Alid kinsmen, were tied by blood to the family of the Prophet. Their collapse thus marked the first time since the overthrow of the Umayyads that the clan of Hāshim did not exercise de jure authority over the entire house of Islam. The continuity that characterized 'Abbāsid rule and, to some extent, 'Alid counterclaims, was at last broken, and with it, the living connection between the origins of Islam and those who commanded the realm.

These five centuries of continuous rule must have seemed incongruous to Ibn Ṭabāṭabā and others like him. At the least, the steadfastness of the ruling house presented the 'Alids and their sympathizers with a vexing problem. If God indeed dispenses justice to the righteous, why were those best qualified for leadership perennially ordained to experience high office from a distance? The mysterious ways of God are without proper explanation; however, the 'Alids were generally resourceful in explaining their lack of good fortune. If their record of resistance to 'Abbāsid rule left much to be desired, it was because they often had to consider the wider interests of the Islamic *ummah*: the preservation of unity among the Faithful. In Ibn Ṭabāṭabā's words, "The best and most pious obeyed it out of religious considerations, the rest out of fear or self-interest." Public order, even when tarnished, is preferable to no order at all.

It can hardly be said that such sentiments were derived from the earliest Islamic experience. The 'Abbāsids themselves were elevated to power in a period of residual anarchic tendencies and messianic anticipation. Their charge was to restore the body politic to the pristine state that allegedly had characterized the age of the Prophet. To that end, they eliminated those responsible for public order in a revolution with far reaching consequences. However, despite dramatic expectations, the 'Abbāsid triumph did not give rise to the millennium, and the party that had destroyed the fabric of government was compelled to establish it anew in circumstances somewhat less idyllic than those of the messianic era.

Divisive ethnic loyalties and demands for regional independence could not be allowed to compromise the powers of the emergent regime. Concessions would have served only to recreate the conditions that had brought down the house of Umayyah. What was required was a polity based on the intensive centralization of power and the cultivation of new political attitudes that would create, for all public elements, a vested interest in the orderly process of government. To give visual expression and continuity to the new order, the ʿAbbāsid Caliphs surrounded themselves with symbolic trappings of authority to a degree hitherto not seen in the world of Islam. So dazzling were the manifestations of ʿAbbāsid rule, that it was difficult, even when the Caliphate declined, for loyal subjects to distinguish form from substance. A sense of continuity had been created and it had taken hold despite the political vicissitudes that gripped the government apparatus.

The basis for an enduring ʿAbbāsid state was thus established with the genesis of the dynasty. Modern observers, viewing what seemed to be an unprecedented concentration of power in the hands of the new ruling family, speak of a transition from "patriarchal to absolute monarchy." It is found perfectly natural that once "a state gained a certain size . . . [absolute] monarchy seemed the only suitable alternative to a rapacious armed oligarchy. . . . The [general] principle . . . was to give one man in the community the disinterestedness of unchallenged supremacy—to make him so highly privileged that no one could hope to be his rival, so that his interests were no longer pitted against those of other individuals but became merged with those of the community as a whole. . . ."[3]

The processes by which the ʿAbbāsids moved towards absolute rule were not simple; they were painstakingly subtle and exceedingly complex. It would seem that the authorities not only showed sympathy to their loyal constituencies; they also anticipated and then catered to their requirements, thereby forestalling the emergence of an organized and identifiable opposition. When the government was later unable to respond to the needs of particular groups, the social infrastructure did not allow for radical changes. There were, to be sure, lateral shifts in authority, but, although the power of the ruling family steadily eroded, the continued presence of the 'Abbāsid Caliphate was taken as axiomatic. Even the encroachment of foreign conquerors—and, in the case of the Būyids, Shī'ites—could not disturb the sacrosanct nature of the Caliphate itself. It is no wonder that Hulākū is reported to have thought carefully before tampering with that which had been divinely ordained.

Nevertheless, even at its height, the 'Abbāsid authority, though highly centralized and always visible, was somewhat short of absolute. Contemporary Islamic society was based more on networks of interpersonal relations than on a well-defined governmental infrastructure. To some extent, this may be regarded as the legacy of the revolutionary experience that propelled the 'Abbāsids to power; others perhaps will see in this the residual effects of tribal identification. In both instances, a high premium was placed on personal loyalty and a narrowly focused group association. A more dramatic interpretation might link this development to the nature of Islam itself, but an explication of such a view must be reserved for another occasion.

The highly personal ties that bound each Caliph to the army and governmental bureaucracy could not always be transferred to his successor with the same intensity. Moreover, the ruling house was soon beset by a number of candidates bearing authentic credentials for supreme rule. Political figures attached to a particular prince were quick to realize that their own fortunes were tied to his. The world of the court became one of intrigue and counterintrigue as many leading clients became provocateurs in an effort to enhance the position of their patron. The army, in turn, was capable of accepting any ruler who satisfied the legal requirements to command the faithful. In the years of declining Caliphal authority, the choice of a candidate was likely to have been less important than the all-consuming ambitions of his promoters.

Although the particular circumstances of a given succession could result in the breakdown of public order, all parties generally showed the desire for a return to normalcy. To paraphrase the political adage of an American public servant: The business of government is business as usual. The weakened Caliphate still remained the single most visible institution that created a sense of cohesion and stability in the wider Islamic community. With each successive blow, it came to share these functions more and more with a burgeoning religious establishment. The diffuse nature of religious institutions in Islam, however, tended to divide loyalties and thus probably delayed the ultimate demise of ʿAbbāsid rule. The Command of the Faithful may have indeed been suffering from a fatal illness, but it clung to life and seemed to linger interminably before wasting away. Over the centuries, the physiognomy of the realm underwent enormous changes. From an empire that extended from Central Asia to North Africa, it gradually shrunk to a truncated regional entity confined largely to its native Iraq.

The most striking characteristic of the ʿAbbāsids is not, however, their declining imperial fortunes, but the duration of their rule. Their longevity was due, in no small part, to policies established by al-Manṣūr and his successors during the formative years of the dynasty. Even after decline had set in, the magnificent government architecture, the elaborate court ceremonial, the careful attention to rank, both as regards position and dress, all created a style of rule that generated a sense of distance and awe. As time passed, these reflected only an illusion of power, but, for the public, they had the operative force of established authority.

The praetorians who eventually wrested power from the Caliphate could not wield symbols of authority in quite the same way. What emerged was a partnership of convenience, one that was eventually to include elements of the religious establishment as well. The military groups that ruled through the Caliph could of course build magnificent structures of their own, palaces that might rival and even surpass that of the ʿAbbāsid sovereign. The Būyid amīr, ʿAḍud al-Dawlah, is said to have spent considerable time studying the Caliphal enceinte in an attempt to emulate the physical surroundings of the Commander of the Faithful. To that end, the Būyid built the spacious Dār al-Mamlakah in the Mukharrim quarter of Baghdad.[4] But, at the moment of his greatest triumph, and in full public view, the actual power at the capital was, in accordance with protocol, asked to kiss the ground before his acknowledged sovereign. Given the impotence of the Caliph in contrast to the real power at the Būyid's disposal, ʿAḍud al-Dawlah was first inclined to refuse. He yielded, however, for he was a man who fully appreciated the consequences of proper social, and hence political, behavior.[5] The Caliph could be manipulated behind the scenes to suit Būyid interests; there was no need to tamper with society's expectations in public.

Ibn Ṭabāṭabā understood these matters only too well.[6] In citing the opponents of the Baghdad regime, he draws attention to the Būyids ('Aḍud al-Dawlah), the Saljūqs (Ṭughril Bak), and the Khuwārizm Shahs ('Alā' al-Dīn), all of whom dominated the city while the 'Abbāsid Caliph seemed powerless. The question of who holds power and how it is held, however, can be exceedingly subtle, as the author points out in a rather ironic passage:

> All of this [tribulation] and yet 'Abbāsid rule continued. No dynasty was powerful enough to put an end to their rule and obliterate the traces of their existence. On the contrary, one of the aforementioned rulers would assemble and lead large armies before arriving at Baghdad. And when he arrived, he would seek an audience with the Caliph; and when admitted to the Caliph's presence, he would kiss the ground before him. His utmost wish was that the Caliph appoint him to some position and present him with a standard and the robe of honor. When the Caliph did that, the ruler would kiss the ground before him and walk astride the Caliph's stirrup, the latter's saddle-cloth tucked under his arm.

That such appearances were still important centuries after the founding of the dynasty and long after the loosening of Caliphal control is a tribute to the firmness with which al-Manṣūr and his successors laid the foundations of future power and influence.

APPENDIX A

PROTO-SHĪᶜITE CONTENDERS

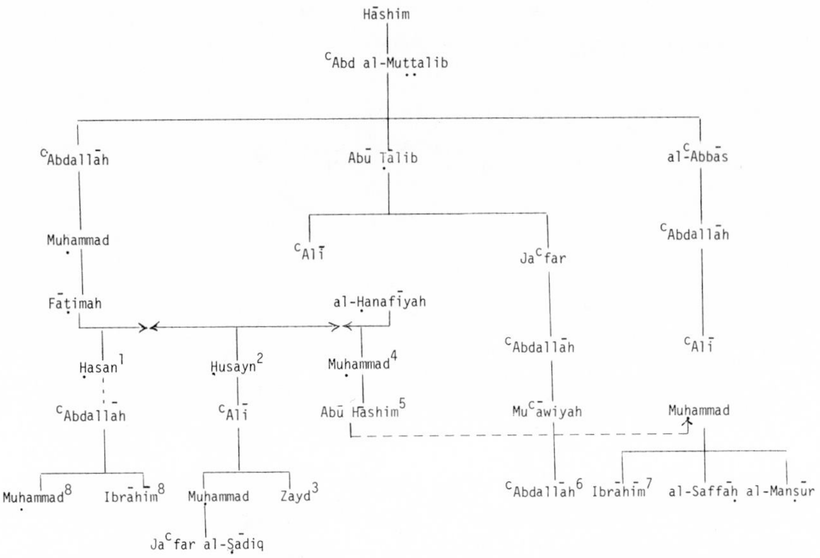

[1] Resigned (661 A.D.)

[2] Killed at Karbalā (680 A.D.)

[3] Killed during revolt at al-Kūfah (740 A.D.)

[4] Imām of Mukhtār's revolt at al-Kūfah (685-87 A.D.)

[5] Transferred authority to ᶜAbbāsids (ca. 716 A.D.)

[6] Killed by Abū Muslim following the revolt against the Umayyads (747 A.D.)

[7] Allegedly killed by the Umayyads (749 A.D.)

[8] Killed in the widespread ᶜAlid revolt of 762 A.D.

APPENDIX B

THE EARLY ABBĀSID CALIPHS

- Al-ʿAbbās, uncle of the Prophet
  - Muḥammad b. ʿAlī (d. 124 A.H./742-43 A.D.)
    - Ibrāhīm al-Imām (d. 132/745)
    - Abū al-ʿAbbās al-Saffāḥ (132-36/750-54)
    - Abū Jaʿfar al-Manṣūr (136-158/754-775)
      - Muḥammad al-Mahdī (158-169/775-785)
        - Muḥammad al-Hādī (169-170/785-86)
        - Hārūn al-Rashīd (170-193/786-809)
          - Muḥammad al-Amīn (193-98/809-13)
          - ʿAbdallāh al-Maʾmūn (198-218/813-33)
          - Abū Isḥāq al-Muʿtaṣim (218-27/833-42)
            - Later Caliphs

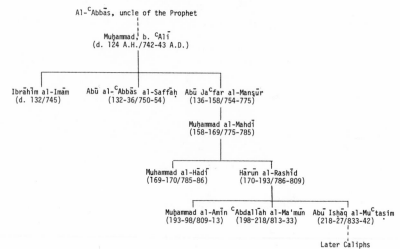

APPENDIX C

THE MANṢŪRID FAMILY

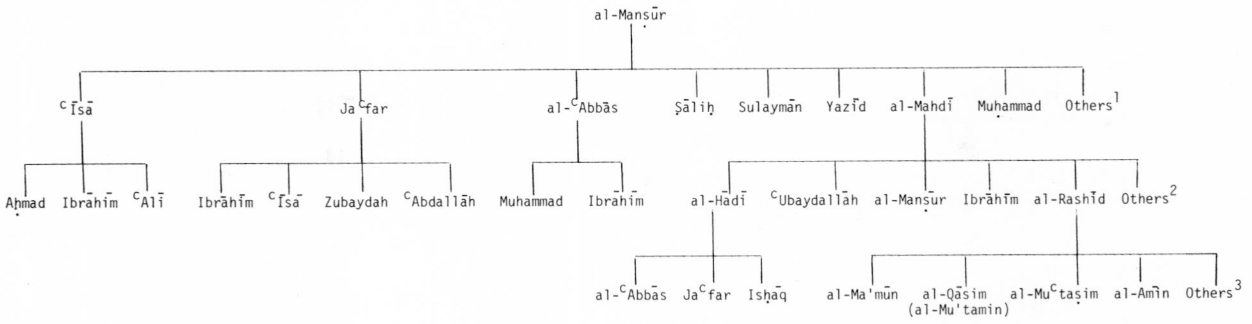

---

[1] Al-Qāsim, Yaʿqūb, ʿAbd al- Azīz: obscure and leave no record of offspring.

[2] Yaʿqūb, Alī, Isḥāq and four daughters.

[3] ʿAlī, Ṣāliḥ, Muḥammad (Abū ʿĪsā), Muḥammad (Abū Yaʿqūb), Muḥammad (Abū al-ʿAbbās), Muḥammad (Abū Sulaymān), Muḥammad (Abū ʿAlī), Muḥammad (Abū Aḥmad), Abū Muḥammad.

APPENDIX D

THE FAMILY OF MUḤAMMAD B. ʿALĪ

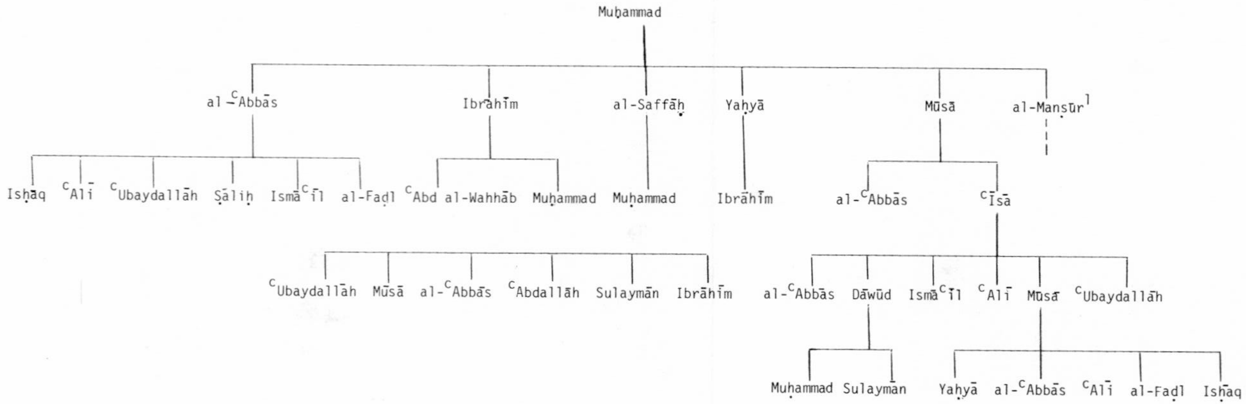

[1] See Manṣūrid Family

APPENDIX E

THE ᶜUMŪMAH

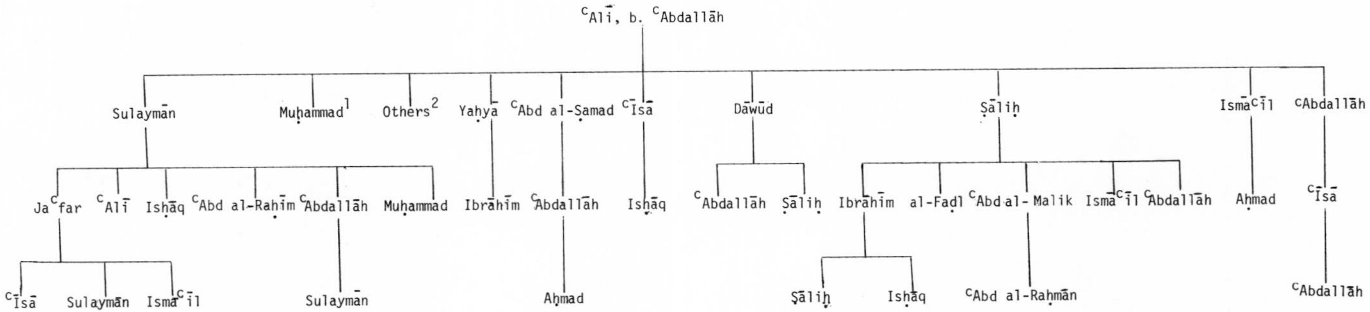

---

[1]Gives rise to ᶜAbbāsid Caliphs. See Appendix B.

[2]Bishr, Aḥmad, Isḥāq, Mubashshir and others. Obscure and leave no offspring.

NOTES

INTRODUCTION

1 J. Wellhausen, *Das Arabische Reich und sein Sturz*, trans. M. G. Weir, *The Arab Kingdom and Its Fall*, 558.

2 Ibid., 543-66.

3 M. Shaban, *The 'Abbāsid Revolution*. One may wish to note his rather sharp remarks concerning the scholarship that preceded his work. Despite the author's dramatic claims, this work is confined essentially to the problem of Arab settlement in Khurāsān and is based on his doctoral dissertation, "The Social and Political Background of the 'Abbāsid Revolution in Khurāsān." The events of the revolution are confined to the last chapter of the book.

4 See F. Omar, *Al-'Abbāsiyūn al-awwā'il: 132-70/750-86* and *The 'Abbāsid Caliphate, 132-70/750-86*. Note the excellent, but as yet unpublished, dissertation of M. Sharon, " 'Alīyat ha-'Abbāsīm la-shilṭōn"; and the dissertation of D. Dennet, "Marwān b. Muḥammad; the Passing of the Umayyad Caliphate."

5 T. Noeldeke, *Orientalische Skizzen*, trans. J. S. Black, *Sketches from Eastern History*, 107-45.

6 M. Shaban, *Islamic History: A New Interpretation*, vol. 2, is an exception because of its conceptual boldness, but it is rather idiosyncratic and not altogether reliable in its documentation.

CHAPTER I

1 For a description of the qualified 'Abbāsid notables, see n. 3.

2 Regarding his birth (A.H. 103), see Ṭabarī, 3/1:328; for Abū Muslim's offer, see Omar, *Caliphate*, 167, 175: Balādhurī, *Ansāb al-ashrāf*, 505a-b; Kūfī, 236b; Ṭabarī 3/1:100, MS A.

3 'Abdallāh b. 'Alī's career as a military and political figure needs no retelling here. It is sufficient to say that he was, except for the Caliph and possibly Abū Muslim, the most powerful figure in the 'Abbāsid state. Dāwūd b. 'Alī emerges as Abū al-'Abbās's most trusted confidant. He introduced the Caliph to the public at the time of Abū al-'Abbās's investiture, and he received the first political appointment of the new 'Abbāsid state when he became governor of al-Kūfah. He later took over the Ḥijāz and al-Yamāmah, relinquishing his post in Iraq to his great nephew 'Īsā b. Mūsā (Ṭabarī, 3/1:33-35, 37, 60, 64). His early death in A.H. 133 may indeed have produced wider ramifications than we shall ever adduce from the sources. 'Abd al-Ṣamad b. 'Alī was the conqueror of al-Mawṣil (Azdī, 134, 145-46) and held a major command under 'Abdallāh b. 'Alī in the

battle for Damascus (Ṭabarī, 3/1:47ff.). During 'Abdallāh's brief revolt, he was designated as heir apparent (Azdī, 163). Ṣāliḥ b. 'Alī also held a major command during the siege of the Umayyad capital and continued with his brother during the Palestine campaign (Ṭabarī, 3/1:48-49). 'Īsā b. Mūsā, before assuming his position at al-Kūfah, was attached to the force of al-Ḥasan b. Qaḥṭabah, which was besieging Ibn Hubayrah at Wāsiṭ (Ṭabarī, 3/1:37). Ismā'īl b. 'Alī, who was a governor in al-Ahwāz (Ṭabarī, 3/1:73), later replaced the Caliph's brother Yaḥyā, who had crushed the Umayyads in al-Mawṣil (Azdī, 145). The fact that this third brother is not mentioned again before his death in 136 is very interesting. Sulaymān b. 'Alī became governor of al-Baṣrah (Ṭabarī, 3/1:72).

4 The late sources Ibn Ṭabāṭabā (Beirut), 160, and Ibn al-Athīr, *Kāmil*, 6:20, for al-Manṣūr's ability as a military figure at Wāsiṭ.

5 Ṭabarī, 3/1:64, 65, 71; *FHA*, 208ff.

6 Ṭabarī, 3/1:56-57, 58, 72, 87; Azdī, 159.

7 *'Uyūn al-akhbār* (Cairo), 1: 206ff.

8 Sharon, " 'Alīyat," 36-75; S. Moscati, "Il testamento di Abū Hāshim," 28-46.

9 Sharon, " 'Alīyat," 237-48; esp. 241, 246.

10 Ibn Khayyāṭ, 2:451, reports that he was the governor of al-Baṣrah sub anno A.H. 140. He therefore must have been a temporary replacement during the period following the removal of Sulaymān b. 'Alī. Muḥammad is later reported to have taken part in the campaign against the 'Alid rebel in al-Madīnah (*FHA*, 241, sub anno A.H. 145). The use of the 'Abbāsid ruling family in this campaign was probably conditioned by political rather than military considerations and thus would not reflect his military prowess (see Chapter III, Section B). I am indebted to Mr. Amikam Cohen for calling to my attention various traditions in Balādhurī's, *Ansāb* that indicate the denigration of Muḥammad. One looks forward to the publication of these traditions by Mr. Cohen.

11 Ṭabarī, 3/1:87ff.

12 It is not clear whether Yaḥyā was eventually replaced for his brutal suppression of the revolt, in which thousands, including women and children, were reported to have lost their lives. There was much plunder and the markets were not operative until three years later. An interesting feature of this event was the presence of a slave (*zanj*) contingent (Azdī, 152ff., 157; concerning the *zanj*, 149). Ismā'īl owned commercial property in the city, including a *funduq* that was in the Sūq al-Ṭa'ām and a bath house that was also situated there. In addition, he possessed considerable agricultural lands in the area (Azdī, 197, sub anno 146). Concerning the history of other royal properties confiscated by al-Rashīd, see Ṭabarī, 3/1:607-608, sub anno 173; Mas'ūdi, *Murūj* (Beirut), 3:337; *FHA*, 242, sub anno 172. This was in reference to al-Baṣrah, where the properties of Muḥammad b. Sulaymān b. 'Alī, totaling about sixty million (dirhams) in assets, were seized. These included not only land and cash assets, but also clothes, furnishings, slaves, animals, and jewels. Only the rubbish (*khurthā*) was left behind. The economics of the royal family and its retainers are well worth serious study. For some brief speculative views, *see* J. Lassner, *The Topography of Baghdad in the Early Middle Ages: Text and Studies*, 184-88.

13 Azdī, 177. The event is recorded in the chronicles of al-Mawṣil, sub anno A.H. 142. Al-Manṣūr, seeking to strengthen his position, had already removed Sulaymān b. 'Alī from his post at al-Baṣrah and transferred 'Abdallāh b. 'Alī from Sulaymān's protective custody to al-Ḥīrah. Concerning the removal of royal governors in A.H. 141, see E. Zambauer, *Manuel de généalogie et de chronologie pour l'histoire de l'Islam*, 20-24. Sulaymān died in al-Baṣrah in A.H. 142 with 'Abd al-Ṣamad praying over him (Ṭabarī, 3/1:14). Note that Ṭabarī, 3/1:421, indicates that Sulaymān b. 'Alī was alive in A.H. 158 and was the recipient of a large grant from the Caliph. The last account mentions several other uncles and probably confuses Sulaymān with 'Abd al-Ṣamad b. 'Alī, who lived until the reign of al-Rashīd. Difficulty with still another uncle is reported in Ya'qūbī, *Historiae*, 2:468 (the event cannot be chronologically fixed). The Caliph apparently feared Ṣāliḥ b. 'Alī, who, as governor of Qinnasrīn, amassed considerable equipment and men. He was therefore recalled to Baghdad and for a while became persona non grata at the court. The Caliph's attitude towards the *'umūmah* apparently mellowed towards the end of his life (was there a political motive?). In A.H. 158, he bestowed enormous sums of money on Ṣāliḥ, Ismā'īl, 'Īsā, and, perhaps, 'Abd al-Ṣamad b. 'Alī (see Ṭabarī, 3/1:421).

14 Regarding the Persian account, see H. Zotenberg, *Chronique de abou Djafer Mo'hammed ben Djarir ben Yazid Ṭabarī*, 4:324. For the *ba'yah* to Abū Ja'far, see *FHA*, 213. However, see Ya'qūbī, *Historiae*, 2:420 (mentions *ba'yah* to Abū al-'Abbās alone); Dīnawarī, 373 (mission unspecified—*yunādhiruhu* [that is, Abū Muslim] *fī ba'ḍ al-umūr*); Ṭabarī, 3/1:61 (mission unspecified), 58 (to consult about the prospective murder of Abū Salamah Ḥafṣ b. Sulaymān).

15 See Sharon, "'Aliyat," 36-75, for the most complete exposition of the circumstances surrounding Abū Hāshim's last will and testament; and S. Moscati, "Il testamento," 28-46. For his prophecy, see Ya'qūbī, *Historiae*, 2:357. Note that al-Manṣūr, although the eldest, was not chosen to succeed Ibrāhīm al-Imām. For a later tradition making Abū al-'Abbās the elder brother, see al-Kūfī, 220b.

16 *Akhbār*, 138; also 139-40.

17 Mas'ūdī, *Murūj* (Beirut), 3:282.

18 Mas'ūdī, *Murūj* (Paris), 6:90.

19 *FHA*, 216; Azdī, 162.

20 Wellhausen, trans. M. G. Weir, 533-34.

21 See B. Lewis, "The Regnal Titles of the First 'Abbāsid Caliphs"; and Khaṭīb (Cairo), 1:92 = Paris, 38, for a similar play on his name. Concerning the difficulties with 'Īsā b. Mūsā, see Chapter II, Section D.

22 Sharon, "'Alīyat," 237-48, esp. 241, 246.

23 Variants of this tradition are found in Ṭabarī, 3/1:1903; and Mas'ūdī, *Murūj* (Paris), 6:217-18. Concerning the claims of 'Abdallāh b. 'Alī based on having taken the field against Marwān, see Ṭabarī 3/1:92-93; Ya'qūbī, *Historiae*, 2:437-38; Azdī, 163ff; Mas'ūdī *Murūj* (Beirut), 3:289. See also Tha'ālibī, *Laṭā'if al-Ma'ārif*, ed. P. DeJong (Leiden, 1867), 58-59.

24 *'Uyūn al-akhbār* (Cairo), 1: 206ff.

25 For the complicated problem of the massacre of the Umayyads, there is S. Moscati, "Le massacre des Umayyades dans l'histoire et dans les fragments poétiques," 88-115.

26 Ya'qūbī, *Historiae*, 2:425-26; and perhaps Balādhurī, *Ansāb*, 763a-b.

27 Moscati, "Le Massacre," 88-99; and Ibn Ṭabāṭabā (Beirut), 151-52.

28 Ibid., 99-106.

29 The list of these officers is preserved in Ṭabarī, 3/1:93. It includes Abū Ghānim al-Ṭā'ī, Khufāf al-Marwarrūdhī, Abū al-Aṣbagh, Ḥumayd b. Qaḥṭabah, Khufāf al-Jurjānī, Ḥayyāsh b. Ḥabīb, Mukhāriq b. Ghaffār, Turārkhudhā (?), and unspecified others from *ahl Khurāsān wa al-Shām wa al-Jazīrah*. Ya'qūbī, *Historiae*, 2:438, emphasizes the compliance of the Syrians but specifies no names. He also indicates that Qaḥṭabah and others from among the commanders testified concerning the pledge of Abū al-'Abbās (p. 437). Concerning the Umayyad treasuries, see *FHA*, 219.

30 Ya'qūbī, *Historiae*, 2:439, reports the defection of Ḥumayd b. Qaḥṭabah, who heard that there was a threat against his life; see also Ṭabarī, 3/1:93-94, 101. It is reported that, when 'Abdallāh b. 'Alī learned that Abū Muslim was marching against him, he felt he could not trust his Khurāsānī troops, and thus killed 17,000 of them. Whether true or not as regards detail, it appears that 'Abdallāh b. 'Alī drove the Khurāsānīs to back al-Manṣūr or, more correctly, to back Abū Muslim. Regarding the more diplomatic handling of these matters by Abū Muslim, see Ṭabarī, 3/1:96. Omar, *Caliphate*, 184-85, citing Balādhurī's *Ansāb*, 762a-b, notes the "hostile relations between Khurāsānīs, Syrians, and Jazirites in 'Abdallāh's very army." He further states that the Khurāsānīs took the oath to 'Abdallāh without enthusiasm and points out that the major appointments were not given to them. However, this last point is not supported by Ṭabarī, 3/1:93, which he also cites. It is very likely that there may have been tension between various constituencies in 'Abdallāh's army. Nevertheless, on the basis of Ṭabarī and Ya'qūbī (see n. 29 above), it appears that the Khurāsānīs initially supported him without reservation. Indeed, it was their testimony about the pledge of Abū al-'Abbās that served as the basis for his ideological claims.

31 One of the first acts of 'Īsā b. Mūsā was to march from al-Kūfah to the Capital in order to secure the treasuries and the administrative apparatus for Abū Ja'far, who was en route from the Ḥijāz (Ṭabarī, 3/1:92).

32 See Ṭabarī, 3/1:90—indicating Abū Muslim's confidence that 'Abdallāh b. 'Alī would not be able to retain the loyalty of his Khurāsānī troops.

33 Ya'qūbī, *Historiae*, 2:438. 'Īsā b. 'Alī had been governor of Fārs in 132 and again in 133-34 (Zambauer, list G).

34 Ṭabarī, 3/1:94-99; Ya'qūbī, *Historiae*, 2:439; Dīnawarī, 375. Note that Ṭabarī, 3/1:98, indicates in a brief statement, which is not preceded by any *isnād*, that Ismā'īl b. 'Alī was pardoned in the aftermath of the war, implying that he also took sides. There is no evidence to support this statement.

35 Ṭabarī, 3/1:122, sub anno 138.

CHAPTER II

1 No full-length study of this subject has yet appeared. There is only the article of F. A. Tuqan, "'Abdallāh b. 'Alī; A Rebellious Uncle of al-Manṣūr," which treats the material in a conventional manner. See also *EI*[2], s.v. 'Abdallāh b. 'Alī. Mr. Amikam Cohen of Hebrew University is now making a study of the first 'Abbāsid Caliph, Abū al-'Abbās, that one expects will shed new light on early 'Abbāsid relations for he has made use of relevant materials in Balādhurī's *Ansāb al-ashrāf* that have not been published.

2 Ya'qūbī, *Historiae*, 2:442; Ṭabarī, 3/1:126-27; *FHA*, 226.

3 Ya'qūbī, *Historiae*, 2:439; Ṭabarī, 3/1:125-26; *FHA*, 226; Jahshiyārī, 104; Azdī, 167.

4 His treachery was eventually hurled back at him by his ideological opponents. See Ṭabarī, 3/1:209-10, sub anno 145; *FHA*, 240-41, Azdī, 182-87. The texts describe an exchange of letters between the Caliph and the 'Alid rebel Muḥammad b. 'Alī. In them the rebel responds negatively to an offer of amnesty, "What guarantees of amnesty will you give me? The guarantee of Ibn Hubaryah, or of your uncle 'Abdallāh b. 'Alī, or that of Abū Muslim." Although the ideological claims of the 'Abbāsids found in these letters apparently became official policy only in the reign of al-Mahdī (*Akhbār*, 164-65), there is no compelling reason to doubt that the letters are authentic and that the breached agreement engendered much embarrassment and cynicism.

5 Ṭabarī, 3/1:330-31; *FHA*, 258-59; Mas'ūdī, *Murūj* (Beirut), 3:304-306.

6 Mas'ūdī, *Murūj* (Beirut), 3:305. For the fact that he was the first to be buried in the cemetery at the Damascus Gate, see also Khaṭīb (Cairo), 1:120-21 = (Paris) 78-79. The cemetery was named after Abū Suwayd, who, along with his son, owned considerable property there. See also Yāqūt, *Mu'jam*, 3:488; Lassner, *Topography*, index.

7 Khaṭīb (Cairo), 10:9.

8 Ibid., 1:73 = (Paris) 11. Note also that floods in Baghdad tended to undermine the foundations of buildings. For example, ibid., 1:76 = (Paris) 16, sub anno 330s; Ibn Miskawayh, 2:8; Ibn al-Jawzī, *Muntaẓam*, 6:300, 315-16, sub annis 328 and 329.

9 Ṭabarī, 3/1:331. Variants of this account are found in *FHA*, 259; and Mas'ūdī (Beirut), 3:306.

10 The account of Mas'ūdī, *Murūj* (Beirut), 3:306, seems to be the earlier version. In it, the question reads: "Do you know a Caliph whose name begins with *'ayn* who killed three great men whose names begin with *'ayn*?" 'Abdallāh replied, "Yes. You, O Commander of the Faithful. You killed 'Abd al-Raḥmān b. Muslim, 'Abd al-Jabbār b. 'Abd al-Raḥmān, and your paternal uncle 'Abdallāh b. 'Alī, upon whom the building fell." The Caliph then asked, "Am I to blame if the building fell upon him?" The reply—"You are not to blame." The Caliph then smiled. The text does not report, as does Ṭabarī, that the populace can spread falsehood; moreover, the direct accusation of guilt here is only implied in Ṭabarī.

11 See Chapter IV, Section A.

12 This is a theme played with many variations. The account here is derived from Ibn Hishām, 1:323-25. The exact date for its provenance cannot be established, but the author of the text was a fixture at the 'Abbāsid court.

13 See the article of J. Schacht, *EI, Supplement* = *EI*, shorter edition, s.v. *Ḳatl*. For a list of the legal authorities at Baghdad, there is L. Massignon, "Cadis et naqībs baghdadiens," 2:258ff. One should be aware, however, that the rules cited may belong to a later systemization of law.

14 Ṭabarī, 3/1:569, 571, and repeated in Ibn Ṭabāṭabā (Beirut), 191 (smothered with a pillow); Suyutī, *Ta'rīkh al-khulafā'* (Cairo, 1888), 109; Ibn Taghrī Birdī, 1:458 (poisoning). The entire issue of al-Hādī's last days is treated in a general fashion by N. Abbot, *Two Queens of Baghdad*, 105-112; regarding his short reign, see S. Moscati, "Le Califat d'al-Hādī," 1-28. The exact location of 'Īsābādh cannot be determined, but it was somewhere near Baghdad, if not in it, on the East Side. According to Yāqūt, *Mu'jam*, 3:752-53, al-Mahdī granted it to his son 'Īsā. A palace (Qaṣr al-Salām) was built there at the cost of fifty million dirhams. The location of 'Īsābādh is important for reconstructing the events of another tradition that implies the Caliph died a natural death after a long illness (see Text below).

15 Ṭabarī, 3/1:569, 578; Qifṭī, 431; Ibn Abī Usaybi'ah, 1:126.

16 Reservations concerning the historicity of 'Abbāsah's murder are listed in the article of J. Horovitz in *EI*[2]; Citing all relevant bibliography, one should add D. Sourdel; *Le Vizirat 'Abbāside de 749 ā 936*, 1:151-181, esp. 159, 167; and Abbot, 195-197. For some general observations concerning 'Abbāsid clientage, see Chapter IV.

17 Dīnawarī, 395; Ṭabarī, 3/2:913-14; Mas'ūdī, *Murūj* (Paris), 6:472-74. Khaṭīb (Cairo), 1:69 = (Paris), 5, indicates he took to the river to divert himself (*tanazzaha*) and was killed there. This is obviously in error for the military situation would hardly have allowed for a pleasure trip. This version seems to be suggested by various stories that indicate that the Caliph delighted in spending his leisure time on the Tigris.

18 Ya'qūbī, *Historiae*, 2:536; Dīnawarī, 395; Mas'ūdī, *Murūj* (Paris), 6:477; Ṭabarī, 3/2:920-21. For the final events of his life, see Ṭabarī, 3/2:919-24; Mas'ūdī, *Murūj* (Paris), 6:478-82; Khaṭīb (Cairo), 1:68 = (Paris), 4.

19 Jahshiyārī, 304.

20 Mas'ūdī, *Murūj* (Beirut), 3:448-49.

21 Ṭabarī, 3/1:37 (besieging Ibn Hubayrah at Wāsiṭ under the command of Ḥumayd b. Qaḥṭabah; more particularly, his role against the 'Alid rebels). See, for example, Ṭabarī, 3/1:230ff; *FHA*, 241ff; and esp. Azdī, 194 (with respect to the great public acclaim given him); Mas'ūdī, *Murūj* (Beirut), 3:296.

22 See Chapter I, Section A.

23 Ṭabarī, 3/1:112-14. On the background of the affair of Abū Muslim, see R. N. Frye, "The Role of Abū Muslim in the 'Abbāsid Revolt," 28-32; and esp., S. Moscati, "Studi su Abū Muslim," 4:323-35, 474-95; 5:89-105; and Omar, *Caliphate*, 163ff.

24 Ṭabarī, 3/1:114-116.

25 Ibid., 116.

26 Ibid., 328-30; *FHA*, 257ff.; Mas'ūdī, *Murūj* (Beirut), 3:305, sub anno 149—a variant of the other accounts but essentially the same plot. See Text and n. 29 below.

27 The most extensive account of the Caliph's dealings with his nephew is found in Ṭabarī 3/1:331-52, and *FHA*, 259-60. Ironically, among the implied threats to the life of 'Īsā b. Mūsā was a situation in which elements of a building came down upon him (Ṭabarī, 3/1:338). Regarding 'Īsā b. Mūsā's original place in the succession, see Chapter I, Section A.

28 Ṭabarī, 3/1:351; *FHA*, 260.

29 Following the version in Ṭabarī, 3/1:328-30. Mas'ūdī, *Murūj* (Beirut), 3:305 gives a somewhat different story.

30 Mas'ūdī, *Murūj* (Beirut), 3:305.

31 The reference is to the great palace at al-Ruṣāfah and not the larger area of the East Side that was known by that name. See J. Lassner, "Why did the Caliph al-Manṣūr build al-Ruṣāfah—A Historical Note," 95-99 = *Topography*, 149-54. This work is in need of some revision as regards ethnic settlements of the upper West Side (97 = 152), but the basic thesis still stands. See also Khaṭīb (Cairo), 1:82-83 = (Paris), 23-25; Yāqūt, *Mu'jam*, 2:783. Note that Ya'qūbī, *Buldān*, 251 gives a date of A.H. 143 for the beginning of construction contra Khaṭīb (Cairo), 82 = (Paris), 23; and Ṭabarī, 3/1:364-65. Ya'qūbī also reports that the Caliph left for Baghdad to trace the (Round) City in A.H. 141, and that this had been completed by 144 when the Caliph left to meet al-Mahdī, who was returning from a mission in Khurāsān (that is, his maiden campaign against the Ṣaqālibah). After meeting with al-Mahdī, he encamped at al-Hāshimīyah (the capital before Baghdad). He returned to Baghdad the following year (*Buldān*, 251; *Historiae*, 2:449-50). Ya'qūbī thus gives the impression that as many as four years may have elapsed between the conception of the city and the actual construction, and that al-Ruṣāfah may have been part of the original plan. Note also Dīnawarī, 379, wherein construction of Baghdad was said to be underway as early as A.H. 139; and K.A.C. Creswell, *Early Muslim Architecture*, 2:19, n. 7, citing Ibn al-Jawzī's, *Muntaẓam*, Aya Sofya MS 3095, 68a—A.H. 142. The dating followed by all other early and late historians is A.H. 145 for tracing the plan, thereby marking the onset of construction, and this is most assuredly correct. The later date for the building of al-Ruṣāfah is therefore undoubtedly also correct. See also Lassner, *Topography*, index, s.v.; and G. LeStrange, *Baghdad During the Early 'Abbasid Caliphate*, index, s.v.

32 Ṭabarī, 3/1:364; and Khaṭīb (Cairo), 1:82 = (Paris), 23.

33 Ṭabarī, 3/1:367.

34 Ibid., 471, sub anno 160; *FHA*, 271.

CHAPTER III

1 For a survey of the content and structure of local histories, as well as a list of authors, see F. Rosenthal, *A History of Muslim Historiography* (1968), 150-72 and 457-86, which contains a fully annotated translation of the section on local

histories from al-Sakhāwī's *I'lān*. For other lists of local histories, see 457, n. 1. The information about the period that is preserved in those texts recently made available tends to be uneven. Al-Azdī's, *Ta'rīkh al-Mawṣil*, which is often cited here, contains some useful information, but much of the material is found in the universal chronicles. About this work, see P. Forand, "The Governors of Mosul According to al-Azdī's *Ta'rīkh al-Mawṣil*," 88-106. I have not been able to obtain a copy of al-Ḥarrānī's history of al-Raqqah (Rosenthal, 469, n.1), but, in view of the importance of the city, particularly in the time of al-Rashīd, it might prove very useful.

2 Concerning these titles, see Sharon, " 'Alīyat," 115-16.

3 Ibid., 236: Kūfī, 226a; Ibn Qutaybah, *K. al-Ma'ārif*, 188. He also assumed the role of paymaster, according to Omar, *Caliphate*, 115: Balādhurī, *Ansāb*, 782a.

4 Ṭabarī, 3/1:19ff.; *FHA*, 196; Jahshiyārī, 57; and Omar, *Caliphate*, 139: Balādhurī, *Ansāb*, 785b.

5 *Akhbār*, 270. The meaning of the text is misunderstood by Omar, *Caliphate*, 145-50. The granting of the territories indicated the geographical scope of revolutionary responsibilities and not the later rewards the revolutionaries were supposed to receive. Once these territories were secured for the 'Abbāsids, Abū Muslim and Abū Salamah administered them.

6 Sharon, " 'Alīyat," 237ff. See Omar, *Caliphate*, 139ff., for a detailed but conventional view; and C. Cahen, "Pointes de vue sur la revolution 'Abbāside," 328ff. The remarks concerning Abū Muslim in this chapter are taken from a more comprehensive study of his career on which I am now working.

7 Omar, *Caliphate*, 153: Balādhurī, *Ansāb*, 806a, concerning the dismissal of Abū Salamah's appointees in the provinces.

8 The most complete treatment is that of Sharon, " 'Alīyat," 117ff.

9 Cahen, "Points de vue," 326.

10 Ṭabarī, 3/1:113-14; Mas'ūdī, *Murūj* (Beirut), 3:291-92; *FHA*, 222-23.

11 These two functions went hand in hand at the outset of the revolt (Ṭabarī, 2/3:1956-58, 1962ff., 1969). When the revolution extended to Iraq, the function of paymaster in that region seems to have been given to Abū Salamah and, later, to Khālid b. Barmak, a client of the ruling family. With the elimination of 'Abdallāh b. 'Alī, Abū Muslim emerged as the leading political influence from among the military. Note that, before Abū Muslim left on his ill-fated visit to the Caliph at al-Madā'in, he paid his troops in order to insure their support (Ṭabarī, 3/1:114).

12 *Akhbār*, 270.

13 Ṭabarī, 3/1:87ff., 99-100, 112; *FHA*, 213. It can be argued that, when al-Manṣūr became Caliph, the large retinue was actually needed for Abū Muslim's protection.

14 Sharon, " 'Alīyat," 131: Balādhurī, *Ansāb*, 285a.

15 Dīnawarī, 373-74; Ṭabarī, 3/1:72. Could this refer to the appointment mentioned in n. 14 above?

16 Dīnawarī, 373; Ṭabarī, 3/1:61.

17 Ya'qūbī, *Historiae*, 2:422; *FHA*, 212-13; Jahshiyārī, 90; S. Moscati, "Studi

su Abū Muslim," 324-31; *EI*², s.v. Abū Salamah; Sourdel, *Le Vizirat 'Abbāside,* 65-73; Omar, *Caliphate,* 152: Balādhurī, *Ansāb,* 793a-b.

18 Ṭabarī, 3/1:67-68.

19 See Chapter I, Section A for 'Abdallāh b. 'Alī; and Jahshiyārī, 94, regarding the relationship of the army to Abū Muslim's power. Note the suggestion of Khālid b. Barmak that the size of the army be reduced by eliminating all non-Khurāsānīs.

20 Ṭabarī, 3/1:61, 85-86, Ibn Ṭabāṭabā (Beirut), 168; Dīnawarī, 373. See also Omar, *Caliphate*: Kūfī, 235b; Jahshiyārī, 93, indicates that Abū al-'Abbās himself felt the pressure of Abū Muslim but gives no details.

21 Ṭabarī, 3/1:86; See also Omar, *Caliphate,* 165; Balādhurī, *Ansāb,* 505a-b, who speaks of still another aborted assassination plot.

22 Ibid., 85.

23 Ibid., 67; *FHA,* 209; and Omar, *Caliphate,* 131: Balādhurī, *Ansāb,* 787a.

24 Ṭabarī, 3/1:90, 100ff. Note, however, *FHA,* 215; also Omar, *Caliphate,* 165-67.

25 Note Omar, *Caliphate,* 167, 175: Balādhurī, *Ansāb,* 505a-b; Kūfī, 236b, 240b; Ṭabarī, 3/1:100. Omar states that, "according to Balādhurī, Kūfī, and Ṭabarī, Abū Muslim instigated the heir apparent 'Īsā b. Mūsā to supplant Abū Ja'far before he established himself firmly on the throne." Only the text of Ṭabarī was available to me. He reports that Abū Muslim went to al-Anbār "*wa da'ā 'Īsā b. Mūsā ilā an yubāya'a lahu faatā. . . .* " Ṭabarī, MS A, reads *faabā,* "and he [Īsā] refused," for the clumsy *faatā,* "and he came." According to Omar, the texts of Balādhurī and Kūfī clearly indicate that Abū Muslim had declared for 'Īsā b. Mūsā, but that the Caliph's nephew refused the offer.

26 Ya'qūbī, *Historiae,* 2:438, indicates that Abū Muslim was less than anxious, at the outset, to oppose 'Abdallāh b. 'Alī. He thought of waiting out the conflict and supporting the winner but succumbed to advice against remaining aloof from the struggle.

27 Ṭabarī, 3/1:58ff.; *FHA,* 212-13; Jahshiyārī, 90.

28 Ṭabarī, 3/1:59, and Jahshiyārī, 90, report that blame was fixed upon the Khārijites. The term *khāriji* may, of course, simply mean rebel, but it is clearly used here in its more technical meaning. Abū Salamah is reported to have been taken unawares, for, in the three days prior to Abū Salamah's assassination, Abū al-'Abbās publicly indicated his satisfaction with him through pronouncements followed by the gift of a ceremonial robe (Jahshiyārī, 90).

29 *FHA,* 217-18, indicated that the entire revolutionary establishment (*ahl al-da'wah*) was employed in the campaign against 'Abdallāh b. 'Alī at Ḥarrān. The elimination of Abū Salamah, who had jurisdiction in Iraq, probably meant that the Khurāsānī army in the region came more directly under the control of the ruling family (most likely through 'Abdallāh b. 'Alī). By turning against the Khurāsānīs, who had originally supported him (see Chapter I, Section D), 'Abdallāh b. 'Alī not only sealed his own fate, but also strengthened Abū Muslim's hand in relation to the Caliph by reinforcing Abū Muslim's ties to the

leading generals. See Ya'qūbī, *Historiae*, 2:439; Ṭabarī, 3/1:93-94, 101. Concerning Abū Muslim's diplomatic skill with the army, see Ṭabarī, 3/1:96.

30 Ṭabarī, 3/1:87, 102-104; *FHA*, 219; Dīnawarī, 375; Ya'qūbī, *Historiae*, 2:439; Ibn Ṭabāṭabā (Cairo), 168-69; Omar, *Caliphate*, 169-70: Balādhurī, *Ansāb*, 520a-b, 564a-b, 764b; Kūfī, 238b-239a.

31 *FHA*, 222. Read *Nīzak*(?).

32 Ṭabarī, 3/1:112-14. One notes that 'Īsā b. Mūsā was, according to various reports, an innocent agent to Abū Muslim's murder in delivering him (or allowing him to go) to the Caliph while under his personal protection. This may have ultimately provided the added advantage of tainting 'Īsā b. Mūsā in the public eye. Note that al-Manṣūr, sometime later, sought to remove 'Īsā from the line of succession.

33 Ṭabarī, 3/1:116-17, notes that Abu Mūslim's death was to be followed by the murder of his chief of intelligence (Abū Isḥāq) and the head of security forces (Abū Naṣr). However, the Caliph eventually decided to use them rather than have them killed. In this matter, al-Manṣūr heeded the advice of Abū al-Jahm, Abū Muslim's former liaison with the court. The former counseled that there was no need for further killing since "his [Abū Muslim's] army is yours."

34 Ṭabarī, 3/1:116.

35 Lassner, *Topography*, 129-30.

36 See Chapter I, Section B.

37 *EI*, s.v. Muḥammad b. 'Abdallāh; *EI*[2], s.v. Ibrāhīm b. 'Abdallāh for a general survey of the events and a bibliography. For the apocalyptic tradition, see Ṭabarī, 3/1:272.

38 Ṭabarī, 3/1:227-28; and Iṣfahānī, *Maqātil*, 267-68.

39 Concerning 'Alid contacts with Egypt see Omar, *Caliphate*, 234-35.

40 Iṣfahānī, *Maqātil*, 268: *Ḥunayn b. Jubayr*.

41 Ṭabarī, 3/1:228; Iṣfahānī, *Maqātil*, 268: I see myself putting my hand in impenetrable armor *faawwalahā bilmadīnah* (as in Ṭabarī, A). For a similar response in Umayyad times, see M. J. Kister, "The Battle of the Ḥarra," *Studies In Memory of Gaston Wiet*, ed. M. Rosen-Ayalon (Jerusalem, 1977), 33-49.

42 Ṭabarī, 3/1:228-29.

43 Ibid., 223-24, 291.

44 For the Wādī al-Qurā; see Yāqūt, *Mu'jam*, 4:81, 878 and other references in 6:225. The Wādī al-Qurā was described as being between al-Madīnah and Syria. It was administered from the Ḥijāz (*min a'māl al-Madīnah*) and contained numerous villages (*qurā*), thereby explaining its name. At one time the villages extended the entire length of the *wādī*, but, already by the middle ages, the wādī had become arid and the area was reduced to ruin. It was used as a pilgrimage route from Syria and was a caravan route in pre-Islamic times. Note also Ṭabarī, 3/1:280, wherein foodstuffs are reported to have been cut off from Egypt in order to bring hardship to the *ḥaramayn*.

45 Ṭabarī, 3/1:291.

46 Mas'ūdī, *Murūj* (Beirut), 3:295.

47 The names of several families are preserved in the account of Mas'ūdī, *Murūj* (Beirut), 3:295. They include the descendants of 'Alī (b. Abī Ṭālib), Ja'far, 'Aqīl, 'Umar b. al-Khaṭṭāb, and al-Zubayr b. al-'Awwām. See also Iṣfahānī, *Maqātil*, 277ff. With regard to the traditional scholars who supported the revolt, see Omar, *Caliphate*, 242, n. 38.

48 Ṭabarī, 3/1:291-92, indicates a similar story in which Budayl b. Yaḥyā, who had previously been consulted on delicate matters by Abū al-'Abbās, suggested that the Caliph garrison the province of al-Ahwāz.

49 Azdī, 187, indicates 4,000 men as does Iṣfahānī, *Maqātil*, 267.

50 The contention of Omar, *Caliphate*, 236, that the Caliph sent 'Īsā b. Mūsā in order to get rid of him makes no sense at all in view of the predicted success of the operation in the Ḥijāz and the probable difficulties in Iraq.

51 Ṭabarī, 3/1:291-92.

52 Ibid., 305-306; Iṣfahānī, *Maqātil*, 325.

53 That is to say, the capital at Madīnat b. Hubayrah, which was situated adjacent to al-Kūfah. For a full description of the 'Abbāsid capitals before the building of Baghdad, see Chapter VI.

54 Ṭabarī, 3/1:304-305. There is the report of Ya'qūbī, *Historiae*, 2:452, that Abū Ja'far, who was then encamped at the building site at Baghdad, wanted to attend to Muḥammad b. 'Abdallāh personally. However, he feared leaving Iraq while Ibrāhīm was still unaccounted for.

55 Iṣfahānī, *Maqātil*, 265-66.

56 Ibid., 344. No mention of the Syrians.

57 Ṭabarī, 3/1:305.

58 Ibid., 292.

59 Ibid., 291.

60 Ibid., 292.

61 See Chapter VI, Section C.

62 Ṭabarī, 3/1:305.

63 Note that Ṭabarī, 3/1:291, explicitly identifies the Syrians as the enemies of the family of Abū Ṭālib (*a'adā' āl Abī Ṭālib*). Needless to say, there were also strong historic memories of the sack of the *ḥaramayn* by a Syrian army in Umayyad times.

64 The reference here is to the letters exchanged between al-Manṣūr and Muḥammad b. 'Abdallāh in which the 'Abbāsids set forth their claims to rule vis-à-vis the 'Alid line by way of Fāṭimah. At the same time, they offered a guarantee of safety for their adversaries. See Ṭabarī, 3/1:209-210; *FHA*, 240-41; Mas'ūdī, *Murūj* (Beirut), 3:295; Azdī, 182ff.; Iṣfahānī, *Maqātil*, 268; and Omar, *Caliphate*, 226ff.

65 'Īsā b. Mūsā was accompanied by Mūsā, the son of Abū al-'Abbās. See Ṭabarī, 3/1:223; Azdī, 187. Iṣfahānī, *Maqātil*, 267, also indicates that some 'Alids traveled with the 'Abbāsids. Their function was to serve as negotiators between the parties. Even Ḥumayd b. Qaḥṭabah was considered friendly to the 'Alid (*Maqātil*, 268, 270). One may also note that somewhat later, in A.H. 149, an 'Abbāsid army fighting against the 'Alid al-Ḥusayn b. 'Alī was led by the

notables of the 'Abbāsid house, including Sulaymān b. Abī Ja'far al-Manṣūr, Muḥammad b. Sulaymān b. 'Alī, Mūsā b. 'Īsā b. Mūsā, and al-'Abbās b. Muḥammad b. 'Alī. This battle also took place in the Ḥijāz at Fakhkh, a wādī in Mecca. Guarantees of safety were originally offered here as well, although carnage is reported to have ensued following the refusal of the 'Alid pretender to accept the offer. See the article by L. Veccia Vaglieri in *EI*², s.v. al-Ḥusayn b. 'Alī, Ṣāḥib al-Fakhkh for further details and bibliography.

66 The relationship of the capital to its general environment is developed in J. Lassner, "Massignon and Baghdad: The Complexities of Growth in an Imperial City," 1-27 = Lassner, *Topography*, 155-77. See also R. Adams, *Land Beyond Baghdad*, esp. 84-111. The studies deal essentially with the hinterland of Baghdad and particularly the Diyala Plains. There are, however, implications as well for the cities of southern Iraq.

67 Ṭabarī, 3/1:306.

68 Ya'qūbī, *Historiae*, 2:455-56; Ṭabarī, 3/1:306. The Medinese women presented to al-Manṣūr are reported to have been Fāṭimah bt. Muḥammad b. 'Īsā b. Ṭalhah (Ya'qūbī: Ṭulayḥah) b. 'Abdallāh, and Umm al-Karīm bt. 'Abdallāh, from the family of Khālid b. Asīd b. Abī al-'Īṣ.

69 Ṭabarī, 3/1:308.

70 Ibid., 307-308. Note the glowing terms in which the Caliph described 'Īsā b. Mūsā (*al-shahm al-najd al-maymūn al-muẓaffar*) as well as the importance which he attached to 'Īsā's mission (*la quwwah liamīr al-mu'minin illā bihi*). The victory in the Ḥijāz and the ultimate success of the heir apparent not only secured al-Manṣūr's position, but brought 'Īsā b. Mūsā great honor. See Ṭabarī, 3/1:230ff.; *FHA*, 241ff.; Mas'ūdī, *Murūj* (Beirut), 3:296; and esp. Azdī, 194, regarding the great public acclaim given to the Caliph's nephew.

71 Ṭabarī, 3/1:309ff.; Omar, *Caliphate*, 244: Balādhurī, *Ansāb*, 225b; *FHA*, 252-53, indicates that 'Īsā b. Mūsā had already stationed his forces between Ibrāhīm and al-Kūfah. If true, the purpose of the proposed diversionary attack may have been to open the road to al-Kūfah for Ibrāhīm's forces by drawing 'Īsā b. Mūsā to the nearby capital. One would have to conclude that the 'Alid read the situation quite accurately. Although this failure to sacrifice the Kūfans was ethically correct, given his point of view, it was militarily damaging. If 'Īsā b. Mūsā had not yet positioned his troops in Iraq, the error was even more grave; for al-Manṣūr, with his limited resources at the capital, would have been extremely vulnerable.

72 Ṭabarī, 3/1:310-11.

73 Ibid., 308.

74 Ibid., 310-11, 312. There is, however, the possibility that the martial etiquette of the 'Alids may, in fact, be a widespread literary convention designed to explain their all too frequent reverses in battle.

75 See Chapter III, Section B.

76 Ṭabarī, 3/1:311: *a'rā*; MS A, *a'dā*; Ibn al-Athīr, *Kāmil*, 5:435: *aghrā*.

77 Ṭabarī, 3/1:312.

78 Concerning the development of the 'Alid sects, see M. Hodgson, "How did the Early Shī'a Become Sectarian," 1-14.

79 See Chapter IV, Section D.

80 Based on Ibn Ṭabāṭabā (Beirut), 154-55. For variants, see Ya'qūbī, *Historiae*, 2:418-19; Mas'ūdī, *Murūj* (Paris), 6:93-96; *FHA*, 196-97.

81 Ya'qūbī, *Historiae*, 2:418, indicates that 'Abdallāh al-Mahd came out in favor of his son Muḥammad. Note the persistent rumors of sedition attached to his name. See Ṭabarī, 3/1:116; Ya'qūbī, *Historiae*, 2:424; and also Omar, *Caliphate*: Balādhurī, *Ansāb*, 792a; Kūfī, 232a; and Iṣfahānī, *Maqātil*, 257ff.

82 Ya'qūbī, *Historiae*, 2:453-54 preserves an account that relates how Ibrāhīm slipped through the Caliph's hands and made his way to al-Baṣrah. For the Caliph's indignation with Ja'far and Sulaymān b. 'Alī, see Ṭabarī, 3/1:306-307.

83 Ṭabarī, 3/1:304 (taxes collected), 309, citing Dāwūd b. Ja'far b. Sulaymān (b. Alī?), notes that the *dīwān* of the Baṣrans listed 100,000 names. Ya'qūbī, *Historiae*, 2:454, reports the seizure of the public treasury (*bayt al-māl*) and the registering of 60,000 names on the *dīwān*. Military expenditures for the campaign against the Caliph are given by Ṭabarī, 3/1:300 at 600,000 (dirhams). Azdī, 188, and Iṣfahānī, *Maqātil*, 324, give a figure of one million dirhams distributed from the treasury. Fifty (forty was the usual figure) dirhams were distributed to each soldier. This makes a total of 20,000 men. See also Omar, *Caliphate*: Balādhurī, *Ansāb*, 625a. Concerning other attempts at raising monies, see Iṣfahānī, *Maqātil*, 332ff.

84 According to Ṭabarī, 3/1:301, 17,000 men were dispatched to Wāsiṭ under the command of al-Ḥakam b. Abī Ghaylān al-Yashkarī.

85 Ṭabarī, 3/1:309. It is not clear whether the men pressed into service were local inhabitants forming an irregular infantry or whether Ibrāhīm b. 'Abdallāh followed the 'Abbāsid principle of recruiting an army according to geographical location.

86 *FHA*, 253; Omar, *Caliphate*, 244: Balādhurī, *Ansāb*, 225b.

87 Ṭabarī, 3/1:313.

88 'Īsā b. Mūsā had 15,000 men and Ḥumayd b. Qaḥṭabah had 3,000 under his command. See Ṭabarī, 3/1:310. Concerning the battle, Ṭabarī, 3/1:311ff.; *FHA*, 253; Azdī, 183.

89 This was clear to al-Manṣūr, for, upon receiving the initial news from the battlefield, he prepared to abandon his capital for al-Rayy in Khurāsān. See Ṭabarī, 3/1:317; Iṣfahānī, *Maqātil*, 346.

90 See *EI*², s.v. Ḳaṣr b. Hubayra. Concerning the dangers of al-Kūfah, note Ṭabarī, 3/1:271-72; and placing him at the site of Baghdad, 278, 281, 284.

91 Ṭabarī, 3/1:304.

92 Ibid., 305, 292.

93 He also refused to be guided around the army of 'Īsā b. Mūsā in order to attack the Caliph near al-Kūfah. See Ṭabarī, 3/1:310.

94 Yāqūt, *Mu'jam*, 1:458 describes Bākhamrā as being located between al-Kūfah and Wāsiṭ, but closer to al-Kūfah. He gives the distance between al-Kūfah and Bākhamrā at 17 *farsakh* (1 *farsakh* = 3 Arabic *mīl* or 6 km). Ṭabarī, 3/1:313, indicates 18 *farsakh*; Mas'ūdī, *Murūj* (Beirut), 3:297, gives 16 *farsakh* in the Ṭaff. For the Ṭaff, see Yāqūt, *Mu'jam*, 3:535.

95 Ṭabarī, 3/1:317; Omar, *Caliphate*, 245: Balādhurī, *Ansāb*, 626b.

96 See Chapter VIII.

97 See Ibn Khayyāṭ, 2:471-73.

98 Ṭabarī, 3/1:484, sub anno 160. Note also his desire to turn over the revenues (*ghallah*) from the Nahr al-Ṣilah region below Wāsiṭ to the ruling house and others. See Ṭabarī, 3/1:522, sub anno 168. On Nahr al-Ṣilah, see Yāqūt, *Mu'jam*, 4:841, who indicates the revenues went to the people of the *ḥaramayn*. The early death of Abū al-'Abbās son, Muḥammad, left that particular branch of the family without a future claimant. In a sense, the line of Abū al-'Abbās continued through his daughter Rayṭah, who married her first cousin Muḥammad al-Mahdī. See *FHA*, 214.

99 See the articles of A. A. Duri in *EI*², s.v. amīr and 'āmil. The division of labor in the provincial administration is indicated by numerous references in the chronicles. The most detailed study of these matters is that of D. W. Biddle, "The Development of the Bureaucracy of the Islamic Empire During the Late Umayyad and Early 'Abbāsid Period."

100 Zambauer, 20, 24, 36, 40, 43; supplemented by Ibn Khayyāṭ, 2:429-32, 460-65, 471-73, 496-501. The rule of al-Hādī is excluded because it was of such short duration. The tables are limited to the paternal side of the 'Abbāsid family and are confined to the central provinces of the empire.

101 This does not include the division of the governorship into various administrative offices in A.H. 156 and 158.

102 This figure includes al-'Abbās b. Muḥammad, the Caliph's brother, who was an "honorary" governor, and his son, Ja'far (al-Miskīn). See Zambauer, G.

103 Yazīd, the son of Abu Ja'far al-Manṣūr, was given the Sawād of Iraq during a divided governorship in A.H. 161.

104 Concerning the development of an 'Abbāsid Khurāsānī army in that region, see Chapter V, Section C.

105 Ṭabarī, 3/2:647, 651-67, 704; Ya'qūbī, *Historiae*, 2:500ff.; Mas'ūdī, *Murūj* (Beirut), 3:351-53; *FHA*, 303ff; A. Chejne, *Succession to the Rule in Islam*, 94-107; F. Gabrieli, "La successione di Hārūn al-Rashīd e la guerra fra al-Amīn e al-Ma'mūn," 344ff.

106 For al-Faḍl b. Sahl, see Sourdel, *Vizirat*, 196-213; and for Abū 'Ubaydallāh, 94-103, and *EI*² s.v.

CHAPTER IV

1 Ya'qūbī, *Mushākalat*, 23; translated and annotated W. Millward, "The Adaptation of Men Into Their Time: an Historical Essay by al-Ya'qūbī," 329-44, esp. 338; Mas'ūdī, *Murūj* (Beirut), 4:223.

2 Some may wish to find traces of Shu'ūbī sentiments in the tradition, but it does reflect the actual situation, particularly if one understands *'arab* to mean Arabs with strong ties to existing tribal organization. On the subject of Arabs and the 'Abbāsid military, see Chapter IV, Section D.

3 See Chapter I, Sections D and E.

4 Note, for example, his audacity in requesting that he be permitted to enter the

great central court (*raḥbah*) of the Caliph's palace at Baghdad, a privilege hitherto reserved only for al-Manṣūr's son and heir apparent al-Mahdī. See Khaṭīb (Cairo), 1:77-78 = (Paris), 17-18, who apparently confuses two accounts: one concerning 'Abd al-Ṣamad, the other concerning Dāwūd b. 'Alī. Dāwūd b. 'Alī, however, died in A.H. 133 before al-Manṣūr's palace at Baghdad was built (Ṭabarī, 3/1:73). A variant in Ṭabarī, 3/1:323 identifies the uncle as 'Īsā b. 'Alī and indicates that he suffered from gout. More seriously, 'Abd al-Ṣamad was removed from his post in the provincial administration when he failed to pay proper respects to al-Mahdī, who was then Caliph. See Ṭabarī, 3/1:498ff., 518; Azdī, 243, sub anno 163.

5 Regarding the famed longevity of his family, see Khaṭīb (Cairo), 1:94-95 = (Paris), 42; Ibn Khallikān, trans. De Slane, 1:296. He is reported to have had the shortest pedigree of his era. His ancestors traced back to 'Abd Manāf were identical in number with those of the Umayyad Yazīd b. Mu'āwiyah, although 121 years separated the time of his death from that of Yazīd.

6 The term, as it is used here, signifies the members of the ruling 'Abbāsid family as distinct from their retainers. It is also not to be confused with the narrow 'Alid interpretation. See Sharon, "The 'Abbāsid Da'wā Re-examined on the basis of the Discovery of a New Source," p. 9, n. 23.

7 Concerning the imagery of father-son relationships with regard to the Khurāsānī army at Baghdad, see Chapter V, Section E.

8 See esp. Chapter I, Section A.

9 Brief summaries can be found in the standard handbooks: G. Bergsträsser-J. Schacht, *Grundzüge des islamischen Rechts*, 38-42; T. W. Juynboll, *Handbuch des ilamischen Gesetzes*, 208ff.; D. Santillana, *Istituzioni di diritto musulmano malichita con riguardo anche al sistema sciafiita*, 1:159-60. An extended description is found in P. Crone, "The Mawālī in the Umayyad Period," 155-215; and I. Goldziher, *Muslim Studies*, 1:101ff.; A. von Kremer, *Culturgeschichte des Orients unter den Chalifen*, 2:154ff.; *EI*, s.v. *mawlā*.

10 Some specific observations on 'Abbāsid historiography will be offered in a work now underway that will be a companion volume to this book.

11 I do not follow, however, the argument of W. Von Soden that attempts to link the *mawlā* with the ancient *muškenum*. See "Muškenum und die Mawālī des frühen Islam," 140. Note also the reservations of B. Kienast, "Zu Muškenum = Maula," 99-103. Concerning Pre-Islamic clientage, see the summary of Crone, 166-188.

12 For *muwālāt* clientage, see Crone, 161-63. The case for this type of association is strongly suggested by P. Forand, "The Relation of the Slave and the Client to the Master or Patron in Medieval Islam," 59-66, esp. 59-60, where he describes the clients of *muwālāt* as "a class important mainly in reference to the 'Abbāsid Caliph and the Muslim community as a whole during the second and third *hijrī* centuries." However, he then goes on to discuss manumitted slaves, a rather different form of clientage. See also the comments of Biddle, 66, which are seemingly based on Forand.

13 See Massignon "Cadis," 106-15, for a list of legal authorities at Baghdad.

One should not, however, exaggerate the systemization of the legal "schools" during this early period.

14 Crone, 183-86; Forand, 60-66.

15 Although in early times it was difficult for the freed client of a tribe to change his patron, there were circumstances in which it was possible. Despite official attempts at controlling the practice, it continued. See Goldziher, trans. Stern, 1:132: Iṣfahānī, *Aghānī* (Beirut), 1:129; 3:141. He also cites the account of Ya'qūbī, *Historiae*, 2:597, in which the Caliph al-Mutawakkil (d. A.H. 247) decreed that a client of the Banū Azd could renounce his relationship and become the client of the Caliph. To be sure, the Caliph had extraordinary leverage in these matters. Nevertheless, there was precedent for his action. It would be very useful to make up a list of those important Umayyad clients who were drawn directly to the 'Abbāsid house, particularly those who served in the government bureaucracy. One would assume that most continued to serve the new regime. The problem of courtiers and major military personnel is somewhat more complicated, because the structure of the court and the army was changed in 'Abbāsid times. In addition, the 'Abbāsids accumulated their own clients. Some preliminary data on the government bureaucracy have been compiled by Biddle.

16 S. D. Goitein, "The Origins of the Vizierate and its True Character," *IC* 16 (1942): 255-62, 380-92; "On the Origins of the Term Vizier," *JAOS* 81 (1961): 425-26. These articles are reproduced in his *Studies in Islamic History and Institutions* (Leiden, 1966), 168-96; Sourdel, *Vizirat*, 41-61.

17 Among his various administrative functions, he, at one time, supervised the distribution of the military payroll (*dīwān al-jund*). See Ṭabarī, 2/3:1964; Jahshiyārī, 87-89; *EI*², s.v. al-Barāmika; Sourdel, *Vizirat*, 71-76.

18 Some later Barmakids are known to have actively participated in various campaigns, but they cannot be correctly identified as members of the regular military establishment. Yaḥyā b. Khālid achieved great fame for his victory against the Byzantines at Samālū. A close reading of the brief account, however, indicates that this was a rather trivial expedition for booty designed to give the future Caliph, Hārūn (al-Rashīd), experience in the field. One notes that quite a few members of the Barmakid family were sent on this campaign to accompany the 'Abbāsid prince and advise him. Their function was perhaps more political than military. It is not likely that the Caliph would have sent his son on any campaign where the outcome of victory was in doubt. See Ṭabarī, 3/1:497-98. Mūsā b. Yaḥyā is pictured as a brave warrior in Ṭabarī, 3/2:675, sub anno 178, but there is no indication of his ability as a military commander. Ṭabarī, 3/1:625, sub anno 176, identifies him with a specific campaign, but his function there was actually that of a moderator. On the other hand, al-Faḍl b. Yaḥyā was given control over a vast network of provinces to the east from A.H. 176 to 179. Although unsuccessful in Armīnīyah (see Ya'qūbī, *Historiae*, 2:516), he made significant gains against Yaḥyā b. 'Abdallāh, the 'Alid in Daylam (Ṭabarī, 3/1:613ff.; Jahshiyārī, 189-90), and the non-Arab populations in Transoxiana (Ṭabarī, 3/2:631). In this last campaign, he created a large client army

of non-Arabs in Khurāsān (*ittakhadha biKhurāsān jund min al-'ajam sammāhum al-'Abbāsiyah wa ja'ala walā'ahum lahum . . .*). The text goes on to indicate that 20,000 of these troops were sent back to Baghdad, where they were known as the Karnabīyah, while the remaining 480,000 stayed to serve in Khurāsān. The numbers are no doubt exaggerated, but the combination of these actions indicate that al-Faḍl had accumulated considerable power. See also *EI*², s.v. al-Barāmika; Sourdel, *Vizirat*, 134-81; L. Bouvat, *Les Barmécides d'après les historiens arabes et persans.*

19 The ease with which control was retained by the central authorities is indicated in Ṭabarī, 3/1:116-17. A brief discussion of the revolts can be found in M. Azizi, *La domination arabe et l'épanouissement du sentiment national en Iran*, 135ff. He views the revolts invoked in Abū Muslim's name as an indication of broad Iranian national sentiment against the Arab regime. Even if true, it should be pointed out that the backbone of the Khurāsānī army was Arab or of mixed ancestry, and that these contingents represented the real power of the central authorities (see Chapter V above). Under no circumstances could these outbreaks be regarded as a major threat to the security of the regime. See also Lassner, *Topography*, 129-30, where the case for Iranian sentiments appears to be overstated. Concerning the legendary history of Abū Muslim, there is the work of I. Melikoff-Sayar, *Abū Muslim le "porte-hache" du Khorassan dans la tradition épique turco-iranienne*; and H. Laoust, *Les schismes dans l'Islam* (Paris, 1965), 62-63.

20 See Chapter V, Section D.

21 Some families, though perhaps not actually *mawālī*, became de facto clients of the 'Abbāsid house as the force of tribal association in Khurāsān and Iraq diminished through assimilation, and the system of patronage developed within the government and the army replaced tribal affiliation as a means of protection and advancement. There were, to be sure, *mawālī* represented in the inner circles of the revolutionary movement. See Sharon, "'Alīyat," 75, n. 21, 110ff. With the emergence of the 'Abbāsid regime, these notables became, in effect, the clients of the ruling family. Concerning the critical government agencies held by old revolutionaries and their descendants, see Biddle, 123ff; and also the extremely interesting comments of Crone, 131-44, esp. 137-40. Her analysis, however, seems more clear-cut than the sources dictate. For the beginning of the 'Abbāsid *ḥaras* and *shurṭah*, see Sharon, "'Alīyat," 181, 183-84. A graphic illustration of sentiments concerning a family sinecure is seen in the remarks of al-'Abbās b. al-Musayyab, who represented the third generation of his family to serve as director of security police (*ṣāḥib al-shurṭah*) for the Caliph. After being removed by al-Ma'mūn for being too old and infirm in A.H. 204, he pleaded: "This is my son, O Commander of the Faithful, my place, my profession (*ṣinā'atī*) and the profession of my father . . . we are the family for it [that is, carrying weapons and hence the *shurṭah*]." See Ibn Ṭayfūr (Cairo), 20.

22 Ibn Khaldūn, *Muqaddimah* (Rosenthal), 1:28-29; *K. al-'ibar* (Bulaq, 1284), 5:436ff.; 6:7.

23 Ṭabarī, 3/1:459, sub anno 159, in which they are described as accompa-

nying a force on the *ṣā'ifah*. These *mawālī* may, however, be political figures and not a military force. The young princes were frequently accompanied by clients on campaigns. See, for example, Ṭabarī, 3/1:496, 503. It is possible, however, the *ḥaras* and *shurṭah* consisted largely of *mawālī*. Note that, following the death of al-Hādī, Khāzim b. Khuzaymah, whose family was long associated with the *shurṭah*, apparently took armed *mawālī* to seize Prince Ja'far, thus assuring al-Rashīd's succession. See *FHA*, 290; Azdī, 262 (text appears corrupt). In later times the Turks, are definitely referred to as *mawālī*, and they are, to be sure, fighting contingents of the army. See n. 63.

24 The phenomenon of shadow governments will be discussed in a separate study. Suffice it to say that the naming of more than one son to the list of succession meant that the *mawālī* attached to the young princes had a vested interest in protecting the position of their young patrons. When the young prince was second in line, there was always the danger that he might later be removed from the line of succession. This was a pattern that occurred often under the early 'Abbāsids. Removal meant at least the temporary decline in influence for the princes' advisors. This process culminated in al-Faḍl b. al-Rabī' pushing al-Ma'mūn into open rebellion against his brother al-Amīn in order to protect the influence of the establishment in Khurāsān. See, in particular, al-Faḍl's speech in Ṭabarī, 3/2:773-74.

25 This was, to be sure, the reason for the slave armies introduced in large numbers by al-Mu'taṣim. They were, in fact, referred to by the term *mawālī*. See n. 63.

26 See Chapter V, Section C.

27 See Chapter I, Section D. In late Umayyad times, the term "Syrian" army may signify forces of a wide geographical distribution. The backbone of the last Umayyad army was formed, in fact, by the veterans of the frontier wars against the Byzantines.

28 *EI*², s.v. Ḳaḥṭaba b. Shabīb.

29 Sharon, " 'Alīyat," 280-83.

30 The text referred to here is the edition of 'Umar Abū al-Naṣr in his *Āthār b. al-Muqaffa'* (Beirut, 1966), 345-61. Regarding the author, see the articles of F. Gabrieli in *EI*², s.v. Ibn al-Mukaffa'; D. Sourdel, "La biographie d'Ibn al-Muqaffa' d'après les sources anciennes," 307-23; and S. D. Goitein, "A Turning Point in the History of the Muslim State," 120-35. This last is reproduced in full in Goitein, *Studies*, 146-67.

31 Ibn al-Muqaffa', 345 (Abū Muslim), 346 ('Abdallāh b. 'Alī). About the dating of the text, see Goitein, 153, n. 3, citing F. Gabrieli, "L'opera di Ibn al-Muqaffa'," *RSO* 13 (1931): 231.

32 G. Richter, *Studien zur Geschichte der älteren arabischen Fürstenspiegel*, esp. 4-32.

33 Ibn al-Muqaffa', 348-49; Goitein, 157.

34 For some recent comments on problems of state and religion under the early 'Abbāsids, see I. M. Lapidus, "The Separation of State and Religion in the Development of Early Islamic Society," 363-85.

35 Ibn al-Muqaffa', 355-66.

36 Khaṭīb (Cairo), 1:68 = (Paris), 4. Close variant in Yāqūt, *Mu'jam*, 1:685.

37 Ṭabarī, 3/2:843-45. Regarding tribal warfare around al-Mawṣil, see, for example, 3/1:609, 624-26, 639, 688; Azdī, 268-69, 279, 289, 296, 332.

38 Ṭabarī, 3/2:1142; Ibn Ṭayfūr (Cairo), 144-45.

39 He stresses the economic drain on the government that resulted from maintaining Syrian forces that were not part of the imperial army.

40 Ibn al-Muqaffa', 347-88.

41 Goitein, 157.

42 Ibn al-Muqaffa', 350.

43 The bracketed words are seemingly implied by the text.

44 Ibn al-Muqaffa', 350.

45 Ibid., 350.

46 Ibid., 347.

47 This included generals such as, Qaḥṭabah b. Shabīb and his sons, who, technically speaking, were not clients of the 'Abbāsid family. Note Khālid b. Barmak's responsibilities in distributing booty and, later, as the director of the military payroll (see n. 17). Concerning the *shurṭah* and *ḥaras*, see n. 21.

48 Ṭabarī, 3/1.129ff., 418-19; *FHA* 227-28; Ibn Ṭabāṭabā (Beirut), 160-61. Dīnawarī, 380, sub anno 142 (attempt to avenge Abū Muslim), which seems confused.

49 As for geography, Ṭabarī, 3/1:82, sub anno 135, indicates that some Rāwandīs from al-Ṭāliqān killed one of Abū Muslim's officers. The reference is to the location in Khurāsān between Balkh and Marwarrūdh. One notes that the vicinity of al-Ṭāliqān was the scene of the first great victory won by Abū Muslim during the revolution. See Yāqūt, *Mu'jam*, 2:129-30, s.v. Junduwayh (one of the villages of al-Ṭāliqān). Al-Ṭāliqān was one of the initial places where the 'Ab bāsid *da'wah* was openly proclaimed by Abū Muslim's agents. See Ṭabarī, 2/3: 1953. Note that Dīnawarī, 380, indicates that the Rāwandīyah sought to avenge the death of Abū Muslim. This is not borne out, however, by the other accounts, which indicate they came to honor the Caliph, who was Abū Muslim's executioner. The heresiographers attest to the existence of various sects invoking Abū Muslim's name. These are considered offshoots of the Rāwandīyah. They hold that the spirit passed either from Abū al-'Abbās directly to Abū Muslim, or from Abū Ja'far al-Manṣūr to Abū Muslim. The sects were referred to by a variety of names. See A. S. Halkin's annotated translation of Baghdādī's, *Al-Farq bayn al-firaq* entitled *Moslem Schisms and Sects*, 74-75.

50 The transmigration apparently extended to the 'Abbāsid agents as well. The spirit of Adam resided in 'Uthmān b. Nahīk, who was chief of the security forces (*ṣāḥib al-ḥaras*), and that of Gabriel rested with al-Haytham b. Mu'āwiyah, a ranking officer in the army. See Ṭabarī, 3/1:129.

51 Ṭabarī, 3/1:418; Ash'arī, *Maqālāt al-Islamīyīn*, ed. H. Ritter (Istanbul, 1929-30), 22-23. For the views held by the Rāwandīyah and similar groups, see Halkin, 74-75, 87-98; and G. van Vloten, *Recherches sur la domination arabe, le chiitisme et les croyances messianiques sous le ḳhalifat des Omayyades*, 48ff.

Concerning the proto-Shī'ite groups in general, see M. Hodgson; W. M. Watt, *The Formative Period of Islamic Thought*, 38-62; and H. Laoust (1965), 30-36. Concerning the relationship of al-Ablaq to the 'Abbāsid *dā'ī* Khidāsh, see n. 54.

52 Ṭabarī, 3/1:418-19. The description of the chronicler indicates that the Caliph was indeed hard pressed by this unexpected turn of events. For the possible influence of the incident on the Caliph's subsequent plans to move the capital to Baghdad, see Chapter VI, Section D.

53 Ṭabarī, 3/1:129ff. The account of Ṭabarī, 418-19, is even more detailed. Though listed sub anno 157, it is reported as an event that took place earlier. Ibn al-Muqaffa' was disgraced and then killed following the *āmān* that he drew up for 'Abdallāh b. 'Alī in A.H. 141. It has been assumed that his death in A.H. 142 may have been caused in part by some of the views presented in the *Risālah*. It seems more likely, however, that the *Risālah* was written in order to ingratiate the author with the Caliph following the decline of his patrons among the *'umūmah*. The critical moment of that decline was the removal of Sulaymān b. 'Alī from his position as governor of al-Baṣrah. This was, in fact, related to the agreement. It is most likely that Ibn al-Muqaffa''s death has little, if any, connection with the substance of his treatise. What defeated him was his framing of the agreement, his connection with the *'umūmah*, and the enmity held for him by the new governor.

54 Ṭabarī, 2/3:1503, 1588-89, 1593, 1639-40; *Akhbār*, 403-404; Balādhurī; *Ansāb*, 292a, cited in Sharon, " 'Alīyat," 92, contains the account that 'Abbāsid agents assassinated him but also preserves the story that he was killed by Asad b. 'Abdallāh al-Qasrī, the Umayyad governor. The event is alternately reported for the years A.H. 109 and A.H. 118. The similarities between Khidāsh and al-Ablaq are noted by van Vloten, 49-53: both were tortured and then killed by Asad b. 'Abdallāh; both preached *istiḥlāl al-huramāt* (one may add that both were known by their nom de guerre). Van Vloten speculates that Khidāsh was, in fact, a Rāwandī, though none of the sources specifically identify him as such. He is merely described as practicing Khurramite beliefs, that is, the beliefs of those who permitted forbidden practices. Note that our understanding of the beliefs held by the proto-Shī'ite groups, as well as the composition of the groups, is extremely confused. See also Wellhausen, 511-17; Azizi, 96-106; Sharon, " 'Alīyat," 91ff.; *EI*, s.v. Khurramiyya.

55 Contra Cahen, "Points devue," 324-25. See the views of Wellhausen, 511-17; and esp. Sharon, " 'Alīyat," 91ff., who attempts to show a link between Khidāsh and 'Alid elements in Khurāsān. He notes, in particular, a tradition in the *Akhbār*, 403-404. The text speaks of a group invoking the name of Khidāsh on behalf of the 'Alids, against the recently established 'Abbāsid regime.

56 This is, to be sure, not a phenomenon unique to the world of Islam. See the fascinating essay on this subject in G. Scholem, *The Messianic Idea in Judaism*, 78-141; and more fully developed in his massive *Sabbatai Ṣevi, The Mystical Messiah*. Concerning the relationship between the Shī'ites and Jewish messianism, see I. Friedlander, "Jewish-Arabic Studies," 1:183ff., 2:482-516, and esp. 3:235ff.

57 Sharon, " 'Alīyat," 280-83.

58 The 'Abbāsid military budgets are discussed in the comprehensive article of W. Hoenerbach, "Zur Heeresverwaltung der 'Abbāsiden. Studie über Abūl-farağ Qudāma: Dīwān al-gaiš," 257-90. In addition, the sources are filled with numerous references to military pay (*'aṭā'*) and allotments (*rizq*). The position of the Khurāsānīs in the early 'Abbāsid *dīwān* is discussed by Sharon, " 'Alīyat," 276-80.

59 The Caliph's patronymic, Abū al-Dawāniq, "Father of the Dāniqs," would seem to indicate that he was a skinflint (the *dāniq* being a weight equal to only 1/16 of a dirham). Stories of his fiscal prudence are legendary; however, there is also reason to believe he was a skillful and innovative financial administrator. See Lassner, *Topography*, 185-86. This theme is developed further in Chapter VIII, Section F. Note that, upon his death, al-Manṣūr left al-Mahdī with a financially sound government and a surplus of approximately one billion dirhams in the public treasury. See *FHA*, 265; Azdī, 230.

60 Ṭabarī, 3/2:924.

61 Ya'qūbī, *Buldān*, 255-56.

62 Ibn Taghrī Birdī (Cairo), 2:208-209; Ṭabarī, 3/2:1101—no mention of Turks.

63 Ṭabarī, 3/2:1539, 1566; *FHA*, 577; Mas'ūdī, *Murūj* (Beirut), 4:60, 77, 90-91. Concerning the slave armies, there are the unpublished notes of D. Ayalon; however, these notes have been circulated privately under the title, *The Military Reforms of al-Mu'taṣim. Their Background and Consequences.* Despite its rough format, Ayalon's paper remains the single most significant statement on the early 'Abbāsid military. It is hoped that the author will someday publish a systematic review of the material. See also his, "Preliminary Remarks on the *Mamlūk* Military Institution in Islam," 44-59.

64 See my forthcoming study on the Caliphate at Sāmarrā.

CHAPTER V

1 Al-Jāḥiẓ, *Risālah ilā al-Fatḥ b. Khāqān fī manāqib al-Turk wa 'āmmat jund al-khilāfah*, ed. A. M. Hārūn, 1:1-86; ed. G. van Vloten, 1-56. Hārūn's edition differs slightly from that of G. van Vloten and is cited throughout the text. See also the article of C. Pellat in *EI*², s.v. al-Djāḥiẓ; and his *Le Milieu baṣrien et la formation de Ğāḥiẓ*. See particularly F. Gabrieli, "La 'Risāla' di al-Ğāḥiẓ sui Turchi," 477-83.

2 Jāḥiẓ, 9-11, 63-64.

3 Ibid., 12-14.

4 Ibid., 31, 33.

5 Ibid., 74-75. The reference here is to the Qeṭūrah genealogy in Genesis, 25:1-4. The account of al-Jāḥiẓ is probably filtered through traditions that are ultimately based on rabbinic material. In the Midrash, Qeṭūrah and Ḥajar are sometimes regarded as the same. In any event, the sons born to Qeṭūrah-Ḥajar were all idolaters and were thus sent by Abraham as far away as possible to the

east. This may serve to explain the later connection with Khurāsān, a land originally inhabited by unbelievers. For a list of the rabbinic sources dealing with Qeṭūrah, see the notes of L. Ginsburg, *The Legends of the Jews*, 5:264-66.

6 The main medieval biographies are the Khaṭīb (Cairo), 12:212-22; Yāqūt, *Irshād al-arīb*, 6:56-80. For a list of recent Arabic biographies, see *EI*[2], s.v. al-Djāḥiẓ, to be supplemented by A. H. Balba', *Al-nathr al-fannī wa āthār al-Jāḥiẓ fīhi* (Cairo, 1969); M. 'A. Khafajī, *Abū 'Uthmān al-Jāḥiẓ* (Cairo, 1965). Concerning the period in which the *Manāqib* was composed, see C. Pellat, "Ǧāḥiẓ à Bagdād et à Sāmarrā," 48-67. See also *GAL*, S, 1:241ff.

7 See O. Pinto, "Al-Fatḥ b. Ḫāqān favorito di al-Mutawakkil," 133-49.

8 Concerning the problems of race and color in Islam, there is B. Lewis, *Race and Color in Islam,* esp. 15-18, on al-Jāḥiẓ. Lewis made use of K. Vollors, "Über Rassenfarben in der arabischen Literatur," 1:84-95; and frequently quotes "an excellent German doctoral thesis" by G. Rotter, *Die Stellung des Negers in der islamisch-arabischen Gesellschaft bis zum XVI Jahrhundert* (Bonn, 1967). I have not seen Rotter's work.

9 Jāḥiẓ, 36.

10 Ibid., 1.

11 Concerning the Arab tribes of Khurāsān serving in the 'Abbāsid army, see Sharon, " 'Alīyat," 138-64, esp. 155ff.

12 Wellhausen, trans. Weir, 493-94; Sharon, " 'Alīyat," 30ff. As regards Arabs speaking Persian, see Ṭabarī, 3/1:16, 50, 65. Note also Ibrāhīm al-Imām's command to Abū Muslim to "kill every speaker of Arabic [in Khurāsān]." See Ṭabarī, 3/1:25. The statement certainly does not mean, however, that every Arab in Khurāsān was to be killed (not even those who spoke pure Arabic). Sharon, " 'Alīyat," 32, 156-59, deals with this and similar traditions (Ṭabarī, 2/3:1974; Dīnawarī, 358) and concludes that they actually signify a policy towards those Arab tribesmen who would not join forces with Abū Muslim. Regarding *lughat Khurāsān*, see Sharon, 32: Jāḥiẓ, *K. al-bukhalā'*, 1:99.

13 See Sharon, " 'Alīyat," 177ff.

14 The organization of an 'Abbāsid protogovernment in Khurāsān is treated in detail by Sharon, " 'Alīyat," 176-85. A full list of the 'Abbāsid operatives in Khurāsān during the clandestine phase of the revolution is preserved in the *Akhbār*, 215-223. It supplements the partial list in Ṭabarī, 2/3:1358. The 'Abbāsid agents are almost exclusively from among the old settlers. The twelve highest ranking agents (*naqīb*) were all from the early Arab settlements around Marw. Forty of the remaining fifty-eight were also from Marw, and there were, to be sure, old settlements elsewhere. The command structure of the army was largely made up of people on these lists, for example, Qaḥṭabah b. Shabīb and his sons al-Ḥasan and Ḥumayd, Khāzim b. Khuzaymah, Muqātil b. Ḥākim al-'Akkī, al-Faḍl b. Sulayman al-Ṭusī, 'Uthmān b. Nahīk and his relatives, and al-Musayyab b. Zuhayr. Concerning the early organization of the *da'wah* in Khurāsān, see Sharon, " 'Alīyat," 105-117.

15 Among the twelve ranking agents (*naqīb*) were the following clients: Abū al-Najm, 'Imrān b. Ismā'īl, Abū 'Alī Shibl b. Tihmān, Abū Ḥamzah 'Amr

b. A'yan. Of the fifty-eight remaining *nuqabā'* of lesser rank, four are listed as *mawālī*. Khālid b. Barmak, who is listed as a replacement (*nazīr*) for a *naqīb*, was a *mawlā*, though he is not listed as such. It is possible that other figures on the lists could similarly have been clients, though there is no certain indication to that effect. Note that Khālid b. Barmak was responsible for the distribution of booty and later became the director of the military payroll. Various clients are also listed among the propagandists (*du'āt*).

16 Not all the Khurāsānīs sided with the revolution. Some forces remained loyal to the encumbent regime, and with grave consequences. During the siege at Nihāwand, the Syrian troops surrendered with a guarantee of safety. Their Khurāsānī compatriots were, however, slaughtered. See Ṭabarī, 3/1:6-8. Regarding the Khurāsānī identity of the army, note the juxtaposition of the terms *ahl Khurāsān* and *ahl al-Shām* in the exhortations to the troops before the first critical battle against Nubātah b. Ḥanẓalah and the main Umayyad contingents. See Ṭabarī, 2/3:2004-2005. Qaḥṭabah's main address, which plays on Iranian sentiments, may be, however, the invention of later times.

17 See Chapter IV, Section D, for a discussion of Ibn al-Muqaffa's *Risālah fī al-ṣaḥābah*.

18 The topography of military settlement at Baghdad is dealt with in detail in Chapter VIII.

19 Ṭabarī, 3/1:1142; Ibn Ṭayfūr (Cairo), 144-45; Kindī, 193, Maqrīzī, 63. Sharon "'Alīyat," 283-87, stresses that al-Ma'mūn had built up an army of non-Arabs from Transoxiana that served as the backbone of his regime vis-à-vis the earlier Khurāsānīs. The latter, largely of Arab stock, had been resettled in Iraq. The policy of removing the Arabs from the *dīwān* was, however, not directed towards the Iraqis, who would not have been registered as Arabs in any case. The Arabs spoken of here are the tribal armies from Syria. Concerning 'Abbāsid attitudes to this last group, see Chapter IV, Section D. Note that al-Mu'taṣim also removed the Arabs from the dīwān in Egypt while introducing the Turks in large numbers to the 'Abbāsid army.

20 Jāḥiẓ, 23-25.

21 Ibid., 14-23.

22 Ibid., 14-16.

23 Ibid., 17-18.

24 Ibid., 16-17. Note Chapter VI, which deals with the subsequent 'Abbāsid decision to establish Iraq as the central province of the dynasty.

25 Ibid., 15.

26 Ibid., 14. The relationship between the early agents and those of Muḥammad b. 'Alī is not coincidental, but part of a well-conceived ideological campaign in which the 'Abbāsids portrayed themselves as the heirs of the Prophet Muḥammad. This is explicitly stated by the author of the *Akhbār*, 215ff., in his description of the organizational structure of the revolutionary underground. Al-Jāḥiẓ's reference (p. 14) to seventy nobles (*najīb*) is probably a reference to the group of Aws and Khazraj that met with Muḥammad at al-'Aqabah. From this group of about seventy, the Prophet chose the twelve agents (*naqīb*) to spread his mes-

sage. The twelve ranking 'Abbāsid agents were similarly chosen from a wider group of seventy. See *Akhbār*, 216. Note that the 'Abbāsids also employed a group of seventy known as the *du'āt* (*Akhbār*, 221-22). To my knowledge, only Sharon, " 'Alīyat," 105-107 and Crone, 132, have recognized the full connection between al-Jāḥiẓ's description of the Khurāsānīs, the Abbāsid revolution, and the pristine era of early Islam.

27 Ṭabarī, 2/3:1952ff. Note that al-Jāḥiẓ's Khurāsānī (p. 15) boasts "Our dress is known [that is, black] and we are the people of the black flags . . . (*wa libāsunā ma'rūf wa naḥnu asḥāb al-rāyāt al-sūd*).

28 Jāḥiẓ, 15 (*ghadhānā bidhālika abā'unā wa ghadawna bihi abnā'anā*).

29 Ibid., 20.

30 Ibid., 21.

31 Ibid., 22. Others listed include: Abū Dāwūd Khālid b. Ibrāhīm, Abū 'Amr Lāhiz b. Qurayẓ, Abū 'Utaybah Mūsā b. Ka'b, Abū Sahl al-Qāsim b. Mujāshi' al-Muzanī. All of the individuals mentioned are to be found on the list of *nuqabā'* in Ṭabarī, 2/3:1358, and the *Akhbār*, 215ff. (see also Text, ns. 13, 14, 15). Mālik b. Ṭawwāf al-Muzanī is listed by al-Jāḥiẓ, as one who functioned as a *naqīb* though not one of them (*yajrī majrī al-nuqabā' wa lam yadkhul fīhim*). He is nevertheless also on the list of the *Akhbār*, p. 218, that denotes the fifty-eight *nuqabā'* directly below the original twelve. Al-Jāḥiẓ also indicates that others from the second category were similarly Arabs but he does not list them by name. Almost the entire leadership of the revolutionary apparatus in Khurāsān consisted of Arabs (see n. 14), as did the central element of the revolutionary army.

32 Jāḥiẓ, 23, also includes Mūsā b. Ka'b, who conquered al-Sind, and Muḥammad b. al-Ash'ath, who conquered Ifrīqīyah, among the Arabs. Both were Khurāsānīs. Both campaigns were conducted with Khurāsānī troops.

33 For 'Abbāsid attitudes towards the Syrians, see Chapter IV, Section D.

34 Jāḥiẓ, 23-25.

35 See Chapter IV, Section C.

36 Ṭabarī, 3/2:1516, 1539; *FHA*, 577; Mas'ūdī, *Murūj* (Beirut), 4:60, 77, 90-91.

37 Jāḥiẓ, 24.

38 Ibid., 23.

39 Ibid., 23-24. The specific indication of the paternal uncles and their offspring (*al-'umūmah wa banī al-a'mām*) may be a very subtle reference to the conversation between 'Abd al-Ṣamad b. 'Alī and his great nephew al-Mahdī. See Ṭabarī, 3/1:534, whose text is the point of departure for chapter IV. The relationship between the ruling family, the Caliph, the *mawālī*, and the army is the central problem of early 'Abbāsid political organization and is thus reflected throughout this study.

40 For some reason, the passage concerning Abū Muslim and Abū Salamah is missing from Hārūn's edition of the text. It is cited here on the basis of G. van Vloten's *Tria Opuscula*, 14. One should remember the *mawālī* were also well represented in the revolutionary apparatus in Iraq. See Sharon, " 'Alīyat," 75-84.

41 Jāḥiẓ, 24-25. Mentioned are the ranking agents (*ru'ūs al-nuqabā'*): Abū

Manṣūr, *mawlā* of the Khuzāʿah, Abū al-Ḥakam ʿĪsā b. Aʿyan, and Abū al-Najm ʿImrān b. Ismāʿīl. All three are listed among the ranking *nuqabā* by Ṭabarī, 2/3:1358; and the *Akhbār*, 216.

42 Jāḥiẓ, 25.

43 Ibid., 25-28.

44 The secondary sources are Wellhausen, 556ff. and A. Mez, *Renaissance of Islam*, 155ff.

45 This information was kindly supplied to me by the author, Professor B. Lewis. The work in question is a short publication of the Société des Études Iraniennes et de l'Art Persan (7) entitled *Salmān Pak et les prémices spirituelles de l'Islam Iranien*.

46 Ibid., 18.

47 Maqrīzī, 72 (according to Massignon, p. 50). Note Section E below, where the Barmakid, Yaḥyā b. Khālid, is identified with a group called the *abnā' al-dawlah*. The reference is, however, vague and certainly does not point to the military institution spoken of by al-Jāḥiẓ.

48 Forand, "Slave," 59-60, who also follows *EI*², s.v.; and Crone, 131-34. Crone speaks of an ʿAbbāsid aristocracy based on early service to the revolution. Hence the *abnā'* are correctly identified as the descendants of those Khurāsānīs who brought the ʿAbbāsids to power; however, her desire to establish clear distinctions between formal groupings of public figures seems to strain the evidence. There were, to be sure, *abnā'* of varied rank and importance, but it appears that was a function of their general duties and background, and not of any specific subgroups in which they claimed association.

49 I. Lapidus, 371 correctly calls the *abnā'* "the descendants of the supporters of the ʿAbbāsid revolution," without further comment or annotation. A fuller exposition is found in the unpublished dissertation of Crone, 131-34, and, more particularly, in that of Sharon, 288-90. The real key to unlocking the puzzle of the identity of the *abnā'* was, however, provided by D. Ayalon, *Reforms*, 6ff. It is his unpublished paper concerning the military reforms of al-Muʿtaṣim that is the foundation of all subsequent studies. With his usual flair for reading a text, he isolated many traditions that make it clear that the term *abnā'* does not simply mean sons, but alludes as well to a well-known military group in Baghdad. See below.

50 Jāḥiẓ, 12.

51 Ibid., 25.

52 Ibid., 26.

53 Ibid., 26.

54 Ibid., 28.

55 Ṭabarī, 3/1:497-98. The apparatus of the text indicates that the term *abnā'* is missing from MS A. Yaḥyā al-Barmakī is also mentioned as one of the *abnā' dawlatihi* (that is, Caliph) in Ṭabarī, 3/2:703, sub anno 189.

56 Crone, 132-34.

57 Regarding this term, see Chapter IV, n. 6.

58 The significance of this marriage is discussed in Chapter IV, Section C.

Other examples of close contacts, that is, foster-brothers of the ruling house, are cited by Crone, 134.

59 Ṭabarī, 3/2:672.

60 Note the brief reference to a contingent of *abnā'* in Ṭabarī, 3/2:732, sub anno 192. The *abnā' dawlatihi* (that is, al-Rashīd) are also mentioned in Ṭabarī, 3/2:703, sub anno 189; however, in that context they are distinct from the army officers (*min ḳufātihi wa anṣārihi wa abnā' dawlatihi wa quwwādihi*).

61 See Ṭabarī, 3/2:817, which indicates that this group was registered in the military roll and was not a makeshift force as the name may imply. The references to the *ahl Baghdād* during the civil war are numerous. Concerning their dominant role in the royalist army, see Ayalon, *Reforms*, 8-10, 36; Ṭabarī, 3/2:831, 858, 865, 866, 898, 1001, 1006, 1013; Ya'qūbī, *Historiae*, 2:532-33, 535, 547, 548.

62 Ṭabarī, 3/2:825, 847, 848, 865, 984, 998, 1000, 1002, 1008-12; Ya'qūbī, *Historiae*, 2:547, 548, 564. See n. 67 below.

63 Ṭabarī, 3/2:934, 935. For references to the people (*ahl*) of the suburbs, see Ṭabarī, 3/2:849, 866, 867, 871, 872, 934, 936.

64 Ayalon, *Reforms*, 6; Iṣfahānī, *Aghānī* (Beirut), 18:61; and the *abnā'* of the Khurāsānī military cantonment (*jund*) in *Aghānī*, 18:100. Ayalon points out that the connection to Iran is also found in the expression "the *abnā'* are the sons of the dihqāns [Iranian gentry]": Khuwārizmī, *Mafātīḥ al-'ulūm*, 119.

65 Ibn Ṭayfūr (Cairo), 80.

66 Ayalon, *Reforms*, 9-10; Ṭabarī, 3/2:824, 826ff. (a force of 20,000 *abnā'* under the command of one of their own officers), 911-12, 922-23, 931, 932 (large force of *abnā'*).

67 Ayalon, *Reforms*, 11-12, surmises that not all the suburban fighters were in fact *abnā'*. "There must have been in Baghdad strong military and paramilitary bodies outside the descendants of the early Khurāsānīs. . . . Admittedly the sources do not make it possible quite often to draw a clear line between various fighting elements defending the 'Abbāsid capital." Furthermore, "from the available data it is impossible to decide whether the *abnā'* lived only in one quarter or were scattered all over the town." There is, however, reason to assume that the backbone of the fighting forces in al-Ḥarbīyah were *abnā'*. With regard to the topography of military occupation in Baghdad, see Chapter VIII.

68 The composition of the imperial army in Khurāsān on the eve of the civil war cannot be determined with certainty. In all likelihood, the Transoxanians were by far the predominant element. The provincial forces, largely Arab at the outset of the regime, were no doubt replenished by captives taken in campaigns to the east. See Ṭabarī, 3/1:631, sub anno 169. Note also the advice of al-Faḍl b. Sahl, the wazīr of al-Ma'mūn, that the latter resist his brother and seek alliances with the Transoxanians (Ṭabarī, 3/2:815ff.). Concerning the problem of *'āṭā'* see n. 73 below. See also D. Ayalon, "preliminary remarks on the Mamlūk Military Institution in Islam," for some general remarks concerning Transoxiana.

69 Jāḥiẓ, 26-28.

70 Concerning the masonry bridges of Baghdad, see Lassner, *Topography*, 321, s.v. *qanṭarah*.

71 Jāḥiẓ, 53; 54. From the passages describing the military skills of the *abnā'*, Ayalon, *Reforms*, 37, concludes: "According to Jāḥiẓ there were amongst the *abnā'* a sizeable body of excellent infantrymen whose weapons and tactics he describes. . . . I did not find any clear evidence corroborating al-Jāḥiẓ's contention. . . ." It is, of course, al-Jāḥiẓ's purpose to compare the abilities of the *abnā'* with the superior fighting skills of the Turks, who specialized in cavalry combat. Nevertheless, there is no reason to suspect al-Jāḥiẓ's analysis. He is not referring to the *abnā'* specifically as foot soldiers, but to the tactics that were imposed upon them by the siege of Baghdad. For reference to the *abnā'* as cavalry, see Ṭabarī, 3/2:817, 911-12.

72 The reference here is to the continuing turmoil in the city after the war was over, particularly the events of A.H. 202-203, when the populace of Baghdad expelled the Caliph's governor, al-Ḥasan b. Sahl, and installed the counter-Calpihate of Ibrāhīm b. al-Mahdī. On the other side of the coin, note the remarks of Ibn Ṭayfūr (Cairo), 80: "It was they [the *abnā'*] who took up the fight against the Commander of the Faithful [al-Ma'mūn], but then they obeyed him and the Caliphate was maintained in good stead owing to them." This last passage is taken from an apocryphal account in which the qualities of the *abnā'* are contrasted with al-Mu'taṣim's Turks and the Transoxanians (*'ajam ahl Khurāsān*) of al-Ma'mūn. The purpose of the discussion was to ascertain which of the three groups was the most proficient and courageous in battle. The disputed issue was resolved in favor of the *abnā'*. The text is essentially the mirror image of the *Manāqib* encapsulated. It indicates that the *abnā'* continued to function as a group and enjoyed support after the Turks were introduced in large numbers by the Caliph al-Mu'taṣim. Note the attempts of the Caliph al-Muhtadī (A.H. 255-256) to create a counterweight to the Turks by using the *abnā'* (Ya'qūbī, *Historiae*, 2:604, 618-19). See also Ayalon, *Reforms*, 34-36.

73 The antagonism of the local Baghdadis to the Turks was the major reason behind al-Mu'taṣim's decision to move the Caliphate from Baghdad. This led eventually to the creation of a new capital at Sāmarrā. When al-Musta'īn later (A.H. 248) wished to free himself of the Turks at Sāmarrā, he quite naturally opted to establish his government at Baghdad. For evidence that the *abnā'* continued to be kept on the military rolls, see Ṭabarī, 3/2:867, 1032-33, 1038, 1112. There are numerous references to the tremendous financial drain caused by the civil war. The shortages continued after the conflict had ended. See, for example, Ṭabarī, 3/2:934ff.; 977, 1012-13, 1014, 1016, 1028, 1030, 1038, 1065; *FHA*, 417, 435, 438; Shabushtī, 148.

CHAPTER VI

1 M. Hinds, "Kūfan Political Alignments and Their Backgrounds in the Mid-7th Century A.D.," 346-67; and A. A. Dixon, *The Umayyad Caliphate 65-86/684-*

705. The question of the complex, political alignments is badly in need of a full and systematic study.

2 Concerning this subject, there is H.A.R. Gibb, *The Arab Conquests in Central Asia*, who describes the later activities of the Arabs in Transoxiana; and Shaban, *The 'Abbāsid Revolution*, esp., 16-52. Despite its title, Shaban's book is largely concerned with the Arab tribes in Khurāsān.

3 Note the attempt to buy the support of the Kufāns by putting them back on the military roll and the negative response of the regular army (*ahl al-Shām*) to this action. See Ṭabarī, 2/3:1855.

4 This is dealt with tangentially throughout the text. For a concise review, see Cahen, "Points de vue," 295-338.

5 Concerning the Kūfah station, see Sharon, " 'Alīyat," 75-84.

6 Ibn Ṭabāṭabā (Beirut), 144, and Mas'ūdī, *Murūj* (Beirut), 3:207. It is doubtful that there is any truth to the account that al-Ḥasan was poisoned. The tradition no doubt found currency in order to establish that the passive al-Ḥasan was no less a martyr than his celebrated brother. See *EI*[2], s.v. al-Ḥasan b. 'Alī b. Abī Ṭālib.

7 Sharon, " 'Alīyat," 203: *Anonymous*, 207a; Ṭabarī, 3/1:1668, 1679, Kūfī, 205a-b; *Akhbār*, 110a (= ed. 231); Wellhausen, 517. Note, not all the 'Alids were prepared to put their faith in the Kūfans. Muḥammad al-Bākir, Zayd's brother, urged caution. See Kūfī, 206b-207a, and the variant in Mas'ūdī, *Murūj* (Beirut), 3:207, in which the litany of Kūfan sins is graphically expressed. For the 'Alid's belated recognition of Dāwūd b. 'Alī's advice, see Ṭabarī, 2/3:1712.

8 *Akhbār*, 231.

9 For the revolt of 'Abdallāh b. Mu'awīyah, see *EI*[2], s.v.; also the interesting views of Sharon, " 'Alīyat," 201ff.; and Cahen, "Points de vue," 329.

10 A brief and descriptive survey of Ḥusaynid-'Abbāsid relations can be found in F. Omar, "Aspects of 'Abbāsid Ḥusaynid Relations," 170-79.

11 Ibn al-Faqīh, 315; Muqaddasī, 293-94; Yāqūt, *Mu'jam*, 2:412; Jāḥiẓ, *Manāqib*, 16; *Akhbār*, 206-207; Sharon, " 'Alīyat," citing Balādhurī, *Ansāb*, 283a. The Arabic text is reproduced by Sharon in appendix B, 1.

12 Summed up by Sharon, " 'Alīyat," 19-36.

13 See Lassner, *Topography*, 126-28.

14 That is to say, when the 'Abbāsids arrived in al-Kūfah, there were still major military campaigns to be fought in Iraq and Syria. The Kūfah region was a most suitable base from which to conduct these efforts. Concerning the purge of the government apparatus, see Chapter III, Section A.

15 See Chapter I, Section A.

16 Ṭabarī, 3/1:26-27; Azdī, 120.

17 *Akhbār*, 410-11.

18 Ya'qūbī, *Historiae*, 2:390 (*ma aḥabba al-ḥayāt qaṭṭu aḥad illā dhalla*).

19 The most complete discussion of this issue is found in Sharon, " 'Alīyat," 237ff. esp. 254-60.

20 Ṭabarī, 3/1:20, 21, 34, 37; Mas'ūdī, *Murūj* (Beirut), 3:253; *FHA*, 201; *Akhbār*, 388; Azdī, 123; Ibn Ṭabāṭabā (Beirut), 146.

21 *Akhbār*, 374-75.

22 Ṭabarī, 3/1:37; *FHA*, 201; Azdī, 124.

23 Ibid. To be contrasted with Ṭabarī, 3/1:21 wherein Abū Salamah is pictured in charge of the operations in the province; Azdī, 124-25.

24 Yāqūt, *Mu'jam*, 3:239.

25 Ṭabarī, 3/1:21.

26 Yāqūt, *Mu'jam*, 2:375, s.v. al-Ḥīrah.

27 Balādhurī, *Futūḥ*, 281.

28 S.A. al-'Alī, "Minṭaqat al-Ḥīrah," *Majallat kullīyat al-ādāb* (Baghdad University), 5 (1962):17-44.

29 Yāqūt, *Mu'jam*, 2:375-76; Ṭabarī, index, 698; *EI*², s.v.; G. Rothstein, *Die Dynastie der Lakhmiden in al-Ḥīra*. See also M. J. Kister, "Al-Ḥīra," *Arabica* 15 (1968):143-69.

30 Ṭabarī, 2/3:1641ff., sub anno 120; Ya'qūbī, *Historiae*, 2:387ff., describing Yūsuf b. 'Umar's seizure of power. I can find no explicit statement that he established al-Ḥīrah as a base for the Syrian army, but this is obvious from the description of Zayd b. 'Alī's revolt, in which the Syrians based in al-Ḥīrah play a prominent role. See Ṭabarī, 2/2:1698-1716, 1699, 1702, 1706, esp., sub anno 122.

31 Wellhausen, 334.

32 Ṭabarī, 2/3:1702.

33 Ibid., 1836-37, 1855.

34 For an overview of this period, see Wellhausen, 370ff.

35 Ṭabarī, 2/3:1854-55.

36 The negotiator was 'Umar b. al-Ghadbān b. al-Qab'atharī. For his effort he was awarded the ceremonial robes of honor and various gifts. In addition, he received a number of sensitive administrative posts. It is not clearly stated that the bonuses helped to quiet matters, but this can perhaps be assumed. See Ṭabarī, 2/3:1855.

37 Ṭabarī, 2/3:1898ff.

38 Ibid., 1854.

39 Ibid., 1898.

40 Ibid., 1899. Concerning the rebellion of al-Daḥḥāq b. Qays, see *EI*², s.v.; it contains a lengthy bibliography.

41 The two similar sounding locations are often confused. See Balādhurī, *Futūḥ*, 287; Yāqūt, *Mu'jam*, 1:680; 3:208; 4:123, 946; Ṭabarī, 3/1:80, 183; Iṣṭakhrī, 85; and Ibn Ḥawqal, 166; Muqaddasi, 53, 115, 121, 130; E. Reitemeyer, *Die Städtegründungen der Araber im Islam*, 49; *EI*², s.v. Kaṣr b. Ḥubayra.

42 Ṭabarī, 3/1:37; Azdī, 124.

43 See Chapter III, Section A.

44 See, for example, the article of J. Lassner in *EI*², s.v. al-Hāshimiyya. Note, however, that it is later corrected by his article, s.v. Kaṣr b. Ḥubayra.

45 Ṭabarī, 3/1:37.

46 Balādhurī, *Futūḥ*, 287.

47 Ṭabarī, 3/1:88, specifies *bi-l-Anbār al-'atīqah fī qaṣrihi*.

48 Ṭabarī, 3/1:80; Ya'qūbī, *Historiae*, 2:249; *FHA*, 211, 214; Dīnawarī, 372; Azdī, 155.

49 Yāqūt, *Mu'jam*, 4:123.

50 The term *madīnah*, which has generally come to mean town or city, is not always clearly defined. It carries with it the nuance of an administrative center, as distinguished from a *qaryah*, "village," which lacks an established authority. The term is sometimes translated here as administrative center.

51 Yāqūt, *Mu'jam*, 4:346.

52 See also Ṭabarī, 3/1:99, 100, 103, 105.

53 *EI*², s.v. al-Anbār.

54 Concerning the course of the 'Īsā, *see* Yāqūt, *Mu'jam*, 4:842; Khaṭīb (Cairo), 1:111-12 = (Paris), 65; Suhrāb, 123 = Ibn Serapion, 14; Muqaddasī, 124; Ya'qubī, *Buldān*, 250; Iṣṭakhrī, 84-85; Ibn Ḥawqal, 164-65.

55 Dīnawarī, 131.

56 Ibid., 372.

57 Neither Ṭabarī, 3/1:80 nor Balādhurī, *Futūḥ*, 287, gives any information of the position of Abū al-'Abbās's capital. Ṭabarī, 3/1:88, which is not cited in the article, indicates that when Abū al-'Abbās died, he was buried in his palace in the old city of al-Anbār (*al-Anbār al-'atīqah*).

58 Dīnawarī, 372 (incorrectly cited in *EI*² as p. 273).

59 Ṭabarī, 3/1:271-72.

60 Ibn Ṭabāṭabā (Beirut), 161. I know of no indication in any source that throws light on this statement.

61 This al-Ruṣāfah, of which almost nothing is known, is not to be confused with the area of that name later developed at Baghdad. See Chapter VIII, Section D. There is no explanation how this complex was used. It is tempting to suppose that it was a military camp like Ruṣāfat Baghdad. Perhaps it housed the garrison of the local governor, 'Īsā b. Mūsā. See the brief entry in Yāqūt, *Mu'jam*, 2:786.

62 Ṭabarī, 3/1:91ff.; Ya'qūbī, *Historiae*, 2:438ff.; *FHA*, 219.

63 His difficulties with the *'umūmah* in al-Jazīrah are discussed in Chapter I, Section A.

64 See Chapter I, Section A.

65 Note that Abū Muslim is reported to have at first backed 'Īsā b. Mūsā, the Caliph's nephew, but the latter declined to promote any claim for the Caliphate.

66 Ṭabarī, 3/1:271; Ibn Ṭabāṭabā (Beirut), 161.

67 See Chapter IV, Section D.

68 When the disturbance broke out, Mālik b. al-Haytham stationed himself at the gate of the palace and declared, "I am the gate-keeper today." That is to say, a senior officer was hastily pressed into service to guard the palace, normally a function reserved for an ordinary soldier. See Ṭabarī, 3/1:130. Another account indicates that the rioters reached the palace itself. They ascended to the audience hall (*khaḍrā'*) and jumped off as if to fly. See Ṭabarī, 3/1:418-19. There may be some confusion here with the Caliph's audience hall at Madīnat al-Salām, also a green (*khaḍrā'*) structure; however, it is very possible that the

basic lines of this last incident are accurate. The Rāwandīyah, who believed in the transmigration of souls, would, by this act, have simply passed on into another existence.

69 Ṭabarī, 3/1:130, specifies the number at 600.

70 See Chapter III, Sections B and C.

71 Ṭabarī, 3/1:308.

72 The name literally means "The City of Peace," but it is sufficiently innocuous as to give rise to all sorts of false etymologies. According to the Khaṭīb (Cairo), 1:60, this name was chosen because the site of Baghdad was adjacent to the Tigris, which was known as Qaṣr al-Salām. On p. 58, the Khaṭīb had reported the same, but with *Wādī* for *Qaṣr*. This last tradition is reported in Ibn al-Jawzī, *Manāqib*, 2; Yāqūt, *Mu'jam*, 1:678; Sam'ānī, *Ansāb*, 86a; Ibn al-Athīr, *Lubāb*, 1:133. A similar explanation is found using *Nahr*. Yāqūt also presents two additional explanations: *Mu'jam*, 1:677, indicates that the name was adopted by al-Manṣūr from an earlier Persian form, *hilid*, which is said to mean in Arabic "leave in peace" (*khallū bi-l-salām*); the second account (p. 678) explains that al-Salām denotes God and what was desired was a name signifying "The City of God." What is significant, however, is that the city was not called al-Hāshimīyah, thereby breaking a precedent that had determined the name of all the previous 'Abbāsid administrative centers. Could it be that Baghdad was to have represented a break with the past in more ways than one?

73 Khaṭīb (Cairo), 1:72 = (Paris), 16.

CHAPTER VII

1 See Lassner, *Topography*, in which a detailed investigation was attempted of these accounts. Recent research has made it necessary to review certain data in order to modify earlier views and to suggest new ideas for consideration. Several modified studies that had appeared earlier are also included in this book. See bibliography under J. Lassner.

2 *Ibid.*, 126-28.

3 Khaṭīb (Cairo), 1:119 = (Paris), 77; regarding the pattern of growth, see Lassner, *Topography*, 155-77.

4 Lassner, *Topography*, 128-37, which is essentially the same as "Some Speculative Thoughts on the Search for an 'Abbāsid Capital. Part II." The views expressed in these works are badly in need of revision and expansion. This is attempted in the present chapter.

5 Ṭabarī, 3/1:272-73, 276; Khaṭīb (Cairo), 1:66; Yāqūt, *Mu'jam*, 1:680; Ibn Ṭabāṭabā (Beirut), 162.

6 The story of Miqlāṣ is similarly reported for the building of al-Rāfiqah, a city that was founded by al-Manṣūr in A.H. 155 and that reportedly contained architectural features comparable to Baghdad. See Balādhurī, *Futūḥ*, 287; Ṭabarī, 3/1:276; Ya'qūbī, *Buldān*, 238; Yāqūt, *Mu'jam*, 2:734-35. Note, however, Ya'qūbī, *Historiae*, 2:430, 445, who states that the city plan was traced during the reign of al-Saffāḥ.

7 See Chapter III, Sections B and C.

8 Ṭabarī, 3/1:278, 281.

9 LeStrange, *Baghdad*, 11.

10 Yāqūt, *Mu'jam*, 2:954.

11 LeStrange, *Baghdad*, 11. Note also the relationship of the name Madīnat al-Salām to the Tigris. See Khaṭīb (Cairo), 1:58, 60; Ibn al-Jawzī, *Manāqib*, 2, based on the Khaṭīb; and Yāqūt, *Mu'jam*, 1:678, 3:112; Sam'ānī, fol. 86a; Ibn al-Athīr, *Lubāb*, 1:133.

12 *Mu'jam*, 1:678; see also Mas'ūdī, *Tanbīh*, 360.

13 Khaṭīb (Cairo), 1:77 = (Paris), 16.

14 Mas'ūdī, *Tanbīh*, 360; Yāqūt, *Mu'jam*, 2:954.

15 Yāqūt, *Mu'jam*, 2:954. Concerning the bent entrances, see Khaṭīb (Cairo), 1:74 = (Paris), 12; Ya'qūbī, *Buldān*, 239, E. Herzfeld and F. Sarre, *Archäologische Reise im Euphrat und Tigris Gebiet*, 2:123; K.A.C. Creswell, *Early Muslim Architecture*, 2:12, and 23ff.

16 Ṭabarī, 3/1:277; Khaṭīb (Cairo), 1:66-67 = (Paris), 1; Yāqūt, *Mu'jam*, 1:682.

17 For a discussion of the literary sources, see J. Lassner, "Notes on the Topography of Baghdad: The Systematic Descriptions of the City and the Khaṭīb al-Baghdādī," 458-469, and, somewhat expanded, Lassner, *Topography*, 25-42. See also Figures 1 and 2.

18 Little is known about the administration of public works in early 'Abbāsid times. See E. Herzfeld, "Die Genesis der islamischen Kunst und das Mshatta-Problem," 60-63; Herzfeld and Sarre, *Archäologische Reise*, 2:117, n. 8; and F. Rosenthal, *The Muslim Concept of Freedom*, 77ff. In recruiting his labor force, al-Manṣūr tapped the adjacent regions of Syria, al-Mawṣil, al-Jabal, al-Kūfah, Wāsiṭ, and al-Baṣrah. See Ya'qūbī, *Buldān*, 238; Ṭabarī, 3/1:276-77. Muqaddasī, 121; Khaṭīb (Cairo), 1:67 = (Paris), 1-2; Yāqūt, *Mu'jam*, 1:681-82.

19 Khaṭīb (Cairo), 1:67 = (Paris), 1; also Ya'qūbī, *Buldān*, 238. There are, however, other references, even in Islamic literature, to round cities. Moreover, the circular plan had been known in Iraq since Assyrian times, particularly in connection with military architecture. See Creswell, 2:18-21; Herzfeld and Sarre, 2:132-33. Creswell's assertion that "it was probably the plan of Darābjird which directly inspired the Round City of al-Manṣūr," cannot be taken at face value. Other Parthian-Sassanian circular cities include Gūr, Hatra, and Ctesiphon (horseshoe). There is no compelling evidence for a direct prototype. See also n. 30.

20 H. P. L'Orange, *Studies in the Iconography of Cosmic Kingship* (Cambridge, 1953), 12.

21 Ibid., 13-14.

22 Italics mine.

23 Khaṭīb (Cairo), 1:72 = (Paris), 10; and Ṭabarī, 3/1:321; Ibn Ṭabāṭabā (Beirut), 163. Note also Creswell's argument that this shape leads to an economy of construction (p. 21).

24 Concerning the problem of Umayyad royal iconography and court cere-

monial, there is the unpublished dissertation of O. Grabar, "The Ceremonial Art of the Umayyads" (Princeton University, 1955).

25 C. Wendell, "Baghdad: *Imago Mundi* and Other Foundation Lore," 99-128.

26 Ibid., 127.

27 Ibid., 126.

28 Ibid., 127.

29 O. Rheuter, "Sassanian Architecture: a History," 575.

30 Wendell, 104ff., concerning cities. For the quotations, see 122-23, 128.

31 Ṭabarī, 3/1:277.

32 That is to say, al-Kūfah was the gateway to the Ḥijāz along the main pilgrimage route to the holy cities. One may note, however, al-Manṣūr's contempt for the political pretensions of the *ḥaramayn*. See Chapter III, Section B.

33 Wendell, 123.

34 Ibid., 119: J. Lassner, "Some Speculative Thoughts on the Search for an 'Abbāsid Capital," 210.

35 Ibid., 123-24.

36 Citing Ṭabarī, 3/1:277.

37 Wendell, 126, 127: Ṭabarī, 3/1:320. The same account appears in Ibn Ṭabāṭabā (Beirut), 157.

38 Ṭabarī, 3/1:320.

39 Ṭabarī, 3/1:276; Khaṭīb (Cairo), 1:70 = (Paris), 7.

40 Khaṭīb (Cairo), 1:67 = (Paris), 1.

41 Ṭabarī, 3/1:277; Yāqūt, *Mu'jam*, 1:682.

42 Ṭabarī, 3/1:320; Ibn Ṭabāṭabā (Beirut), 157. Note, however, the opposite sentiment in Ṭabarī, 3/1:325.

43 Wendell, 127.

44 Construction on al-Tāj is also reported to have begun in the reign of al-Mu'taḍid (A.H. 279-289), who then abandoned the project. See Yāqūt, *Mu'jam*, 1:109, 808-809; Ibn al-Jawzī, *Muntaẓam*, 5/2:144; Khaṭīb (Cairo), 1:99 = (Paris), 48; and, G. Makdisi, "The Topography of Eleventh Century Baghdad: Materials and Notes," 134, n. 2; LeStrange, *Baghdad*, index, 368; map 8, ref. no. 2.

45 Yāqūt, *Mu'jam*, 1:109, 808-809.

46 Ibid., 109-110. For al-Buḥturī, see *EI*², s.v.

47 The solid construction of the Sassanian building apparently made this possible. Even the battlements were made of burnt brick (*ājurr*) and thus could be used in foundation work, for burnt brick combined with quick lime (*ṣārūj*) served to prevent seepage. Indeed, Yāqūt indicates that the battlements were reused in constructing the quay (*musannāh*) of the palace. See *Mu'jam*, 1:809.

48 Italics mine. See Lassner, *Topography*, 132, where this misleading concept is articulated.

49 Ibid., 129-31.

50 Ṭabarī, 1/3:2491-92.

51 Ṭabarī, 3/1:321; Khaṭīb (Cairo), 1:75 = (Paris), 13-14; Yāqūt, *Mu'jam*, 2:952.

52 Ṭabarī, 3/1:321. Note, however, Herzfeld and Sarre, 2:128, who hold that it was placed in the outer gateway of the Baṣrah Gate.

53 *EI*², s.v. al-Hadjdjāj b. Yūsuf.

54 O. Grabar, "Al-Mushatta, Baghdad and Wāsiṭ," 99-108; Lassner, *Topography*, 134-37; Wendell, 117-19.

55 Balādhurī, *Futūḥ*, 290; Ya'qūbī, *Buldān*, 322; Ibn Rustah, 187; Khaṭīb (Cairo), 1:73, 107-109; Yāqūt, *Mu'jam*, 4:885.

56 F. Safar, *Wāsiṭ the Sixth Season's Excavations*. See also M. 'A. Muṣṭafā, "Al-Tanqīb fī al-Kūfah," 3-32.

57 Grabar, 106; Creswell, 1:31.

58 Grabar, 106.

59 Oral communication of P. Soucek.

60 See Chapter IV, Section D.

61 Khaṭīb (Cairo), 1:73 = (Paris), 10-11 describes the representation of a horseman surmounting the dome. Note, however, Yāqūt, *Mu'jam*, 1:683, who regards the story of the horseman as a popular rather than mechanical invention. Nevertheless, a mechanical device based on the details of the horseman is described and illustrated in Jazarī's, *K. fī ma'rifat al-ḥiyal al-handasīyah*. See F. J. Martin, *The Muslim Painting of Persia, India and Turkey*, 2: pl. 2. Martin describes the horseman as St. Michael.

62 Khaṭīb (Cairo), 1:73 = (Paris), 11.

63 Khaṭīb (Cairo), 1:73 = (Paris), 11; Ṣūlī, *Akhbār* (London), 229, sub anno 330; Ibn al-Jawzī, *Muntaẓam*, 6:317.

CHAPTER VIII

1 Khaṭīb (Cairo), 1:115-17 = (Paris), 71-73; Lassner, *Topography*, 173-76, 280-81.

2 Ya'qūbī, *Buldān*, 237-38.

3 Khaṭīb (Cairo), 1:71-75 = (Paris), 8-14, Ya'qūbī, *Buldān*, 238-39; Ṭabarī, 3/1:278, 321, 322; Yāqūt, *Mu'jam*, 1:681; Ibn Rustah, 108; Muqaddasī, 121; Herzfeld and Sarre, 108-109, 119ff.; Creswell, 2:8ff.; and Figure 3. Regarding the dimensions of the walls, see Herzfeld and Sarre, 108-109, 121, and the corrections of Lassner, *Topography*, 240-41, ns. 25, 26, which are based not on the conflicting and obviously erroneous statements of the literary sources, but on the ruined wall structure of al-Raqqah, which was reportedly similar to that of Baghdad. See also Creswell, 2:39-42. Al-Raqqah, which was somewhat smaller than Baghdad (1,500 meters to a side as opposed to 2,000 meters from gate to gate), featured a main wall almost 6 meters thick (12 cubits) and an outer wall 4.5 meters thick. The walls of al-Raqqah are not sufficiently well-preserved to give an indication of height, but a ratio of 1 : 7 seems about right. The inner wall of Baghdad could therefore have reached a height of about 40 meters. The protective wall featured thirty-eight towers, which were probably hollow projecting towers with rooms for fighting men rather than simple buttresses. The wall was surmounted by battlements, which

shielded a walkway encompassing the city. See Lassner, *Topography*, 238, n. 17. Access to the walkway was obtained via a ramp that could be blocked at various stages by closing a system of gateways. See Ya'qūbī, *Buldān*, 239-40. The ramp inclined in the haunches of a vault constructed partly of burnt brick cemented with gypsum. The inside of the vault served as a room for the guard. See also Creswell, 15-16.

4 See Figures 2 and 3.

5 There is no indication of the width of the moat in any of the published texts. Dūrī, in his article on Baghdad in *EI*², mentions that it was 40 cubits (60 feet) wide. This is presumably based on the Mashhad MS of Ibn al-Faqīh. Note that the moat at al-Raqqah, whose fortifications were modeled after Baghdad, was also approximately 40 cubits wide. See Creswell, 2:41. Herzfeld and Sarre, 119, and Creswell, 2:10-11, were all unaware of Ibn al-Faqīh when they estimated the width of the water barrier at 12 to 22 cubits, and their figures must be emended accordingly. Ya'qūbī, *Buldān*, 239, reports that the base of the city wall was lined with a quay (*musannāh*) of burnt brick cemented with quicklime. Ibn Rustah, 108, indicates that the walls of the moat were constructed of burnt brick and gypsum (*qad banā ḥāfatāhu bi-l-jaṣṣ wa al-ājurr*). The outer gateway featured a bent entrance and was 30 cubits wide (45 feet) and 20 cubits long (30 feet). See Khaṭīb (Cairo), 1:74 = (Paris), 12; Herzfeld and Sarre, 123; and Creswell, 12. For examples of bent entrances, see Creswell, 23ff. The outer gateway led to a court 60 cubits wide (90 feet). From this court, there were entrances to the first *faṣīl*, and, at the end of the court, there was the second gateway that protected the inner wall of the city. This was a two-story structure that was about 30 cubits long (45 feet) and 40 cubits wide (60 feet). The lower story contained the main protective gates of the city; the upper story housed an audience hall of the Caliph and was allegedly surmounted by a green dome. See Khaṭīb (Cairo), 1:74-75 = (Paris), 12, 13; Ya'qūbī, *Buldān*, 238-39; Herzfeld and Sarre, 125; Creswell, 12.

6 See Figures 2, 3, 5, and 6.

7 Ya'qūbī, *Buldān*, 240. The building was a large portico (*saqīfah*) raised on columns of burnt brick cemented with gypsum. The author indicates that, in his time, that is, the ninth century, the portico was used as a place of prayer (*muṣallā*), thus suggesting that it was the Dar al-Qaṭṭān mentioned by the Khaṭīb (Cairo), 1:108-109 = (Paris), 60-61. That is to say, that in A.H. 260 or 261, when there was no longer sufficient room in the principal mosque, the former headquarters of the security police was converted into a place of prayer. The Caliph had long ceased to occupy the original Manṣūrid palace and was, in fact, living in Sāmarrā. The structure of a portico (surrounding a court) would have been ideally suited for conversion into a place of prayer. The notion of the Caliph's personal domain is discussed in great detail by J. Lassner, "The Caliph's Personal Domain: The City Plan of Baghdad Reexamined," 105ff.; which is essentially the same as his *Topography*, 138-48.

8 Ya'qūbī, *Buldān*, 240.

9 Ibid. The older children, princes of the ruling family, received land grants outside the Round City to serve as their estates.

10 Ibid.

11 It is reported that the gates were sufficiently high to allow for the entry of a mounted horseman holding a lance (Ya'qūbī, *Buldān*, 238-39). Herzfeld stated that the long lance of the modern bedouin is 10 cubits long. He therefore assumed that the doorway was of comparable height. He apparently did not consider the height of the horse, the point at which the lance was held, the possibility that the lance spoken of might be of a different size, or that the expression might be an idiom. See Herzfeld and Sarre, 121-22. The massive gates required a company of men to open and close them. One notes that during a riot in A.H. 307, the populace allowed the prison inmates (in the Round City) to escape. However, the iron gates of the city were still intact and were shut. The security forces pursued those who had broken out of prison until they captured the entire lot, without a single prisoner escaping. See Khaṭīb (Cairo), 1:75-76 = (Paris), 14. The reference here is presumably to the fortress-like Maṭbaq Prison that was situated on the street of the same name, between the Kūfah and Baṣrah Gates (Ya'qūbī, *Buldān*, 240). Riots broke out that year on the West Side because of rising prices and shortages. The report of the Khaṭīb is no doubt connected with these events. See Hamadhānī, 21-42, 149-73, 185-216; Ibn al-Athīr, *Kāmil*, 8:85-86. Note also the use of gates to seal off the Caliph's domain at al-Hāshimīyah during the disturbance of the Rāwandīyah.

12 Khaṭīb (Cairo), 1:76, 77 = (Paris), 16, 17. The large arcades are reported as 200 cubits (300 feet) in length and 15 cubits (22.5 feet) in width. There were fifty-four arcades in all. Herzfeld and Sarre, 129, followed by Creswell, 2:16, who is of the opinion that the length of the arcades indicated by the Khaṭīb does not leave sufficient room for a guard of 1,000 men. Consequently, the arcades are arbitrarily lengthened in his reconstruction. There is no reason to assume, however, that the men were actually quartered in the flanking rooms, although they may very well have stayed there while on duty. The likelihood is that they resided in streets designated for the *ḥaras* and *shurṭah* (Ya'qūbī, *Buldān*, 240). The commandant of the Damascus Gate was Sulaymān b. Mujālid; of the Baṣrah Gate, Abū al-Azhar al-Tamīmī; of the Kūfah Gate, Khālid al-Akkī; and of the Khurāsān Gate, Maslamah b. Suhayb al-Ghassānī.

13 See Figure 1; LeStrange, *Baghdad*, map 2; *Baghdād: 'araḍ ta'rīkhī muṣawwar* (Baghdad, 1969) ed. M. Jawad et al., 21.

14 See Lassner, *Topography*, 138-41. Somewhat similar distinctions between administrative areas and civilian centers of occupation are referred to by W. Barthold in his description of pre-Islamic cities in Iran and Turkestan. These cities comprised a citadel and town proper. The market was outside the town (*berun = rabad*). In some instances the suburbs were enclosed by a second wall. See W. Barthold, *Turkestan to the Mongol Invasion*, 18; and W. Barthold, *Mussulman Culture*, 31-32. These references are cited in G. von Grunebaum, *Islam* (Leiden, 1955), 148.

15 Khaṭīb (Cairo), 1:77 = (Paris), 17.

16 Ibn Rustah indicates that the domes were green, that is, the same color as the cupola that surmounted the Qaṣr al-Dhahab. Like the cupola of the central structure, the domes of the gateways featured a mechanical device. See Khaṭīb (Cairo), 1:73, 75 = (Paris), 10-11, 13. Creswell, 2:13, describes the gateway domes as "gilt." This is, however, probably based on a misreading of *muzakhrafah*, which in this case means "ornamented." Concerning the symbolic meaning of the green dome, see Chapter VII, Section C. The room was reached by an external stairway. Thus, the Caliph would not have been required to mix with the traffic entering the city gates. An account in Ya'qūbī suggests that the upper chamber could be reached by way of an (enclosed) ramp. The details are missing, but it seems probable that this structure connected with the inner wall. See Ya'qūbī, *Buldān*, 239-40. Note that all the audience halls were part of two superposed structures of equal dimensions. The gateway room, which was 12 cubits (18 feet) in width and 20 cubits (30 feet) in length, rested on a vaulted structure of similar dimensions. One may assume (following Creswell) that the domed chambers and the vaulted hall below were of equal height. If one cubit is allowed for the apex of the dome and one for the apex of the vault (according to Creswell, 2 cubits), a total of 50 cubits (75 feet) is obtained, the very height designated by the Khaṭīb for the cupola. Similarly, the domed audience hall of the Qaṣr al-Dhahab, which was 20 by 20 cubits, was surmounted by a structure of identical dimensions. Allowing the walls and zone of transition to represent twice the width, one obtains a figure of 40 cubits for the walls of each chamber, and a total height of 80 cubits (120 feet), the very figure designated by the Khaṭīb for the cupola of the Qaṣr al-Dhahab.

17 The sources conflict in reporting the total area that was circumscribed by the walls of the structure; there are no fewer than six reports giving figures ranging from 576,000 to 64,000,000 square cubits. Within this range, I am inclined to accept the report that is attributed to Rabāḥ. See Khaṭīb (Cairo), 1:71 = (Paris), 8. Rabāḥ indicated that the distance between each of the city's (symmetrically arranged) gates was one *mīl* (2,000 meters). This figure is also accepted by Herzfeld and Sarre, 107; and Creswell, 2:8. For a review of all the statistical data on the size of the Round City, see Lassner, *Topography*, 235, n. 2.

18 See R. Adams, *Land Beyond Baghdad*, which is based essentially on an analysis of surface remains. The figure for Ctesiphon may, however, be much too small, for the government center of the Sassanids was part of a wider urban occupation that included the older city of Seleucia across the Tigris.

19 Ṭabarī, 3/1:322-23; see also Khaṭīb (Cairo), 1:77-78 = (Paris), 17-18. See also Chapter IV n. 4.

20 This expression may, however, also refer to the first court encountered upon entering the wall system of the city (see Figure 3). Note the variant in the Khaṭīb (Cairo), 1:77-78 = (Paris), 17-18, in which the initial reference seems to be to the outer gateway. However, the account of the Khaṭīb is clearly confused.

21 That is to say, the third *intervallum* of the city marking the limit of the residential section. See Figures 3 and 4.

22 Concerning the guards in the arcades, see Khaṭīb (Cairo), 1:76 = (Paris), 15.

23 Variants of this last account are found in Ṭabarī, 3/1:323, 324; Khaṭīb (Cairo), 1:78-79, 80 = (Paris), 18-19, 21. Yāqūt, *Mu'jam*, 4:254.

24 See Figure 7.

25 Khaṭīb (Cairo), 1:76 = (Paris), 15, indicates that the width of the arcade was 15 cubits (23 feet) and that flanking the passageway were 106 rooms. Creswell estimates these rooms as 8 cubits (12 feet) in width and 12 cubits (18 feet) in length. This is sufficient for local shops and small manufacture, but it hardly seems large enough to provide services for the entire urban area. See Creswell, 2:16; and Herzfeld and Sarre, 129; and Figure 3.

26 The old market of the West Side (Sūq Baghdād) was situated in al-Karkh. See Ṭabarī, 2/2:910, 914. The position of this market is fixed by Balādhurī as somewhere near Qarn al-Ṣarāt, the point at which the Ṣarāt empties into the Tigris. See *Futūḥ*, 246.

27 Khaṭīb (Cairo), 1:77 = (Paris), 16-17. Note that, when the Caliph al-Amīn attempted to flee the city while it was under siege in A.H. 198, there was apparently no such passage known to him. His options were either to break out of the city escorted by armed cavalry or to surrender to the rival forces. See Lassner, *Topography*, 234, n. 17.

28 Khaṭīb (Cairo), 1:78-79 = (Paris), 18-19.

29 Ibid., 78 = (Paris), 18.

30 The variant in Ṭabarī, which is the more expansive of the two, is also followed by the account of the Byzantine Patrikios, but it does not mention the construction of water conduits. See Ṭabarī, 3/1:322-23.

31 Ya'qūbī, *Buldān*, 239.

32 According to Ibn Rustah, 108, the walls of the moat on both sides were cemented with gypsum (*jaṣṣ*).

33 See R. J. Forbes, *Studies in Ancient Technology* (Leiden, 1955) 1:72-74.

34 Khaṭīb (Cairo), 1:79 = (Paris), 19.

35 Ya'qūbī, *Buldān*, 238. The bricks were reportedly assembled on the island that subsequently became known as al-'Abbāsiyah. This is explicitly stated in the deed to the property, which was turned over to the Caliph's brother al-'Abbās. See Yāqūt, *Mu'jam*, 3:600.

36 Khaṭīb (Cairo), 1:79 = (Paris), 19.

37 Ibid. = (Paris), 19-20.

38 See Yāqūt, *Mu'jam*, 3:600; Ya'qūbī, *Buldān*, 242-43; Khaṭīb (Cairo), 1:91 = (Paris), 37. This fief is not to be confused with the estate of that name that was situated on the East Side. See Ya'qūbī, *Buldān*, 252. Access to the island was gained by three bridges spanning the Lesser Ṣarāt. See Khaṭīb (Cairo), 1:112 = (Paris), 66.

39 See Section F.

40 Khaṭīb (Cairo), 1:80 = (Paris), 21-22.

41 Ṭabarī, 3/1:322-23.

42 Ṭabarī, text: *madīnatika*; MS B: *baytika*.

43 The term *ṣanf* only later acquires the meaning of guild. This is not the meaning intended here. For a brief summary of the dating of guilds in medieval Islam, see C. Cahen, "Y a-t-il eu des corporations professionelles dans le monde musulman classique," 51-63; and, in the same volume, the study of S. M. Stern, "The Constitution of the Islamic City," 36ff. contra B. Lewis, "The Islamic Guilds," 20-37, and L. Massignon, "Les corps de métier et la cité Islamique," 473-88; *EI*, s.v. *ṣinf*. See also A. A. Duri, "Nushū' al-aṣnāf wa al-ḥiraf fī al-Islam," 133ff.

44 Ṭabarī, 3/1:324.

45 Ṭabarī, 3/1:324; Khaṭīb (Cairo), 1:79ff. = (Paris), 20-21.

46 Concerning this revolt, see Chapter III, Sections B and C.

47 Ṭabarī, 3/1:325.

48 This was particularly true beginning with the period of the Būyids (A.D. 945-1055). See, for example, Ibn al-Jawzī, *Muntaẓam*, 8:140-42, 149-50; and Ibn al-Athīr, *Kāmil*, 9:373-74, 395-96. A systematic study of this problem is very much needed. See the sketchy remarks in the introduction to the Paris edition of the Khaṭīb by G. Salmon, 61ff. and M. Canard, "Baghdad au IVe siècle H.," 281ff.; also Makdisi, "Topography," 178-97, 281-309. The frequent altercations resulted in great losses of property and goods and even led to the creation of protective walls around the large quarters inhabited by these groups. See also C. Cahen, "Mouvements populaires et autonomisme urbain dans l'Asie musulmane du moyen âge," 5:225-50; 6:25-26, 233-65.

49 Khaṭīb (Cairo), 81 = (Paris), 23. The Shī'ite settlement in the market suburbs may go back to the earliest period of the city. Note the account describing the seditious activities of Abū Zakariyā', the *muḥtasib* of the city markets, which links him with the supporters of former Shī'ite rebels.

50 Ṭabarī, 3/1:325.

51 Khaṭīb (Cairo), 1:75, 80 = (Paris), 14, 21; Ya'qūbī, *Buldān*, 245.

52 Khaṭīb (Cairo), 1:92 = (Paris), 38-39; Ya'qūbī, *Buldān*, 245. The fief of 'Īsā b. 'Alī, one of the *'umūmah*, seems, however, to be situated farther inland near Bāb al-Muḥawwal. See Ya'qūbī, *Buldān*, 244; Yāqūt, *Mu'jam*, 4:143, location not indicated. The Bāb al-Muḥawwal was a vaulted gateway situated somewhere below the junction of the two Ṣarāt Canals. See Ya'qūbī, *Buldān*, 245; Yāqūt, *Mu'jam*, 1:451; 4:432. With the decline of the city, it gave its name to the surrounding area, which became a separate urban entity. Its inhabitants were Sunnite and were frequently in conflict with the inhabitants of al-Karkh. The text of the Khaṭīb may be corrupt. A suggested reading is found in Lassner, *Topography*, 260-61, n. 71.

53 The political ramifications associated with the construction of this East Side palace are discussed in Section D.

54 *Mu'jam*, 3:279; and Ya'qūbī, *Buldān*, 245.

55 Ibid.

56 Ya'qūbī, *Buldān*, 245.

57 *Mu'jam*, 3:279.

58 Ṭabarī, 3/1:324; Khaṭīb (Cairo), 1:79 = (Paris), 20.

59 Ya'qūbī, *Buldān*, 245. The existence of a principal mosque, together with a judicial authority, ordinarily specifies a separate municipal entity. There is no specific indication when the mosque at al-Sharqīyah was turned over to public use. The assumption here is that the move to al-Khuld, together with the continuing construction at al-Ruṣāfah, enabled al-Manṣūr to use the mosque originally intended for al-Mahdī's palace as the major place of prayer for the populace of al-Karkh. This is only an assumption, but it seems eminently plausible. Concerning the relationship of the mosques at Baghdad to the overall organization of the city, see Section E.

60 Ṭabarī, 3/1:364ff., 460; Khaṭīb (Cairo), 1:82-83 = (Paris), 23-25; Yāqūt, *Mu'jam*, 2:783. Note, however, the peculiar date for the beginning of construction of al-Ruṣāfah given by Ya'qūbī, *Buldān*, 251. He indicates that it was begun in A.H. 143, two years before the founding of Baghdad, according to most authorities. The main water supply for al-Ruṣāfah was the Nahr al-Mahdī. See Khaṭīb (Cairo), 1:115 = (Paris), 71.

61 Balādhurī, *Futūḥ*, 295; Mas'ūdī, *Tanbīh*, 360; Khaṭīb (Cairo), 1:83 = (Paris), 25; Yāqūt, *Mu'jam*, 3:677.

62 Ṭabarī, 3/1:365ff., sub anno 151.

63 Ṭabarī, 3/1:380; Khaṭīb (Cairo), 1:115 = (Paris), 71. Pontoon bridges (*jiṣr*) were used to connect East and West Baghdad, because the inundation of the winding river made masonry bridges (*qanṭarah*) impractical. The pontoon bridges also had the advantage of being mobile and easy to repair. In times of strife the bridges could be dismantled and traffic between the two sides cut. Conversely, the bridges were also easy to erect so as to facilitate the transfer of men and materials. See, for example, Ibn al-Jawzī, *Muntaẓam*, 8:56-57, 132. The bridge mentioned in Ṭabarī and the Khaṭīb is identified by G. LeStrange as Jisr al-Awwal, the lower bridge connecting the two sides. See LeStrange, *Baghdad*, 175 and map 4; Ya'qūbī, *Buldān*, 254; and M. Canard, *Histoire de la dynastie des Hamdanides de Jazira et de Syrie*, 1:168. There is no doubt, however, that this was the prototype for the main public bridge (*Al-Jisr*) connecting al-Khuld with Bāb al-Ṭāq. Regarding the complicated question of the city bridges, see Lassner, *Topography*, 173-76, 280-81.

64 Khaṭīb (Cairo), 1:116 = (Paris), 71.

65 For the location of Bustān al-Zāhir in the vicinity of the main bridge on the East Side, see Khaṭīb (Cairo), 1:107, 116 = (Paris), 59, 70; and Ibn al-Jawzī, *Muntaẓam*, 8:132, sub anno 450, which states that a bridge was erected at Bāb al-Ṭāq (the original bridgehead) in order to give access to the wazīr al-Basāsīrī's troops, who were encamped at Bustān al-Zāhir. Concerning the alleged gardens of al-Khuld, see Khaṭīb (Cairo), 1:75 = (Paris), 14. Al-Khuld was reportedly named because of its likeness to the *Jannat al-Khuld*, "The Garden of Eternity." The allusion is to the Qu'ran 25:16, which mentions the Palace of Eternity (*Khuld*) that is promised to the God-fearing. See also LeStrange, *Baghdad*, 101-105.

66 Ya'qūbī, *Buldān*, 251, 253; Khaṭīb (Cairo), 1:92, 93 = (Paris), 38, 40.

67 Khaṭīb (Cairo), 1:93 = (Paris), 41. Originally it was called the Market of Satiety (*Sūq al-Riyy*), but this name was superceded by the Market of Thirst (*Sūq al-'Aṭash*). It was reportedly built for al-Mahdī by Sa'īd al-Ḥarrashī, who was made responsible for the collection of taxes in the markets in A.H. 167. See Khaṭīb (Cairo), 1:81 = (Paris), 22. The name al-Ḥarrashī is often confused in the texts with other variants, that is, al-Jurshī, al-Khursī. See Lassner, *Topography*, index, 312; 'Arīb, 43d; Ṭabarī, index, 230. According to Ya'qūbī, *Buldān*, 252, it was situated near the Fief of Badr, the location of which is not indicated. Suhrāb, 130 = Ibn Serapion, 22, fixes the location of the market somewhere in al-Mukharrim. By the time of Yāqūt, it was completely destroyed and its previous location unknown. However, he mentions it as being in the general area between Nahr al-Mu'allā and al-Ruṣāfah, that is, al-Mukharrim. Another account cited by him places it between al-Ruṣāfah and Bāb al-Shammāsīyah near the dyke of Mu'izz al-Dawlah. See Yāqūt, *Mu'jam*, 3:194. 'Arīb, 28-29 and Ṣūlī, *Akhbār* (London), 90, place it near the main bridgehead. All these references indicate a location in the upper East Side. Ya'qūbī, *Buldān*, 252 likens it to al-Karkh. Sūq al-'Aṭash was thus the major market area for the upper East Side, just as al-Karkh serviced the lower West Side, and Sūq al-Thalāthā', the lower East Side. Concerning the disposition of the city markets, see Lassner, "Massignon," 1-27, which is essentially his *Topography*, 155-77. See esp. 170ff. This market must have been in the same area as Sūq Yaḥyā, which was situated in the vicinity of the main bridge between the palaces of the amīrs and wazīrs. Sūq Yaḥyā served the specific area of Bāb al-Ṭāq. See Khaṭīb (Cairo), 1:93 = (Paris), 40; Ya'qūbī, *Buldān*, 253; the description of Ibn 'Aqīl in Ibn al-Jawzī, *Manāqib*, 17, 26; Ibn al-Jawzī, *Muntaẓam*, 5:146; 9:82; and Yāqūt *Mu'jam*, 3:195. See also G. Salmon, *L'Introduction topographique à l'histoire de Baghdad*, 65; LeStrange, *Baghdad*, 199-201, 206. M. Canard, *Histoire*, 1:161, 164; G. Makdisi, "Topography," 186, n. 6; Lassner, *Topography*, 262, n. 5.

68 Khaṭīb (Cairo), 1:96 = (Paris), 44. The exact location of 'Īsābādh is not known. According to Yāqūt, *Mu'jam*, 3:752-53, al-Mahdī originally granted it to his son 'Īsā. Later he built a palace there (Qaṣr al-Salām) at a reported cost of fifty million dirhams. At first, temporary quarters were built of mud brick; later, the permanent residence was built of burnt brick. According to Ṭabarī, the foundations were laid in A.H. 164 and the Caliph took up residence there two years later. See Ṭabarī, 3/1:517.

69 See the judgment of the Khaṭīb (Cairo), 1:119 = (Paris), 76-77.

70 See Ṭabarī, 3/1:606-607, 610, sub anno 171, indicating the Caliph's disenchantment with Baghdad; Ṭabarī, 3/2:645, sub anno 180; Azdī 289, 290, 291; *FHA*, 301, indicating the move to al-Rāfiqah. This was clearly more than a temporary visit, although, for official purposes, the capital might have remained at Baghdad (*wa fīhā shakhaṣa Hārūn . . . ilā al-Rāfiqah fanazalahā faawṭanahā . . .*). Note that al-Rāfiqah was better positioned for use as a base in the Caliph's campaigns against the Byzantines (*wa fīhā awṭana al-Rashīd al-Rāfiqah wa ghazā minhā . . .*). The Caliph went to Baghdad in A.H. 184, but then returned to al-

Rāfiqah in A.H. 185. See Ṭabarī, 3/2:649, 651. Note that the Barmakids apparently had properties and considerable monies in al-Rāfiqah as well as in Baghdad. See Ṭabarī, 3/2:679, sub anno 187. The relationship of al-Rāfiqah to Baghdad in the period of the early 'Abbāsid Caliphs is a subject worthy of serious attention.

71 Detailed information on the distribution of palace personnel is found in the Khaṭīb (Cairo), 1:99-100 = (Paris), 49-50; and, more particularly, Hilāl al-Ṣābi', *Rusūm*, 8-9. The latter indicates that, in the time of al-Muktafī (A.H. 289-295), there were 20,000 *ghilmān al-dār* and 10,000 Blacks and Slaves. In addition, there was the Ḥujarite Guard (*al-ḥujrīyah*) numbering many thousands. These palace servants were also called *ghilmān al-ḥujar* and *ghilmān al-dār*. According to Canard, they were so called because they resided in quarters designated as *al-ḥujar*, "the chambers." A better explanation, perhaps, is that they were attached to the palace precincts. They also seem to have joined the Caliph in his campaigns. They were first formed by al-Mu'taḍid (A.H. 279-285) and placed under the command of the chief eunuchs or their assistants. See Canard's commentary and translation of Ṣūlī's *Akhbār* (Algiers) 12:49, n.3: Ṭabarī, 3/3:2262, 2265; and Ṣābi', *Wuzarā'*, 12-13. The security patrol (*nawbah*) consisted of 5,000 troops (*rajjālat al-muṣaffiyah*), 400 security personnel (*ḥaras*), and 800 room servants (*farrāsh*). The city garrison (*shiḥnat al-balad*) was under the supervision of the police (*sāḥib al-ma'ūnah*) and numbered 14,000 cavalry and infantry.

72 Khaṭīb (Cairo), 1:100ff. = (Paris), 49ff.; Ibn Miskawayh (Cairo), 1:53-55; Ibn al-Jawzī, *Muntaẓam*, 6:143-44; Ibn al-Athīr, *Kāmil*, 8:79; and particularly Ṣābi', *Rusūm*, 11ff. and Ibn al-Zubayr, 131-139. The lengthy passage of the Khaṭīb was translated and discussed by G. LeStrange, "A Greek Embassy to Baghdad in 917 A.D.," 35-45. See also M. Hamidullah, "Nouveaux documents," 293-97.

73 The palace was on the east bank of the Tigris, presumably in al-Shammāsīyah, the northernmost section of the East Side. See Ṣābi', *Wuzarā'*, 262, 431. For Sa'īd b. Makhlad, see Sourdel, *Vizirat*, 1:315ff.

74 That is to say, the capital situated adjacent to al-Kūfah. The complicated problem of identifying the early 'Abbāsid capitals is discussed in Chapter VI.

75 See Chapter III, Section C.

76 Ya'qūbī, *Buldān*, 237-38; Ṭabarī, 3/1:272-73, 276-77; Muqaddasī, 115-120, Yāqūt, *Mu'jam*, 1:680-81. For examples of western authorities, see Noeldeke, trans. J. S. Black, 129-30; LeStrange, *Baghdad*, 6-10; M. Streck, *Die alte Landschaft Babylonien*, 54; Reitemeyer, *Städtegründungen*, 50-51; and Lassner, *Topography*, 126ff.

77 Ṭabarī, 3/1:272; Ibn Ṭabāṭabā (Beirut), 161.

78 In recruiting his labor force, al-Manṣūr tapped the regions of Syria, al-Mawṣil, al-Jabal, al-Kūfah, Wāsiṭ, and al-Baṣrah. See Ṭabarī, 3/1:276-77; Muqaddasī, 121; Yāqūt, *Mu'jam*, 1:681. No mention is made of Egypt or Khurāsān. See also Chapter VII n. 18.

79 General statements on the typology of Islamic towns and cities can be found in G. Marcais, "Le conception des villes dans l'Islam," 517-33, and E.

Pauty, "Villes spontanées et villes créées en Islam," 52-75. An analysis of the distinction between spontaneous and created cities as it applies to the *amṣār* and Baghdad, is found in Lassner, *Topography*, 138ff.

80 Khaṭīb (Cairo), 1:70 = (Paris), 6-7, Yāqūt, *Muʿjam*, 1:683. See also A. Udovitch "The Bronze Coinage of the ʿAbbāsids," 20ff. Udovitch notes that payment to certain types of workers was fixed according to weights, that is, *qīrāṭ, ḥabbah, dāniq*; H. Sauvaire, "Materiaux pour servir à l'histoire de la numismatique et de la metrologie musulmane," 251, 256; and W. Hinz, *Islamische Masse und Gewichte*, 11, 12, 27. According to Udovitch (citing the Khaṭīb), "It is inconceivable that these minute pieces of silver were weighed out every evening in order to pay thousands of laborers. . . . The small sums were obviously paid in copper or bronze coins, the denomination created expressly for this purpose. The weight divisions of the dīnār (gold) and dirham (silver) were monies of account pegged to the fluctuating and diversified value of the fals (copper coin). The *dāniq*, *qirāṭ*, and *ḥabbah* were, both for official and private purposes, the only standard way to express small sums of money." See also E. Ashtor, *Histoire des prix et des salaires dans l'Orient médiéval*, 64ff. Ashtor believes that the favorable relationship between salary and purchasing power was not maintained for long. Although the evidence is slight, I am inclined to favor this view on the assumption that prices and wages may have been controlled to attract laborers during the years of construction.

81 Yaʿqūbī, *Buldān*, 238, indicates 100,000 laborers; the Khaṭīb (Cairo), 1:67 = (Paris), 1, indicates many thousands.

82 Ṭabarī, 3/1:272, 278, 322; Yaʿqūbī, *Buldān*, 241. The reference here may, however, be to suburban development.

83 Yaʿqūbī, *Buldān*, 241-42, 246.

84 Ṭabarī, 3/1:322, relates that an official was thrown into prison for a paltry sum. The account demonstrates the Caliph's well-documented tightness with money, but it reveals as well the efficiency of the accounting system used during the construction of the city.

85 Yaʿqūbī, *Buldān*, 246, does seem to indicate the possible existence of a cantonment (*jund*) in al-Karkh, but no such place is described by him or any other author. With respect to the topographical sources, see J. Lassner, "Notes on the Topography of Baghdad: The Systematic Descriptions of the City and the Khaṭīb al-Baghdādī," 458-69, which is essentially the same as his *Topography*, 25-42.

86 Note Yaʿqūbī, *Buldān*, 250, where the author admits that there are many locations not included in his description of the topography and toponymy of the city.

87 Yaʿqūbī, *Buldān*, 246ff.; Iṣṭakhrī, 83; Ibn Ḥawqal, 164; Khaṭīb (Cairo), 1:85 = (Paris), 28; Suhrāb, 134 = Ibn Serapion, 27; Yāqūt, *Muʿjam*, 4:485; LeStrange, *Baghdad*, 127-28.

88 Yaʿqūbī, *Buldān*, 254.

89 Ibid., 251-54.

90 See n. 68.

91 The first of the great palaces of the lower East Side, which later became the Dār al-Khilāfah, was originally built at great expense by al-Ma'mūn's tutor, Ja'far al-Barmakī, for his own pleasure. Fearing that the Caliph (al-Rashīd) might not look with favor on so magnificent an edifice, he turned the palace over to the Caliph's son, al-Ma'mūn. The name was subsequently changed from Qaṣr al-Ja'farī to Qaṣr al-Ma'mūnī. Al-Ma'mūn undertook extensive renovations and expanded the palace grounds into the surrounding area. He added a hippodrome and zoological garden and dug a canal leading from the Nahr al-Mu'allā to provide drinking water. An eastern gate was constructed to give access to the unoccupied land beyond, and nearby residences were built for his special personnel and his companions. Following the civil war, it was occupied first by al-Ḥasan b. Sahl and then by al-Ḥasan's daughter Būrān, thus the name Qaṣr al-Ḥasanī. See Khaṭīb (Cairo), 1:99ff. = (Paris), 47ff.; Yāqūt, *Mu'jam*, 1:806-808; *EI*, s.v. al-Ḥasan b. Sahl; *EI*[2], s.v. Būrān. See also LeStrange, *Baghdad*, 243-46.

92 When al-Ma'mūn returned to Baghdad from Khurāsān in A.H. 204, he set up quarters for himself in al-Ruṣāfah and then built two more residences for himself on the left bank in al-Mukharrim. One of these was near his regnal palace, the Qaṣr al-Ma'mūnī, the second was near Bustān Mūsā. See Ibn Ṭayfūr (Cairo), 9-10; Khaṭīb (Cairo), 1:98 = (Paris), 47. The exact location of Bustān Mūsā is not indicated, but it is clear from the account of the Khaṭīb that it was between the Qaṣr al-Ma'mūnī and the dwellings of the family of Wahb that reached the main bridge (*al-jisr*). The original palace of al-Mu'taṣim was also situated there adjacent to the dwelling of his brother. The area also contained numerous other residences of the ruling family and their followers. For the palace of al-Mu'taṣim, see also Suhrāb, 130 = Ibn Serapion, 22.

93 This palace was situated near al-Khuld above Qarn al-Ṣarāt, the point at which the great canal entered the Tigris. See Khaṭīb (Cairo), 1:87, 92 = (Paris), 30, 39; LeStrange, *Baghdad*, 102-103.

94 This problem of military settlement in Baghdad is briefly discussed by A.S. al-'Alī, "The Foundation of Baghdad," 92-101.

95 Ya'qūbī, *Buldān*, 247-50. The single exception is the Fief of the North Africans (*Qaṭī'at al-Afāriqah*).

96 Ibid., 247-48.

97 Text: *Asbīshāb, Ishtakhanj.*

98 The presumption here is that the *ra'īs* was in charge of the payroll.

99 Ṭabarī, 3/1:631.

100 Ya'qūbī, *Buldān*, 248.

101 Ibid., 249. These cantonments are mentioned together with the names of various military commanders: Būzān b. Khālid al-Kirmānī, Kharfāsh al-Ṣughdī, Māhān al-Ṣāmaghānī, and Marzubān Abī Asad b. Marzubān al-Fārayābī. Thus far, I have not been successful in identifying any of them. It is of course possible that the estate of al-Balkhī retained its name long after his death, thus suggesting that the entire description of the area may be a later interpolation.

102 This particular area was situated along the Dujayl Road adjacent to the

property of Abū al-'Abbās al-Ṭūsī. See Khaṭīb (Cairo), 1:85 = (Paris), 27; Suhrāb, 134 = Ibn Serapion, 27; Yāqūt, *Mu'jam*, 4:485.

103 Khaṭīb (Cairo), 1:85 = (Paris), 27. Yāqūt, *Mu'jam*, 2:750; Ya'qūbī places the location of this name between the Kūfah and Damascus Gates. See Ya'qūbī, *Buldān*, 246.

104 See Chapter V, Section C.

105 Concerning the early 'Abbāsid attitudes towards the Arab tribal armies of Syria see Chapter IV, Section D.

106 See Chapter III, Section D.

107 Ṭabarī, 3/1:365-68.

108 It is the assumption here that all the Baghdad-based troops were from Khurāsān, including those allegedly divided according to tribal grouping. It is inconceivable that the Arab tribal armies of Syria that supported 'Abdallāh b. 'Alī against the Caliph would have been permitted to settle at Baghdad.

109 This general pattern seems to be borne out by Ya'qūbī's description of the area. See *Buldān*, 251. The reference to *al-jisr* signifies the Main Bridge, which connected al-Ruṣāfah with the area of al-Khuld. Concerning the great market at Sūq Yaḥyā, which was situated at Bāb al-Ṭāq, that is, near the bridge, see n. 67. The Mosque of Khuḍayr presumably was situated in or near the suwayqah of that name. The suwayqah was situated on the road leading to the Fief of al-Faḍl b. al-Rabī'. Khuḍayr was a client of Ṣāliḥ Sāḥib al-Muṣallā and was responsible for the distribution of land grants in the area. It is reported that waterjars (*jirar*) and imported curios from China (*ṭarā'if al-ṣīn*) were sold at Suwayqat Khuḍayr. By the thirteenth century, it had given its name to the entire quarter, which was known as al-Khuḍayrīyah. See Khaṭīb (Cairo), 1:93 = (Paris), 40; Ya'qūbī, *Buldān*, 253; Ya'qūt, *Mu'jam*, 2:453; *Marāṣid*, 1:357; also LeStrange, *Baghdad*, 173, 197-98; Ya'qūbī, *Buldān*, trans. Wiet, 41, n. 3. I can find no other reference to the Road of the Skiffs.

110 Ya'qūbī, *Buldān*, 251-54; Khaṭīb (Cairo), 1:93 = (Paris), 40-41.

111 Ya'qūbī, *Buldān*, 253.

112 See Chapter IV, Section D.

113 Ṭabarī, 3/1:272; Ibn Ṭabāṭabā (Beirut), 161.

114 Concerning these two figures, see Chapter III, Section A.

115 This metaphor is seemingly used in connection with 'Abd al-Ṣamad b. 'Alī's complaint concerning the influence of the *mawālī*. See Chapter IV, Section A.

116 See n. 19; Chapter IV n. 4.

117 It was originally the Archway (*Ṭāq*) of Asmā', the daughter of al-Manṣūr, and then passed into the possession of 'Alī b. Jahshiyār. It was situated between the two palaces (*bayn al-qaṣrayn*), that is, her palace and that of 'Ubaydallāh, the son of al-Mahdī. It later gave its name, Bāb al-Ṭāq, to the entire area between al-Ruṣāfah and Nahr al-Mu'allā, that is, al-Mukharrim, but, most specifically, to the upper part of al-Mukharrim near the bridge. See Khaṭīb (Cairo), 1:93 = (Paris), 40; Yāqūt, *Mu'jam*, 1:445; 3:489. Concerning the topographical problems arising in identifying this location, see LeStrange, *Baghdad*, 218, 320;

Makdisi, "Topography," 185, n.4; Lassner, *Topography*, 173ff. Similarly, *bayn al-qaṣrayn*, which originally signified the area between the palaces of the notables from the ruling family, became in time an identifiable section. See Yāqūt, *Mu'jam*, 1:799.

118 Concerning the name Madīnat al-Salām, see Chapter VI, n. 69. For variants of the name Baghdad and its etymology, see the article of A. A. Duri in *EI*[2], s.v. Baghdad. For the name al-Zawrā', see Chapter VII, Section C.

119 See Lassner, "Massignon," 1-27, which is essentially the same as his *Topography*, 155-77, esp. 169ff.; and his "Municipal Entities and Mosques: More on the Imperial City," 53-63 = Lassner, *Topography*, 184-88. The data in these earlier studies is further refined here.

120 Khaṭīb (Cairo), 1:71 = (Paris), 7. Originally "The Straw Gateway," Bāb al-Tibn became known as a large neighborhood (*maḥallah*) in Baghdad along the Ṭāhirid Trench opposite the Fief of Umm Ja'far. By the time of Yāqūt, it had become farmland. The area adjoining the nearby complex of cemeteries, which contained the tombs of several important individuals, including the Shī'ite Saint Mūsā al-Kāẓim and his grandson, continued, however, to be occupied and even had a protective wall of its own. See Yāqūt, *Mu'jam*, 1:443; Khaṭīb (Cairo), 1:71, 121 = (Paris), 7, 79; Lassner, *Topography*, 285-86, n. 1.

121 Sometimes referred to simply as al-Qaṭī'ah, "The Fief." It is also identified with al-Zubaydīyah after Umm Ja'far Zubaydah, the wife of al-Rashīd. It is not to be confused with a southern fief, called al-Zubaydīyah, which was situated in the general area of al-Karkh at Nahr al-Qallā'īn. For the southern fief, see Khaṭīb (Cairo), 1:89, 110 = (Paris), 34, 64, which confuses it with the northern fief; Yāqūt, *Mu'jam*, 2:917; 4:141. The Fief of Umm Ja'far above the Round City was the northernmost area of the upper West Side. It was bounded by Bāb al-Tibn on the west and the Tigris to the east. The southern boundary was formed by the Ṭāhirid Trench where it emptied into the river above the upper harbor; although at one time, part of al-Zubaydīyah may have extended farther south into the Fief of the Baghayīn. See Ya'qūbī, *Buldān*, 250; Suhrāb, 132 = Ibn Serapion, 24; Khaṭīb (Cairo), 1:114 = (Paris), 67; Yāqūt, *Mu'jam*, 4:141, who, following the Khaṭīb (Cairo), 1:89 = (Paris), 34, situates it between the Khurāsān Gate and Shāri' Dār al-Raqīq, that is to say, south of the trench. Note that Yāqūt considers al-Zubaydīyah as a specific location within the fief.

122 This is not a direct translation, but the notion of a city proper is implied as explained below.

123 The Kabsh (Ram) and Asad (Lion) consisted of two large quarters (*shāri'*) near al-Naṣrīyah approaching the Ṭāhirid Trench. See Yāqūt, *Mu'jam*, 4:233; LeStrange, *Baghdad*, 133.

124 See Khaṭīb (Cairo), 1:75-76 = (Paris), 14, referring to the riot of A.H. 307, in which the iron gates of the city were closed to prevent the prisoners from escaping. For details on the background of this event, see n. 11.

125 For the southern canal of al-Karkh, see the article of Lassner in *EI*[2], s.v. 'Īsā, Nahr.

126 With respect to the dimensions of Baghdad, see Lassner, "Massignon," 3ff., which is equivalent to his *Topography*, 157ff.

127 See n. 130 below.

128 Khaṭīb (Cairo), 1:110 = (Paris), 63-64. This account is discussed in detail by Lassner, "Entities," 61-63, which is equivalent to his *Topography*, 182-83.

129 The Khaṭīb refers to a Fief of Umm Ja'far in Nahr al-Qallā'īn, although, as the text goes on to indicate, he clearly means the fief that was beyond Khandaq Ṭāhir and that separated Qaṭī'at Umm Ja'far from the rest of the city. His error stems from the identification of Umm Ja'far's fief with al-Zubaydīyah. There were two locations by the name of al-Zubaydīyah: one situated in the general area of al-Karkh at Nahr al-Qallā'īn, another situated north of the Round City and identified with the Fief of Umm Ja'far. See n. 121.

130 A discussion of these matters can be found in the *K. al-fiqh 'alā al-madhāhib al-arba'ah, qism al-'ibādāt*, 2nd edition (Cairo), 346-48. I am indebted to a responsum of the late Joseph Schacht on the laws applying to the establishment of a principal mosque.

131 See Ibn Ṭayfūr (Cairo), 132-33; and Lassner, *Topography*, 181, noting the principal mosque and qāḍī of al-Karkh, institutions that ordinarily indicate the existence of a municipal entity.

132 Khaṭīb (Cairo), 1:75 = (Paris), 20. The chapter on hydrography (111-15) = (Paris, 65-71) is reported on the direct authority of 'Abdallāh b. Muḥammad b. 'Alī al-Baghdādī, whom I have not succeeded in identifying. It is, however, virtually identical in content and language with the scientific geography of Suhrāb, *'Ajā'ib*, 123-24, 131-34 = Ibn Serapion, 14-15, 24-26. The account of the *'Ajā'ib* can be dated on the basis of internal evidence as ca. A.D. 925. Concerning the decline of the canals, see Miskawayh (Cairo), 2:406, sub anno 369, but actually describing an earlier breakdown in canalization. The Khaṭīb also does not mention some new canals, which were subsequently dug, for example, those reported in Ibn al-Jawzī, *Muntaẓam*, 7:168, sub anno 382; Ibn al-Athīr, *Kāmil*, 8:518.

133 Mas'ūdī, *Murūj* (Beirut), 4:172-73, describes his death and indicates that his tomb was situated adjacent to the Bāb al-Anbār and the quarter (*shāri'*) known as al-Kabsh wa al-Asad. Concerning Ibrāhīm al-Ḥarbī, see *EI*², s.v.

134 Khaṭīb (Cairo), 1:71 = (Paris), 7-8.

135 I have not succeeded in identifying al-Naṣrānī.

136 See Makdisi, "Topography," 185-97, 281-309, for a collection of material on these developments. As for al-Kabsh wa al-Asad, Makdisi, citing Ibn al-Jawzī, *Muntaẓam*, 8:181, and *Mir'āt al-Zamān*, folio 266, argues that it was still a populated quarter fifteen years before the death of the Khaṭīb (A.D. 1071), because it is listed among the various places that were damaged in the great conflagration of A.H. 445 (Makdisi, "Topography, 283 n. 5). He does note, however, a variant reading in the Paris manuscript of the *Mir'āt*, which substitutes *al-kutubiyīn* for *al-Kabsh*, and also in the *Bidāyah*, 12:71, which has *al-kanīs*, but he believed those to be copyists' errors. Of all the identifiable places mentioned in the account of this fire, none, with the exception of Bāb al-Sha'īr, is in the

general vicinity of al-Naṣrīyah, where al-Kabsh wa al-Asad stood (see n. 123). All are in or near al-Karkh, south of the Round City. Al-Kutubiyīn was situated in the eastern part of al-Karkh. See Ya'qūbī, *Buldān*, 245 (*ashāb al-kutub*). The reading of the Paris manuscript may therefore be the more correct, and the assessment of the Khaṭīb would thus remain accurate.

137 Khaṭīb (Cairo), 1:111 = (Paris), 64-65.

138 Yāqūt, *Mu'jam*, 2:254.

139 Khaṭīb (Cairo), 1:76 = (Paris), 16. Note similar floods reported in Miskawayh (Cairo), 2:8; Ibn al-Jawzī, *Muntaẓam*, 6:300, 315-16.

140 Khaṭīb (Cairo), 1:73 = (Paris), 11; Ibn al-Jawzī, *Muntaẓam*, 6:317; Ṣūlī, *Akhbār* (London), 229, sub anno 330.

141 A general overview of legal matters pertaining to the urban environment can be found in R. Brunschvig, "Urbanisme médiéval et droit musulman," 127-55.

142 Khaṭīb (Cairo), 1:67-68 = (Paris), 3. The astrologer who is the source of this account is identified by Yāqūt, *Mujām*, 1:684, as Abū Sahl b. Nawbakht. Ya'qūbī, *Buldān*, 238, 241, indicates that Nawbakht was assisted by other court astrologers. See *EI*, s.v. Nawbakht.

143 Ya'qūbī, *Buldān*, 258-59.

144 Ibid., 259. On the West Side of Baghdad, the term *suwayqah* is used exclusively in the area north of the Ṣarāt. I have no references to any location so designated in the market suburb of al-Karkh to the south of the canal.

145 Ibid., 248.

146 Ibid., 242.

147 Khaṭīb (Cairo), 1:91ff. = (Paris), 37ff.; Yāqūt, *Mu'jam*, 2:760. Salmon identifies the Patrikios as Tarasius the Armenian, who later defected to the Muslims at the battle of Maleh in A.D. 781. See his *Histoire*, 120, n. 2, citing Ibn al-Athīr, *Kāmil*, 6:42. Note, however, that, according to Yāqūt, the Byzantine died in A.H. 163/A.D. 779-80.

148 See *EI*, s.v. mahdī.

149 See the brief remarks of Sharon, " 'Alīyat," 18-19.

150 For a similar tradition playing on the Caliph's regnal title and the coming of the Messiah, see Chapter I, Section B.

151 See Khaṭīb (Cairo), 1:91ff., 112 = (Paris), 37ff., 66; Ya'qūbī, *Buldān*, 243; Suhrāb, 132 = Ibn Serapion, 24; Yāqūt, *Mu'jam*, 2:760; *Marāṣid*, 1:463.

152 Salmon, in his annotated translation of the Khaṭīb, regards the second 500,000 dirhams indicated in the text as "sans doute une repetition superflue du passage precedent." See also his *Histoire*, 38, n. 2. The language of Yāqūt, *Mu'jam*, 2:760, makes it clear that this is not the case, and that, in fact, the gift was doubled.

153 Ya'qūbī, *Buldān*, 243, 254, who indicates that one hundred millstones were used there.

154 Khaṭīb (Cairo), 1:79ff. = (Paris), 20ff.

155 Ṭabarī, 3/1:323-24; Balādhurī, *Futūḥ*, 295; Yāqūt, *Mu'jam*, 2:254.

156 Ya'qūbī, *Historiae*, 2:481; Khaṭīb (Cairo), 1:80 = (Paris), 22; Yāqūt, *Mu'jam*, 2:254.

157 Sourdel, *Vizirat*, 1:94ff.; F. Løkkegaard, *Islamic Taxation in the Classic Period*, 124.

158 Ṭabarī, 3/1:323.

159 Yāqūt, *Mu'jam*, 2:254.

160 Ya'qūbī, *Buldān*, 254.

161 With respect to Ḥanafite views concerning various types of commercial arrangements, see A. L. Udovitch, *Partnership and Profit in Medieval Islam*, esp. 249ff. It is no accident that the great Ḥanafite jurist al-Shaybānī, who was a qāḍī in Baghdad during the eighth century, wrote a book in praise of trade. The publication of such a tract did not signify the need for a new attitude toward commercial ventures; it simply ratified objective realities.

162 Ya'qūbī, *Buldān*, 251.

163 Khaṭīb (Cairo), 1:79-80 = (Paris), 20-21.

164 See Khaṭīb (Cairo), 1:79 = (Paris), 20, for a list of the canals. Various locations along the inner canals of al-Karkh are found in his chapter on hydrography, 113 = (Paris), 67-68. This description is the same as Suhrāb, 132-33 = Ibn Serapion, 25-26. Note that one of these canals, Nahr Ṭābaq, stems from pre-Islamic times, according to some authorities. See Ṭabarī, 3/1:280; Khaṭīb (Cairo), 1:91 = (Paris), 36; and Yāqūt, *Mu'jam*, 3:486; 4:841, in which it is indicated that it was originally named after Bābāk b. Bahram b. Bābāk. According to Ya'qūbī, *Buldān*, 250, it was named after Ṭābaq b. al-Ṣamīh. See Lassner, *Topography*, index, 320.

165 Ya'qūbī, *Buldān*, 252.

166 Khaṭīb (Cairo), 1:83 = (Paris), 23-24; Yāqūt, *Mu'jam*, 1:142.

167 Salmon, *Histoire*, 113, 114, n. 1.

168 Khaṭīb (Cairo), 1:73 = (Paris), 10.

169 Lassner, *Topography*, 72.

170 Yāqūt, *Mu'jam*, 1:799. Note the similar construction *bayn al-qaṣrayn*, which literally means "between the two palaces." It refers to an area between the palaces of Asmā' and 'Ubaydallāh, which is later identifiable as a large neighborhood (*maḥallah*). See also n. 117.

171 Ya'qūbī, *Buldān*, 245.

172 It was situated near the Suwayqah of Abū al-Ward in the fief of Ibn Raghbān. The Anbārites referred to here were scribes in the *dīwān al-kharāj*. See Balādhurī, *Futūḥ*, 296; Ya'qūbī, *Buldān*, 244-45; Khaṭīb (Cairo), 1:79, 89 = (Paris), 20, 33; Yāqūt, *Mu'jam*, 1:142; and LeStrange, *Baghdad*, 61, 95; map 4, ref. no. 6.

173 Ṭabarī, 3/1:279; Khaṭīb (Cairo), 1:88 = (Paris), 32; Yāqūt, *Mu'jam*, 4:142, reads *Bayāwarī* as in MS B of the Khaṭīb. No entry can be found for either name.

174 Suhrāb, 123 = Ibn Serapion, 15. This is equivalent to the Khaṭīb (Cairo), 1:112 = (Paris), 66; and Yāqūt, *Mu'jam*, 1:460-61.

175 Ṭabarī, 3/1:280.

176 *EI*², s.v. Dihkān.

177 Khaṭīb (Cairo), 1:88 = (Paris), 32. The Suwayqah of Ghālib is mentioned by Yāqūt as a place in Baghdad, but the precise location is not given. See *Mu'jam*, 3:201; and 4:919, based on the Khaṭīb.

178 Yāqūt, *Mu'jam*, 4:843.

179 Ibid.; and *EI*², s.v. al-Karkh.

180 See Section B.

181 Ya'qūbī, *Buldān*, 252.

182 Ibid., 245; and Suhrāb, 133 = Ibn Serapion, 26; Khaṭīb (Cairo), 1:79, 88, 113 = (Paris), 20, 32, 33, 67; LeStrange, *Baghdad*, index, 362.

183 Khaṭīb (Cairo), 1:88 = (Paris), 33.

184 Ya'qūbī, *Buldān*, 242-43, 252; Khaṭīb (Cairo), 1:95 = (Paris), 43.

185 *Mu'jam*, 3:600-601.

186 Mashhad MS, Cat. 17:1, 2: Photo Berlin MS sim. or 48. Photographs of this manuscript are appended to the Georgian work of O. K. Tsikitshvilli, *On the City Baghdad*, and are paginated separately. The text under review is on p. 25. For this addition to the geographical literature on Baghdad, see Lassner, *Topography*, 29; *JA*, 204 (1924):149ff—list of materials in report of meeting held in 1924: S. Janicsek, "Al-Djaihani's lost *Kitab al-masalik val-mamalik*: is it to be found at Mashhad?" *BSOAS*, 5 (1928-30):15-25; A. Z. Validi, "Der Islam und die geographischen Wissenschaft," *Geographische Zeitschrift*, 40 (1934):368; P. Kahle, "Islamische Quellen zum chinesichen Porcellan," *ZDMG*, 88 (1934): 34-35; V. Minorsky, "A False Jayhānī," *BSOAS*, 13 (1949-50):89, n. 5; and A. Miquel, *La Geographie humaine du monde musulman jusq'au milieu du 11ᵉ siecle* (Paris, 1967), 153ff.

187 The account of Yāqūt is apparently based on Ibn al-Faqīh and is corrupt. Yāqūt reads: *fakānū yunsabūna ilahyi ribḥ al-'Abbās*, "They were named after him the profit (*ribḥ*) of al-'Abbās." This last statement appears totally out of context and makes no sense as it stands. Note that, without any diacritical marks, *ribḥ* and *zanj* cannot be distinguished in Arabic script.

188 Yāqūt, *Mu'jam*, 3:601; Ya'qūbī, *Buldān*, 242-43; also Khaṭīb (Cairo), 1:91 = (Paris), 37.

189 Ya'qūbī, *Buldān*, 263-64. Agricultural exploitation at Sāmarrā reportedly yielded an income (*ghallah*) of 400,000 dīnārs yearly. Even at the canonical exchange rate of 1 : 10 this would have amounted to 4,000,000 dirhams.

POSTSCRIPT

1 Ibn Ṭabāṭabā (Beirut), 140ff.

2 Note that in the tenth century, there was the concurrent 'Alid (Fāṭimid) Caliph holding sway in Egypt and North Africa and their dependencies.

3 M.G.S. Hodgson, *The Venture of Islam* (Chicago, 1974), 1:281-82, 84.

4 Regarding the palaces of the Būyid amīrs, see Lassner, *Topography*, 271, n. 1.

5 Ṣābi', *Rusūm*, 31.

6 Ibn Ṭabāṭabā (Beirut), 141.

BIBLIOGRAPHY

The bibliography is alphabetically ordered, but no consideration is given to the Arabic definite article *al-*, which is often prefixed to a given name. Thus, the chronicler al-Ṭabarī appears as though his name were written Ṭabarī. Works are listed under the name of the author, with the exception of compilations and editions of anonymous works, which are entered by title. When an author is known by two names, for example, Ibn al-Ṭiqṭaqā, who is also referred to as Ibn Ṭabāṭabā, the name is cross-listed. The bibliography is limited essentially to those works cited in the text and is therefore not to be considered all-inclusive. It is divided into primary and secondary sources; translations of the original texts that are copiously annotated are listed among the primary sources.

Abbreviations

AO	Acta Orientalia
AIEO	Annales de l'Institut d'Études Orientales
ArO	Archiv Orientální
BAHG	Bibliothek Arabischer Historiker und Geographen
BGA	Bibliotheca Geographorum Arabicorum
BI	Bibliotheca Islamica
BIFAO	Bulletin d'Études Orientales de l'Institut Français d'Archéologie Orientale
BSOAS	Bulletin of the School of Oriental and African Studies
EI	Encyclopedia of Islam
EI²	Encyclopedia of Islam, 2nd edition
FHA	Fragmenta Historicorum Arabicorum
GAL	C. Brockelmann, Geschichte der Arabischen Litteratur
GMS	Gibb Memorial Series
IC	Islamic Culture
IJMES	International Journal of Middle East Studies
JA	Journal Asiatique
JAOS	Journal of the American Oriental Society
JESHO	Journal of the Economic and Social History of the Orient
JNES	Journal of Near Eastern Studies
JQR	Jewish Quarterly Review

JRAS	Journal of the Royal Asiatic Society
MIDEO	Mélanges de l'Institut Dominicain d'Études Orientales
MIFAO	Mémoires de l'Institut Français d'Archéologie Orientale du Caire
MSOS	Mitteilungen des Seminars für Orientalische Sprachen
MW	Muslim World
PIEO	Publication de l'Institut d'Études Orientales
PIFAO	Publication de l'Institut Français d'Archéologie Orientale du Caire
PIFD	Publications de l'Institut Français de Damas
RAAD	Revue de l'Académie Arabe (Majallat al-majma' al-ilmī al-'arabī)
REI	Revue des Études Islamiques
RSO	Rivista degli Studi Orientali
WZKM	Wiener Zeitschrift für die Kunde des Morgenlandes
ZA	Zeitschrift für Assyriologie
ZDMG	Zeitschrift der Deutschen Morgenländischen Gesellschaft

Primary Sources

Akhbār al-dawlah al-'Abbāsīyah. Edited by 'A. 'A. Dūrī. Beirut, 1971.

'Arīb b. Sa'd al-Qurṭubī. *Ṣilat ta'rīkh al-Ṭabarī*. Edited by M. J. De Goeje. Leiden, 1897.

al-Azdī, Yazīd b. Muḥammad. *Ta'rīkh al-Mawṣil*. Cairo, 1387/1967.

al-Baghdādī, 'Abd al-Mu'min b. 'Abd al-Ḥaqq. *Marāṣid al-iṭṭilā' 'alā asmā' al-amkinah wa al-biqā'*. Edited by T.G.S. Juynboll. 6 vols. Leiden, 1852.

al-Baghdādī, 'Abd al-Qāhir b. Ṭāhir. *Al-farq bayn al-firaq*. Edited by M. Badr. Cairo, 1910; translated and annotated as *Moslem Schisms and Sects*. 2 vols. K. Seelye, vol. 1. New York, 1920 and A. Halkin, vol. 2. Tel-Aviv, 1935.

al-Balādhurī, Aḥmad b. Yaḥyā. *K. futūḥ al-buldān*. Edited by M. J. De Goeje. Leiden, 1866.

Bal'amī, Muḥammad b. Muḥammad. *Tarīkh-i Ṭabarī*. Edited by M. Mashkūr. Teheran, 1959; translated by H. Zotenberg. *Chronique de abou Djafer Mu'hammad ben Djarir ben Yazid Tabari*. 4 vols. Nogent-le-Rotrou, 1874-76.

al-Dhahabī, Muḥammad b. Aḥmad. *K. tadhkirat al-ḥuffāẓ*. 5 vols. Hyderabad, 1915-16.

al-Dīnawarī, Aḥmad b. Dāwūd. *K. al-akhbār al-ṭiwāl*. Edited by V. Guirgass. Leiden, 1888; indices by I. Kratchkovsky (1912).

Fragmenta Historicorum Arabicorum. Edited by M. J. De Goeje. 2 vols. Leiden, 1869.

al-Hamadhānī, Muḥammad b. ʿAbd al-Malik. *Takmilat ta'rīkh al-Ṭabarī*. Edited by A. J. Kannān in *al-Mashriq* (1955): 21-42, 149-73; (1957): 185-216.

Ibn Abī Uṣaybiʿah, Aḥmad b. al-Qāsim. *ʿUyūn al-anbā' fī ṭabaqāt al-aṭibbā'*. Edited by A. Müller. Cairo and Königsberg, 1882-84.

Ibn al-Athīr, ʿAlī b. Muḥammad. *Al-Kāmil fī al-ta'rīkh*. Edited by C. J. Tornberg. 12 vols. Leiden, 1851-76.

———. *Al-Lubāb fī tahdhīb al-ansāb*. 3 vols. Cairo, 1357/1938.

Ibn al-Faqīh, Aḥmad b. Muḥammad. *K. al-buldān*. Edited by M. J. De Goeje. Leiden, 1855. *BGA* 5. Fragment from fuller version of Mashhad MS appended to O. K. Tsikitschvilli. *On the City Baghdad* (Georgian). Tiblisi, 1967.

Ibn Ḥawqal, Abū al-Qāsim al-Naṣībī. *K. al-masālik wa al-mamālik*. Edited by M. J. De Goeje. Leiden, 1897, *BGA* 2.

Ibn Ḥazm, ʿAlī b. Aḥmad. *K. al-faṣl fī al-milal*. Cairo, 1317/1903; translated and annotated by I. Friedlander. "The Heterodoxies of the Shiites." *JAOS* 28 (1907):1-80; 29 (1908):1-83.

Ibn Hishām, ʿAbd al-Malik. *K. sīrat Rasūl Allāh*. Edited by F. Wüstenfeld. 3 vols. Göttingen, 1858-60.

Ibn al-Jawzī, ʿAbd al-Raḥmān b. ʿAlī. *Manāqib Baghdād*. Edited by M. M. al-Atharī. Baghdad, 1923; partially translated and annotated by G. Makdisi. *Arabica* 6 (1959):185-95.

———. *Al-Muntaẓam fī ta'rīkh al-mulūk wa al-umam*. Edited by F. Krenkow. vols. 5^2-10. Hyderabad, 1938-39.

Ibn Kathīr, Ismāʿīl b. ʿUmar. *Al-Bidāyah wa al-nihāyah*. 14 vols. Cairo, 1932-40.

Ibn Khallikān, Aḥmad b. Muḥammad. *K. wafayāt al-aʿyān wa anbā' abnā' al-zamān*. Cairo, 1881; translated and partially annotated by M. G. De-Slane. *Ibn Khallikan's Biographical Dictionary*. 4 vols. Paris and London, 1843-71.

Ibn Khayyāṭ, Khalīfah al-ʿUṣfurī. *Ta'rīkh*. Edited by A. al-ʿUmarī. 2 vols. Najaf, 1967.

Ibn Miskawayh, Aḥmad b. Muḥammad. *K. tajārib al-umam*. Edited and translated by H. F. Amedroz and D. S. Margoliouth. 7 vols. London, 1920-21. Includes the chronicles of Abu Shujāʿ and Hilāl b. al-Muḥassin.

Ibn al-Muqaffaʿ. *Risālah fī al-ṣaḥābah*. Edited by ʿUmar Abū al-Naṣr in *Āthār b. al-Muqaffaʿ*. Beirut, 1966.

Ibn al-Nadīm, Muḥammad b. Isḥāq. *K. al-fihrist*. Edited by G. Flügel. 2 vols. Leipzig, 1871-72.

Ibn Qutaybah, ʿAbdallāh b. Muslim. *K. al-maʿārif.* Edited by F. Wüstenfeld. Göttingen, 1850.

Ibn Rustah, Aḥmad b. ʿUmar. *K. al-aʿlāq al-nafīsah.* Edited by M. J. De Goeje. Leiden, 1892. *BGA* 7.

Ibn Serapion: see Suhrāb.

Ibn Ṭabāṭabā, Muḥammad b. ʿAlī. *al-Kitāb al-fakhrī fī al-ādāb al-sulṭāniyah wa al-duwal al-islāmīyah.* Edited by H. Derenbourg. Paris, 1895; Beirut, 1386/1966; translated and annotated by E. Amar. *Histoire des dynasties musulmanes depuis la mort de Mahomet jusqu'à la chute du Khalifat ʿAbbāside de Baghdadz.* Paris, 1910.

Ibn Taghrī Birdī, Yūsuf. *Al-nujūm al-zāhirah fī mulūk Miṣr wa al-Qāhirah.* Edited by T.G.S. Juynboll and B. F. Mathes. Vol. 1. Leiden, 1855-61; Cairo, 1929.

Ibn Ṭāhir al-Baghdādī: see al Baghdādī, ʿAbd al-Qāhir.

Ibn Ṭayfūr, Aḥmad b. Abī Ṭāhir. *K. Baghdād.* Cairo 1368/1949; edited, annotated, and translated by H. Keller. *Sechster Band des Kitāb Baghdād.* 2 vols. Leipzig, 1908.

Ibn al-Ṭiqṭaqā: see Ibn Ṭabāṭabā.

Ibn al-Zubayr, al-Rashīd. *Al-Dhakhā'ir wa al-tuḥaf.* Edited by S. al-Munajjid. Beirut, 1959.

al-Iṣfahānī, ʿAlī b. al-Ḥusayn. *K. al-aghānī.* 20 vols. Beirut, 1390/1970. Vol. 21. Edited by R. Brünnow. Leiden, 1888.

———. *Maqātil al-Ṭālibiyīn.* Teheran, 1365/1946.

al-Iṣfahānī, Ḥamzah b. al-Ḥasan. *Tawārīkh sinī mulūk al-arḍ wa al-anbiyā'.* Edited by J.M.E. Gottwaldt. 2 vols. Leipzig, 1844, 1848.

al-Iṣṭakhrī, Ibrāhīm b. Muḥammad. *K. al-masālik wa al-mamālik.* Edited by M. J. De Goeje. Leiden, 1870. *BGA* 1.

al-Jāḥiẓ, ʿAmr b. Baḥr. *K. al-Bukhalā'.* Edited by A. Bak and ʿA. Bak. 2 vols. Cairo, 1938-39.

———. *Risālah ilā al-Fatḥ b. Khāqān fī manāqib al-Turk wa ʿāmmat jund al-khilāfah* in ʿA. M. Hārūn, *Rasā'il al-Jāḥiẓ.* Cairo, 1964-65; 1: 1-86; and the slightly different version of G. van Vloten, *Tria Opuscula.* Leiden, 1903: 1-56.

al-Jahshiyārī, Muḥammad b. ʿAbdūs. *K. al-wuzarā'.* Edited by M. al-Ṣafā et al. Cairo, 1357/1938.

al-Khaṭīb al-Baghdādī. *Ta'rīkh Baghdād.* 14 vols. Cairo, 1931; topographical introduction edited, translated and annotated by G. Salmon as *L'Introduction topographique à l'histoire de Baghdadh.* Paris, 1904.

al-Khuwārizmī, Muḥammad b. Aḥmad. *K. mafātīḥ al-ʿulūm.* Edited by G. van Vloten, Leiden, 1895.

al-Khuwārizmī, Muḥammad b. Mūsā (Ahmad?). *K. ṣūrat al-arḍ.* Edited by H. von Mžik, Leipzig, 1926. *BAHG* 3.

al-Kindī, Muḥammad b. Yūsuf. *K. al-wulāt wa kitāb al-quḍāt*. Edited by R. Kast. Beirut, 1908.

K. al-ʻuyūn: see *Fragmenta*.

al-Maqrīzī, Aḥmad b. ʻAlī. *K. al-nizāʻ wa al-takhāṣum fīmā bāynā Banī Umayyah wa Banī Hāshim*. Edited by M. ʻArnūs. Cairo, 1937 (?).

Marāṣid: see al-Baghdādī, ʻAbd al-Mu'min.

al-Masʻūdī, ʻAlī b. al-Ḥusayn. *Murūj al-dhahab wa maʻādin al-jawāhir*. Edited and translated by C. Barbier de Meynard and P. de Courteille as *Les prairies d'or*. 9 vols. Paris, 1861-77; edited by Y. A. Dāghir. 4 vols. Beirut, 1385/1965.

———. *K. al-tanbīh wa al-ishrāf*. Edited by M. J. De Goeje. Leiden, 1894. *BGA* 8.

al-Muqaddasī, Muḥammad b. Aḥmad. *K. aḥsan al-taqāsīm fī maʻrifat al-aqālīm*. Edited by M. J. De Goeje. Leiden, 1877. *BGA* 3.

al-Nawbakhtī, al-Ḥasan b. Mūsā. *Firaq al-Shīʻah*. Edited by H. Ritter. Istanbul, 1931. *BI* 4.

Qazwīnī, Ḥamdallāh Mustawfī. *Nuzhat al-qulūb* (Persian). Edited by G. LeStrange. London, 1915. *GMS* 23; translated by G. LeStrange, *The Geographical Part of the Nuzhat al-Qulūb of Qazwīnī*. London, 1919.

al-Qifṭī, ʻAlī b. Yūsuf. *Ta'rīkh al-ḥukamā'*. Edited by J. Lippert. Leipzig, 1903.

Qudāmah b. Jaʻfar. *K. al-kharāj*. Edited and translated by M. J. De Goeje. Leiden, 1899. *BGA* 6.

al-Ṣābi', Hilāl b. al-Muḥassin. *K. al-wuzarā'*. Edited by A. Farrāj. Beirut, 1958.

———. *Rusūm dār al-khilāfah*. Edited by M. ʻAwad. Cairo, 1963.

al-Sakhāwī, Muḥammad b. Aḥmad. *Al-Iʻlān bi-l-tawbīkh liman dhamma ahl al-tawārīkh*; translated by F. Rosenthal in *A History of Muslim Historiography*. Leiden, 1952; 2d ed. 1968.

al-Samʻānī, ʻAbd al-Karīm b. Muḥammad. *K. al-ansāb*. Edited by D. S. Margoliouth. London, 1912. *GMS* 20.

al-Shābushtī, ʻAlī b. Aḥmad. *K. al-diyārāt*. Edited by K. ʻAwad. Baghdad, 1951; translated by E. Sachau, *Vom Klosterbuch des Shābushtī*. Berlin, 1919.

al-Shahrastānī, Muḥammad b. ʻAbd al-Karīm. *K. al-milal wa al-niḥal*. Cairo, 1317/1899-1321/1903.

Suhrāb. *ʻAjā'ib al-aqālīm al-sabʻah*. Edited by H. von Mžik. Leipzig, 1930. *BAHG* 5; section on hydrography = Ibn Serapion. *Description of Mesopotamia and Baghdad*. Edited and translated by G. LeStrange. London, 1895; originally in *JRAS* of that year.

al-Ṣūlī, Muḥammad b. Yaḥyā. *Akhbār al-Rāḍī wa al-Muttaqī*. Edited by J. H. Dunne. London, 1935; translated and annotated by M. Canard. 2 vols. Algiers, 1946, 1950. *PIEO* 10 and 12.

———. *Ash'ār awlād al-khulafā' wa akhbāruhum*. Edited by J. H. Dunne. London, 1936.

Sūsah, Aḥmad. *Aṭlās Baghdād*. Baghdad, 1952.

al-Ṭabarī, Muḥammad b. Jarīr. *K. Akhbār al-rusul wa al-mulūk (Annales)*. Edited by M. J. De Goeje et al. 13 vols. Leiden, 1879-1901.

al-Tanūkhī, Abū 'Alī al-Muḥassin b. 'Alī. *Nishwār al-muḥāḍarah wa akhbār al-mudhākarah*, Pt. 1: edited and translated by D. S. Margoliouth. *The Table Talk of a Mesopotamian Judge*. London, 1921 (Oriental Translation Fund, n.s. 27 and 28). Pt. 2: text in *RAAD* 12 (1932); 13 (1933-35); 17 (1942); translation in *IC* 5 (1931):169-93, 352-71, 559-81; 6 (1932):47-66, 184-205, 370-96. Pt. 3: text in *RAAD* 9 (1930); translation in *IC* 3 (1929):490-522; 4 (1930):1-28, 223-28, 363-88, 531-57.

al-Ya'qūbī, Aḥmad b. Abī Ya'qūb. *K. al-buldān*. Edited by M. J. De Goeje. Leiden, 1892. *BGA* 7; translated and annotated by G. Wiet. *Les Pays*. Cairo, 1937. *PIFAO* 1.

———. *Mushākalat al-nās lizamānihim wa mā 'alayhim fī kull 'aṣr*. Beirut, 1962; translated and annotated by W. Millward. "The Adaptation of Men into Their Time: an Historical Essay by al-Ya'qūbī." *JAOS* 84 (1964): 329-44.

———. *Ta'rīkh (Historiae)*. Edited by M. Th. Houstma. Leiden, 1883.

Yāqūt, Ya'qūb b. 'Abdallāh. *Irshād al-arīb ilā ma'rifat al-adīb (Mu'jam al-udabā')*. Edited by D. S. Margoliouth. London, 1907-31. *GMS* 6.

———. *Mu'jam al-buldān*. Edited by F. Wüstenfeld. 6 vols. Leipzig, 1866-73.

———. *Mushtarik*. Edited by F. Wüstenfeld. Göttingen, 1846.

Secondary Sources

Abbot, N. *Two Queens of Baghdad*. Chicago, 1946.

Adams, R. *Land Beyond Baghdad*. Chicago, 1965.

al-'Ali, S. A. "Minṭaqat al-Ḥīrah." *Majallat kullīyat al-ādāb*. Baghdad University 5 (1962):17-44.

———. *Al-Tanẓīmāt al-ijtimā'īyah wa al-iqtiṣādīyah fī al-Baṣrah fī qarn al-awwal al-hijrī*. Baghdad, 1953.

———. "The Foundation of Baghdad." *The Islamic City*. Edited by A. H. Hourani and S. M. Stern, Oxford, 1970:87-101.

Ashtor, E. *Histoire des prix et des salaires dans l'Orient médiéval*. Paris, 1969.

———. "L'évolution des prix dans le Proche-Orient à la basseépoque." *JESHO* 4 (1961):15-46.

Ayalon, D. "Preliminary Remarks on the Mamlūk Military Institution in Islam." *War Technology and Society in the Middle East.* Edited by V. J. Perry and M. E. Yapp. Oxford, 1975:44-58.

———. *The Military Reforms of al-Mu'taṣim. Their Background and Consequences.* Private Circulation. Jerusalem, 1964.

Azizi, M. *La domination arabe et l'épanouissement du sentiment national en Iran.* Paris, 1938.

Barthold, W. *Turkestan to the Mongol Invasion.* Translated by H.A.R. Gibb. 2d ed., London, 1948.

———. *Mussulman Culture.* Calcutta, 1934.

Bergsträsser, G. and Schacht, J. *Gründzüge des islamischen Rechts.* Berlin, 1935.

Biddle, D. "The Development of the Bureaucracy of the Islamic Empire During the Late Umayyad and Early 'Abbasid Period." Ph.D. dissertation, University of Texas/Austin, 1972.

Bouvat, L. *Les Barmécides d'après les historiens arabes et persans.* Paris, 1912.

Brunschvig, R. "Urbanisme médiéval et droit musulman." *REI* 15 (1947): 127-55.

Cahen, C. "L'évolution de l'iqṭā' du IXe au XIIIe," *Annales* 8 (1953):25-52.

———. "Mouvements populaires et autonomisme urbain dans l'Asie musulmane du moyen âge." *Arabica* 5 (1958):225-50; 6 (1959):25-26; 233-65.

———. "Points de vue sur la revolution Abbāside." *Revue Historique* 230 (1963):295-338.

———. "Y a-t-il eu des corporations professionelles dans le monde musulman classique." *The Islamic City.* Edited by A. H. Hourani and S. M. Stern. Oxford, 1970:50-63.

———. "Zur Geschichte der städtischen Gesellschaft im islamischen Orient des Mittelalters." *Saeculum,* 9 (1958):59-76.

Canard, M. "Baghdad au IVe siècle H." *Baghdad, publié à l'occasion du mille deux centième anniversaire de la fondation = Arabica* 9 (1962): 267-87.

———. *Histoire de la dynastie des Hamdanides de Jazira et de Syrie.* 2 vols. Paris, 1953.

Chejne, A. "Al-Faḍl b. al-Rabī'—A Politician of the Early 'Abbāsid Period." *IC* 38 (1962):167-81, 237-44.

———. *Succession to the Rule in Islam.* Lahore, 1960.

Creswell, K.A.C. *Early Muslim Architecture,* 2 vols. Oxford, 1940.

Crone, P. "The Mawālī in the Umayyad Period." Ph.D. dissertation, University of London, 1973.

Dennet, D. "Marwān b. Muḥammad; the Passing of the Umayyad Caliphate." Ph.D. dissertation, Harvard University, 1939.

Dietrich, A. "Das politische Testament des zweiten 'Abbāsiden Kalifen al-Manṣūr." *Der Islam*, 30 (1952):33-65.

Dixon, A. A. *The Umayyad Caliphate 65-86/684-705*. London, 1971.

Dūrī, 'A. 'A. "Nushū' al-aṣnāf wa al-ḥiraf fī al-Islām." *Majallat kullīyat al-ādāb*. Baghdad University 1 (1959):133ff.

Forand, P. "The Governors of Mosul According to al-Azdī's *Ta'rīkh al-Mawṣil*." *JAOS* 89 (1969):88-106.

———. "The Relation of the Slave and Client to the Master or Patron in Medieval Islam." *IJMES* 2 (1971):59-66.

Friedlander, I. "Jewish-Arabic Studies." *JQR*, n.s. 1 (1910-11):183-215; 2 (1911-12):482-516; 3 (1912-13):225-300.

Frye, R. "The 'Abbāsid Conspiracy and Modern Revolutionary Theory." *Indo-Iranica* 5/3 (1952-53):9-14.

———. "The Role of Abū Muslim in the 'Abbāsid Revolt." *MW* 37 (1947):28-38.

Gabrieli, F. "La 'Risāla' di al-Ǧāḥiẓ sui Turchi." *Scritti in onore di G. Furlani*. Rome, 1957 (= *RSO* 32):477-483.

———. "La successione di Hārūn al-Rashīd e la guerra fra al-Amīn e al-Ma'mūn." *RSO* 11 (1926-28):341-97.

Gibb, H.A.R. *The Arab Conquests in Central Asia*. New York, 1970.

Ginsberg, L. *The Legends of the Jews*. 6 vols. New York, 1963.

Goitein, S. D. "A Turning Point in the History of the Muslim State, Apropos of Ibn al-Muqaffa''s Kitāb aṣ-Ṣaḥāba." *IC*, 23 (1945):120-35; reprinted in his *Studies in Islamic History and Institutions*. Leiden, 1966.

Goldziher, I. *Muhammedanische Studien*. 2 vols. Halle, 1895-90; analytical translation by L. Bercher. *Études sur la tradition islamique*. Paris, 1952. English translation and annotation by S. M. Stern. *Muslim Studies*. 2 vols. Chicago, 1966. London, 1971.

Grabar, O. "Al-Mushatta Baghdad and Wāsiṭ." *The World of Islam: Studies in Honor of P. K. Hitti*. Edited by J. Kritzek and R. B. Winder. New York, 1959.

Halkin, A. S., trans. *Moslem Schisms and Sects*. Tel-Aviv, 1935.

Hamidullah, M. "Nouveaux documents." *Arabica*, 7 (1960):293-97.

Herzfeld, E. and Sarre, F. *Archäologische Reise im Euphrat und Tigris Gebiet*. Vol. 2. Berlin, 1921.

Herzfeld, E. "Die Genesis der islamischen Kunst und das Mshatta-Problem." *Der Islam* 1 (1910):60-63.

Hinds, M. "Kufan Political Alignments and Their Backgrounds in the mid-7th Century A.D." *IJMES* 2 (1971):346-67.

Hinz, W. *Islamische Masse und Gewichte*. Leiden, 1955.

Hodgson, M. "How Did the Early Shī'a Become Sectarian." *JAOS* 75 (1955):1-13.

Hoenerbach, W. "Zur Heeresverwaltung der 'Abbāsiden. Studie über Abulfarağ Qudāma: Dīwān al-ğaiš." *Der Islam* 29 (1950):257-90.

Juynboll, T. W. *Handbuch des islamischen Gesetzes*. Leiden, 1910.

Kienast, B. "Zu Muškenum = Maula." *ABAW*, n.f. 75 (1972):99-103.

Kritzeck, J. and Winder, R. B., eds., *The World of Islam: Studies in Honor of P. K. Hitti*. New York, 1959.

Lapidus, I. M. "The Separation of State and Religion in the Development of Early Islamic Society." *IJMES* 6 (1975):363-85.

Lassner, J. "Massignon and Baghdad: The Complexities of Growth in an Imperial City." *JESHO* 9 (1966):1-27.

———. "Municipal Entities and Mosques: More on the Imperial City." *JESHO* 10 (1967):53-63.

———. "Notes on the Topography of Baghdad: The Systematic Descriptions of the City and the Khaṭīb al-Baghdādī." *JAOS* 83 (1963):458-69.

———. "Some Speculative Thoughts on the Search for an 'Abbāsid Capital. Part 1. *MW* 55 (1965):135-141; part 2: 203-10.

———. "The Caliph's Personal Domain: The City Plan of Baghdad Reexamined." *The Islamic City*. Edited by A. H. Hourani and S. M. Stern. Oxford, 1970: 103-18.

———. "The *Ḥabl* of Baghdad and the Dimensions of the City: A Metrological Note." *JESHO* 6 (1963):228-29.

———. *The Topography of Baghdad in the Early Middle Ages: Text and Studies*. Detroit, 1970.

———. "Why did the Caliph al-Manṣūr Build ar-Ruṣāfah—A Historical Note." *JNES* 24 (1965):95-99.

LeStrange, G. "A Greek Embassy to Baghdad in 917 A.D." *JRAS*, 1895.

———. "Description of Mesopotamia and Baghdad." *JRAS*, 1895.

———. *Baghdad During the 'Abbasid Caliphate*. London, 1900.

———. *Lands of the Eastern Caliphate*. Cambridge, 1905.

Lewis, B. *Race and Color in Islam*. New York, 1971.

———. "The Islamic Guilds." *Economic History Review* 8 (1937):20-37.

———. "The Regnal Titles of the First 'Abbāsid Caliphs." *Dr. Zaḳir Husain Presentation Volume*. New Delhi, 1968.

Løkkegard, F. *Islamic Taxation in the Classic Period with Special Reference to Circumstances in Iraq*. Copenhagen, 1950.

L'Orange, H. P. *Studies in the Iconography of Cosmic Kingship in the Ancient World*. Cambridge, 1953.

Makdisi, G. "Autograph Diary of an Eleventh Century Historian of Baghdād." *BSOAS* 18 (1956):9-31, 239-60; 19 (1957):13-48, 281-303, 426-43.

———. "The Topography of Eleventh Century Baghdad: Materials and Notes." *Arabica* 6 (1959):185-97, 281-309.

Marçais, G. "La conception des villes dans l'Islam." *Revue d'Alger* 2 (1945):517-33.

Martin, F. J. *The Muslim Painting of Persia, India and Turkey*, 2 vols. London, 1912.

Massignon, L. *Mission en Mésopotamie (1907-1908)*. Vol. 2. Cairo, 1912 *MIFAO* 2.

———. "Cadis et naqībs baghdadiens." *WZKM* 51 (1948): 106-15; reprinted in his *Opera Minora*. Edited by Y. Moubarac. 3 vols. Beirut, 1963.

———. "Les corps de métier et la cité islamique." *Revue Internationale de Sociologie* 28 (1920):473-88.

———. *Salmān Pāk et les prémices spirituelles de l'Islam iranien*. Tours, 1934.

Mélikoff-Sayar, I. *Abū Muslim le "porte-hache" du Khurassan dans la tradition épique turco-iranienne*. Paris, 1962.

Mez, A. *Renaissance of Islam*. London, 1937.

Millward, W. "The Adaptation of Men into Their Time: an Historical Essay by al-Ya'qūbī." *JAOS* 84 (1964):329-44.

Moscati, S. "Il testamento di Abū Hāshim." *RSO* 27 (1952):28-46.

———. "Le Califat d'al-Hādī. *SO* 13/4 (1946):1-28.

———. "Le Massacre des Umayyades dans l'histoire et dans les fragments poétiques." *ArO* 18 (1950):88-115.

———. "Nuovi studi storici sul califatto di al-Mahdī." *Orientalia*, 15 (1946):155-79.

———. "Studi storici sul califatto di al-Mahdī." *Orientalia*, 14 (1945):300-354.

———. "Studi su Abū Muslim." *Rendiconti Lincei*, ser. 8, 4 (1949-50):323-35, 474-95; 5 (1950-51):89-105.

Muṣṭafā, M. 'A. "Al-Tanqīb fī al-Kūfah." *Sumer*, 12 (1950):3-32.

Noeldeke, T. *Orientalische Skizzen*. Berlin, 1892; translated by J. S. Black. *Sketches from Eastern History*. London, 1892.

Omar, F. *Al-'Abbāsīyūn al-awwā'il: 132-70/750-86*. 2 vols. Beirut, 1390/1970.

———. "Aspects of 'Abbāsid Ḥusaynid Relations," *Arabica* 22 (1976):170-79.

———. *The 'Abbāsid Caliphate, 132-70/750-86*. Baghdad, 1969; a slightly shortened version of his *al-Abbāsīyūn*.

Parry, V. and M. Yapp. *War Technology and Society in the Middle East*. Oxford, 1975.

Pauty, E. "Villes spontanées et villes crées en Islam." *AIEO* 9 (1951):52-75.

Pellat, C. "Ǧaḥiẓ à Bagdād et à Sāmarrā." *RSO* 27 (1952):48-67.

———. *Le Milieu baṣrien et la formation de Ǧāḥiẓ*. Paris, 1953.

Pinto, O. "Al-Fatḥ b. Ḫāqān favorito di al-Mutawakkil." *RSO*, 13 (1931-32):133-49.

Reitemeyer, E. *Die Städtegründungen der Araber im Islam*. Leipzig, 1912.

Rheuter, O. "Sassanian Architecture: a History." *Survey of Persian Art*. Edited by A. U. Pope. New York, 1964-65, 1:491-578.

Richter, G. *Studien zur Geschichte der älteren arabischen Fürstenspiegel*. Berlin, 1932.

Rosenthal, F. *A History of Muslim Historiography*. Leiden, 1952; 2d ed., 1968.

———. *The Muslim Concept of Freedom*. Leiden, 1960.

Rothstein, G. *Die Dynastie der Laḫmiden in al-Ḥīra*. Berlin, 1895.

Safar, F. *Wāsiṭ, the Sixth Season's Excavations*. Cairo, 1945.

Salmon, G. *L'Introduction topographique à l'histoire de Baghdadh*. Paris, 1904.

Santillana, D. *Istituzioni di diritto musulmano malichita con riguardo anche al sistema sciafiita*. 2 vols. Rome, 1926-38.

Sauvaire, H. "Matériaux pour servir à l'histoire de la numismatique et de la métrologie musulmane." *JA*, ser. 7, 14 (1879):455-533; 15 (1880):228-77, 421-28; 18 (1881):499-516; 19 (1882):23-97, 281-327.

Scholem, G. *The Messianic Idea in Judaism*. New York, 1971.

———. *Sabbatai Ṣevi, the Mystical Messiah*. Princeton, 1973.

Shaban, M. *Islamic History: A New Interpretation*. 2 vols. Cambridge, 1971, 1976.

———. *The 'Abbāsid Revolution*. Cambridge, 1970.

———. "The Social and Political Background of the 'Abbāsid Revolution in Khurāsān." Ph.D. dissertation, Harvard University, 1960.

Sharon, M. "Alīyat ha-'Abbāsim la-shilṭōn." Ph.D. dissertation, Hebrew University, Jerusalem, 1970.

———. "The 'Abbāsid Da'wā Re-examined on the Basis of the Discovery of a New Source." *Arabic and Islamic Studies*, Bar-Ilan University 1 (1973):21-41.

Sourdel, D. "La Biographie d'Ibn al-Muqaffa' d'après les sources anciennes." *Arabica* 1 (1954):307-23.

Sourdel, D. *Le Vizirat 'Abbāside de 749 à 936.* 2 vols. Damascus, 1959-60.

Stern, S. M. "The Constitution of the Islamic City." *The Islamic City.* Edited by A. H. Hourani and S. M. Stern. Oxford, 1970:25-50.

Streck, M. *Die alte Landschaft Babylonien.* Leiden, 1900.

Tuquan, F. "Abdallāh b. 'Alī, A Rebellious Uncle of al-Manṣūr." *Studies in Islam,* 6 (1967):1-26.

Udovitch, A. L. *Partnership and Profit in Medieval Islam.* Princeton, 1970.

———. "The Bronze Coinage of the 'Abbasids." Unpublished paper, American Numismatic Society, Summer Seminar, 1961.

Van Vloten, G. *De Opkomst der Abbasiden in Khurasan.* Leiden, 1890.

———. *Recherches sur la domination arabe, le chiitisme et les croyances messianiques sous le khalifat des Omayyades.* Amsterdam, 1894.

Vollors, K. "Über Rassenfarben in der arabischen Literatur." *Centenario della nascita di Michele Amari.* Palermo, 1910, 1:84-95.

Von Grunebaum, G. "The Structure of the Muslim Town." *Islam Essays In the Growth and Nature of a Cultural Tradition.* Chicago, 1955:141-55.

Von Kremer, A. *Culturgeschichte des Orients unter den Chalifen.* 2 vols. Vienna, 1875-77.

Von Soden, W. "*Muškenum* und die Mawālī des frühen Islam." *ZA,* n.f. 22 (1964):133-42.

Watt, W. M. *The Formative Period of Islamic Thought.* Edinburgh, 1973.

Wellhausen, J. *Das Arabische Reich und sein Sturz.* Berlin, 1902; translated by M. G. Weir, *The Arab Kingdom and Its Fall.* Calcutta, 1927; the translation is cited throughout this work.

Wendell, C. "Baghdad: *Imago Mundi* and Other Foundation Lore." *IJMES,* 2 (1971):99-128.

Zambauer, E. *Manuel de généalogie et de chronologie pour l'histoire de l'Islam.* Hanover, 1927.

Zotenberg, H., trans. *Chronique de abou Djafer Mo'hammad ben Djarir ben Yazid Tabari.* 4 vols. Nogent-le-Rotrou, 1867-74.

NOTE: It is not unusual that, after a manuscript is completed for press, materials of importance become available. Regrettably, it is not always possible to integrate these materials within the body of the text. Of these works, special notice should be made of T. Nagel's *Untersuchungen zur Entstehung des abbasidischen Kalifates,* Bonn, 1972.

Index

The definite article (*al-*) in Arabic and the genealogical designations (b.) and (bt.) are not considered in the alphabetical arrangement.

Library of Congress Cataloging in Publication Data

Lassner, Jacob.
The shaping of 'Abbāsid rule.
(Princeton studies on the Near East)
Bibliography: p.
Includes index.
1. Islamic Empire—Politics and government.
2. Abbasids. 3. Iraq—History—634-1534. I. Title. II. Series.
DS38.6.L37 909'.09'767101 79-84000
ISBN 0-691-05281-6